Universities in the Business of Repression

Universities in the Business of Repression

The Academic-Military-Industrial Complex and
Central America

Jonathan Feldman

South End Press   Boston, MA

    Manufactured in the United States.
    Cover design by Bob Gill.
    Typeset and design by the South End Press collective.

Library of Congress Cataloging-in-Publication Data
    Feldman, Jonathan, 1959-
    Universities in the business of repression : the academic-military-industrial complex and Central America / Jonathan Feldman.
        p. cm.
    Bibliography : p.
    Includes index.
    ISBN 0-89608-355-1 : $30.00 -- ISBN 0-89608-354-3 (pbk.) : $14.00
    1. Central America--Relations--United States. 2. United States--Relations--Central America. 3. United States--Foreign relations--1945-   4. Education, Higher--Political aspects--Central America--History--20th century. 5. Education, Higher--Economic aspects--Central America--History--20th century. 6. Corporations, American--Central America--History--20th century. 7. Industry--Political aspects--History--20th century. 8. United States--Military policy. I. Title.
    F1436.8.U6F45   1989
    303.4'8273'0728--dc19   89-4156
                                               CIP

    1 2 3 4 5 6 7 8 9 10   89 90 91 92 93 94 95 96 97 98

South End Press, 116 Saint Botolph Street, Boston, MA 02115

Tempted by lucrative government contracts, many universities—especially the big and famous ones—have become neglectful of their paramount responsibilities and have gone dangerously far toward becoming servants of the state. Because the major source by far of government contract funds is the military establishment, the universities have been drawn primarily into military, or military useful, research in physical and social sciences, becoming in the process card-carrying members of the military-industrial complex.

—Senator J. William Fulbright
Speech at Denison University, April 18, 1969

It is obvious that we cannot discuss the relations between government, industry and universities without taking into account the rapid evolution—or should I say revolution—in the attitudes of students and staff and the academic community in general. In part, the upheavals may have been engineered by a group of well-organized and thoroughly indoctrinated agitators. Their avowed aim is to destroy our present society; they attack the universities because these are both vulnerable and important. These agitators are joined by irresponsible mischief-makers—raising hell has always been the students' prerogative—and by a curious group of slightly paranoic types who see the evil influence of big business lurking around every corner and who suspect the most sinister conspirations every time a professor and an industrialist meet on friendly terms.

—H.B.G. Casimir, "Industries and Academic Freedom,"
Research Policy, November 1971

Table of Contents

List of Tables and Figures

Acknowledgements

Writing a book can be an isolating and lonely experience. However, I had the good fortune to meet many people in the course of my research. Among the many who have helped with encouragement and ideas for this project are: David Allen, Deborah Barry, Chuck Bell, Larry Birns, Marie Bloom, John Cavanagh, Noam Chomsky, Frank Clairmonte, Steven Colatrella, Christina Courtright, Rainer G. Daxl, Daniel Del Solar, Tod Ensign, Mary Ann Fiske, Rachel Feldman, Lisa Foley, Jonathan Fried, Tom Gervasi, James Goetsch, Eva Gold, Van Gosse, Oscar Hernandez, Dominique Hoppe, Dan Karan, Mel King, Noa Kleinman, Jonathan Lind, Beth Marcus, Robert Mathews, Leonard Minsky, Monty Neil, John O'Connor, Adele Oltman, Rachel Ovyrn, Leslie Parks, Arn Pearson, Tony Palomba, Dave Raymond, Juan Jose Rodriguez, Roque Sanchez, Eric Shultz, Jenny Shriver, Leonard Sklar, Sandy Smith, Carol Somplatsky, Jonathan Soroko, Gary Stern, Gary Stone, Annie Street, Francisco Szekely, Jack Trumpbour, America Ugarte, and Ken Walters.

The development of my ideas on "selective divestment" and "dependency" in Central America was assisted greatly, both in agreement and disagreement, by conversations and feedback from Robert Armstrong, Ramon Borges-Mendez, Randall Dodd, John Gerassi, Marc Herold, Edwin Melendez and Jorge Sol. My knowledge of the warfare state and economy grew from a year of research work and discussion with Greg Bischak, Robert Krinsky, Seymour Melman, Mario Pianta, Paul Quigley, and Michael Renner.

This study has built on the work of many other activists and scholars. In particular, I have found essential reading in the work of Noam Chomsky, Michael Klare, Seymour Melman, and David Noble as well as the critique of corporate intervention in Central America developed by Tom Barry, Allan Nairn, Deb Preusch, and Beth Wood. In addition, I have also benefited from David Bull, David Weir, and Mark Schapiro's studies of agro-chemical companies.

Martin Diskin and Michael Albert's early suggestions were essential in helping to pull things together. In producing this book, I am especially indebted to the South End Press collective for their support throughout the years of this project. South End's Cynthia Peters deserves a special mention for her abilities, diligence and patience. I also thank Bob Gill for his excellent work on the cover and his interest in this project. Finally, my parents and friends, I thank you for your emotional, ideological and material support.

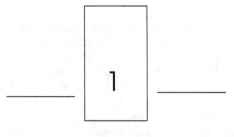

Introduction:
The Tripartite Alliance

On February 13, 1987, the newsletter *Enfoprensa* reported on a war being waged in Guatemala:

> On February 1 and 2, airplanes and helicopters of the Guatemalan Air Force indiscriminately bombed the *parcelamientos* "La 14" and "La Resureccion," in the northwestern *departamento* of El Quiche, according to...the Guatemalan Human Rights Commission (CDHG). The CDHG demanded that President Cerezo see that these repressive actions against non-combatant civilians immediately cease.[1]

Some months later, on May 6, 1987, an Associated Press (AP) wire story appeared. Titled "U.S. Helicopters Used to Fly Guatemalan Troops to Battle," *The New York Times* reported in two and one half column inches how:

> [T]hree Army helicopters and their crews were sent this week to airlift Guatemalan soldiers for a counterinsurgency operation...The operation began on Sunday and ended Monday after the craft had transported about 300 soldiers from Guatemala City to the town of Playa Grande.[2]

This version of events, based on a May 5 Pentagon press release, placed the Guatemalan soldiers in northern Quiche, the same region as the February massacre. *El Grafico,* a leading Guatemalan newspaper, recounted that the soldiers were taken to the Peten, Guatemala's northernmost department. An army offensive had just ended in northern Quiche and one had just begun in the Peten.[3]

This episode highlights the direct role of the U.S. government in assisting the war against the people of Guatemala. But the trail of terror marked by this helicopter attack against Guatemalan peasants also leads to other questions: Who manufactured the helicopters, sold them to the U.S. government and supplied them to the Guatemalan military? Who designed their deadly technology? Who trained the pilots? What role do U.S. corporations play in supporting the Guatemalan government and its allies in the oligarchy? The answers to these questions reveal that the system of terror in Central America is propelled by more than just the actions of government officials and war planners. The cast of supporting actors extends even further, encompassing not only the U.S. government but also a larger network involving arms contractors, transnational corporations and universities.

Guatemala's fleet includes numerous Bell helicopters flown by members of the Guatemalan Air Force trained at Bell's Fort Worth facilities.[4] The corporate connections of Bell's parent firm, Textron, ties U.S. universities to the system of political intervention in Central America. For example, the March 15, 1988 Proxy Statement for the Textron Corporation reveals that then president of Brown University, Howard R. Swearer, had been a Textron corporate director since 1978. In sum, the leader of a major university has been tied to a corporation which profits from sales to a brutal dictatorship (Bell sent helicopters to Guatemala during 1980-82 as well as spare parts in 1984).[5]

Brown is not alone in its links to Textron; numerous universities have invested their endowments in this company, profiting directly from arm sales to nations like Guatemala.[6] Textron is just one example of the connections between universities and repression in Central America.

The anti-apartheid movement has recognized the pivotal role of U.S. transnational investment in supporting a racist society that denies the majority of its people political freedom and access to economic resources. The South African government is considered so morally reprehensible that activists feel free to criticize any and all institutions involved with the South African state, including universities with investments in companies doing business in South Africa. If we believe that the brutal military states of Guatemala and El Salvador should also be considered pariah nations, then we can begin to question the role foreign investment plays in supporting these governments; accordingly, we can begin to consider the argument for corporate divestment.

Several political campaigns have shown how U.S. corporations support repression in the region. One campaign, launched by the New Mexico-based Global Justice, exposed how General Foods' purchases of Guatemalan and Salvadoran coffee have been used by these nations to finance arms imports. The International Union of Food and Allied Workers (IUF) helped organize an international campaign of boycotts and other union actions in support of a Guatemalan labor union's struggle with a Coca Cola franchise that carried out a campaign of political harassment against the workers. These two organizing efforts demonstrate how solidarity actions have expanded their critique of repression in Central America beyond the actions of the U.S. government and particular officials.

Universities are also linked to another important player in the region. Agro-chemical companies, based in the United States and Europe, have extensive commercial links with Central American agriculture. The pesticide trade has led to the deaths of thousands of Latin Americans through the poisoning of water supplies and the exposure of farmers to aerial spraying. U.S. agro-chemical companies have furthered Third World nations' dependency on fertilizers, pesticides and other technologies which squeeze poor farmers, exacerbating social inequality and driving peasants off their land.

Universities also contribute to U.S. government war planning and research. Consider again the example of U.S. helicopters in the region. Pentagon planners are tirelessly seeking to advance military technologies to gain the edge over their "adversaries." A 1981 report described efforts by the Pentagon and the National Research Council to establish a fellowship system "to help steer students away from lucrative jobs in industry and into doctoral studies in technical fields in demand by the military." The program was created to address shortages in such technical specialties as computer sciences, advanced materials research, vertical-lift (helicopter) technology and vacuum-tube research. The fellowship was designed to support seventy-five to one hundred graduate students, with stipends of $10,000 to $12,000, beginning in the 1982 fiscal year.[7] Universities also engage in millions of dollars worth of research for the military and allow war contractors and the armed forces to openly recruit on campus. Faculty also act as consultants for military contractors and the armed forces.

1.1 Challenging the Institutions of Intervention

Theft and murder are the two central characteristics which define our relations with Central America. The former is expressed as the transnational corporations' interest in the region as a collection of banana republics. Investment directed by corporate administrators takes the form of low-paid labor under the gun of local thugs called "democrats" and "new democrats." The latter, murder, is the objective result of government-waged counter-insurgency war. When there is popular opposition to theft, the government responds with a "depopulation" program. There can be no opposition if there are no opponents.

Hundreds of thousands have died in Central America, murdered by client states that receive their support from the United States or surrogates themselves dependent on U.S. assistance. But the war waged daily against the people of Central America is part of a general pattern that shapes U.S. relations with the Third World. During the Vietnam War, schools, hospitals and civilian areas in North Vietnam were repeatedly bombed by the United States.[8]

The opposition to U.S. intervention in the Third World has taken new forms in recent years, yet *effective* opposition has been hindered in a number of ways. Some participants in opposition movements insist on treating each country in Central America as a distinct issue. Others look to South Africa and forget about Central America; the reverse is also common. Still other targets of U.S. intervention, like Haiti, South Korea and the Philippines, are largely ignored.[9] The Pentagon projects power over a global U.S. empire; we must oppose oppressive U.S. policies with a global perspective.

As long as the United States is helping to deny other people freedom, we cannot be free. The forces of centralized power that are working to deny Central Americans their freedom are also limiting and constraining our choices. Preparation for war is a daily occurrence in the United States; it is the livelihood of millions of citizens. The dependence on military spending is evidenced in the growth of war research in the universities, in the militarization of the industrial base, in the growing incompetence of manufacturers to make anything but weapons, in newspapers that chronicle Pentagon press releases and in national media that treat the Commander-in-Chief's words as the words of a God.[10]

We cannot be free as long as the people of the Third World are not free because those who wish to carry out a policy of intervention and repression abroad are more than willing to devise plans to suspend the Constitution if opposition *in the United States* should arise in conflict with their war plans.[11] If morality, the U.S. Constitution and international law can be suspended by militarists tackling only the Nicaragua "problem," then this thinking is bound to shape their psychology about life in general and politics in the United States. What runs through the mind of someone who can rationally support the contras who randomly rape and murder must be frightening. These are the same men, and they are mostly men, who are shaping the destinies of millions of Americans from their offices in Washington, D.C.

Our freedom and the freedom of Central Americans are closely bound, because as we work to limit the grasp of the military on our own economy and institutions there will be less reason for war thinking and war planning. Our freedoms are linked because as we work to limit the centralized power of the national security agencies and the transnational corporations, we facilitate dissent and freedom of expression. A movement against intervention in Central America *is* a good place to start, but there are clear ways to build alliances with groups opposing intervention in South Africa, the military-industrial complex in Israel, and the militarization of daily life in the United States. This book addresses these questions and analyzes the problem of the institutional basis of intervention. Unless we remove the root causes of war in these institutions, we will be left to harvest the next Vietnam and the next Central America.

The focus here is not on how military planners have shaped U.S. policy in Central America; this question has been given full treatment by other writers.[12]

Rather, this study examines how greater leverage can be gained to stop U.S. military intervention and provide support for popular opposition movements in Central America—how political leverage can be gained to reduce the likelihood of both theft and murder. The underlying principle of this study is that, as Jean-Paul Sartre would have it, institutions are "serialized groups," i.e. the institutions which support the war machine have publics which can be mobilized in these very same institutions. The potential constituency to be mobilized by a university-based anti-intervention, disarmament and conversion effort is vast: there are 3,340 colleges and universities across the nation with an enrollment of more than twelve million students, employing 710,000 professors.[13]

My focus is on how universities are part of a complex web of intervention and militarism: the university as participant in both the U.S. war system and the transnational economy. These links define the possible "handles" for organizing against political intervention and militarism. They are *starting points* from which we can build the political base for larger social movements that address issues of arms reductions, military intervention, economic conversion and democratic planning in universities, the workplace and society as a whole.

In Chapter Two, I document how U.S. policies have been based on murder in Central America and examine the responsibility of transnational corporations and U.S. war planners in this enterprise. Part One of this book details the responsibility of these two political actors for repression in Central America. Some attention is paid to how students and academics have suffered in the region as a way to underline the moral responsibility of North Americans to address the burdens faced by their counterparts abroad. This section provides one basis for the argument that churches, unions and universities should not invest their monies in institutions linked to terror in Central America.

Part Two further examines the role of transnationals in Central America. Chapter Three chronicles the role of agro-chemical companies in the Third World. This chapter documents their responsibility for the poisoning of Central Americans. It explains how these very same companies are developing technologies which will increase the economic dependency of Central American farmers, and the economy as a whole, on technologies imported from the transnationals. This section lays the basis for arguments that institutional ties to these corporations should be questioned and it examines the research links between universities and such companies.

Chapter Four addresses the economic role of transnationals in Central America as a whole. Do transnationals contribute to equitable economic development in Central America? After addressing this question in Chapter Four, I examine in Chapter Five how university links to corporate investments in Central America could be used to challenge U.S. policy in Central America. A theory of "selective divestment" describes how divestment actions used to mobilize opposition to U.S. support for apartheid could be applied to Central America.

Part Three examines in detail how universities are part of a larger "warfare state" defined by the collective agencies which carry out war planning and production. Chapter Six begins by examining the central role of the warfare state and "geopolitical" interests in shaping military intervention in Central America. It details how universities contribute to this warfare state and which companies export arms to Central America.

Chapter Seven examines universities' increasing dependency on military funding and the political and economic forces which drive the "militarization" of research and development activities in the United States. It looks at how the diverse constituencies of faculty, students and youth outside the university are co-opted and conscripted in service to the warfare state. The economic relationships detailed here define the barriers to action designed to sever university links to the military economy. Such relationships also define the necessity for economic conversion planning, a program for providing alternative civilian resources for those constituencies dependent on the war economy.

Chapter Eight examines current efforts to reduce the military's influence on the university. This chapter describes how universities can initiate conversion planning and join efforts with a larger movement for converting the national economy and disarming the institutions of intervention.

The universities are part of a division of labor linking them to both transnationals and the warfare state. Administrators, faculty and students often act in ways which make them appear autonomous from larger political and economic spheres. However, the results of their actions are clear: university research, investment and political affiliations contribute significantly to the war-making institutions that lie behind intervention and repression in Central America.

An appreciation of the power of the Pentagon and allied agencies does warrant strategic concentration of energies, but the focus should not be limited to regions. It should encompass these institutional realities.

Part 1

State and Corporate Repression in Central America

2.1 Terrorism and the State

El Salvador

In El Salvador today, formal political power is divided between two political parties intrinsically linked to a terror campaign against the civilian population. Of the more than 45,000 non-combatant deaths since 1980, most took place during the first term of Napoleon Duarte, the Christian Democratic Party leader. During this term, Duarte was unable to prevent the murder of his own fellow Christian Democratic mayors.[1] Observing Duarte's role during this period, foreign policy scholar Noam Chomsky noted that by joining the March 1980 junta, Duarte would be working with people he had himself accused of being death squad members.[2]

The alternative right-wing ARENA (Nationalist Republic Alliance) which won a majority in the National Assembly in March of 1988 has been linked to death squad killings. An article in *The New York Times,* December 2, 1987, described ARENA leader Roberto d'Aubuisson as "the best known rightist politician in El Salvador" and the object of repeated accusations of "directing political killings and of plotting to eliminate the American Ambassador in 1984." The story described evidence which links d'Aubuisson to an intricate terror network.[3]

President Duarte held only formal power in El Salvador. His primary source of leverage against the military and the death squads was the legitimacy he held with U.S. and European governments and corporate leaders. He combined token reformism with democratic rhetoric as a means of securing U.S. military and economic assistance. But Duarte was not the major force which defined political authority. Instead, political realities have been shaped by a "parallel government" in which right-wing violence and military repression hold back most political rights and liberties.[4]

The parallel government links the army and the country's death squads in an alliance which carries out the policies of violence behind the backs of government leaders. While the government has sanctioned much of the violence, much power lies in forces which cannot be controlled by elections or arm twisting by Congressional delegations or State Department initiatives. These forces include death squads and their political affiliates in right-wing organizations. In fact, the U.S. government, as discussed below, has been instrumental in the organization of state terror in Central America. A U.S. Embassy spokesman in San Salvador explained the parallel government as follows: "If you pursue the squads it is going to cut so far back into the fabric of Salvadoran society you may face the destabilization of the society."[5] A January 16, 1986 article in the *The New York Times,* showed the legitimacy granted terror by reporting that "Salvadoran military officials said…that two army officers, linked by Washington to right-wing death squads and later sent into exile under United States pressure, have received promotions…"[6]

The ties between the Salvadoran government and terrorism are betrayed in countless episodes, documented by human rights groups and researchers. Amnesty International charged in a November 3, 1983 report that the death squads "act with the implicit or explicit warrant of the Salvadoran security forces."[7] A military official interviewed in a March 3, 1984 article in *The New York Times,* reported that "Government officials routinely ordered the police and soldiers to stay out of areas where political murders were about to take place" and that they helped assassins to get to refuges in neighboring Guatemala.[8]

In February of 1986, Ricardo Ernesto Castro, a former Salvadoran army officer, publicly stated that he participated in death squad killings. He was the first Salvadoran officer to make such a public statement and said that he personally commanded four assassination missions, claiming about a dozen lives. As noted in the *The Boston Globe* on February 13, 1986, Castro's statements supported claims made by private human rights groups that the Salvadoran military killed tens of thousands of civilians in the early 1980s.[9] A former Captain in the Salvadoran army testified before the U.S. Congress that the death squads were:

> made up of the security forces, and acts of terrorism credited to these squads such as political assassinations, kidnappings, and indiscriminate murder are, in fact, planned by high-ranking military officers and carried out by members of the security forces.[10]

One of the worst incidents of military repression occurred during the Duarte junta's attack on civilians in the Morazan Province in December of 1981 when during a ten day period "more than 1,009 peasants were assassinated."[11]

While Duarte passed "strict rules about aerial bombardment," the military command in El Salvador has engaged in "heavy and repeated bombing" of rural zones. As a result of such bombing, one-third to one-half of the peasant population in the targeted zones was massacred during 1984 by air attacks.[12] The bombings are part of the heaviest air war in the Western Hemisphere. As popular support for the guerrilla and opposition movement, the Democratic Revolutionary Front/Farabundo Martí Front for National Liberation (FDR/FMLN), has spread, and the rebels have become more successful in blocking government forces on the ground, the army has stepped up its attacks on civilian areas. Modeled after "Operation Phoenix," the U.S. strategy in Vietnam, the El Salvadoran government uses saturation bombing, inch-by-inch patrols, and complete encirclement of civilian villages as a means to force civilians from caves where they hide from government planes. Hundreds of sick and hungry persons have turned themselves into the army, which then transfers them to privately-sponsored refugee camps with a warning that if they return to their shattered homes they will be killed.[13]

Since 1984, the air war has been the principal cause of injury, starvation and displacement of rural civilians in El Salvador. In the first half of 1984 alone, 1,300 civilians were reported killed by aerial bombardment. The Council On Hemispheric Affairs reports that "close to 3,000 civilians have died in rural areas in the first half of 1985 as a result of the air war." The air war has aggravated the country's refugee problem: within El Salvador there are approximately half a million displaced persons (10 percent of the population); 750,000 have fled abroad. A 1987 report in *The New York Times,* stated that in September "the air force bombed and strafed several villages, setting back plans to resettle about 5,000 refugees displaced by the civil war."[14]

Beginning on January 10, 1986, two Salvadoran military battalions, trained and advised by the United States, began a "sweep" of Guazapo volcano, fifteen kilometers from the capital, San Salvador. Guazapo has long been a stronghold of the FMLN as well as the home of thousands of civilians. Working in conjunction with U.S.-supplied helicopter gunships and A-37 bombers, ground troops carried out a "scorched earth" campaign designed to not only clear out the FMLN, but also the civilians in the region. One thousand civilians were surrounded for over two weeks by the military. The Red Cross was denied access and no food or water was let into the area. At least sixty people were "arrested" for giving material or "spiritual" aid to the the guerrillas. Four hundred more were forcibly removed to strategic hamlets, armed camps controlled by the military.[15]

The air war, while ostensibly designed as a military operation to eliminate support for the guerrillas, has become another form of direct State violence against the people. Observers note that the rebels have learned to avoid aerial bombardment, but that the civilian population has fewer resources and thus receives the brunt of the attacks. Given the desperation of the military (or perhaps because of their whole-hearted identification with the nation's elite), they are willing to accept the enormous civilian cost involved in the massive bombardment of rural regions and the scorched earth policy.[16]

Guatemala

Guatemala is ruled by what has been called a "bureaucracy of death."[17] The State stands ready to murder, kidnap or deport any reformer in a country where the concentrated patterns of land ownership bring starvation to hundreds of people every day. More than thirty years of military rule has led to the murder of 85,000 to 100,000 Guatemalans. More than 200,000 children have become orphans from violence since 1978. Some 150,000 refugees live in Southern Mexico.[18] Like El Salvador, extreme poverty based on income inequality and underdevelopment has led to movements for reform, which in turn have been opposed by the government. Thus, the Guatemalan state depends on genocide: "Guatemala has been ruled for three decades by governments which must murder large numbers of their own citizens simply in order to survive."[19]

State Department and journalistic accounts portray political violence as the result of a sinister war between right- and left-wing extremists, with the country's peasant population caught in the middle. However, most of those who suffer from violence are not political leaders or party functionaries. A study of the victims of political violence from 1966-76 demonstrated that more than 65 percent were peasants and rural workers. Further, the popularity that the guerrilla movement has enjoyed belies attempts to betray civil strife as the outcome of conflicts between fringe ideological groups.[20]

The link between government sanctioned and supported violence and the repression of the civilian population has been documented over and over again by human rights organizations. According to Amnesty International,

> the so-called "death squads" operating in urban areas are in fact made up of reservists or off-duty regular security and military personnel in plain clothes, acting under orders from high level officials of the Guatemalan Government.

In 1981, a leading Guatemalan businessman and adviser to the Lucas Garcia regime acknowledged the character of death squad activity as state repression: "The death squads were organized under the patronage and approval of the government and the army because it was the only way to fight the guerrillas."[21]

The Boston Globe noted in February 1987 that "unofficial records compiled by diplomats and other sources indicate that more than 1,200 people were murdered in Guatemala during the first nine months of democratic rule, a 40 percent increase over the same period in 1985." A news release that month by the Council On Hemispheric Affairs described how the Commander of the Guatemalan Armed Forces referred to the Cerezo government as "a project" of the military and stated how Cerezo's rule had left the power centers of political and economic repression in place:

> Unremitting political violence and the murder of dissidents…continues to plague the country…Up to this point, the disproportionate power of the conservative business elite and the military barely have been affected by the Cerezo government.[22]

The New York Times later reported that "although trade unionists and other protestors have greater freedom to organize than in the past," in Cerezo's Guatemala, "men in uniform still exercise ultimate political authority."[23] The President's failure to revoke the military's General Amnesty Decree 8-86 provides evidence for this blunt assessment. The decree, issued by the armed forces just before it relinquished power in January 1986, freed the military from legal responsibility for all crimes committed from 1982 through Cerezo's inauguration.

Other actions by Cerezo reveal his unwillingness to push for human rights reforms that would restrict the military's authority. On October 22, 1986, he attempted to veto a human rights measure by the Guatemalan congress. Cerezo also refused to accept demands by the Mutual Support Group in May of 1986 that a non-government commission be formed to investigate cases of disappearances under the former military regimes. By September 1986, Cerezo was to declare that, "since the electoral campaign, I said we were not going to bring military men to trial, that I would practice normalization and that agreements cannot be reached by punishing one sector." Other reports note that Cerezo has described the army as the promoter of democracy.[24]

Honduras

Honduras is becoming more and more like its neighbors, El Salvador and Guatemala. A February 1984 report by a coalition of human rights groups detailed growing repression as increased intervention by the American military machine has contributed to polarization and a climate of suspicion and fear:

> Critics of government policies are commonly stigmatized as "subversives" or Sandinista sympathizers. Thus, for example, even criticism of the Honduras Government's recent decision to "postpone" a planned

literacy program was publicly labelled by government officials as an effort to destabilize the government.[25]

From 1981 to 1984, eighty-five Honduran labor and *campesino* leaders were murdered by death squads; nine priests were also killed.[26]

During the reign of former President Roberto Suazo Cordova, at least twenty-three Hondurans were shot to death, apparently for political reasons, according to the Committee for the Defense of Human Rights in Honduras (CODEH). Thirty other people were kidnapped. In 1984, the Committee listed fifty-three political prisoners. In addition to several death squads, which the military lets operate freely, the Honduran army had a hand in the May 14, 1980 massacre of 600 refugees. Honduran soldiers prevented the refugees from crossing the Rio Sumpul River into Honduras. "Approximately 600 refugees were killed, trapped between the Hondurans who wouldn't let them step on shore and the Salvadoreans who shot them down as they struggled back."[27] This incident was just one of many in which Honduran security forces were responsible for the deaths of refugees from El Salvador. Ten months after the Sumpul River massacre, another large-scale slaughter took place when Salvadoran peasants were killed as they fled across the Lempa River.[28]

According to CODEH, "138 individuals of different nationalities, mostly Salvadorans and Nicaraguans, disappeared between 1981 and 1984."[29] In September 1985, *The New York Times* reported on an attack by eighty Honduran army soldiers on a UN camp for Salvadoran refugees. The soldiers wounded thirteen and kicked and beat twenty-five others with rifle butts. Previous to the raid, soldiers had entered the camp, "shouting that the refugees were Salvadorans who did not belong in Honduras and that they should leave or be killed." Among those murdered was a two-month old girl kicked to death by a soldier and among those wounded were two four-year olds and a seventy-year old deaf mute. One witness to the attack said "she had watched Honduran soldiers torture the 10 refugees who were seized, beating them in their faces with rifle butts, kicking them on the ground, dragging them by the hair, and in one case cutting a man with a knife." Witnesses to the attack included five international relief officials, some belonging to the United Nations High Commissioner for Refugees. The army's August 1985 attack on the Colomoncagua refugee camp left two Salvadoran refugees dead, fifty people wounded and ten imprisoned.[30]

A comprehensive review of the human rights situation in Honduras during the first ten months of 1986 by CODEH documented twelve cases of torture; seventy-one illegal detentions (of which the Department of National Investigation was responsible for twenty-four, the Public Security Force twenty-two, and the army sixteen); and the evictions of hundreds of families in urban and rural zones. The evictions, mostly carried out by the Public Security Force (FUSEP), in some cases involved violent evictions, the burning and destruction of homes, and the killing of children. CODEH reported on death squad activity that year as follows:

> Some 65 persons have died violently at the hands of unknown assailants, principally in Tegucigalpa and San Pedro Sula. We are not referring to people who died as a result of a fight, rather those who turn up dead in a very suspicious fashion, as the victims of "paramilitary corps" or "death squads" in Guatemala or El Salvador usually appear.[31]

CODEH and other Honduran groups have linked the Honduran government to such death squad activity and political murder. Much of the Government repression is linked to the Department of National Investigation (DNI) which holds suspected "subversives," who are arrested without due process, in *incommunicado* detention. DNI has been linked to death squad activity.[32]

Perhaps the most dramatic revelation in the mainstream press about the Honduran government's link to terror in recent years was a news story in *The New York Times,* May 2, 1987, which described how "the Honduran Army high command maintained a network of secret jails, special interrogators and kidnapping teams who detained and killed nearly 200 suspected leftists between 1980 and 1984." The report stated that army and police units were "authorized" to organize death squads and were trained by Argentinians and Chileans in kidnapping and "elimination" techniques.[33] These reports were given greater attention when the Inter-American Court on Human Rights put the Honduran government on trial for "maintaining army death squads that caused the 'disappearance' of civilians suspected of being leftists."[34]

This terror system follows the general pattern in Central America; it is a system of insurance to shut off all dissent in a nation where economic wealth is concentrated in the hands of a political elite. A March 1982 report noted that "ten percent of the population receives eighty percent of the gross national product and only five percent of the population controls sixty percent of the land."[35] The rural population of Honduras comprises over 60 percent of the population, yet only 10 percent benefit from electricity:

> Seven out of ten Hondurans live in conditions of desperate poverty, and less than fifteen percent of rural Hondurans have access to drinking water. Eight out of ten rural Hondurans live in wretched hovels, and fifty children die each day from preventable diseases.

Like El Salvador and Guatemala, the inequitable distribution of land has contributed to economic underdevelopment. Over 40 percent of rural Hondurans are without land and 80 percent suffer from malnutrition.[36]

2.2 The Repressive State: The Case of Central American Universities

In Central America, the attacks of death squads and armed forces on universities stand as a model for how the institutions of democratic participation have been subverted by government-sponsored terrorism. In El Salvador, the violence has involved coordinated attacks by the armed forces:

> On July 30, 1975, a peaceful student demonstration in San Salvador, protesting military intervention of the university campus in Santa Ana, was attacked by National Police, National Guard and Army Forces. An unknown number of students were killed. Ambulances followed behind the tanks and the armored cars, to pick up the dead and wounded. Behind the ambulances came street sweepers to wash the blood away.[37]

The universities of Central America have played an important role in promoting democracy and human rights; they have historically been viewed as sanctuaries, free from government interference and control. The university traditionally served as a refuge for the political opposition and functioned as a center of political debate in El Salvador. But, as the contradictions of the region have grown, dissension is met with repression; any challenge to the ruling military machine of El Salvador meets with government violence.

The repression of the Salvadoran people has escalated the cycle of violence in the country. A report in 1980 described the process by quoting a leader of El Salvador's teachers' union, ANDES:

> Fifteen years ago the teachers' union was organized in response to economic circumstances...The growth of the trade union led the Government to force teachers employed in the capital to take jobs in distant provinces. Our first mobilizations were in opposition to the power of the administrators over the teachers. Beginning in 1970, secondary school teachers were organized by ANDES in opposition to government-controlled policy changes. Between 1970 and 1975, Government repression took the form of taking and dispersing militant teachers to remote areas, taking prisoners and an occasional assassination or prisoner disappearance.[38]

As the union gained more members and developed a political perspective on the country's problems, government repression grew worse. The junta killed 181 school teachers between October 15, 1979 and July 31, 1980.[39] Government repression of teachers is just one example of a concerted attack on the educational system in El Salvador. More recent attacks on the University betray a cynical disregard for any vestige of democratic participation in or control over society.

On June 26, 1980, the army—with helicopters, tanks and 900 troops—invaded the campus of the University of El Salvador (UES). The attack was launched by the government in response to what was seen as an intolerable level of subversive activity. The American Embassy estimated that close to fifty were killed in the attack. The condition of the University after the armed attack and subsequent vandalism serves as a symbol of political life in El Salvador. The social-science library was bombed and burned, its books reduced to pulp and ash.[40] Three-fourths of the University's volumes were sold or burned. The military destroyed and sacked many University buildings, including the medical school's laboratory and classroom. "Solidiers...removed everything that could be sold, from sophisticated computers to basic laboratory equipment."[41] Twenty thousand students were trapped on campus, as military officers examined student identification and those from rural areas were taken aside and interrogated by officers. Later, students who returned to such areas were kidnapped and killed during attacks from death squads. After the invasion, buses and vehicles on campus destroyed by the army were found spray painted with slogans such as "the death squad goes here" and "Fuerzas Armadas," the Armed Forces of El Salvador.[42]

In late May of 1984, in response to international pressures against the closing of the University and its destruction, President Duarte reopened the campus. Power was handed over to the Superior University Council to govern the University. The Council is evenly divided between faculty and students and had been the governing body of UES before it had been closed down. An observer of the situation in August of 1984 explained that despite the reopening, a climate of repression and government control surrounded the University. While classes were being held, the current school budget was only half of what it was before the attack. Bombed-out buildings still stood as a reminder of the limits of the University's renewal. In the middle of June of 1984, the chair of the University's medical department was assassinated. The army still patrolled the campus. The Council was negotiating with the government in order to end the activities of death squads and secret police who have attacked and spied upon students and faculty. The Council was also attempting to negotiate new faculty contracts and university political autonomy from the government.[43]

Despite the apparent movement towards reform, the shadow government of the death squads still threatens the campus. The London *Economist* noted in July 1985 that there were renewed threats by the death squads intimidating people at the University to leave the country or be assassinated, "a reminder that the right-wing terror machine is still in running order."[44] A November 6, 1985 report noted that students, professors and employees have been regularly arrested at the University.[45] Throughout 1985, there was continued harassment of the University. At the start of July, an advertisement was published in various papers listing eleven students and professors and suggesting that they leave the country by July 20, 1985. The Secret Anti-Communist Army, an underground terrorist organization which targeted the groups, is a right-wing death squad which students have linked to the Duarte government. The death list was published shortly after a demonstration in July 1985 by several thousand UES students, teachers and employees who were protesting government underfunding of the University.[46] On June 15, 1987, a death squad threatened to kill fourteen students and teachers at the National University which it has called a "sanctuary of the communists." On June 30th, another six students and faculty were threatened.[47]

Repression against universities has also been directed against the Catholic University of America in San Salvador. In a 1985 interview, the vice-rector, Father Ignacio Martin Baro said that "during the past four or five years we have lost between 40 and 60 percent of our faculty...students have been killed, my house has been blown out several times..."[48]

U.S. policy makers have glossed over the repression of Central American universities such as UES. Instead, a propaganda campaign, sponsored by the United States Information Agency (USIA), was launched which will send more than 150 college students from seven Central American countries to the United States. The $3.8 million scholarship program was an outgrowth of a presidential commission headed by Henry A. Kissinger, former Secretary of State. It recommended the aid as a way "to build lasting links between Central America and the United States." The Central American Program for Undergraduate Scholarship is billed as an opportunity to assist poorer students who are unable to afford attendance at U.S. universities. In conjunction with a companion plan backed by the Agency for International Development, the USIA expects to bring more than 4,000 undergraduates from Central America to the United States to study for bachelor's degrees by the early 1990s.[49]

In contrast to an effort which might be interpreted as an attempt to replace Central American education with one "made in the U.S.A.," progressive groups within the United States are attempting to help rebuild the University of El Salvador. The Washington, D.C.-based U.S. Campaign for the University of El Salvador was formed to mobilize the academic communities in the United States in support of higher education in El Salvador. The task is especially critical because UES has long been the only accessible institution of higher learning for 90 percent of the Salvadoran people. In response to threats by Salvadoran military officials to remilitarize the UES if professors and students "keep up" their demands for a fair budget and academic freedoms, Salvadoran educators and students have appealed for international support for two basic demands:

> that the University be given an adequate budget to function and begin reconstruction; [and] that the Salvadoran government and its various military and paramilitary forces respect the University's autonomy,

neither invading the campus, nor threatening and attacking members of the UES community.[50]

The U.S. Campaign has organized a material aid effort to help the University obtain supplies and has also sent delegations to El Salvador to monitor conditions at UES and observe human rights violations. Similar efforts are also being organized by groups such as the New England Central America Network (NECAN) and the Committee in Solidarity with the People of El Salvador (CISPES), based in Washington, D.C. Over thirty universities or student governments in the United States have declared themselves either sister organizations with the General Association of Salvadoran University Students or have become sister universities with the UES. Since the University reopened in 1984, over 500 students from the United States have visited the UES.[51]

As in El Salvador, the Guatemalan University faces severe repression. "In October 1978, shortly after the publication of a 'death list' naming (among others) twenty-three academics as targets, the military's education minister declared that the country could 'do without' teachers who 'agitate.' "[52] In 1981, a major attack was launched against the University of San Carlos (USAC) in which *deconocidos,* unidentified people, killed nine and left fourteen wounded. During the attack, the director of the University Cultural Center and the University's sports director were killed by machine-gun fire.[53] In September 1983, the rector of the University of San Carlos said that some thirteen members of the University had been murdered or abducted by death squads over the previous few weeks, and he held the government publicly responsible for their fate.[54]

In 1985, Raul Molina, member of the Guatemalan Opposition (RUOG) and former president of the University of San Carlos, explained a number of incidents in the repression of Guatemalan universities:

Mario Dary, President of the University of San Carlos of Guatemala (USAC), the national university, elected for the period 1981-1985, was assassinated on the university campus in December 1981. Saul Osorio, the previous President elected for the period 1978-1982, had to resign in 1980 and leave the country to save his life. Leonel Carrillo Reeves, who served as interim President after Osorio left and who conferred the presidency on Dary, was assassinated on the university campus in December 1983. Deans of three colleges of the ten major colleges of USAC (Architecture, Law and Medicine), resigned in 1980 and 1981 and went into exile. From 1979 to the present, more than 150 professors have been killed or been caused to disappear, including three deans of USAC's Schools of Psychology, Law and Economics...From 1979 to the present, more than 500 students have been killed or been caused to disappear...[55]

Protests against price hikes of basic goods and urban transport fares in September of 1985 accelerated government repression of the University. In the early evening of September 3, 1985, more than 500 soldiers illegally occupied the installations of San Carlos University, as students held a general assembly. This violation marked "the formal end of university autonomy, even though the new constitution had guaranteed it." During its occupation of the University, the army carried out a search of all installations and destroyed documents, technical equipment and buildings, with damage estimated at more than $1.5 million.[56]

Honduras also has not escaped the violence that faces the academic community. In June 1982, sixty student and trade union leaders were arrested.[57] *Honduras Update* reported in its November-December 1983 issue that several university students who spoke out against government harassment in the academic community had been tortured.[58] The publication also stated that, "Currently, academic freedoms at the universities and the preparatory schools are suspended and a campaign is underway to murder selected leaders of peasant, labor, student and church organizations."[59]

2.3 The U.S. Warfare State: Manager of Regional Repression

During the Vietnam War, military planners and their liberal sympathizers depicted the South Vietnamese government as a victim of aggression from the North and the guerrillas operating in southern Vietnam as agents of the Soviet Union, Communist China and North Vietnam. However, radical historians at the time carefully documented the origins of the South Vietnamese state in a campaign orchestrated by the United States to gain a military and political foothold in Asia. In short, the Vietnamese War was not a "civil" conflict between two warring nations. Rather, the South Vietnamese government was a creation of the United States warfare state, a puppet government with domestic allies sustained by a capital fund amounting to billions of dollars, artificially keeping the government apparatus afloat.[60] The fall of "South Vietnam" to the Viet Minh and North Vietnamese forces after the withdrawal of U.S. military forces in 1975 demonstrated the validity of radical historians' belief that the South Vietnamese government was backed by a narrow class of individuals dependent on U.S. intervention.

The contras' economic sabotage campaign and alliance with right-wing elements in Nicaragua follows the pattern already seen in Vietnam. In the end, the objective is to make a U.S.-backed force appear as the legitimate authority and confuse elite needs with popular interests. In Nicaragua, the contras' primary allies are holdovers from the oligarchy which had supported Somoza until the last years of his rule. Sectors of the country's business elite and oligarchy are given moral and political support by contra attacks which have wreaked havoc on the nation's economy. By demonstrating that Nicaragua's economy "does not work," these conservative elements seek to gain support for their vision of Nicaragua, a vision of a society ruled by contra factions and business interests untrammeled by economic policies designed to aid rural or urban workers.[61]

The contras' political capital is in the first instance based on terror. In testimony before the World Court, contra leader Edgar Chamorro decribed how the contras attempted to win supporters in Nicaragua:

> FDN [Nicaraguan Democratic Force] units would arrive at an unde-fended village, assemble all the residents in the town square and then proceed to kill—in full view of the others—all the persons suspected of working for the Nicaraguan Government or the FSLN [Sandinista Front for National Liberation]. In this atmosphere, it was not difficult to persuade all those able-bodied men left alive to return with us to Honduras.[62]

The most recent data since the "cease fire" signed in March 1987 (the Sapoa Accord) show "over 1,000 civilians kidnapped by contra forces. In the first three weeks of July [1988] alone, 35 Nicaraguans were killed in contra attacks, 8 of them civilians."[63]

The U.S. warfare state has also wielded power over Nicaragua by leading a loan embargo against Nicaragua.[64] The President's media influence has historically been used to support intervention. On November 3, 1969, 72 million television viewers heard President Richard Nixon's defense of the Vietnam intervention in his speech which claimed that a "silent majority" backed the War.[65] More recently, the Reagan administration made countless national ap-peals, through television and radio, with dutiful coverage in the print media supporting the contras.[66]

The warfare state's Vietnam project is also useful for understanding the evolution of the contras as a political force. The role they play in Nicaragua is similar to the one played by the South Vietnamese government; they are contract laborers for the warfare state. The contras were organized as a mercenary army in 1981. Former UN Ambassador Jeane Kirkpatrick explained one rationale for the use of mercenaries, arguing that the contras could be portrayed as "Nicara-guans fighting against Nicaraguans."[67] Peter Kornbluh, author of *Nicaragua: The Price of Intervention*, explains another reason why warfare state planners funded the contras:

> by working through a surrogate force, Washington could invoke a "plausible denial" of responsibility for the contras' actions, shielding the administration from accountability to Congress and the American public.[68]

The contras' dependency on U.S. military planners was explained by their former leader Edgar Chamorro: "the *contras* are a creation of the U.S. government and are accountable to it. They don't make their own decisions."[69] In short, the contras have been a front organization of the U.S. warfare state.

In tandem with the contras, the Central Intelligence Agency (CIA) has been the central agent of the warfare state's attempted creation of a "new Nicaragua" in the South Vietnamese mold. The effort to create this "new Nicaragua" began with CIA actions under President Jimmy Carter's administration when the Agency provided financial assistance to opposition elements within the country and expanded intelligence operations.[70] Shortly after Reagan took office, the CIA worked towards the re-establishment of the defeated National Guard, "the instrument that had protected U.S. interests in Nicaragua for fifty years."[71]

The contras have failed to win a military victory against the Nicaraguan government. As a result, they have sought to promote "reconciliation" and "peace" as a means of gaining popular support in Nicaragua. The contras and conservative interests have blamed the continuation of the war on the Sandinistas who are unwilling to bargain for "peace."[72] By the Spring of 1988, high level negotiations between the Nicaraguan government and the contras suggested the possibility of an end to the military conflict and contra assaults on civilians. However, the contras have used the language of "peace" as a weapon to extract political concessions that would create a Nicaragua in the image of their U.S. and domestic business allies. In sum, without the dissolution of the contras or a Sandinista military victory, a political settlement is likely to become an instrument of U.S. warfare state designs on the political and economic structure of Nicaragua.

In El Salvador, the U.S. government also plays a central role, as a "super-government" which directs and controls the country's military and political programs.[73] From 1979 to 1985, the United States invested a total of $1.835 billion in the country. As the authors of a University of El Salvador report noted:

> In the old days the armed forces ran the country for the benefit of the oligarchy; now the Christian Democratic Party runs the country for the benefit of the Reagan Administration.[74]

Washington's sponsorship of elections and political-military endorsement of the Christian Democratic Party in elections between 1982 and 1985 helped bring Duarte to power as president and gave his party a majority in the legislative assembly and control of most mayoralties. The Reagan administration pushed the Christian Democrats to adopt economic policies which aid in the production of non-traditional exports such as seafood, clothing, textiles and food processing. In part, these policies are designed to promote Salvadoran business interests tied to U.S. markets. These forces are more responsive than the old oligarchy has been to the policy objectives of the U.S. government.

The U.S. government has used military and economic aid as a central prop in its exercise of power over the Salvadoran state. Such aid has been made contingent on changes in the nation's economic policies such as the devaluation of the Salvadoran currency, drastic cuts in public expenditures and the adoption of economic policies designed to favor the private sector. In the interim, President Duarte sanctioned the directive role of the U.S. government in order to give himself room to maneuver with the oligarchy and the right wing.[75]

Repression in El Salvador has been organized and assisted by the United States, through both government agencies and personnel. U.S. Green Berets have been linked to the instruction and commission of torture in El Salvador.[76] U.S.-supplied jets have engaged in direct attacks on peasants and U.S. advisors have directed troops engaged in mass murder missions. The U.S.-trained elite battalions such as Atlacatl and Ramon Belloso engaged in the worst of the massacres. One of the first reports linking the United States to the death squads appeared in a March 22, 1984 story in *The New York Times* which revealed how the "head of Salvador's Treasury Police [had] been a paid [CIA] informant since the late 1970s."[77] The Treasury Police have been a major organizer of death squad activities. Journalist Allan Nairn has also explained the U.S. government role in creating the death squads in El Salvador. In a May 1984 article in *The Progressive,* he described how:

> Early in the 1960s, during the Kennedy Administration, agents of the U.S. Government in El Salvador set up two official security organizations that killed thousands of peasants and suspected leftists over the next fifteen years.[78]

These organizations, guided by U.S. operatives, developed into the death squads described above. Over the past twenty years or so officials of the State Department, CIA and U.S. armed forces "conceived and organized ORDEN, the rural paramilitary intelligence network" which uses terror against government opponents. The Mano Blanca, or "White Hand" death squad developed from ORDEN and was described by a former U.S. ambassador to El Salvador as "nothing less than the birth of the Death Squads."[79]

Michael McClintock, a researcher for Amnesty International, has also detailed how the U.S. played a direct role in expanding the links between the official armed forces in El Salvador and the death squads. ORDEN developed side by side with El Salvador's armed forces. The country's rural police or National Guard "worked closely with the Army's military reserves and recruitment appparatus to screen potential ORDEN members."[80] In 1980, members of ORDEN regrouped as part of the new "Civil Defense" forces. U.S. military advisors later urged that the army work more closely with such forces in order to limit and control guerrilla activity.[81]

The United States also conceived and organized the elite presidential intelligence service ANSESAL. This organization gathered files on Salvadoran dissidents and worked closely with the country's death squads. The United States also "supplied ANSESAL, the security forces and the general staff with electronic, photographic, and personal surveillance of individuals who were later assassinated by Death Squads."[82]

The U.S. warfare state's influence has been equally dramatic in shaping the lives of the Guatemalan people. In 1954, a coup organized and directed by the CIA toppled the democratically elected Jacobo Arbenz government in Guatemala. The coup has shaped the country's political structure by helping to institutionalize the power of the oligarchy and army, retarding any independent political development of more liberal social forces. By the early 1980s, the U.S. warfare state had spent close to $45 million to keep in power a military machine whose primary enemy was its own people. Organized under the banner of "counter-insurgency," the U.S. government supported the suppression of domestic liberties with $4.4 million in police training and supplies from 1957 to 1974. The U.S.-trained "elements of the police specializing in political repression and the Mobile Military Police, later implicated in many massacres."[83] The ruler, Mendez Montenegro, invited U.S. military advisors into Guatemala the day after his inauguration. These advisors oversaw a counter-insurgency campaign, carried out from 1966 to 1968, which included death-squad killing and "led to the slaughter of perhaps 10,000 peasants with the help of American Green Berets; also napalm bombing by US planes based in Panama, according to Guatemalan vice-president [Marroquin] Rojas."[84]

Political power in Honduras is shaped by a dynamic similiar to that found in El Salvador and Guatemala. Civilian leaders do not have the power or will to stop domestic repression. The Honduran military exerts control over state violence, and, as in El Salvador, the United States exerts a large degree of control over the Honduran state. This control can be seen in the large-scale dependency of Honduras on U.S. military and economic aid. In addition, reports have identified the role of U.S. state authorities in monitoring political institutions. For example, in 1987, former Armed Forces Chief of Staff Walter Lopez told the Honduran press that when he assumed office he learned that the CIA was infiltrating all levels of his country's military and government. An editorial in the Honduran daily *El Tiempo*, on December 4, 1986 also noted that the U.S. Ambassador regularly attends Honduran Security Council meetings.[85]

Honduras has served the warfare state directly as the region's major U.S. military outpost. In 1954, U.S. Secretary of State John Foster Dulles used Honduras as a military base for CIA-trained exiles who overthrew Arbenz in Guatemala. Throughout the 1980s, Honduras has served as the major military base for the contras. Contra aerial and naval raids, with U.S. assistance, origi-nated from Honduran airfields and ports. An April 23, 1984 report in *The New York Times* noted Pentagon disclosures that "American pilots at bases in Honduras and Panama now provide regular tactical support for Salvadoran Army units by flying reconnaissance missions over battle zones." The Palmerola, Honduras, air base has also been used to shuttle U.S. helicopters in military transport missions to Guatemala. But the use of such facilities is not just to provide direct military aid. In addition, the build up in Honduras is designed to create a "trip wire" for a U.S. military intervention. As New Mexico Senator Jeff Bingaman explained:

> The more people you have on the spot, the more chance you have of casualties and the more chance you have of confrontation with Sandinista troops...or the Salvadoran guerrillas...The risk-taking has increased and so have the chances of an incident that would be used to justify direct military involvement.

The danger of such a confrontation could be seen in March of 1986 when the Honduran Armed Forces, under pressure from the United States, deployed its troops to the Nicaraguan border in order to defend the contras from reprisals by the Sandinistas. The contras also played a role in provoking similar tensions in March of 1988 when 3,500 U.S. troops were flown to Honduras and positioned forty-two miles from the Nicaraguan border.[86]

2.4 The Transnationals: Partners in Repression and Intervention

El Salvador

While government repression has ensured that Central America will be profitable for companies eager to employ cheap labor and receive government tax breaks, the situation for foreign investments is complicated by political turmoil which encourages capital flight and disinvestment (see Section 4.4). The recent history of El Salvador offers an interesting illustration of the relationship between poverty, repression and U.S. investment. The Molina government, that ruled El Salvador from 1972 to 1977, developed a system of generous tax breaks and credits, in conjunction with severe repression of the workers' movement in the city and countryside.[87] The San Bartolo free trade zone was also born. A company which established two plants in this zone in the early 1980s explained the profitability of El Salvador as follows:

We cannot meet the competition of the Japanese in Europe with supplies from the U.S. The U.S. cost of production is higher than the selling price in Europe. But we can compete from Central America.[88]

However, since the "Civil War" began in 1979, more than thirty-five transnational corporations have left the country. U.S. investment dropped from $150 million that year to about $50 million in 1984.[89] Capital goods imports declined from $87 million in 1978 to approximately $32 million in 1982. From 1979 to 1981, over $1.5 billion in capital fled El Salvador.[90]

Despite the process of disinvestment, U.S. corporations have important interests in El Salvador. A 1980 report said that U.S. direct investment accounted for approximately 56 percent of total foreign investment in El Salvador. However, by 1985, U.S. direct investment was—by one account—less than one-fifth of U.S. economic aid (see Tables 4-8 and 4-9). U.S. banks have played a crucial role in financing coffee and cotton production in El Salvador. Exports of these products have helped the country purchase weapons from the United States. Citibank, a leading agribusiness bank in El Salvador, has financial connections with three non-financial firms doing business in El Salvador: Kimberly-Clark, Phelps Dodge, and Monsanto (see Table 5-11).[91]

In order to increase his administration's legitimacy and influence at home and abroad, President Duarte attempted to stem the tide of disinvestment by appealing to U.S. business leaders. In 1981, Duarte addressed corporate and government leaders of Caribbean/Central American Action (C/CAA). The C/CAA is one of the main organizers of multinational investment in Central America. Among other activities, C/CAA helped organize meetings between chambers of commerce members in U.S. cities and their counterparts in Central America. Among the corporate supporters of C/CAA during Duarte's meeting were the Bank of America and Coca-Cola; Castle & Cooke later became a supporter of C/CAA.

In July 1984, Duarte addressed a meeting of business leaders in New York City and urged them to invest in El Salvador. The meeting was sponsored by the Council of Americas Society, whose chair, David Rockefeller, is also chair of C/CAA. Among the Council of Americas members are companies which have been linked to political repression in Central America. These include Bank of America and Coca-Cola (in Guatemala) and Castle & Cooke (in Honduras). Members also include companies whose weapons have ended up in Central America such as E.I. Du Pont de Nemours & Co. (owner of Remington Arms), United Technologies, General Electric, Olin Corporation and Rockwell International (owner of North American). Companies linked to the pesticide trade in Central America are also members, such as Du Pont, Monsanto, Dow Chemical Latin America, American Cyanamid Company and the Standard Oil Company of California (Chevron).[92]

Several U.S. multinationals have been linked to right-wing forces and the system of political repression in El Salvador. According to a report in *The New York Times,* "over 40 major pharmaceutical corporations...have donated to right-wing aid campaigns in El Salvador." Among such companies are: Parke-Davis, Eli Lilly, Upjohn and Searle.[93] Evergreen Helicopters, located in McMinnville, Oregon, has provided logistical support to help the government win the civil war. Since December 1981, the company "has been helping to repair power lines damaged in El Salvador's civil war through contracts financed by the Agency for International Development." The company has also provided training with clear military implications. The AID contract calls for Evergreen to provide "in-service training to Salvadoran helicopter pilots and mechanics." In a letter to Evergreen Vice-President Donna Nelson, a coalition of human rights groups explained the link between U.S. corporate investment and political repression in El Salvador as follows:

> Restoration of orderly power service [in El Salvador] plays a crucial political function in upholding a government involved in the systematic denial of human rights.

Oregon's Pledge of Resistance campaign, together with a coalition of anti-war groups, organized protests at Evergreen's facilities.[94]

Another solidarity action also protested the role U.S. corporations play in Central America. In Fall 1986, the California Board of the Amalgamated Clothing and Textile Workers Union adopted the Salvadoran Textile Workers as a "sister union" and organized to support a group of workers who were on strike at a San Salvador factory where Levis jeans are made. A group of 250 Salvadoran workers, mostly women, occupied the jeans factory for a number of weeks. They halted production in a protest over dismissal of union representatives and wages which at $4 a day made them hard-pressed to feed their families.[95]

In addition to these firms which help perpetuate the political system of terror and economic repression in El Salvador, other U.S. multinationals have played a direct role in the slaughter of civilians through their supply of weapons employed in the government's devastating air war. Dave Raymond, a researcher based in Berkeley, has compiled a detailed listing of the companies involved in the air war and the use to which U.S. supplied weapons are put. Among the leading firms supplying the Salvadoran armed forces are: Textron, Colt Industries, Rockwell International and McDonnell Douglas (see Chapter Six and Appendix One).

Guatemala

As in El Salvador, transnationals have played an important role in political life in Guatemala. The 1954 coup was not the final episode in state repression

Table 2-1: Bank of America's Right Wing Clients

El Salto: El Salto is a sugar plantation owned by Roberto Alejos Arzu. During a labor dispute over the minimum wage in 1980, nine workers were killed at El Salto. One of Alejos' plantations was used as a training ground for the CIA's Bay of Pigs invasion. Alejos is co-founder of the Guatemalan Freedom Foundation. The Foundation is an ultra-right organization that had lobbied for the resumption of military aid to Guatemala and for the deletion of human rights restrictions on aid.

Pantaleon: Pantaleon is a large sugar plantation owned by the Herrera family. They are one of the richest families in Guatemala and have extensive holdings in industry and agribusiness. The Herreras have served on the directorate of the National Liberation Movement, Guatemala's ultra-right party that claims to have its own army. A dozen workers were killed at Pantaleon during the labor strikes of 1980.

Technica Universal: Technica Universal is a company that imports and services agro-industrial products. Its president, Juan Maegli, is a key member of the Amigos del Pais, and was one of the founders of Mano Blanco, Guatemala's most feared death squad.

Hotel Camino Real: Hotel Camino is a luxury hotel owned by Edward Carette, a member of Amigos del Pais, who has lobbied extensively in Washington for military aid to Guatemala. In 1979, an engineer employed at the hotel was killed for labor organizing.

Productos de Kenaf: Productos de Kenaf, or "PROKESA," is a privately held corporation whose general manager is Fred Sherwood, a long-time resident of Guatemala and one of the company's few stockholders. Six people were killed at PROKESA in the first half of 1980 for union organizing. "Why should we be worried about death squads?" Sherwood said in a CBS documentary. "They're bumping off the Commies, our enemies...The death squads? I'm all for it."

SOURCE: "Bank of America: Banking on Repression," *Guatemala!*, Vol. 4, No. 1, January-February 1983; Rebecca Bogdan, "Bank of America in Guatemala: Bankrolling the Rightwing," *Multinational Monitor*, October 1982.

linked to transnational actors. In the 1980s, the Bank of America (BOA) has been one of the strongest and most influential supporters of the political dictatorship in Guatemala. It is "the only bank with full service facilities in Guatemala."[96] It is "second only to the Guatemalan government itself as a source of capital for the export sector."[97] BOA was owed 13 percent of the total Guatemalan government debt to banks of industrialized nations in 1981.[98] The Bank has acted directly to prop up the Guatemalan economy and thereby its government. This twin political and economic role in supporting the dictatorship was described by a Council On Hemispheric Affairs report in February 1982:

> The bank is well aware of its leadership role in the Guatemalan political economy. In the fall of 1980, following what had been the worst year of political repression in the nation's history, the bank sought to counter widespread reports of U.S. capital flight by announcing that it would increase its loans to Guatemala. In doing so, according to [manager of BOA operations in Guatemala] Parker, the bank intended to say, "We will show you where our confidence is, and we're going to bring in another million dollars."

BOA is the "only foreign firm which is known to have been granted membership in Amigos del Pais." Amigos is an exclusive club of right-wing Guatemalan businessmen and professionals. "Some Amigos members have even been directly linked to the financing of death squads."[99] Prior to 1984, BOA was also a member of the American Chamber of Commerce in Guatemala, the organization that testified before Congress for military aid for Guatemala.[100] Local officials of BOA, such as Keith Parker (quoted above), have been apologists for the military:

> When you've got a situation like you have here you need the strongest government you can get. If you use human rights in a country with guerrillas, you're not going to get anywhere.[101]

Parker further suggests that the Guatemalan government should counter its poor image abroad by killing off its enemies:

> What they should do is declare martial law...There you catch some-body; they go to a military court. Three colonels are sitting there; you're guilty, you're shot. It works very well.[102]

The BOA gave loans to both Guatemala's armed forces and to businesses led by death squad supporters. Bank of America documents list the Institute of Military Planning, an agency of the Guatemalan army, as one of the Bank's government accounts. The Institute manages military retirement funds and a military bank, and built a residential housing project for military officers. BOA loaned $750,000 to Lucas Garcia when he was Guatemala's Minister of Defense and political leader.[103] Table 2-1 lists Bank of America customers (past and present) and details the Bank's ties to Guatemalan death squad supporters and the country's far right.

Because of the Bank of America's role in Guatemala, church groups such as the United Church Board for World Ministries and the Interfaith Center for Corporate Responsibility (ICCR) filed shareholder resolutions and organized a public inquiry into the Bank's operations. The California State Teachers Retirement System, the state's Public Employee Retirement System, St. Clara College and the Unitarian Universalist Service Committee also registered shareholder complaints against BOA. Faced with the prospect of a public confrontation at BOA's annual meeting in April 1982, the Bank moved to dissuade religious investors from proceeding with their inquiry. According to Robert Morris of ICCR:

> The Bank of America corporate secretary even tried to intimidate one of the religious investors by asking that they consider what would happen to their representatives in Guatemala should the stockholder action be made public.[104]

Like the Bank of America, Coca-Cola has also played a role in political repression in Guatemala. Food processors such as Coca-Cola have an important influence on the economies of Latin American nations. Such food companies draw over 50 percent of their revenue from international operations. Through its various brand names, Coca-Cola accounts for 42 percent of the soft drink sales in Mexico. With operations in El Salvador, Guatemala, Costa Rica, Panama and Nicaragua, Coke is one of the major corporations active in Central America.[105]

The Coca-Cola franchise bottler, Embotelladora Guatemalteca, SA (EGSA), was long a symbol of the brutality of Guatemalan society. Guatemalan labor leaders have singled out the union-busting campaign that was led by the plant's management as the most violent example of labor repression in Guatemala. Ten directors of the plant's union, the Guatemala Bottling Plant's Workers Union (STEGAC), were assassinated between 1975 and 1980. One former American manager of the Coke franchise, John Trotter, "was a leading member of the Freedom Federation, a right-wing corporate interest group with ties to the military and death squads." In 1980, EGSA workers launched a strike at the plant to demand the return of twenty-seven kidnapped labor activists seized by the police. "In response, on July 1, 1980, approximately eighty armed riot police were called into the plant and began to beat the striking workers."[106]

In response to the workers' action and pressure from international union and church groups against Coca-Cola headquarters in Atlanta, the parent company agreed to change the ownership and management of the Guatemalan bottler. Political pressure included an international boycott, begun April 15, 1980, which included several European countries, Canada, Australia, New

Zealand, Mexico and Venezuela. In Mexico, a street demonstration supported the demands of Guatemalan Coca-Cola workers; in Venezuela, the Beverage Workers' Federation staged fifteen-minute stoppages in all five Coca-Cola bottling plants.[107]

In July 1980, the International Union of Food and Allied Workers Association (IUF), negotiated an agreement on behalf of STEGAC with Coca-Cola. "The settlement was based on a commitment of the Coca-Cola company to buy out the independent franchise of owners and to finance the new owners, while retaining management control for five years."[108] The agreement also provided a loan to Anthony Zash and Roberto Mendez to acquire EGSA.[109]

On February 17, 1984, the plant's union, STEGAC, was informed, with the acquiescence of Coca-Cola in Atlanta, that the plant was bankrupt and would close the next day. Workers responded by occupying the plant, "believing that the business had been intentionally destroyed through complex financial schemes by the owners."[110] The conflict took on both a national and international significance. First, the union and workers' struggle at EGSA became an important symbol to those resisting political and economic repression in Guatemala. Second, the struggle against the plant closure represented a stand by Guatemalan workers to fight for trade union rights against their abuse by multinationals in Third World countries. The closure of the plant would have represented a serious blow to international trade union solidarity. A closure would have set a dangerous precedent for transnational companies that wanted to break labor contracts in Third World nations.

Coca-Cola in Atlanta was directly implicated in the management attempt to shut down the plant and the socio-economic attack on Guatemalans that this represented:

- The July 1980 agreement constituted "an unprecedented acknowledgment by a multinational corporation of responsibility for the actions of its franchise holders."[111]
- According to the IUF, Coca-Cola in Atlanta, since the 1980 agreement, has always had control over what happened at the EGSA plant.
- The market for Coke products in Guatemala was determined in Atlanta. Coke also supplied the EGSA plant's syrup.
- Since the plant itself was used as the collateral for the original loan to Zash and Mendez, and since this loan was not paid off, the plant was technically owned by Coke.
- When the EGSA union, STEGAC, and the IUF contacted Coke about the economic deterioration of the plant, Atlanta failed to intervene against the franchise and never explained why capital and goods were being removed from the plant.[112]

Documentation by the IUF and Locker/Abrecht Associates shows that Zash and Mendez "had structured the company in order to drain it of its resources through mutliple conflicts of interest...They had burdened the company with excessive costs, in part to benefit themselves and their families."[113]

In May 1984, Coca-Cola executives met in Costa Rica with Rodolfo Robles, head of STEGAC. Coke executives also met with other leaders of the union at their Guatemala plant. As a result of these meetings an agreement was reached in May 1984 between STEGAC and Coca-Cola in Atlanta. The agreement contained guarantees of the workers' job security by Coke until new owners were found for the plant. Some observers argued that Coke signed the agreement as part of a plan to defuse the controversy. On June 22, 1984, the National Committee of Labor Unity in Guatemala accused Coke of violating the May agreement, arguing that the company had failed to pay retroactive wages to the plant's workers and had also failed to compensate relatives of Coca-Cola employees in Guatemala who have disappeared or were murdered.[114]

The threatened closure of the EGSA plant brought the same international pressures which had changed Coke policy in 1980. Food and beverage workers' unions in Norway, Sweden and Finland threatened to launch a boycott on May 7, 1984. The IUF called on its affiliates worldwide to support the Guatemalan Coke workers to the fullest extent possible. The United Food and Commercial Workers Union, an IUF affiliate, "played an active role in challenging Coca-Cola over the closing of the Guatemalan franchise at a stockholders' meeting in Houston, April 18."[115] A labor solidarity group in Portland, Oregon, organized a demonstration at a Coke plant.[116]

On February 1, 1985, an agreement was signed between the STEGAC union and the new Coca-Cola franchise holders in Guatemala. Plant ownership was turned over to a Guatemalan investor group headed by the Porras family. STEGAC agreed to terminate the legal relationship with the former company and the obligations set forth in the May 1984 agreement. The Coca-Cola Interamerican Corporation and the Coca-Cola Company also were a party to this agreement which was to lead to the re-opening and operation of the plant by new owners, employment guarantees for 265 workers and recognition of a new union by Guatemalan authorities and the new franchise holder.[117]

The Coke campaign is instructive for future efforts which target corporate complicity in intervention, especially as the Coke workers continue to face formidable obstacles. The current owners have attempted to employ the techniques of "Transactional Analysis in meetings to make the union representatives feel like 'infants,' incompetent and therefore dependent on an effective 'father,' i.e., management." Furthermore, the Coke plant is now vulnerable to competition from Pepsi. The Coke workers' union has accused Pepsi of sending out people to threaten Coke salesmen making deliveries.[118]

Other companies have been implicated in repression as well. The union at the U.S.-owned Duralux factory, where several trade unionists have been killed or kidnapped, also faced a possible plant closure. The subsidiary of Warner-Lambert, Productos Adams in Guatemala City, "recently closed down one of its plants and reopened under another name to block union organizing." The parent considers Guatemala a key location for making Chiclets.[119]

Honduras

U.S. multinational intervention has helped make the Honduran rural oligarchy the poorest and weakest in all of Central America. U.S. investment in the banana and mining industries slowed the local economy's growth and fostered underdevelopment. Even today, "the country's five largest firms are wholly owned subsidiaries of U.S. corporations." The dominance of U.S. capital over the Honduran economy has led "many Honduran scholars to believe that a national state has never been able to coalesce in Honduras."[120] The weakness of the Honduran oligarchy in turn has contributed to the autonomy of the armed forces. The army has become an independent political force. This independence of the military from civilian control was established in 1957. Ever since then, the armed forces have become formally independent of any elected government. In fact, "the military wrote into the constitution the right of the head of the armed forces to disobey presidential orders it [sic] considered unconstitutional."[121]

The indirect impact which U.S. multinationals have had in strengthening the Honduran military has come full circle to "benefit" the U.S. military; the Honduran army's independence from civilian authority helped make it more susceptible to U.S. control. This mutually supportive pattern of economic and military intervention highlights the complex of interests which defines political intervention throughout the region. U.S. military intervention can also be seen as a means of supporting regional economic interests. The precursor to the elaborate defense pact which has made Honduras a U.S. base was a military treaty signed on May 25, 1954. The United States promised military aid in exchange for "unlimited access to Honduran raw and semi-processed materials" if it faced deficiencies in its own resources.[122] U.S. multinationals have manipulated the Honduran government to make maximum profits at minimum cost:

> The few advances the Honduran government has made to extract benefit from the banana industry have been whittled away by the TNCs [transnational corporations] which continually threaten to fire workers and leave the country if their demands are not met.

A recent illustration of such threats occurred when Rosario Resources, a gold-and-silver-mining subsidiary of AMAX, laid off 120 unionized workers in 1985. The company also blamed its decision on low profitability, but the company's union argued that Rosario's plan was to replace higher paid union employees with lower paid temporary workers. After firing the Honduran workers, "Rosario turned around and hired sixty Nicaraguans, among them former members of Somoza's National Guard." By April 1987, *La Prensa* reported that the company had closed down its operations. Texaco has also put pressure on the Honduran government by stopping refinery operations as a way to force the government to raise the price of petroleum sold in Honduras.[123]

Perhaps the most dramatic example of U.S. corporate involvement in political repression in Honduras involves the actions of the Castle & Cooke Company in the late 1970s. The authors of *State for Sale,* a critical treatment of U.S. policy in Honduras, note that the growth of U.S. influence in Honduras was closely related to the growth of a number of fruit companies which expanded operations in the country at the turn of the century. Within fifteen years of operating in Honduras, the banana companies represented two-thirds of Honduran exports and controlled the national railroad.[124] With U.S. investment by firms such as Standard Fruit (originally the Vaccaro brothers), Cuyamel Fruit and United Fruit, the banana industry grew rapidly. By 1913, bananas accounted for 66 percent of exports. In 1918, 75 percent of the banana lands were controlled by the three U.S. firms.[125]

Beyond economic control, the U.S. agricultural multinationals have exercised direct influence over Honduran political life. The multinational fruit companies were instrumental in the overthrow of reformer Ramon Villeda, who served as president from 1957 to 1963. Villeda's economic policies were designed to grant some measure of economic independence for the country by expanding the internal market and reducing Honduran dependence on the imports of manufacturing goods. A 1962 agrarian proposal challenged the rights of landlords to leave their land unfarmed. Under this plan, fruit companies such as United Fruit were threatened with the seizure of thousands of acres of uncultivated land. This prompted the intervention of Charles Burrows, then U.S. ambassador, who told Villeda not to allow the reform to pass as law until the State Department had granted its approval.[126] On many other occasions the multinationals influenced national political life. Lopez Arellano, a military president in 1975, was removed from office for his alleged involvement in a $1.25 million bribe from United Fruit.[127]

In 1981, Castle & Cooke, owner of Standard Fruit, controlled 8,800 acres of banana land in Honduras and 15,000 to 17,000 acres in Costa Rica through associate producer arrangements. While the company has sold much of its land to local producers in these countries, contracts with associate producers keep the banana land under company control without the expense and political difficulties of direct ownership.[128] Castle & Cooke owns the Dole fruit company; 25 percent of Dole's bananas come from Honduras. This follows a larger pattern in which "U.S. corporations control the production of virtually all Central

American bananas and United States consumers eat 56 percent of the bananas produced in Central America."[129] In recent years Castle & Cooke has owned as many as 148,000 acres in Honduras.[130] But, the transfer of land to associate producers has not ended the company's political influence in Honduras. Since associate producers are dependent on Castle & Cooke's distribution and marketing contracts for their livelihood, they have come to be political allies of the company in its relations with the Honduran government. The company's influence is magnified by its relations with this local aristocracy.[131]

Castle & Cooke has been an ally of military governments in Central America and has worked with them "to crush unionization and worker organizing."[132] Standard Fruit President Don Kirchoff has argued that corporate leaders should "take the offensive" in a "guerrilla war against the opponents of business."[133] What he meant can be seen in an essay describing the company's actions, written by Larry Rich for the Interfaith Center for Corporate Responsibility:

> Probably the most controversial questions about C&C's relationship to both independent producers and a government are focussed on an incident in Honduras. The Las Isletas peasant-run banana cooperative was prospering with a sales volume of $10.5 million. There was discussion of its seeking marketers other than Castle & Cooke's Standard Fruit. On February 13, 1977, a Honduran military detachment under the command of Lt. Colonel Alvarez arrived at Las Isletas in Standard Fruit vehicles to arrest and imprison the cooperative's leaders. Later, a document was produced showing that the Colonel (as well as other officials and journalists) were listed as recipients of "Special Payments" in Standard's own records.[134]

After the leaders of the cooperative at Las Isletas were arrested, the army appointed new directors. With the old leadership arrested and out of power, the new directors "quickly signed a ten-year agreement binding them to sell all their production to Castle & Cooke."[135]

President Kirchoff said that he has paid army personnel in Latin America, "much as you might hire off-duty policemen."[136] In October 1982, Standard Fruit pulled its operations out of Nicaragua without leaving any notice, contributing to that country's economic destablization. The pullout was a direct political attack on the Sandinista government. Not only were 3,500 employees thrown out of work, but the company also "launched a campaign to spread the word that Nicaragua's bananas were chemically contaminated and inferior."[137] Castle & Cooke has also found allies in the Honduran government's offices in its dealings with the country's labor movement. In December 1976, a new military government came to power. "The senior legal advisor to the new government was none other than the head of the law firm representing Castle & Cooke and United Brands in Honduras. Another member of the same law firm soon became minister of labor."[138] In 1977, 1978 and 1979, Castle & Cooke received share-holder proposals filed by church groups concerned with the company's policies in Latin America and other regions.

A more recent episode illustrates that Castle & Cooke continues to contribute to economic repression in Honduras. In late 1984, "Standard Fruit threatened to fire 500 workers because it was losing money." The company's union argued that the company was financially sound and only wanted to avoid paying a wage increase scheduled in the contract. The union also charged that Standard Fruit "switched its pineapple division over to another corporate division as a way to break its contract with the union." The dispute ended with the 500 workers keeping their jobs after the government agreed to suspend the company's taxes for a year.[139]

Part 2

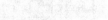

Agro-chemical Companies:
From Napalm in Vietnam to Pesticide Poisoning in Central America

3.1 Napalm and Agent Orange: Agro-chemical Companies in Vietnam

In recent years, universities have entered into elaborate contracts with multinational agro-chemical companies, the same firms that, during the 1960s, manufactured napalm used against the Vietnamese people and today promulgate the use of pesticides in Central America, poisoning thousands each year. The expansion of these economic ties is partly based on universities' need to generate new sources of revenue in the face of fiscal pressures and partly by agro-chemical companies seeking the sources of basic research they need to promote the development of biotechnology. In this chapter, we look at the relationship between universities and agro-chemical companies against the backdrop of the latter's unsavory role abroad. As David Bull of OXFAM estimates, at least 750,000 people in the Third World suffer pesticide poisoning yearly, 13,800 of them fatally.[1]

During the Vietnam War, agro-chemical companies such as Dow, Hercules and Monsanto helped produce chemical weapons for the U.S. government. In 1965, Dow Chemical Company began producing napalm. First discovered by Harvard researchers in the early days of World War II, napalm is a deadly chemical weapon which kills by burning and by carbon monoxide poisoning. It also gives rise to keloid scars which ultimately become cancerous. According to the Pentagon, more than 100,000 tons of napalm were used from the early years of the Vietnam War up to the beginning of 1968.[2] In 1966, at the price of 14.5¢ per pound, Dow received $43 million for 300 million pounds of polystyrene which was converted into napalm.[3] The polystyrene within napalm is a plastic which makes the chemical adhere to the skin as it burns. A monograph on chemical and biological warfare published in the 1960s reported that:

> A close study of Pentagon contract awards between June, 1966, and March, 1967, showed that the Michigan-based firm received at least $18 million worth of contracts for the supply of napalm, herbicides, and other chemical agents.[4]

Napalm was not the only chemical weapon used in Vietnam. Throughout the war, the U.S. government "dumped the equivalent of six pounds of toxic chemicals for every man, woman and child in South Vietnam."[5] Another type of chemical weapon employed in Vietnam was herbicides (or chemical defoliants). In 1967, the Pentagon awarded $57.7 million to U.S. chemical companies, including Dow, Hercules and Monsanto, for defoliants used to destroy forests and ground cover in Vietnam so that the U.S. Army could defend itself against ambushes and "demarcate boundaries." Herbicides were directly linked to counter-insurgency operations:

> Defoliation would be used to clear gun emplacements, open up fields of fire, mark areas of bombing, or test whether or not a particular area was camouflage or actual vegetation.[6]

U.S. scientists investigating herbicide use in South Vietnam estimated that by the end of 1970, "about one-seventh of that nation's land area had been sprayed with herbicides, and that 20 percent of its forests had been defoliated."[7] Herbicides were the major cause of the poisoning of some 300,000 people in Vietnam every year from 1966 through 1969.[8] From January 1962 to February 1971, the Defense Department used 107 million pounds of assorted herbicides in South Vietnam in order to defoliate forests and destroy crops.[9]

The mixture of 2,4-D and 2,4,5-T esters, better known as Agent Orange, became the standard jungle defoliant used in Vietnam. 2,4,5-T is contaminated with dioxin. "It is estimated that a single drop of dioxin, if it could be divided equally among 1,000 people, would kill them all."[10] Dioxin is a member of a class of chemicals which increase the frequency of cancer in subject populations. It can suppress the activity of the immune system and cause neurological damage at relatively low doses. Dioxin is not simply carcinogenic. It also increases the body's vulnerability to other carcinogens, i.e., it is cancer-producing. During the Vietnam War, the United States dumped over 57,000 tons of Agent Orange on Vietnam. Between 1962 and 1971, some 10.6 million gallons of Agent Orange were sprayed from planes at treetop level. Agent Orange was sprayed directly on food crops in Vietnam.[11]

The Vietnamese people were not the only victims of this chemical warfare. The dangers of Agent Orange and other defoliants were never properly communicated to U.S. servicemen. In fact, "several veterans have told stories of jokingly spraying each other with Agent Orange."[12] Thousands of Vietnam veterans have suffered injuries from dioxin poisoning linked to herbicides. Veterans have suffered from cancer, various neurological disorders and have had children born with congenital birth defects.[13] By 1982, 84,000 Vietnam veterans had approached the Veterans Administration for physical tests related to Agent Orange exposure.[14]

In the late 1960s, Dow Chemical helped squash a report by the private Bionetics Laboratory (and commissioned by the National Cancer Institute) which linked Agent Orange to birth defects and cancer. The government was afraid that the release of this information would help the anti-war movement. "FDA [U.S. Food and Drug Administration] officials cited pressure from chemical companies, especially Dow Chemical, as the main force keeping the truth from the public."[15] Although scientists at Dow (and at the Hercules Corporation) had knowledge that 2,4,5-T contained "surprisingly high" amounts of toxic impurities and caused damage to the skin and liver, Dow and other companies continued to tell the public that herbicides were completely safe and posed no health threat throughout the 1960s.[16]

In 1983, the activities of Dow and other chemical companies were being investigated by a House subcommittee. The committee was looking into whether Dow and the Chemical Manufacturers Association, with help from the Environmental Protection Agency, "were able to bypass regular channels and exert improper influence on the U.S. position on the international marketing of toxic chemicals." Donald R. King, the director of the State Department's environmental office, was fired shortly after a Dow executive complained to one of King's superiors that King "would support a policy on the international regulation of chemicals that would not be acceptable to the United States chemical industry."[17]

Protests against Dow Chemical's complicity in the production of chemical weapons used against the Vietnamese became an important focus of student organizing efforts in the 1960s. A graduate student at New York University in the 1960s drew the links between the company and repression in Vietnam as follows:

> Dow has...institutionalized murder. Our university, through the use of its facilities, is aiding them to recruit people. By doing so, it declares itself accomplice directly to the maintenance of the United States policy in Vietnam.[18]

Such statements showed a consciousness about universities' role in a "military division of labor," in spite of universities' claims to be neutral parties in political affairs.[19]

Acting on these links, students began to organize in the fall of 1967. Thousands demonstrated against the company's recruitment efforts on campuses across the country. In many cases the protests led Dow to cancel job interviews of prospective student employees. By mid-November, *Science Magazine* noted the importance of the corporation as a political target:

> [I]ts image is suffering. Next to LBJ, Dean Rusk and Hubert Humphrey, Dow, the manufacturer of napalm, has become the most popular target for campus anti-war protests.[20]

The protests were confrontational and helped radicalize students on many campuses. A report in the October 23, 1967 issue of *New Left Notes* described the dramatic action at the University of Wisconsin earlier that month:

> Students and police fought with fists, rocks, sticks and tear gas for two and a half hours...The rioting between some three to four thousand students and city police followed what began as a peaceful demonstration against the presence of the Dow Chemical company on campus.

The demonstration escalated when six students were dragged by police from a 350-person strong sit-in at a university building where Dow was recruiting. After the arrested students were placed in a police van, the van's windows were smashed by the crowd, the air was let out of the van's tires, cars were rolled in front of it, students stretched themselves out in its path and a picket line was set up at the only available exit some fifty feet away. The conflict progressed into a pitched battle after police threw tear gas bombs at the students who later responded by using "rocks, bricks, shoes and anything else" they could get their hands on.[21]

Such protests, including a boycott of Dow's Saran Wrap, did not hurt the company's sales, because only 8 percent of the company's revenues came from consumer goods at that time. However, the protests did provide leverage against Dow by upsetting corporate recruitment efforts. As Raymond F. Rolf, Director of Corporate Recruiting, had explained: "You just don't know what it's doing to the quality of students we're talking to."[22] More importantly, perhaps, was the damage to the company's name among consumers and the wider public. A March 15, 1969 article in *Forbes* noted that "the antiwar protestors have given Dow a bad name by labeling it the country's No. One war profiteer." The article continued:

> But Dow's problem with napalm is not completely one of fate. One reason Dow may be so vulnerable is that Dow executives never have been very concerned about their company's image. Dow's experience

proves that corporate image-making these days is not mere management busy-work. If a company does not create a public image, somebody else may. As Dow has found, such images may be hard to destroy.[23]

The full weight of the anti-Dow protests, as well as organizing efforts by veterans who had been pressing legal action against Agent Orange manufacturers, can be seen in present day company reactions to military solicitations to participate in chemical weapons production. Companies with high risk of exposure to consumer boycotts and larger firms which are more concerned with the impact of adverse publicity appear most likely to avoid activities that could provide grounds for protests. A 1985 news story in *The New York Times* highlighted these points, describing corporate reactions after the army solicited companies to manufacture the first battlefield nerve gas to be produced by the military in sixteen years. Although the army had $1.5 billion to spend for new chemical weapons, most companies shunned the business. Of the Fortune 500 chemical companies, only Olin Corporation entered the bidding for the contracts. A major reason why the companies avoided the contracts was their "fear of bad press and liability." As the *Times* explained:

> Memories of consumer boycotts (including one of Saran Wrap) and expensive litigation and settlements that the Dow Chemical Company endured in the aftermath of its manufacture of the incendiary napalm and the defoliant Agent Orange, both used by the military in Vietnam, have made executives leery of any involvement with military poisons.

Dow in particular has been shaped by these calculations. "There is a clear consensus among top management," said Robert W. Charlton, the company's Washington public affairs manager. "We have virtually no interest in that line of business. The experiences with Agent Orange and napalm have been enlightening in that regard."[24]

In 1984, Dow was one of seven companies involved in a $180 million settlement with veterans who had pressed legal damages against companies tied to the manufacture of Agent Orange. The settlement was the largest award ever received by a class of litigants claiming wrongful injury. Even so, the settlement gave the families of Vietnam veterans poisoned by their own government very little financial compensation. Only $3,500 was awarded to the family of deceased veterans and no awards were granted to wives suffering from miscarriages or children suffering from birth defects linked to Agent Orange. About 60,000 wives had established claims against the agro-chemical companies; a larger number of children also had claims. These were legally voided by the settlement.

Dow executives say that liability is one of the key problems that keeps them away from chemical weapons manufacture, but smaller firms appear willing to take the risks involved. The Vertac Chemical Corporation, for example, explained that boycotts were not a problem because "We don't have exposure in the commercial range."[25]

3.2 The Pesticide Problem in Central America

Many of the same companies which produced chemical weapons during the Vietnam era are now involved in producing and distributing dangerous pesticides in Central America. Many of these deadly chemicals are banned in the United States. Agro-chemical companies as well as some farmers claim that pesticides eliminate pest damage to crops and raise agricultural productivity. However, they also generate a self-defeating cycle in which more and more pesticides are needed, adding to costs and serious health hazards.

Pesticides enter the food chain directly by being sprayed on crops while Central American farmworkers labor in the fields. In Central America, "surveyors recorded crops with residues of aldrin up to 2000 times above the level permitted in the United States."[26] Lou Falcon, an entomologist, described how farmworkers are treated in Central America:

> The people who work in the fields are treated like half-humans, slaves really. When an airplane flies over to spray, they can leave if they want to. But they won't be paid their seven cents a day or whatever. They often live in huts in the middle of the field, so their homes, their children and their food all get contaminated.[27]

The people of Central America also risk pesticide poisoning through exposure during production. The multinationals "set up production plants that are clearly inferior to operating standards back in the United States, Europe and Japan."[28]

Water pollution is another primary cause of pesticide poisoning. Many farmworkers and their families "bathe in irrigation canals or streams contaminated with still more agro-chemicals, or try to wash off with water stored in a discarded pesticide drum."[29] In February 1983, high levels of toxic chemicals were discovered in the drinking water supply of Limon, Costa Rica, the country's third largest urban center. The water treatment plant which supplies Limon with water is one and one-half miles downstream from a corporate-owned banana plantation. "Heavy pesticidal applications are made throughout the year on the plantation. These applications are mainly aerial and a large percentage of the toxic substances used enter the water by means of dumping, runoff or aerial drift."[30]

The combined effects of air and water pollution and direct exposure during production and application to crops has produced dramatic statistics on poisoning. The Agency for International Development estimates that the annual per capita pesticide poisoning rate for Central Americans is 1,800 times greater than that of U.S. citizens.[31] Pesticide poisoning can lead to birth defects, cancer and nervous disorders as well as short-term low-level illnesses. In Guatemala, DDT levels in mothers' milk are the highest in the Western world, ninety times as high as the limits allowed in the United States. Guatemalans have thirty-one times more DDT in their blood than U.S. citizens. Parathion, which is sixty times more toxic than DDT, has been responsible for 80 percent of Central America's reported pesticide poisonings in recent years. One nurse in a clinic in Guatemala's cotton region reported that thirty to forty people had to be treated each day for pesticide poisoning.[32]

The worst pesticide poisoning in Central America occurs in cotton-growing regions. A report in the late 1970s noted that 10 percent of the total population of El Salvador, Honduras, Guatemala and Nicaragua lived "in rural areas where at least 1 percent of the county's surface [was] planted with cotton." In 1975, 700,000 people lived in these high pesticide risk areas. That same year, 2,284 poisonings were reported in the cotton-growing areas. In past years, as much as one-fifth of all parathion used in the world has gone into El Salvador's cotton production. As a result, El Salvador has suffered from the greatest number of poisonings. "There were 1,280 cases in 1974, of which 6 resulted in the death of the person. The poisoning rate was 5.16 cases per thousand rural inhabitants of prime cotton zones."[33] A report in 1984 noted that Central America imports close to 90 percent of the methyl parathion exported by the United States. This pesticide is sold freely in Central American stores even though it is highly toxic, carcinogenic and closely related to a nerve gas developed by Nazi Germany.[34]

The living conditions of workers in cotton regions have exacerbated the problem of pesticide poisoning. A 1974 survey of life in Guatemala's cotton region showed that most of the buildings where people lived had no floors; many had no running water. Buildings made with wooden walls, mostly planks with empty spaces between them, also offer little protection against insecticide drift.[35]

Pesticide-related hazards not only affect farmworkers and their families in Central America, but are also passed on to U.S. citizens through imports of crops produced in pesticide-using countries. Although developed industrial nations have established maximum allowable levels of specific pesticide residues in food, these regulations have failed to protect consumers. In 1979, the Government Accounting Office reported that "pesticide use patterns in foreign countries clearly indicate that a large portion of food imported into the U.S. may, in fact, contain unsafe pesticide residues."[36] In 1983 and 1984, the Natural Resources Defense Council (NRDC) investigated pesticide residues in food, and found that the U.S. Food and Drug Administration (FDA) used analytical methods which were incapable of detecting two-thirds of the pesticides registered by the Environmental Protection Agency for use on food. In samples of fresh fruits and vegetables, the NRDC found that 44 percent contained residues of nineteen different pesticides. Several of these were suspected or known carcinogens.[37]

U.S. multinational corporations have profited from a multi-billion dollar pesticide trade with the Third World. In 1981, $14 billion was spent worldwide on pesticides. Pesticide use worldwide each year is about one pound in weight for every man, woman and child on earth. The Third World uses about 15 percent of all pesticides and some 30 percent of the world's insecticides. The pesticide market is dominated by multinationals in the United States and West Germany, which are also the biggest exporters. "Of the 160,000 tons of pesticide annually produced in West Germany, more than 90 percent are for export; United States exports are estimated at about 40 percent of production."[38] European companies control roughly two-thirds of world exports of pesticides. U.S. companies control about 10 percent. In the mid-1960s, Central America imported 40 percent of all U.S. pesticide exports. Table 3-1 shows the growing value of insecticide imports in Central America and trade patterns for pesticides in the region.[39]

Table 3-2 describes the activities of a number of agro-chemical companies in Central America. Links are established through exports from the United States, ownership of subsidiaries or satellite manufacturing firms in Central America and licensing of pesticide products produced by second party manufacturers. Exports by U.S. transnational corporations (TNCs) to Central America are less important than these other marketing connections.

3.3 Corporate Responsibility and the Misuse of Pesticides in the Third World and Central America

A first step in developing an organizing agenda which attempts to regulate the TNC role in pesticides is to document corporate responsibility for the problems facing Central Americans. An immediate question that arises is the benefits—both real and perceived—of pesticide use in the Third World. Pesticides *do* bring the promise of higher crop yields, more food for the hungry and freedom from diseases spread by insects. Without the use of pesticides, it is estimated that 50 percent of Third World cotton production would be destroyed.

But, frequently, statistics that seem to make the case for pesticides miss the point. Pesticide researchers reciting these numbers cannot predict how much production would be lost if *alternative* pest controls were used. Furthermore, they do not take into account the tremendous economic and social costs

Table 3-1: The Pesticide Trade in Central America†
Estimated Dollar Value of Imports of Insecticides, For Retail [5911]

Year	El Salvador	Guatemala	Costa Rica	Nicaragua
1980	3,267,000	7,893,000	4,637,000	11,467,000
1981	9,994,000	9,519,000	11,134,000	12,290,000
1982	8,649,000	16,655,000	2,311,000	5,233,000
1983	9,377,000	13,149,000	8,936,000	12,768,000
1984	13,178,000	20,199,000	8,246,000	20,077,000
1985	6,236,000	12,290,000	5,100,000	6,215,000
1986	2,493,000	3,652,000	4,439,000	6,953,000

Dollar Value of Exports of Insecticides, For Retail [5911]

Year	El Salvador	Guatemala	Costa Rica
1983	3,438,000	15,856,000	5,539,000
1986	NA	124,000	2,982,000

Estimated Dollar Value of Imports of Herbicides, For Retail [5913]

Year	El Salvador	Guatemala	Costa Rica	Nicaragua
1980	1,337,000	4,378,000	11,155,000	4,423,000
1981	2,484,000	4,172,000	7,007,000	4,994,000
1982	2,340,000	8,330,000	6,559,000	4,378,000
1983	4,528,000	6,136,000	10,056,000	13,787,000
1984	5,064,000	7,202,000	11,977,000	13,011,000
1985	4,340,000	6,503,000	8,048,000	6,289,000
1986	4,940,000	3,626,000	7,030,000	5,964,000

† See Note 39.
NA: Not Available

SOURCE: *1984 International Trade Statistics Yearbook*, Volume II, (New York: United Nations, 1986), pp. 488-489; *1986 International Trade Statistics Yearbook*, Volume II, (New York: United Nations, 1988), pp. 488-489.

Table 3-2: Corporate Links to Pesticide Production and Exports to Central America

Company/Location	Pesticide Trading Link
American Cyanamid Inc., Wayne, NJ	Owns two pesticide subsidiaries in Central America: Cyanamid Inter-America Corp in Costa Rica; Cyanamid Inter-American in Guatemala. (A)
Bayer, Leverkusen, West Germany	Pesticide exporter to Costa Rica. (B) Registrant and manufacturer of pesticides in El Salvador. (C)
Castle & Cooke Los Angeles, CA	Occasional pesticide exports to Central America especially Honduras and Costa Rica. (D)
Chevron Corp. San Francisco, CA	Owns pesticide manufacturing subsidiary in Costa Rica: Quimicas Ortho de California. (A) Most pesticides sold have technicals produced in the U.S. and export to distributors in various countries of Central America. Sells products in Costa Rica, Guatemala, Honduras and El Salvador (in descending order of sales importance). (E)
Ciba-Geigy Basel, Switzerland	Pesticide manufacturer, products used in Central America. (C)
Dow Chemical Co. Midland, MI	Owns two subsidiaries: Dow Quimica de Centroamerica, a pesticides distributor in Costa Rica; Tecnica Petroquimica de Centroamerica, a pesticide firm in Guatemala. (A) Exporter of pesticides to Costa Rica. (B)
E.I. DuPont de Nemours & Co. Wilmington, DE	Owns pesticides firm in Guatemala, Quimica DuPont de Centroamerica. (A) Pesticide sales of about $6 million to Central America, with sales to: Costa Rica, El Salvador, Guatemala and Honduras. Latin American sales of about $80 million. (F)
FMC Corporation Chicago, IL	Owns two pesticides subsidiaries: FMC International in Costa Rica and FMC Guatemala in Guatemala. (A) Pesticide trading links with Costa Rica, El Salvador, Guatemala and Honduras. (G) Exporter to Costa Rica. (B)
Hercules, Inc. Wilmington, DE	Owns two subsidiaries: Hercules de Centroamerica (a pesticide firm in Guatemala) and Hercules de Centroamerica in Nicaragua, a manufacturing facility. (A)

Hoechst, Frankfurt,
West Germany
Somerville, NJ

Register of pesticides used in Central America
through Salvadoran subsidiary. (C)

Monsanto Company
St. Louis, MO

Owns two pesticides subsidiaries: Monsanto de
Costa Rica (also involved in agricultural technical
services) and Monsanto de Guatemala in Guatemala. (A) Pesticide trade links to Costa Rica, El Salvador, Guatemala and Honduras. The company
had plans, as of late 1986 to expand its trade in
the region. (H)

Rohm & Haas Co.
Philadelphia, PA

Owns subsidiary: Rohm & Haas Centro-America,
an insecticides manufacturer in Costa Rica. (A)

S.C. Johnson & Son
Inc. Racine, WI

Owns subsidiary in Costa Rica, SC Johnson de
Centroamerica, an insecticides manufacturer. (A)

Shell Oil Company
Houston, TX

Owns subsidiary in El Salvador, Shell Quimica de
El Salvador, a manufacturer of pesticides. (A)(C)

Union Carbide
Danbury, CT

Owns two subsidiaries linked to the pesticide
trade: Union Carbide Centro-Americana in Costa
Rica, and UNICAR in Guatemala. (A)

Uniroyal
Middlebury, CT

Owns Uniroyal Chemical, pesticides subsidiary in
Costa Rica. (A) Also has trading links to Guatemala. (I)

Velsicol Chemical
Rosemont, IL

Has distributor in Costa Rica but has not exported
pesticides to Costa Rica in over a year but within
the last two years. Exports throughout Latin America coordinated by office in Brazil. (J)

SOURCES AND REFERENCES:

(A) Tom Barry and Deb Preusch, *The Central America Fact Book*, (New York: Grove Press, 1986).

(B) Ministry of Agriculture, Government of Costa Rica, 1978 data on imports of selected pesticides in Costa Rica, as published in: David Weir and Mark Schapiro, *Circle of Poison: Pesticides and People in A Hungry World*, (San Francisco: Institute for Food and Development Policy, 1981).

(C) M.C. Victor Manuel Rosales, University of El Salvador, Department of Biology, "Problemas de Contaminacion Asociados a las Areas y los Productos Usados en el Cultivo del Algodon," in *Memoria-I Seminario Centroamericano Sobre Ambiente Y Desarrollo Con Enfasis En Agroquimicos*, Universidad De San Carlos De Guatemala, 6 al 8 de mayo de 1986, Guatemala.

(D) In a January 7, 1985 phone interview, Anthony Hepton, Director of Research for the Packaged Products Division of Castle & Cooke indicated that the company does conduct pesticide-linked business in Central America. Another phone interview in January of 1985 with Dr. J. D. Dement at the company's Boca Raton, Florida facility indicated the above information listed for the pesticide trade. However, a later communication from company offices in Boca Raton in answer to a November 1986 letter from the author stated that "Castle & Cooke Inc. does not produce, sell or distribute pesticides in any Central or South American country." This information contradicts a January 13, 1986 letter to the author from Jack D. DeMent, Vice President for Research & Agriculture of Castle & Cooke's Dole Fresh Fruit Company subsidiary which states: "since we export pesticides to Central America only for use in our operations, such information is company confidential."

(E) January 30, 1986 letter to author from Ira J. Ravel, Chevron International Chemicals Ltd., San Francisco, California.

(F) January 6, 1985 phone interview with Leon De Leon, Marketing Manager for Agricultural Produce in Central America; November 20, 1986 letter to author from J. R. Perdomo, Marketing Coordinator, Caribbean, DuPont Latin America, Coral Gables, Florida.

(G) October 1986 survey response from FMC Corporation, Philadelphia, Pennsylvania.

(H) December 1986 survey response from Lidio Parra, Product Development Manager, Latin America North, Monsanto Co., St. Louis, Missouri.

(I) October 1986 survey response from Uniroyal Chemical Co., Inc., Middlebury, Connecticut.

(J) May 18, 1989 phone interview with Maritza Bermudez, International Sales Department, Velsicol Chemical, Rosemont, Illinois.

NOTE: *C/CAA's 1989 Carribbean and Central American Databook* confirms Central American operations of these firms in these countries: Americam Cyanamid (Guatemala, Nicaragua); Bayer, AG (Costa Rica, Guatemala); Castle & Cooke (Costa Rica); Chevron (Costa Rica, El Salvador); Dow (Guatemala); DuPont (Guatemala, Honduras); Hercules (Guatemala, Nicaragua); Monsanto (Guatemala, Nicaragua); Rohm & Haas (Costa Rica); and SC Johnson & Son (Costa Rica).

of hazardous pesticide use. For example, a UN Commission in 1977 examined the costs and benefits associated with pesticide use in Nicaragua, estimating:

> insecticide-caused environmental and social damage cost Nicaraguan society a yearly total of $200 million in foreign exchange, while cotton earned a maximum of $141 million in 1973.

A 1977 study by the Central American Institute of Investigation and Industrial Technology estimated that a 10 percent reduction in pesticide use would result in a 20 percent reduction in pesticide poisonings.[40]

The traditional use of pesticides is coming under increasing criticism by development economists and environmentalists. Adding pesticides to an agro-ecosystem "may kill many of the natural enemies of the target pest or else the population of natural enemies may take longer to recover from the pesticide application than do the pests." Extended pesticide usage may also kill "large numbers of the natural enemies of a species other than the target pest, but having pest potential." A previously unnoticed insect, a "new" pest, may then be able to reproduce without constraint and destroy a farmer's crops.[41]

Table 3-3 illustrates this problem of the "pesticide treadmill." A pest is the food supply of its own predators. If pests are killed in sufficient numbers, then their predators may themselves die off (from starvation or poisoning) leading to a later outbreak of the pest. This pest resurgence will likely encourage some farmers to spray even more pesticides. This practice, in turn, may lead to more problems, and more pesticide applications, "until the farmer must run forever faster in order to stay in the same place." The problems grow worse as pest species develop resistance to pesticide applications.[42]

The pesticide treadmill aggravates farmers' economic dependency on transnationals selling these high-priced items. At one point, pest control accounted for 50 percent of cotton production costs in Central America.[43] The treadmill, leading to ever larger pesticide applications, also increases the health

Table 3-3: Increase in the Number of Species of Insects and Acarids Resistant to Insecticides

Year	Resistance in Crop Pests	Resistance Among Livestock Pests	Total
1908	1	--	1
1918	3	--	3
1928	5	--	5
1938	5	2	7
1948	9	5	14
1955	13	12	25
1960	65	72	137
1967	127	97	224
1976	225	139	364
1978	246	146	392
1980	261	171	432

SOURCE: A.A. Arata, "The use of pesticides in agriculture and public health—The point of view of human ecology," *Folia Entomologica Mexicana*, No. 59, pp. 139-185, 1984 as published in Angelo Z. Trape, "The impact of agrochemicals on human health and the environment," *Industry and Environment*, Vol. 8, No. 3, July-August-September 1985, United Nations Environment Programme, Paris, France.

risks for farmers and their communities. In Central America, the treadmill cycle has taken its toll in the cotton region. In the 1940s and 1950s, farmers were troubled by at most three pests and used pesticides about eight times per season. By the early 1970s, there were eight important pest species and pesticide applications had reached forty per season in some regions.[44]

Furthermore, whatever extra production might result from pesticide use "brings no direct increase in the supply of food available to the poor."[45] Ultimately servicing the transnationals and more affluent consumers of the developing and developed nations, "nearly all agricultural uses of pesticides...[have] been on cash crops, with cotton representing at least half of all use."[46] Pesticide use further reinforces economic dependency by draining foreign exchange earnings. By the late 1960s, more than 30 percent of the foreign exchange earned from cotton exports in pre-Sandinista Nicaragua was being spent on imported pesticides and on energy for their application. While the economically disadvantaged receive fewer financial benefits from pesticide use, they face a much greater health risk since they are the ones that usually apply the pesticides.

A study in the early 1970s examining Nicaragua, Guatemala, El Salvador and Honduras found that average pesticide use levels were 38 percent above the optimum and that farmers' profits would be improved by a rational reduction in pesticide use. Promotional efforts by the TNCs are one reason why farmers use more pesticides than they should. These efforts, together with pesticide labeling, are two of the primary channels by which information about pesticides reaches users in the Third World. A third channel, governmental advice and extension services, is inadequate in most countries and is hard-pressed to compete with the better financed agro-chemical companies.[47]

Agro-chemical firms serving the Third World also encourage the misuse of pesticides and are responsible for the health hazards that result from products labeled in the wrong language or providing false or insufficient information:

> Company sales promotions are often sophisticated and well financed and in many countries appear to be the most effective channel for reaching the farmer. It is therefore absolutely crucial that the sales promotions are used not merely to sell a product, but to provide usable information on pesticide safety and pest management. In fact, the opposite is very often the case.[48]

A report in the early 1980s found that 50 percent of the pesticides sold in Mexico were incorrectly labeled. Sometimes labels do not list antidotes or provide first aid instructions. In other cases, information on safety procedures, such as the need to wear rubber gloves, boots and goggles and an air purification mask, is not matched by the availability of these products in local stores. The same problem of unavailable resources faces pesticide poisoning victims; they "cannot call a doctor as labels recommend if there is not one available."[49]

Agro-chemical companies may provide some information regarding the safe use of pesticides. However, as the above examples show, the utility of safety information is determined by ancillary conditions such as: literacy, availability of protective equipment, availability of money or credit, negotiating power for workers assigned to apply pesticides, job security and access to clean water. For most pesticide users in Central America, especially smaller farmers and workers without land, these conditions do not exist and will not exist unless social conditions are radically transformed.

Companies also promote pesticides as panaceas. For example, the ICI company has advertised pesticides in Central America through notices which claim that if you have a pest problem, a chemical is the solution. Heptachlor, which is almost completely banned in Europe and the United States, has been promoted in past advertisements in Central America by the Velsicol company. In Guatemala, Bayer advertised tamaron, mentioning no hazards even though this chemical (methamidophos) is classified as "highly hazardous" by the World Health Organization. Some companies attempt to give farmers the false impression that a pesticide "guarantees or virtually guarantees higher yields and profits." For example, in one advertisement, Dow in Guatemala claimed that lorsban (chlorpyrifos) "guarantees a good harvest." The company included no safety instructions in the advertisement.[50]

Table 3-4 identifies the links between specific agro-chemical companies and pesticides exported or manufactured internationally and in Central America. As can be seen, the agro-chemical companies have promoted dangerous pesticides, including those that should be banned outright and are too dangerous for safe use regardless of safety precautions. A study in 1984 found that about "seventy-five percent of the pesticides applied in Central America are either banned, restricted or unregistered in the United States." In mid-1986, workers at Standard Fruit filed a suit against Dow and Shell Oil, claiming that they had continued to export the deadly pesticides to Costa Rica after their use was prohibited in the United States.[51]

3.4 Alternatives to Corporate Agro-chemical Policy in the Third World

An emerging alternative to mass pesticide applications is the adoption of Integrated Pest Management (IPM) techniques which attempt to exploit the advantages of the natural resource base. In IPM, emphasis is placed on the need "to protect and preserve naturally occurring biotic mortality agents such as parasites, predators and pathogens." When agro-chemicals, such as pesticides, are needed to supplement natural agents, "they are employed in as selective a

Table 3-4: Company Links to Pesticide Products

American Cyanamid Inc., Wayne, New Jersey

Malathion: In Central America, American Cyanamid licenses the chemical "malathion 57% E," a product which is manufactured by Quimica Agricola Insectral in Guatemala. Malathion is a "non-systemic organophosphate" insecticide. Malathion has a low mammalian toxicity level and is not restricted in the United States. However, the chemical is an active stomach and contact cholineserase poison. It is toxic when swallowed or inhaled. In India, malathion was transferred onto the banned list of pesticides.

Bayer, Leverkusen, West Germany*

Malathion: Bayer of El Salvador also manufactures malathion 57% E (see above).

Chevron, San Francisco, California

Monitor: Chevron sells the pesticide "monitor" throughout Central America. Monitor's generic name is "methamidophos." In January 1981, the U.S. Environmental Protection Agency restricted the use of methamidophos to application by certified trained applicators or those under their direct supervision. The chemical was restricted because of its extremely high acute dermal toxicity and its residue effects on birds. Methamidophos is not listed in the recommended sheets "Chemical Compounds Used as Pesticides: Recommendations for Safe Use in United Kingdom." It is harmful or fatal if swallowed, inhaled or absorbed through the skin. It is absorbed through the skin very rapidly.

The World Health Organization classifies the liquid and Class Ib form of Methamidophos as "highly hazardous." Methamidophos is among the chemical group called "Organophosphates," the most widely used group of insecticides. This chemical group causes the largest number of reported acute systemic illnesses or poisonings every year in California among farmworkers exposed to pesticide residues. Poisoning from these compounds occurs because organophosphates interfere with an enzyme cholinesterase (the enzyme responsible for nerve transmission).

Orthocide: Chevron also distributes "orthocide" throughout Central America. The chemical fungicide is better known by the generic name, "captan." In solid form, captan is unlikely to present an acute hazard in normal use, according to the World Health Organization. However, in Finland, the license for captan was not renewed by the Plant Protection Institute because of evidence that this substance is carcinogenic. Captan is also on the list of restricted pesticides in India.

Ciba-Geigy, Basel, Switzerland*

Galecron 50 EC: In Central America, Ciba-Geigy manufactures the pesticide galecron 50 EC. This chemical's generic title is "chlordimeform." This chemical is an insecticide-acaricide and ovicial agent. It is generally used on cotton to control bollworm and tobacco budworm. Chlordimeform was voluntarily withdrawn from the U.S. market in 1976. It was put back on the market by its manufacturers in 1978 with severe restrictions. Chlordimeform was removed from the U.S. market because tests showed that it caused malignant tumors in mice. In May 1975, inadequately protected workers in Tennessee who were packaging chlordimeform suffered severe bladder irritations; a medical investigation showed that chlordimeform was responsible. The product is toxic to fish and wildlife. It is toxic to human beings if swallowed or absorbed through the skin.

The *Multinational Monitor* reported in 1985 that "Chlordimeform is notorious for industry's 1976 'field experiment' performed on six Egyptian teenagers to determine its effects on humans." Galecron is also part of the Pesticide Action Network's "Dirty Dozen" campaign.

Dow Chemical, Midland, Michigan

Ethylene Dibromide [EDB]: While no documentary evidence links Dow to the production, export or distribution of EDB in Central America, a 1985 report described the company as a principal manufacturer of this product which is part of the Pesticide Action Network's "Dirty Dozen" campaign. EDB is an extremely potent carcinogen and mutagen that also damages male and female fertility. A fumigant used widely on soil, grains and citrus fruits, EDB penetrates human skin, rubber and plastic, as well as the skin of many crops and has contaminated groundwater throughout the United States.

E.I. DuPont de Nemours & Co., Wilmington, Delaware

Lannate: DuPont manufactures lannate 90 percent in Central America. This chemical is sold in Costa Rica and there is local formulation in Guatemala. Lannate is known by the generic name "methomyl." Methomyl is a relatively non-persistent pesticide not known to bioaccumulate. However, according to the National Wildlife Federation in the United States, the chemical is highly toxic and has been responsible for hundreds of poisonings in areas of high use. The liquid may be harmful if swallowed, poisonous if inhaled.

FMC Corporation, Chicago, Illinois

Furadan: FMC Corporation is linked to the distribution of furadan in El Salvador, Costa Rica, Guatemala, Honduras and Brazil. Furadan is better known under the generic title, "carbofuran." On August 8, 1979, carbofuran was restricted in the United States to use by certified applicators or those under their direct supervision. Carbofuran was restricted because of its acute inhalation toxicity and because of its very high oral toxicity. The chemical is extremely toxic to birds, fish, shrimp, crab and other wildlife. Carbofuran can be fatal if swallowed or if absorbed through the eyes. In June and July of 1987, the Ministry of Health surveillance system in Leon, Nicaragua, reported an epidemic of 548 pesticide poisonings caused principally by furadan and another pesticide (methamidiphos).

Hoechst, Frankfurt, West Germany*

Fundal 500 EC Hoechst licenses the chemical fundal 500 EC which is used in Central America. Fundal is known by the generic name "chlordimeform" (see description under galecron 50 EC above).

Monsanto, St. Louis, Missouri

Parathion: While no documentation exists linking Monsanto to the distribution of parathion in Central America, a 1985 report links the company to the manufacture of this chemical. The Pesticide Action Network's "Dirty Dozen" campaign has identified parathion as responsible for perhaps as much as half of the pesticide poisonings in the world today. The chemical is so acutely toxic that a teaspoon spilled on the skin can be fatal.

Shell, Houston, Texas

Aldrin and Dieldrin: While no documentation exists linking the Royal Dutch/Shell Group to the distribution of these chemicals to Central America, a 1985 report links the company to the manufacture of these products. The Pesticide Action Network's "Dirty Dozen" campaign has focused on Shell because these chemicals are acutely and indiscriminately lethal. The "drins" kill beneficial insects along with target pests. They also pose serious chronic hazards, including cancer in test animals. Environmentally persistent, they have been found in rain water, soil and food crops.

Azodrin 5: Shell manufactures azodrin 5 in El Salvador through its Shell Quimica de El Salvador subsidiary. Azodrin 5 is better known by the generic name "monocrotophos." This chemical is used to control insects and mites. It acts systematically and on contact as a foliage treatment on a variety of plants such as cotton, tobacco, sugar cane and peanuts. The National Wildlife Federation notes that monocrotophos is restricted in the United States because of its acute dermal toxicity and its residue effects on birds and mammals. From 1966 to 1981, it was implicated in fifty-nine poisoning incidents involving 101 people. Two deaths were reported from poisoning (in the United States).

The liquid class Ib form of this chemical is classified as "highly hazardous" by the World Health Organization. In Great Britain, the chemical is not in the recommendation sheets "Chemical Compound Used as Pesticides: Recommendations for Safe Use in the United Kingdom." In India, monocrotophos appears on the list of restricted pesticides.

* Indicates that the firm has a U.S. subsidiary.

SOURCES: Reports on corporate manufacturing and distribution links to specific pesticides come from: M.C. Victor Manuel Rosales, University of El Salvador, Department of Biology, "Problemas de Contaminacion Asociados a Las Areas Y Los Productos Usados en el Cultivo del Algodon," in *Memoria-I Seminario Centroamericano Sobre Ambiente Y Desarrollo Con Enfasis En Agroquimicos,* Universidad De San Carlos De Guatemala, 6 al 8 de mayo de 1986, Guatemala; Letter to author from Ira J. Ravel, Chevron International Chemicals Ltd., January 13, 1986 and accompanying brochure, "Ortho: An International Guide to Crop Protection"; Letter to author from Ira J. Ravel, Chevron International Chemicals Ltd., January 30, 1986; Author's survey received from FMC Corporation, October 1986; Survey with attached letter received from J.R. Perdomo, Marketing Coordinator, Caribbean, DuPont Latin America, Coral Gables, Florida, November 20, 1986. Reports on chemical generic names, pesticide hazards, health warnings and regulation come from: "The Dirty Dozen: Pesticides We Can Live Without," *Multinational Monitor,* September, 1985 as reprinted from "The Dirty Dozen," booklet published by the Pesticide Action Network; "34 Pesticides: Is Safe Use Possible?: A Handbook of Pesticides Regulated in the United States," National Wildlife Federation, National Audubon Society, December 1984; *The Pesticide Handbook: Profiles for Action,* Second Edition, (Penang, Malaysia: International Organization of Consumers Unions, 1986), distributed by the Institute for Food and Development Policy, San Francisco, CA; Rob McConnell, M.D., "An Epidemic of Furadan and Methamidiphos Poisoning in the Cultivation of Corn; Northern Pacific Nicaragua," Division of Occupational and Environmental Medicine, Mount Sinai Medical Center, New York, NY, draft, 1989.

manner as possible and only when their use is economically and ecologically justified."[52]

IPM systems have proven highly effective against pests which have developed resistance to pesticides, as in the cotton industries in Central America. In the early 1970s, Nicaraguan agricultural workers successfully applied IPM techniques by carefully monitoring cotton fields. They also examined the condition of plants, the number and kinds of pests and the presence or absence and abundance of their natural enemies. These examinations were used so that pesticides were applied only when needed rather than on a set schedule. Cotton planting was planned so that the period when crops were most vulnerable to damage would overlap "with the period of lowest activity and/or abundance of the key pests."[53]

Under the Sandinista government, IPM was reinstituted, together with new techniques such as the planting of "trap" crops early in the cotton season which attract pests when no cotton plants are prominent. A September 1985 report noted that the Sandinista IPM program led to a 40 percent reduction in pesticide use since the program's inception in 1981, "while maintaining and in some cases increasing, production." The Sandinistas have also taken important steps to restrict the use of hazardous chemicals, eliminating the import of DDT, endrin, dieldrin and DBCP by 1982. The country also recently banned the import of chlordimeform which had been used in ten commercial products registered in Nicaragua. Unlike many other Third World nations, the Nicaraguans have

prohibited the import of pesticides which are banned in the country of manufacture. The Ministry of Labor has conducted over 4,000 classes on workplace
safety since 1979, concentrating on problems of pesticide safety in the countryside. The Ministry of Health has also monitored workers' exposure to pesticides.[54]

Some transnationals have adopted IPM techniques, but most agro-chemical companies have little incentive to encourage a technique that ultimately
decreases their sales. According to Consumer Union's Dr. Michael Hansen:

> Any corporation included in the search for a classical biological control
> would rapidly find itself out of business; since the product rapidly
> reproduces itself for free, the company is left with nothing to sell.

In some cases, corporate competitors have helped to sabotage IPM programs.
In Nicaragua, before the downfall of the Somoza regime, pesticide companies
paid higher wages to pesticide salesmen than the government could to IPM
technicians. The technicians became salesmen and the program deteriorated.[55]

The bad faith of the agro-chemical companies in the regulation of
pesticides is also underscored by their activities in Brazil. A controversy there a
few years ago led Dow Chemical to actively resist efforts to control the hazards
involved in the use of pesticides in the state of Rio Grande do Sul. Together with
other multinational agro-chemical companies, Dow Chemical broke pesticide
Law 7747 which required companies to give state officials data on the toxicity
of their pesticides.

Brazil is the world's fifth-largest pesticide consumer and suffers from
pesticide poisoning in its forests, fauna and flora as well as in the population at
large. Brazil represents a classic example of a nation caught on the pesticide
treadmill; a 1985 report noted that the consumption of pesticides had increased
in Brazil by 421 percent over a fifteen year period, but the crop productivity had
increased only 4.9 percent over this same period. In a 1985 interview, Magda
Renner, an environmental activist in Brazil, described 144 deaths and 2,320 cases
of toxic contamination which occurred in just one Brazilian state during the
planting and spraying season.

According to Roque Sevilla, the Latin American coordinator of the Pesticide Action Network (PAN), "aldrin, dieldrin, heptachlor, paraquat, and lots of
other substances which are banned or severely restricted elsewhere are freely
available and uncontrolled in Brazil." A 1979 report showed that in the main
market in Sao Paulo, 10 percent of the vegetables analyzed and 13.5 percent of
the fruit contained residues of banned pesticides. Brazil's pesticide industry
association, ANDEF, is challenging Law 7747 which bans all organo-chlorine
pesticides and all those "not authorised in their country of origin."[56] Dow,
Monsanto, DuPont and Hercules all belong to ANDEF and have worked to fight
the law by lobbying federal authorities and initiating legal action in the Supreme

Federal Court in Brasilia.[57] Jose Lutzenberger, an environmental leader in Brazil, says that multinationals dominate the regulation of the pesticide industry in his country:

> Unfortunately, the multinational corporations, whether from the U.S. or Europe, are so strong that they managed to transform the Department of Plant Protection in our Ministry of Agriculture into a true subsidiary of them. Those people take orders from them and carry them out.[58]

A February 16, 1984 report in *Latinamerican Press* revealed that at least forty persons were killed and countless others were injured in an "ecological disaster" in the Brazilian state of Para. The State Electrical Company, Electrobas, sprayed "Tordon-155" and "Tordon-101," both produced by Dow Chemical, along a 500-mile electrical line in order to prevent the growth of plant life that obstructs it. These chemicals contain the same basic elements as Agent Orange. Some 150 citizens, mostly *campesinos,* filed suit against both Electrobas and Dow.[59]

The resistance of agro-chemical companies to IPM and their economic interest in promoting agro-chemicals in the Third Word becomes clearer when we examine the current patterns of biotechnology development and its probable impact on the Third World.

3.5 The "Biorevolution": Fostering Third World Dependency and Underdevelopment

The agro-chemical companies which serve Latin American pesticide markets have also been the driving force behind new developments in agricultural technology which have increased their power in the Third World. In the past few years, these companies have taken advantage of new advances in DNA recombination research and other breakthroughs in molecular biology leading to a "biorevolution" in the organization of biotechnology and the international organization of agriculture. The methods employed in chemical and pharmaceutical production, pollution and waste control, energy generation, food processing and plant and animal breeding are being reorganized in a dramatic fashion. The international revolution in microelectronics and the global factory have their counterparts in new methods of agriculture:

> Shell, Mobil and British Petroleum approached the Massachusetts Institute of Technology (better known as MIT) early in the seventies to conduct a study advising them of new areas of high-technology in which to invest. The answer that came back was the "genetics supply" industry—livestock and plants. Not only could the seed industry

expand its commercial potential enormously to take a much bigger bite out of the US $50 billion market but the agricultural applications of new genetic engineering technologies could open up a new market capable of reaping another US $100 billion by the end of the century.[60]

The biorevolution is producing innovations—such as self-fertilizing corn, vegetables that require less water and bacteria that aerate the soil—which could dramatically boost food production. These advances in technology, together with discoveries that allow cows to superovulate and vaccines which prevent hoof and mouth disease in cattle, could help Third World nations and regions such as Central America. However, the agro-chemical companies behind the biorevolution have developed a monopoly on the new technologies which are replacing older methods in animal and plant husbandry, making Third World nations even more dependent on technological inputs from the transnationals.[61]

The Plant Variety Protection Act, passed in the U.S. Congress in 1980, and Supreme Court decisions which permit patenting of genetically modified life forms, have enabled multinationals to monopolize the results of their research findings.[62] This monopoly guarantees corporate profits by limiting competition and access to the new technologies. For example, the Food and Agriculture Organization of the United Nations (FAO) "estimates that by the year 2000, 67 percent of the seeds used in the underdeveloped countries will be the 'improved' varieties, which in most cases are vulnerable to pests."[63] The agro-chemical companies hope to sell "the seed and the chemical [herbicide] as a pair." They are developing new strains of seeds which are more resistant to herbicide use. "Annual sales of herbicide-resistant seeds could reach $2.1 billion by the year 2000."[64] About twenty companies, including DuPont, Ciba-Geigy and Monsanto, are funding efforts to develop major crops, such as tobacco and soybeans, that will be resistant to herbicides.[65]

The new seed varieties are going to monopolize Third World markets because the Third World is becoming "dependent on the gene banks in industrialized countries for their genetic resources."[66] The new technology has shifted the breeding ground of plant varieties and gene plasm from the Third World nations to the gene banks of the Western industrial nations. How will this changeover be consummated?

> Researchers are attempting to develop new crop varieties that are reproductively unstable so that the farmer cannot save his seed and plant it the next growing season; the development of reproductively unstable hybrids will force the farmer into the market each year.[67]

The economic dependency of Third World farmers on the developed nations is likely to be aggravated by the new agricultural technology because "basic raw materials like sugar and soybeans could lose ground to bioengineered substitutes." Economies dependent on such crops for export would be at a disadvantage in world trade. Farmers purchasing the seeds, animal hormones and chemicals that are beginning to dominate world agriculture will be vulnerable to the pricing policies of agro-chemical TNCs. Most farmers will not "be able to afford these products, exacerbating the division between wealthy and poor farmers."[68] Similarly, many Third World nations will not be able to directly exploit the advances that biotechnology offers because few of them can afford the investment in equipment that major programs in the field entail. Also, "some nations lack sufficient trained scientists to staff such programs." In sum, agricultural biotechnology "contrasts sharply...with conventional plant-breeding programs, which require relatively modest capital investment."[69]

The new plant varieties are more vulnerable to diseases (and require more herbicides) because they are more genetically uniform. The decrease in the number of plant varieties makes them more susceptible to corporate control. This control has also increased since agro-chemical companies such as FMC, Monsanto and Ciba-Geigy have been "buying traditional seed supply firms, and their patentable 'commodities,' at an alarming rate." Between 1968 and 1978, multinationals bought thirty major seed companies.[70] The lack of cold storage and agricultural research facilities in the underdeveloped world has prompted Third World nations to send certain crop seeds to seed banks in the advanced nations. Nicaragua, for example, stored its seed stocks in a gene bank in Colorado. When President Reagan enacted a trade embargo against Nicaragua in 1985, he prevented these seed stocks from returning to Nicaragua. While Nicaragua eventually obtained sixty-four samples of the Nicaraguan plants, many that they did receive were dead and the rest had a very low rate of germination. Countries like Nicaragua fear that they are losing control of their seed stocks to the developed world. The Third World holds less than one-third of all known varieties of genetic stocks, while industrialized countries hold more than 90 percent.[71]

The U.S. government has encouraged this concentration of genetic material essential to the world's food supply. The Reagan administration opposed plans drawn up by representatives of more than 100 countries which would have established a new global system for collecting and storing endangered genetic sources of plants, including rootstocks, seeds and tissues. The plan proposed at the 23rd Conference of the FAO called on industrial nations to provide up to $100 million annually to Third World countries interested in collecting and storing rare plant varieties that have valuable genetic characteristics.[72]

3.6 Universities and the Agro-chemical Companies: Faculty Links to the Transnationals

The biorevolution and the rapid advance of agro-chemical technologies depends to a large extent on increased corporate research and development expenditures. The new technologies in microelectronics as well as biotechnology depend on scientific research work carried out by corporate and university laboratories. "DuPont tripled its investment in bioengineering between 1980 and 1983" and companies such as Dow, Ciba-Geigy and Arco are making similar commitments. Monsanto has the largest plant biotechnology program among private U.S. corporations and had invested $100 million in agricultural biotechnology development by 1986.[73] This company, like other agro-chemical firms, is dependent on non-corporate laboratories to gain access to state-of-the-art technologies.

Universities have become a central resource for expanding corporate biotechnology research:

> In the 1983-84 school year, agribusinesses gave universities an estimated $40 million for bioengineering research, a sum expected to increase as much as tenfold by 1990. In January [1984], for instance, Standard Oil of Ohio (Sohio) donated $2 million for bioengineering research at the University of Illinois.[74]

A study by Harvard University found that biotechnology companies invested $120.7 million in university biotechnology research in 1984. This figure represents about 30 percent of aggregate industrial funding of academic research and about 20 percent of all "extramural" funding of biotechnology research in higher education in 1984. The Harvard report found that 46 percent of biotechnology firms surveyed supported biotechnology research at universities. Of 800 biotechnology scientists polled by the Harvard researchers, 23 percent received grants or contracts from private companies.[75]

Universities have not only received research contracts from agro-chemical companies, they have also set up corporate sponsored research institutes which have increased agro-chemical firms' control over their research. Universities, such as the University of Wisconsin, Cornell, MIT, Stanford and Harvard (through its Medical School), have developed or are developing corporate-financed institutions to conduct research in biotechnology or related fields. At Stanford, a new Institute of Biological and Clinical Investigation is being developed. The founders of the Institute "propose to develop a long-term continuous collaboration with the chemical, pharmaceutical and engineering industries."[76] Some of the ties which universities have developed to agro-chemical-linked firms are described in Table 3-5.

Agro-chemical contracts directly employ faculty to carry out corporate policy. In the biotechnology field, university connections to corporations are especially close. The legal decisions which permit the patenting of laboratory-created micro-organisms have intensified university and corporate interest in joint efforts to exploit biotechnology. Huge profits have led to "an unprecedented level of university-corporate collaboration," leading critics to argue that the mission of basic biological science has been virtually subordinated to commercial interests: "the availability of corporate funds influences the direction of biological research to the extent that less and less research is undertaken which does not serve the ends of industry." Talented scientists have become "hot property," and "nearly every molecular biologist" has been signed up as a corporate consultant or board member, while others are hired full-time by industry.[77]

The universities' corporate-sponsored biotechnology research programs are just one part of a larger system linking academia to transnational interests. For example, Kenneth Smith, Associate Provost and Vice-President of Research at MIT writes that:

> our faculty are accorded the privilege of consulting one day per week; and, particularly in the school of engineering, this work is viewed as part of one's professional obligation.[78]

Table 3-5: University Ties to Agro-chemical Companies

Ciba-Geigy   **Michigan State University**

Ciba-Geigy has attempted to develop pesticide-resistant plants by funding the work of molecular biologists Lee McIntosh and Joseph Hirschberg at Michigan State University. These two researchers have identified and isolated a gene that enables plants to survive heavy treatments of the herbicide atrazine. They are attempting to transfer the gene to soybeans, wheat and other crops so that farmers will be able to use the chemical on a wider basis.

DuPont   **Harvard Medical School**

In 1978, DuPont spent $140,000 at ten universities for toxicology grants to support research by graduate students and postdoctoral fellows. In 1981, DuPont began a five-year, $6 million contract with Harvard Medical School for genetics research.

Union Carbide, Eastman Kodak   **Cornell University**
and General Foods

The Cornell University Biotechnology Program, established in 1982, governs two administrative units, the Biotechnology Institute and the New

York State Center for Biotechnology. The Institute is a collaboration between Cornell and Union Carbide, Eastman Kodak and General Foods. These three sponsors are expected to provide $7.5 million in funding over six years to support the Institute. These three companies are all weak in biotechnology research and the Institute allows them to explore new areas for future development without having to make significant long-term commitments.

Hoechst   Harvard University

In 1980, Hoechst signed a ten-year $70-million agreement with the Massachusetts General Hospital (MGH) of Harvard University in which the former guaranteed a minimum annual funding level that increased up to $6 million per year in the last seven years of the agreement. The company funds basic research in what has developed into a new Department of Molecular Biology. Research is focused on improved medical care through eukaryotic cell gene regulation, somatic cell genetics, virology, immunology and plant molecular biology. Under the agreement, research manuscript drafts are submitted to Hoechst at least thirty days prior to submission for publication. If the two institutions agree to apply for a patent, the applications will be MGH's property but Hoechst receives an exclusive world-wide license. A 1986 report by the Government-Industry-University Research Roundtable notes that "the agreement is unusual in that Hoechst provides funds of approximately $18 million for renovation of a temporary facility, and for construction of equipment for a new facility to house the department."

Chemical Manufacturers Association,   MIT/
Dow, DuPont, Monsanto and Exxon   Harvard University

An MIT-Harvard Joint Program on the Impact of Chemicals on Human Health and the Environment was formed in 1979. The program was established to study the effects of manufactured chemicals and was designed as part of an industry campaign against regulation. Chris DeMuth, a program participant from Harvard, claimed that "there is a growing agreement among scholars that the process of adversarial regulation suffers from inherent shortcomings." These include, he said, "disregard of fundamental economic aspects of regulation and a well-nigh universal suppression of innovation and competition, and protracted and unnecessary disputes between business and government over information disclosures, plant inspections, etc." DeMuth and his colleagues have suggested that alternatives to regulation such as economic incentives for nonpolluters should be explored. The Joint Program has been funded by the Chemical Manufacturers Association, Dow, DuPont, Monsanto and Exxon.

The Whitehead Institute   MIT

The Whitehead Institute is an autonomous, private, non-profit organization which is devoted to research in molecular genetics and developmental biology. Three of the Institute's trustees come from MIT and three are selected with MIT's approval. The Whitehead Institute is linked to Squibb and Celanese, two multinational pharmaceutical companies, through interlocking directorates. Celanese has acquired seed companies such as Cepril Inc., Moran Seeds and Harris Seeds. Examples of MIT's corporate contracts in the early 1980s include a $200,000 program on technology transfer sponsored by Monsanto, a Dow-funded $342,650 program on structural materials and a $243,453 program on fundamental research in mechanical engineering with DuPont.

Michigan Research Corp.   University of Michigan

The Whitehead Institute has served as a model for the University of Michigan's attempts to forge stronger links between the University and private industry. The Michigan Research Corporation (MRC) was proposed to subsidize faculty entrepreneurs whose research has commercial potential. The University has planned to provide the MRC with more than $1 million in funding.

Monsanto   Washington University

A program was developed between Monsanto and Washington University to close the gap between basic research carried out at the University and product development carried out by the company. The contract provides the University with $23.5 million (in 1982 dollars) over five years. The grant was expected to expand to $8.7 million in annual funding by 1987. The funded research areas (the study of the proteins and peptides regulating cellular communication and function) are of commercial interest because they are expected to lead to the development of therapeutic drugs. The University Roundtable report stated that, "the most striking characteristic of the program is the close relationship between company and university scientists. Dozens of Monsanto scientists are involved in the research. University scientists also use Monsanto facilities and expertise in certain chemical fields and in molecular biology." In early 1985, the program supported eighteen full professors, eight associate professors and twelve assistant professors. In 1980, Monsanto named Howard Schneiderman, Dean of the School of Biological Sciences at the University of California at Irvine, to be its new Senior Vice-President for Research and Development.

SOURCES: David Noble, "The Selling of the University," *The Nation*, February 6, 1982; David Noble and Nancy E. Pfund, "Business Goes Back to College," *The Nation*, September 20, 1980; David E. Sanger, "Corporate Links Worry Scholars," *The New York Times*, October 17, 1982, Section Three, p. 4; Frederick H. Buttel, Martin Kenney and Jack Kloppenburg, Jr., "From Green Revolution to Biorevolution," *Cornell Rural Sociology Bulletin*, Bulletin No. 132, August 1983; *Going for Broke*, (Ann Arbor, MI: Committee for Nonviolent Research, 1982); Ruth Ruttenburg and Randall Hudgins, *Occupational Safety and Health in the Chemical Industry*, 2nd Edition, (New York: Council On Economic Priorities, 1981); Kenneth A. Smith, "Industry-University Research Programs," *Physics Today*, February 1984; Government-University-Industry Roundtable, *New Alliances and Partnerships in American Science and Engineering*, (Washington, D.C.: National Academy Press, 1986).

The problem of university consulting is not unique to MIT and is growing. A September 1983 feature in *The New York Times Magazine*, "Academic Research and Big Business: A Delicate Balance," reported that:

So many academics have been hired as part-time consultants to industry that, a year or two ago, an investment company looking for an unaffiliated nuclear biologist reportedly approached 20 researchers before it found one without a commercial tie.[79]

However, the consulting pattern is not new. "From the late 19th century on, professors of chemistry have served as consultants to chemical firms, often moving back and forth between industry and academe."[80] Yet, the lines between the university and corporation are further broken down when MIT faculty are granted a leave of absence for periods of up to two years, "during which the faculty members can be committed full-time to an outside position."[81] Corporations are aggressively pursuing new ties to universities. The larger firms, especially in the petrochemical industry, are beefing up their "university affairs departments" to promote good public relations with university faculty.[82]

What do universities hope to gain from cooperative programs with industry? During the 1970s and 1980s, universities became more and more aware that in numerous fields the cost of doing research was growing while budget deficits and a Reagan administration desire to "privatize" national research threatened government support for research and development.[83] The universities have looked to cooperative programs with industry as a way of supplementing federal research assistance. Kenneth Smith from MIT says, "For the university, the money is certainly always important." Smith also justifies the university's role in cooperative programs with industry since "most students seek employment in industry" and "industry is, after all, the agent through which the benefits of science and technology are usually transferred to the public."[84]

Against the backdrop of university links to intervention in Central America, one must ask: Given the role that transnationals play in promulgating inappropriate technologies which poison Third World nations and increase their economic dependency, what is the responsibility of academic scientists who contemplate serving these concentrated centers of power? How does the increased power of corporations over academic research affect academics seeking autonomy from transnational influence in research which is appropriate to the needs and interests of the Third World? How can students, faculty and the larger community of workers inside and outside academia increase their own influence in shaping the direction of academic research?

Industrial funds for research and development at universities and colleges increased from $84 million in 1973 to $194 million in 1979, and further to $370 million in 1983. However, corporate funding is still under 5 percent of total university R&D budgets.[85] On the other hand, numerous testimonies by academics and the emergence of new "hybrid" neo-corporate institutions on campus reveal a consistent pattern of increasing corporate authority albeit within the parameters of varying levels of faculty autonomy.[86]

Even though their contributions to university R&D are low, corporations can still significantly shape university life. Robert H. Malott, Chair of the Board at the agro-chemical-linked FMC corporation, advises corporations to be very selective about supporting academics. He believes transnationals should keep funds away from faculty who fail to subscribe to corporate ideology:

> In exercising our responsibilities in managing publicly held corporations, do we have the right to establish a philosophical screen to determine how shareholders' money is to be donated? I maintain that we not only have the right and capability to do so, but also that we have the obligation to do so.[87]

Given the control of universities by such trustees, it is not surprising that many critics of the corporate world are denied tenure on a regular basis. Corporations shape how the resources of universities are used and whether they are used for the benefit of the powerful or the disenfranchised. Not only Third World farmers suffer from the advance of agricultural technologies. The California Rural Legal Association sued the University of California and charged that "the University's research on agricultural machinery serves only the interest of large growers at the expense of small growers and farm workers."[88]

The increasing dependency between universities and corporations represents a point of leverage for those in the academic community concerned with challenging university links to intervention and limiting the scope of corporate influence. Two observers of the new university-industry alliances observe a growth in university public relations activity:

> Many universities are behaving as if they believe that corporate funding is dependent in good part on a favorable public image. Indeed, journalists refer these days to "press conference science." Public relations, in effect a form of advertising, often emphasizes the spectacular promises of research to attract corporate funds.[89]

Universities are not only vulnerable to political damage which threatens their lucrative links to the transnationals; they also are potentially wary of disruptive influences on their public relations image. Such vulnerability portends both increased repression to cut off dissent (a phenomenon noted in increased cases of harassment and firings of faculty)[90] *and* universities' potential willingness to concede to organized demands to strengthen research programs which are more socially responsible.

3.7 Pitfalls and Possibilities of Agro-chemical Regulation

A strong international movement for the safe use of pesticides must include actions that target the agro-chemical/university connection. Such a movement should be combined with efforts to increase popular control over academic research and the development of technology, and to push for the development of alternatives to intensive pesticide use. A first step in such efforts is to discuss and publicize the links universities have to corporations which have investments, trustee ties and institutional affiliations with the agro-chemical companies. Churches could also apply pressure on corporations in which they have investments. "The International Code of Conduct on the Distribution and Use of Pesticides" provides a partial framework for demanding corporate reforms in pesticide abuse in the Third World. This international agreement was adopted on November 22, 1985 at the 23rd Session of the Conference of the FAO.

Among the provisions in the Code of Conduct are guidelines on pesticide management, trade, promotion and handling. Clause 4.1 states that pesticide manufacturers are expected to ensure that "each pesticide and pesticide product is adequately and effectively tested" and that "the data produced by such tests, when evaluated by competent experts, must be capable of showing whether the product can be handled and used safely without unacceptable hazard to human health, plants, animals, wildlife and the environment." Clause 10.2 says that industry should use labels that "include recommendations consistent with those of the recognized research and advisory agencies in the country of sale." Such labeling is critical in the reduction of pesticide poisonings for "worker ignorance of pesticide hazards and the failure to use adequate protective measures account for a major proportion of occupational injuries and illnesses."[91] The Organizacion Regional Internacional de Sanidad Agropecuaria (ORISA), following FAO recommendations, issued guidelines governing the labeling of pesticide products in Central America. A plan was drafted in a meeting in San Jose, Costa Rica, of Central American nations to provide specific color-coded labels for pesticides of different levels of toxicity. Nicaragua has adopted the ORISA guidelines and all industrial pesticide containers have detailed labels which discuss toxicity and instructions for use.[92]

Clause 11.1.2 of the Code of Conduct states that industry should ensure that:

advertisements do not contain any statement or visual presentation which directly or by implication, omission, ambiguity or exaggerated claim is likely to mislead the buyer, in particular with regard to the safety of the product, its nature, composition, suitability for use, or official recognition or approval.[93]

Another strategy for campus organizing regarding university ties to the agro-chemical companies is to make demands that universities sever links with companies which fail to provide information about their pesticide labeling, advertising and general activities in the Third World countries. Campus and community groups could demand that universities cut links to all agro-chemical companies involved in the pesticide trade, or those companies responsible for pesticides which have been banned by regulatory authorities in the United States and other developed nations.

Intermediate reforms centered around the International Code of Conduct must be supplemented by other demands on the agro-chemical companies.[94] The relations of dependency (as discussed in the next chapter) and repression place serious constraints on pesticide reform and regulation. In Nicaragua, efforts to develop pesticide health and safety programs have been slowed by the contra war. A report in 1986 described how 175 civilian professionals—including agronomists, ecologists, teachers and health care workers—had been killed by the contras since 1982. In 1983, defense mobilizations increasingly drew away health and safety inspectors from the Ministry of Labor.[95] Tom Barry, in his study, *Land and Hunger in Central America*, explains how repression limits pesticide regulation:

> Right-wing elements consider charges of pesticide misuse to be a strategy to incite poor farmworkers, and have issued death threats in both Guatemala and El Salvador against people expressing public concern about the dangers of insecticides. In Guatemala, death squads kidnapped a doctor who had reported on the harm inflicted by chemicals on that country's agricultural workforce.

Barry also says that Central American governments tend to ignore farmworkers' complaints partly because they do not want to encourage conflicts between workers and managers.[96]

Nicaragua's attempts to develop a responsible pesticide program have also been constrained by the war economy and the need to pay off foreign debts: "The possibility that new policies might briefly disrupt foreign earnings is a powerful brake against implementing alternative courses of action." The war economy and debt payments have drained human and capital resources needed to conduct research, planning, training and implementation of pesticide regulation policies.[97] As a result of this political context, effective pesticide reforms depend on a strong solidarity movement working to provide an alternative to repression and underdevelopment in the region. If activists can point to concrete models of responsible pesticide use in Central America, they will be aided in campaigns designed to pressure TNCs. Care International's

"Pesticide Health and Safety Program," based in Managua, Nicaragua, has provided workplace health and safety equipment, medical training and illness monitoring and training for workers and communities in the safe use of pesticides. TNCs active in Nicaragua could be lobbied to provide more economic assistance for such projects.[98] In addition, they can be pressured to provide aid for similar projects in other Central American nations. Here, administration of such programs by Western or U.S.-based Non-Governmental Organizations (NGOs) or governments might ensure protection for such projects from repression.

Student and faculty efforts in challenging transnational influence in the university can be aided by establishing networks with other groups concerned with the domestic and international activities of the agro-chemical companies. Important links can be forged by supporting the work of PAN, an international network founded in 1982 to combat "the indiscriminate sale and misuse of hazardous chemical pesticides throughout the world."[99] PAN's "Dirty Dozen" campaign has reached across the world to further these goals by seeking a ban on the use of twelve extremely hazardous pesticides wherever their safe use cannot be assured. PAN's efforts in Ecuador led the Minister of Agriculture to sign a decree prohibiting and cancelling all import licenses and registrations of twenty-three pesticides, including ten of the "Dirty Dozen." Brazil responded to the PAN campaign by prohibiting the use, distribution and sale of all organochlorine pesticides and restricting advertising, distribution and use of paraquat. In the United States, PAN is affiliated with the San Francisco-based Pesticide Education and Action Project. Corporate changes in this country include a Monsanto announcement that it would phase out ethyl parathion production and cooperation by Ciba-Geigy in an independent review of the pesticide "chlordimeform."[100]

The United Farmworkers of America has also challenged the relationships which put farmworkers and consumers in our country at risk to pesticides dangers. The union has encouraged consumers to boycott fresh grapes from California. A principal demand of the boycott is to win a joint grower-farmer testing program to test for consumer exposure to poisonous pesticide residues. The union also wants a ban on the five most dangerous pesticides which their workers are exposed to: captan, parathion, phosdrin, dinoseb and methyl bromide.[101]

Another important group of farmworkers in pesticide reform is the Farm Labor Organizing Committee (FLOC), based in Toledo, Ohio. The Committee launched a successful eight-year boycott against Campbell's Soup Company in 1979 that led to the creation of a labor relations commission which provides labor with a forum for negotiating grievances. FLOC is now pressuring farm managers and the company to halt the use of two pesticides, "maneb" and "bravo," which pose a health threat to FLOC workers. Bravo, whose common name is chlrothalonil, was described by the Environmental Protection Agency as having "oncogenic" (tumor-causing) potential.[102] Chlrothalonil was implicated in one death through exposure at a golf course.[103]

The United Farmworkers campaign has focussed on how the use of pesticides has led to health problems for citizens in the developed world. Current efforts in the environmental movement are focusing on stricter enforcement of the so-called Delaney Clause of the 1958 Food, Drug and Cosmetics Act. This clause prohibits any cancer-causing chemical residues that concentrate in processed food. Another organization working to build a national network for pesticide safety and alternatives is the National Coalition Against the Misuse of Pesticides in Washington, D.C. This group monitors dangerous pesticides and provides resources for community groups and activists concerned with the pesticide problem.

Solidarity activists can build ties with groups fighting agro-chemical companies' links to the creation of toxic waste dump sites throughout the country. U.S. firms generate more than 100 million tons of toxic waste each year, or about 833 pounds of toxic waste per person. According to the Council on Economic Priorities eight out of ten U.S. citizens, or some 190 million people, live near a source of toxic waste or a toxic waste dump.[104] These dumps have created numerous health hazards for communities faced with poisoned ground water and exposure to dangerous chemicals stored at the sites.

The agro-chemical transnationals are major generators of toxic waste chemicals. For example, a Council on Economic Priorities study of hazardous solid and liquid waste generation by major firms found that Dow was second to DuPont in total tonnage of waste generated: 2,238,001 tons in 1983. A report in November 1985 found that Dow had been named a responsible party at nine Superfund sites, large chemical waste areas which receive government clean-up assistance.[105] Monsanto was named as a responsible party at sixteen such sites. Union Carbide generates an estimated 2,537,427 tons of solid and liquid hazardous waste each year, according to a 1984 report.[106] The National Campaign Against Toxic Hazards, based in Boston, Massachusetts, together with the Citizen Action Network, have taken a leadership role in the fight to clean up toxic waste polluters. Common ground can be found with environmentalists concerned with deterioration of the ozone layer. Chlorofluorocarbon chemicals (CFCs) released by refrigeration units, insulating foams and industrial solvents, are the primary cause of ozone loss. DuPont is one of the major producers of CFCs.[107]

Important alliances can also be forged if pesticide reform activists make links to groups seeking divestment from South Africa. Appendix One lists the ties of U.S.-based agro-chemical firms to South Africa.

The Environmental Project on Central America, affiliated with the Earth Island Institute in San Francisco, has investigated in detail the environmental impact of U.S.-supported militarization. For example, "in the northern province of Chalatenango," in El Salvador, "government raids have destroyed forests and fields, making cultivation impossible." Military attacks resemble those in Vietnam: Dr. John Constable, a leading U.S. burns surgeon visited El Salvador in 1984 and found "perfectly classical, clear-cut cases of napalm bombing of civilians."[108] However, like the Vietnam period, U.S. agro-chemical firms are not innocent parties in such counter-insurgency attacks.

A report in early 1989 described the use of Monsanto's roundup herbicide as a defoliant in Guatemala. Starting in the spring of 1987, U.S. pilots from Belize, under the cover of an anti-drug campaign, targeted for spraying regions which "are precisely those where government troops are battling three leftist guerrilla armies." Guatemalan opposition spokesman Frank LaRue argues that the defoliation campaign wipes out peasant crops in order to destroy the insurgents' food supply. Another result is that Indian peasants seeking food are forced into zones controlled by the military.[109] While Monsanto's role in this campaign might be considered minimal, it is important to note that TNCs are attempting to develop seed strains that are not vulnerable to such chemicals.[110] In sum, the control of technology by the TNCs is a key variable. As agronomist Pat Roy Mooney explains: "There can be no true land reform—no true agrarian justice of any kind—and certainly no national self-reliance, if our seeds are subject to exclusive monopoly patents and our plants are bred as part of a high-input chemicals package in genetically uniform and vulnerable crops."[111]

4

Foreign Capital: Dependency or Development?

4.1 Growth with Hunger: Central American Agriculture

Transnational corporations are a central force promoting the economic hardships that lie behind the political revolution in Central America. But solidarity activists, whose strategy is to challenge TNCs (and university support for them) will face many obstacles. The most common argument against applying a divestment strategy to Central America will come from advocates of the position that U.S. corporate investment significantly contributes to the employment and economic well-being of Central Americans and should not be hampered in any way.[1] While foreign investment may make some contribution to the economic infrastructures of Guatemala, El Salvador and Honduras, TNCs must also take responsibility for the severe constraints placed on the ability of each country to develop industry, agriculture and trade, and to bring high income levels or stable employment to the majority of the region's people.

Turning first to the agricultural sector, it is clear that economic growth and development have increasingly led to impoverishment for the vast majority of Guatemalans, Salvadorans and Hondurans. One of the ways that multinational capital is most damaging to Third World nations is that it leads countries into food dependency. In Central America, for example, people rely less on themselves for food production and depend more on developed nations for food supplies. Central American governments have encouraged food dependency by supporting export agriculture. Resources allocated for agricultural production for the domestic market have been redirected toward the foreign market, resulting in increased need for imports, including basic foodstuffs to supply domestic needs. In addition, the financial sector has rewarded agro-export crops at the expense of basic grains. For example, in Honduras, in 1980, an assessment of agricultural loans at the end of the year showed that 77 percent were for export crops and livestock, while only 13 percent went to basic grains production.[2] In Central America, the agrarian sector represents about 25 percent of Gross Domestic Product and roughly 70 percent of exports.

The economic well-being of the Central American people has been tied to the fate of the agricultural sector. In 1978, 64 percent of the Honduran, 57 percent of the Guatemalan and 52 percent of the Salvadoran labor force were employed in agriculture.[3] At the same time, the Caribbean region has the highest level of malnutrition of any major region in Latin America; in Costa Rica, about 34 percent of the population is malnourished.[4] Economic growth has not led to either greater food security or the elimination of malnutrition. The reason for this division between the development of capital and the economic security of the population is based on several patterns of development common throughout the developing nations.

In the Third World, farm workers were lured away from food production by landed interests who wanted the agricultural sectors to be devoted to cash crops. Tariffs were removed from imported food, making it less expensive than domestically produced goods, thereby impoverishing local farmers.[5] While food accounts for about a third of the exports of Asia, Africa and Latin America, almost all of this food is destined for North America, Europe and Japan. As an Oxfam America report concluded: "this agricultural flow of wealth from the Third World to the industrialized nations is one of the main reasons why half a billion people in the world today are hungry."[6] In Latin America, the schism between food for export and food for domestic use is most dramatic:

> Although the region possesses some of the continent's best land and water resources...Central America and the Caribbean were the only parts of Latin America where the rates of population increase between 1950 and 1975 were estimated to have outstripped rates of growth in home market agriculture.[7]

The problems of hunger cannot be reduced to population growth or the fate accompanying regional resources. China, South Korea and Japan have eliminated malnutrition, even though they have a third or less of Central America's per capita arable land resources.[8]

Some development economists celebrate foreign investment as a source of foreign exchange needed to buy critical imports to fuel the rest of the economy. Yet, rising food *imports* in Central America have actually increased the shortage of foreign exchange. Table 4-1 shows the growing level of food imports in Guatemala, El Salvador and Honduras. In 1980, total food system imports reached $313.1 million in Guatemala, $251.3 million in El Salvador and $226.7 million in Honduras (in current U.S. dollars).[9] The Central American agricultural economy generates foreign exchange "but not food." The high levels of malnutrition in the military states of Central America again reveal the failure of these governments to provide for their people. Malnutrition persists despite increased export levels as the lack of self-sufficiency in basic grains is causing a nutrition crisis.[10]

While Central Americans go hungry, U.S. corporations profit from food sales at home. Some 90 percent of Central America's beef exports have gone to the United States despite the U.S. media and textbook claims that "America feeds the world." The United States imported more food than any other country, according to 1981 statistics. Most of these food imports come from the Third

Table 4-1: Food System Imports Selected Central American Countries 1960-1980
(Millions of Constant 1970 US Dollars)

		Guatemala	El Salvador	Honduras
1960	Food & Agriculture*	33.8	19.9	12.0
	AI, forest and fish**	12.7	2.7	0.5
	Total	46.5	22.6	12.5
1970	Food & Agriculture	32.1	30.8	25.7
	AI, forest and fish	24.4	43.6	27.6
	Total	56.5	74.4	53.3
1978	Food & Agriculture	65.9	68.9	53.6
	AI, forest and fish	58.4	59.7	59.1
	Total	124.3	128.6	112.7
1980	Food & Agriculture	63.6	89.9	87.6
	AI, forest and fish	91.4	40.9	54.9
	Total	155.0	130.8	142.5

* Food and other agricultural products.
** Agricultural inputs and machinery, forest and fish products.

SOURCE: FAO 1971, 1980 *Production Yearbook*; FAO 1971, 1980, *Trade Yearbook*; as published in Table 3a, Solon Barraclough and Peter Marchetti, "Agrarian Transformation and Food Security in the Caribbean Basin." In *Towards an Alternative for Central America and the Caribbean,* edited by George Irvin and Xabier Gorostiaga (London: George Allen & Unwin, 1985), p. 161.

World.[11] The United States imported $4.7 billion worth more of food and live animal products than it exported in 1986.[12] Although exports are not *ipso facto* a cause for impoverishment, TNCs and associated elite groups have monopolized much of the profit from these exports so that the wealth they create is not available to the peasants and working people of Central America.

Guatemala's cotton economy exemplifies a shift from mass food production to production for profit. The massive "drive to increase cotton exports [was] achieved at the expense of domestic capacities to produce food for the population."[13] In 1950 and 1967, "only 38 percent of the value of agricultural production was for internal consumption, the rest being for export."[14] While the overall average growth rate for the country's five major export crops was 5 percent, between 1961 and 1973, the annual increase in corn production averaged only 1.6 percent and wheat production grew 2.3 percent, and bean production grew 4.8 percent. Here, it is critical to note that these three staple items constitute the lion's share of the basic diet of *campesinos*.[15] In El Salvador, also, the profits from export crops far exceed those of crops produced for local consumption. For example, in 1971, a hectare planted in coffee produced $774 worth of goods, but a hectare of beans produced only $150 and corn $75.[16] The higher profits of the international market encouraged the encroachment of export farming on lands once used by local food producers.

The pattern of food dependency is the same in Honduras. During the 1970s, coffee and beef exports more than doubled. Cotton, pineapples, citrus fruits and palm oil became major exports. In this same period, there was a decline in the production of every major food crop which was consumed locally. Since 1976, Honduras has become a net importer of corn, rice, sorghum and beans. As in Guatemala, these staples constitute the basic part of most workers' diet (see Table 4-2). While beef production more than doubled between 1960 and 1980, and beef exports increased 505 percent, the per capita consumption of beef declined more in Honduras than any other Central American country.[17]

In Honduras, 61 percent of the population is malnourished, according to studies by the United Nations' Economic Commission on Latin America (ECLA). The Public Health Ministry has estimated that malnutrition affects 70 percent of all Hondurans.[18] Malnutrition is rooted in the low-income of the population, deficiencies in the food marketing and distribution system, and the improper physiological utilization of food due to infectious and contagious diseases. All of these roots of malnutrition can be traced to the government policies and TNC interests which have assigned a low priority to the food crisis and encouraged agro-exports as opposed to the basic grains consumed by the majority of the population. The latter form of agricultural production "gets little support (credit, agricultural extension services, subsidies, etc.) either from the public or private sectors, hence its primitive and traditional features," i.e. low productivity.[19] The lack of government support has encouraged backward systems of agriculture

Table 4-2: Sources of Calories in Honduras
(Percent from Each Basic Food Source)

	Main Cities (1800 Units)	Other Urban Areas (1700 Units)	Rural (1500 Units)
Corn	39	45	54
Beans	8	11	13
Rice	10	8	8
Fats	13	10	10
Sugar	7	8	7
Meats	9	6	3
Others	14	12	5

SOURCE: Document No. 42A/83 "Food Consumption and Nutrients Intake by Socio-Economic Groups in Honduran Households" of the project "Study of the Affects of Agricultural Development Policies of Food Consumption in Central America" SIECA/ECID, as published in Mario Ponce, "Honduras: Agricultural Policy and Perspectives," in *Honduras Confronts its Future*, (Boulder, CO: Lynne Rienner Publishers, Inc., 1986), p. 134.

leading to food shortages of basic foodstuffs. Estimated foodstuffs production in 1982 reached only 80 percent of the 1969-71 yield.[20]

In Guatemala, El Salvador and Honduras patterns of land use and monopolization further explain why domestic consumption fared so poorly relative to production in the agro-export sector. In Guatemala, from 1961 to 1973, "the amount of arable land devoted to export crops expanded by 6.5 percent per year, while arable land for food production increased by only 1.7 to 2.0 percent per year."[21] In Honduras, 67 percent of the population is limited to only 12 percent of arable land.[22]

Furthermore, the concentration of capital in the hands of giants like United Fruit encouraged the destruction of small farms as the TNCs bought up lands. The increased use of seed varieties requiring pesticides has made the ability to afford such chemicals a primary requirement for farmers. As noted in Chapter Three, multinationals, with U.S. government encouragement, have contributed to the promulgation of these chemicals and the monopolization of seed varieties in Central America. Mechanization (tractors) and irrigation systems are now considered a must for cost-effective production but, of course, are only affordable to large landowners. The fact that TNCs control the major intermediate agricultural inputs (tractors, pesticides, fertilizers, etc.) means that they have tremendous influence over the agricultural relations of production. The result of TNC and domestic elite control of technological inputs has been further displacement of the average poor farmer. A 1981 United Nations report summarized the problem as follows:

> The high prices charged by oligopolistic enterprises for basic inputs (fertilizers and pesticides, fuel, seeds, and machinery) have...sharpened the predicament of the smaller and medium-sized farmer. In the absence of countervailing power, the trend to concentration assumes a momentum which presages the further elimination of the smaller producers in the 1980s. The conjunction of these influences...lends credence to the contention of a leading Mid-Western banker that "the control of agriculture is moving to those who control capital."[23]

TNC control over agricultural inputs is just one side of the equation. TNCs also benefit at the expense of Central Americans through their control of markets and marketing agencies. Table 4-3 details corporate control of the global commodity trade in some of the commodities most critical to Central America. In El Salvador, the largest profits in export agriculture are made in marketing. The control of distribution by U.S. agricultural brokers diverts wealth away from the region's people:

> ...for the stages of picking and packing *alone,* "rejects" of melons in Honduras amounted to 81%, for cucumbers in Guatemala 82% and for melons in El Salvador 90%! Production costs were frequently much higher than revenues and US brokers...sometimes refused up to a third of all deliveries. Brokers only accept the produce "on consignment" when they accept it at all; this means the producer bears the risk of spoilage or failure to sell right through to the final purchaser. Under these circumstances, producers are lucky to recoup their costs, much less make a profit.

Table 4-3: Corporate Control of the Global Commodity Trade (1980)

Commodity	% Marketed by the 15 Largest TNCs
Coffee	85-90
Bananas	70-75
Cotton	85-90
Sugar	60

SOURCE: UNCTAD estimates as published in Table 4 of John Cavanagh and Frederick Clairmonte, *The Transnational Economy,* (Washington, D.C.: Institute for Policy Studies, 1984), p. 17.

In sum, TNC control over input industries and marketing agencies helps explain why "ties to the international market result in profits being drained out of the country, despite the land itself being owned by Salvadorans."[24] Chapter Five examines the TNCs' role in the banana and coffee industries in detail.

U.S.-dominated business interests have encouraged poverty in Central America not only through their control over the agro-export system, but also through their influence over domestic political life. By opposing radical and reform efforts at land and income redistribution, multinationals have helped further the conditions of impoverishment. Corporations such as Castle & Cooke, Del Monte and United Brands (in the guise of United Fruit) each have opposed efforts to redistribute land and income, and have worked to reinforce the system of oligarchic rule and the subordination of the rural work force inherited from colonial Spain. Foreign capital has also supported oligarchic rule (the monopolization of land in the hands of a few) through investment and economic ties which provide elites with economic resources. In Latin America, contracts with large multinational food distributors have given an advantage to larger firms and the oligarchy at the expense of smaller firms.[25] The access to multinational markets has led to the three tiers of economic power in traditonal Central American society, with multinational interests sitting on top, their associates who control capital and industry in the local economy vying for power with the landed oligarchy in the middle, and then, at the bottom, the peasantry.[26]

4.2 Dependent Industrialization and Foreign Control

U.S. investment has also dominated industrial development in Central America as firms have moved operations overseas to take advantage of lower wages in the region. In the 1960s, U.S. banks and financial corporations gained increased financial control of Central American industry. Until 1959, about 60 percent of U.S. direct investment had been located in economic activities such as export agriculture, railroads, harbors and electric power. Investment in *manufacturing* went from $14.6 million in 1959 to $232.8 million in 1969. After 1961, all new industry was predominantly North American. In 1959, the book value of foreign direct investment represented .8 percent of the manufacturing sector in Guatemala, 1.6 percent in El Salvador and 6.0 percent in Honduras. By 1969, these figures had jumped to 43.6 percent, 38.1 percent and 11.2 percent respectively.[27]

Manufacturing in Central America (excluding Panama and Mexico) grew from 16.4 percent of U.S. direct investments of $420 million in 1966 to 40.7

percent of U.S. direct investments of $698 million in 1977. In 1982, manufacturing represented 37.4 percent of U.S. direct investments of $814 million.[28] Recently, the disruption caused by war has encouraged much foreign capital to leave the region, but there have been times in the past when about three-fourths of Central American products traded were produced in factories either under direct U.S. ownership or in which the majority of capital was North American. In 1986, manufacturing accounted for one-sixth of real GDP and one-fourth of total exports in El Salvador.[29]

The advance of industrialization in Central America has not brought increased economic independence for Central Americans. Some attempts were made to follow the model of "import substitution" carried out in Argentina and Mexico. Products which were once imported became manufactured domestically: "infant industries" were given a chance to grow through trade controls which kept out lower priced goods imported from advanced industrial nations. Through the domestic production of goods, import-substituting industrialization was designed to create "new incomes which may enlarge the market for a number of additional final demand goods to the point where their domestic production becomes, in turn, feasible." A central goal was that the expansion of imported inputs would open up "new opportunities for the establishment of domestic manufacturing facilities turning out these inputs."[30] However, as we shall see, this model never worked in the Central American context because of U.S. interference and the weakness of local markets. Central America never experienced an "authentic" import substitution policy. Industrial expansion has been highly influenced by foreign investment.[31]

Why has U.S. domination of industry placed limits on the generation of employment and social wealth for the majority of people in Central America? Since 1954, industrialization in Guatemala has encouraged the denationalization of property and resources as industries have been taken over by U.S. capital. The Guatemalan government oversaw this process with laws such as the Industrial Promotion Law of 1959 which created generous fiscal incentives to lure foreign investment including exemptions from income taxes and duties on machinery and raw materials imports. These government giveaways contributed to a loss of tax revenue for national development. The use of imported rather than local raw materials was also rewarded.[32]

Industrial development also failed to bring employment to all regions. In 1968, 69 percent of industry was located in and around Guatemala City. While there have been high levels of migration from rural areas to the cities, the industrial sector dominated by U.S. interests has not absorbed significant numbers of workers displaced from agriculture: "from 1950 to 1962 industrial employment rose an average of 1.5 percent per year, while urban population increased at an annual rate of 5.1 percent." A study in 1969 found that "foreign corporations employed a mere two percent of the work force."[33]

Nor has the significant level of foreign investment in El Salvador done much to bring employment to the large numbers of displaced farmers.

Between 1961 and 1971 the manufacturing sector in El Salvador grew by 24 percent, but the number of people employed in industry increased by only 6 percent. Furthermore, by the end of the 1970s, due to the economic crisis, many workers previously employed in industry were no longer employed. It was estimated that by this time 11 percent of the urban industrial workers had lost their jobs in Guatemala and Costa Rica, and 21 percent in El Salvador.[34]

Investments in advanced technology raised productivity and helped expand production. However, the failure to develop a system to redistribute resulting profits limited equitable economic development.

Foreign investment has not provided *stable* employment even in labor intensive industries. TNC investment in *maquiladoras* (or export manufacturing plants) have had low rates of tenure; they can easily pick up and leave a region. El Salvador has "become a base for *re-runaway* industries," which have fled other low-wage havens after conditions were no longer favorable. For example, in the same year that Texas Instruments shut down its Curacao plant, it launched production in El Salvador.[35] To attract such assembly plants, the Salvadoran government granted tax concessions and built extensive infrastructure such as roads and housing. However, this $20 million dedication to TNC investment came at the cost of social programs and by 1979 led to the creation of only 5,000 jobs.[36]

The industrial sector is limited in its ability to provide greater numbers of jobs because TNCs, under the leadership of the U.S. government, have enforced economic relationships which weakened the links between assembly operations in Central American industry on the one hand, and domestic suppliers and producers on the other. Multinational capital has also represented an "economic drain" on local capital in Central America. As a result, the growth and the extension of domestic industrial capacity has been held back.[37] This development has its roots in U.S. policies governing the Central American Common Market (CACM) in the 1950s.

The Central American nations developed a common market to provide larger markets, which were otherwise unavailable, because domestic demand was constrained by the impoverishment of the local population. Economic planners hoped that this would encourage growth through trade. The original common market proposals developed by ECLA emphasized job creation to raise the income of the poor, and projects which would make the Central American economies less vulnerable to the sharp changes which affected world commodity prices. As a result, the ECLA plan stressed the importance of production for local markets rather than export. This initial common market plan sought to ensure these goals by limiting foreign investment in any one industry to a 49 percent interest. ECLA also proposed a planning commission which would guarantee each Central American nation a share of newly created industry.[38] In the 1950s, U.S. government and industry leaders demanded that U.S. capital be allowed to enter Central America on its own terms. Central American nations were asked to eliminate the very controls which might have made foreign capital investment more beneficial to national development. The key decisions were made when U.S. interests sought to reshape the CACM:

> In a series of meetings with government officials from the Central American countries, U.S. officials promised substantial financial assistance—provided that regulations governing the common market were modified. Restrictions on foreign investment and free trade should be eliminated; the gradual process of tariff elimination between the five countries should be accelerated with tariffs eliminated immediately; and monopoly priviledges and the integration industries concept, which interfered with the free flow of investment and with competition, should be discarded.[39]

The U.S. government saw provisions for planning and limits on foreign control of industry as inimical to the operations of TNCs. These provisions were dropped although they were necessary to help ensure the growth of industry geared to local needs. Conservative local elites sided with the United States and "saw any form of economic planning as one step removed from Bolshevism."[40] Tariffs were needed in order to protect the growth of industries using domestic resources as in the import substitution industrialization model. In the original common market plan, industries having a natural monopoly in the region (so called "integration industries") would have been protected from competition for ten years.

The benefits of trade protection for the region were noted in a 1966 study which suggested that constraints on imports furthered growth:

> During the last twenty years, industrial production has increased at a faster pace than the rest of the Central American economy, thanks to the impetus afforded by a number of circumstances: the restriction of imports during the war and the early postwar period; the active protective policy followed by most of the nations; and, until the mid-1950s, the rapid increase in export earnings.[41]

However, a barrier emerged which prevented the Central American economies from taking an independent course. The U.S. government was able to control the key Central American economic integration agencies such as SIECA and the Central American Bank for Economic Integration. In El Salvador, the Bank worked to support U.S. transnational interests:

> Through 1967 this bank loaned $46 million to infrastructure projects, such as roads and dams. Many of these projects directly benefited the multinationals. In some cases the bank would loan directly to Ameri-

can firms, such as the $1.1 million loaned to Phelps-Dodge to expand its Salvadoran wire-making plant. Many of these loans were to buy US goods which had to be shipped in US ships.[42]

The U.S. government provided generous support for the Bank and was able "to exercise a decisive influence over the particular strategies and institutions of integration."[43]

The original approach to integration favored by ECLA had called for policies designed to overcome the historical inequalities within the region and an increased government role in planning. U.S. government control led to policies giving free rein to private enterprise and "investment decisions based purely on market considerations." Consequently, foreign investors flocked to the more developed nations of Guatemala and El Salvador, leaving Honduras with relatively little industrial development.[44]

Although the common market treaty provided that all members would raise tariffs on outside goods to a level agreed upon by all, tariffs were eliminated *between* member nations.[45] Given weak investments in Honduras, such tariff elimination helped keep Honduran industry backward. In sum, "the United States had succeeded in divesting the common market of the controls posed by the principles of balanced growth and government planning" which had been favored by ECLA.[46]

The U.S.-controlled "import substitution" industrialization helped promote production geared for foreign interests at the expense of domestic needs. The changed character of the CACM shows how earlier patterns of development inherited from colonization were reinforced by U.S. government and TNC manipulation and control. Legal and financial structures were put in place which created few incentives for local entrepreneurs to use local materials or produce consumer necessities for domestic markets. The development of the CACM led to a tremendous increase in the volume of intra-regional trade and "a shift in the composition of that trade from un-processed agricultural surpluses to non-durable consumer goods often produced by the 'new' foreign investors."[47] The bias against the use of local inputs in turn helped foster economic stagnation. One critic of CACM noted that "only an estimated 5 to 20% of manufacturing of 'Salvadoran' products was actually done in El Salvador."[48]

A number of factors have combined to draw capital away from Central American economies and into the coffers of the multinational firms. Economists in the region have termed the impact of foreign investment "parasitic" precisely because foreign investors took over domestic industry and repatriated millions of dollars. In the process, Central American industries were transformed into assembly operations of foreign-made parts.

Edelberto Torres-Rivas, a leading critic of U.S. investment's impact on the region, argues that foreign capital has held back the development of economic institutions which would benefit most Central Americans. The rising presence of foreign capital led to the "replacement of finished products by their semi-finished components." Basic production was increasingly carried out in the more advanced industrial nations. Not only did foreign business interests separate production from assembly, they also worked to the detriment of local industrialists by taking control of local markets through joint ventures or acquistions. Much of this TNC control of local business was bought with locally raised capital.[49] In the 1960s, multinationals in El Salvador contributed to balance of payments problems by buying out local corporations. When TNCs borrowed from local banks to buy out such companies, they diverted capital from local investors who often generate more jobs than the multinationals.[50]

An estimate in 1970 found that about half of the largest U.S. companies in Guatemala started operations by buying up local firms. Reports in 1969 and 1974 noted the displacement of Central American private capital through acquisition by TNCs and that about 28 percent of U.S. foreign investors entered the Central American market through the acquisition of previously existing firms. In El Salvador, joint ventures made up three-fourths of new investments between 1960 and 1978.[51] In Guatemala, "the very term 'U.S. investment' is quite misleading...insofar as the net effect for Guatemala is a capital outflow rather than inflow." Only half of total foreign direct investment from 1962 to 1969 represented new capital inflows, "the other half coming from reinvested profits, local bank loans, etc." A large proportion of profits made in Guatemala is sent back to parent corporations: 39 percent in 1962, 45.5 percent in 1968 and 42 percent in 1969.[52] The parasitical role of foreign capital also suggests that the region might do better without foreign investment:

> Accounting for both new investments and profit repatriation by TNCs, the net contribution of foreign private capital in the 1970s was a negative $180 million—meaning that TNCs had taken out $180 million more than they put into the Central American economy.[53]

U.S. Department of Commerce statistics have shown that "for every dollar that U.S. companies invest in Latin America, an estimated three dollars accrues to the United States in income."[54] Multinationals have several competitive advantages which allow them to drive their indigenous competitors out of business. Among these are: superior economies of scale, management, selective access to new product developments, trained personnel, markets and financing. Multinationals also "recruit the most talented labor, raise labor costs for all firms, make independent ventures unattractive, and induce indigenous management personnel to manage a subsidiary rather than compete with it."[55]

Foreign investment capital has limited the number of jobs which industry is able to provide to Central American workers. One reason is the weakness of backward linkages to domestic suppliers, i.e., the links to native producers of raw materials suppliers and intermediate goods are weak. These weak linkages, together with the absence of signigicant production levels for the home market, has limited the number of jobs that might have been created had more of the inputs to assembly operations come from within Central America itself. The lack of an "internal market," a basis for domestic demand for industrial products, is rooted in both the poverty of Central American workers *and* the dedication of industrial production to overseas markets. The weakness of the "internal market" has resulted in stagnation: "over half of the industrial plant of Central America stood idle in the mid-1970s for lack of effective demand."[56]

Foreign investment actually decreases the ability of industry to provide jobs. For example, the tire industry had a value added of more than 50 percent before foreign investments were undertaken in Central America. It dropped to below 40 percent with the entrance of the TNCs and the enlargement of trade among the Central American nations. In Guatemala, a study of products manufactured by sixty-eight multinationals showed a foreign-import factor ranging from 70 to 85 percent.[57] Other data compiled from a 1972 report reveal that increasing levels of foreign participation in ownership reduced the contribution of Central American inputs as a percentage of total inputs in a survey of twelve firms.[58] Table 4-4 shows that the massive entrance of foreign firms in the pharmaceutical industry caused a drop in the contribution of domestic producers towards the total value of production. This occurred despite the increased levels of output and intra-regional trade.[59]

The predominance of agricultural export interests has also limited industrial growth. Agricultural export firms compete with industry for scarce credit

Table 4-4: Estimated Value Added as a Percentage of Production in the Central American Pharmaceutical Sector, 1962 and 1968

Country	1962	1968	Variance
Guatemala	41	26	-15
El Salvador	39	32	-7
Honduras	36	30	-6
Nicaragua	36	34	-2

SOURCE: ICAITI, *Informe sobre la Industria Farmaceutica en Centroamerica,* December 1969, as published in Table 26, C.V. Vaitsos, *The role of transnational enterprises in Latin American integration efforts: Who integrates, and with whom, how and for whose benefit?* UNCTAD, January 6, 1983.

and contribute to the "inability of industrialists to develop pressure groups" capable of advancing their needs before the government.[60] In periods of declining credit, agriculture "has been given precedence over industry, as well as paying lower interest charges." In El Salvador, there was little economic or political leadership for industrialization as long as coffee remained a profitable cash crop.[61]

4.3 Cycles of Dependency: Trade, Debt, Austerity

Confronted by a cycle of rising trade deficits, increased debt to foreign banks and the International Monetary Fund (IMF), and resulting austerity, the military states of Central America have faced declining rates of growth (see Table 4-5). This cycle also has been aggravated by a "war economy" and economic sabotage. For the people of Central America, the cycle of dependency has meant increased economic hardship. The cycle can be largely traced to the structure of agricultural and industrial development elaborated above. In this structure, agriculture is most critical, comprising a large share of exports and national income.

Dependence on agricultural exports has led to a decrease in national purchasing power, as primary product export prices have widely fluctuated. The terms of trade have worked against Central American nations as the value of their exports have been driven down by fierce international competition. Such competition is the result of shrinking demand, itself a product of the global recession which began in the early 1970s. In the 1980s, developing countries have competed directly with each other as exporters of a narrow range of

Table 4-5: Growth Rate of Gross Domestic Product
(Rates Expressed as Geometric Annual Averages at 1950 Prices)

	El Salvador	Guatemala	Honduras
1969-1974	4.9	6.4	3.5
1974-1979	3.5	5.3	5.2
1979-1982	-8.1	.8	.5

SOURCE: Victor Bulmer-Thomas, "Central American Trade Diversification and the World Market," Chapter 11 in *Towards an Alternative for Central America and the Caribbean*, edited by George Irwin and Xabier Gorostiaga, (London: George Allen & Unwin, 1985).

primary products. As a result, "separate efforts by each to expand shipments in the face of stagnant or weak demand often led to price reductions for all."[62] Falling prices for agro-exports has contributed to a serious loss of foreign exchange earnings. This loss comprises a large share of the debt burden as countries face balance of payments difficulties. They must borrow from overseas lending agencies as the value of exports drops and the cost of imports has increased. Table 4-6 shows how falling export earnings have led to trade and debt problems in the region. The ability of Central American countries to expand sales of key exports has also been hindered by European agreements which favor the imports of their former colonies.[63]

As marketer and direct producer, the TNCs have linked Central American nations to an international economy in which the terms of trade have worked against them. TNCs have reinforced dependence on food imports but "dependence on food imports for survival means that a country can never hold out just prices for its exports."[64] In the face of TNC control, the developing nations are limited in their ability to increase the price of their agricultural goods through the creation of cartels or producers' associations.

The weak trading position of Central American nations is also part of their dependence on imported machinery: "Where it took 160 bags of coffee to purchase a tractor in 1960, it took 400 bags to buy the same tractor in 1970."[65] The reliance on foreign sources for such imports is part of the structure of Central American industry noted earlier. Here, TNC penetration has led to the decreased contribution of native industries towards production (value added). But the other side of such low-content production is the increased imports of

Table 4-6: Loss of Export Earnings Due to Commodity Price Changes, 1981-1983

	cummulative loss/debt accumulation	cummulative loss/current account deficits	average loss/ 1980 imports
El Salvador	121.3	106.1	23.1
Guatemala	150.4	97.8	24.4
Honduras	87.3	56.5	14.0
Nicaragua	26.9	32.5	17.4

SOURCE: Table 13 in United Nations Conference on Trade and Development, *Trade and Development Report*, (New York: United Nations, 1985), UNCTAD/TDR 15, p. 79.

semi-finished products and industrial machinery which has worsened the trade balance. From 1963 to 1969, the aggregate Central American imports of machinery and equipment exceeded $500 million.[66]

While agricultural export prices have been falling, the prices of key imports and financial services have been rising. The value of oil imports has risen dramatically since 1973. In 1972, El Salvador's balance of payments was a positive $12 million; by 1974 the country faced a deficit of $134 million. The role of oil in this turn around can be seen in the dramatic oil price increases initiated by the OPEC cartel in the 1970s. In 1973, $16.1 million worth of oil was imported, increasing to $62.1 million in 1975, and $167.8 million (or 16 percent of the value of imports) in 1981.[67]

TNCs have played a direct role in aggravating the trade deficits of Central American nations because they contribute little by way of direct investment and wages and have repatriated large amounts of profit. Third World export manufacturing has worked against achieving a healthy balance of payments and external balance "by holding down both the quantity of labor and the wage it receives, and therefore the inflow of foreign exchange to pay local labor."[68] In Central American nations, the average annual deficit was $177 million from 1968 to 1970, but the remittance of profits by foreign companies in 1970 totaled $120 million.[69]

Although certain problems are specific to the region, Central America has followed the general pattern which defines the debt burden of developing nations:

> The essentials of the debt problem may be found in the scissor-like movements taken by key monetary and real variables: rising interest rates and falling commodity prices; rising debt service payments and falling capital inflows; rising trade balances and falling investments...[70]

Trade deficits have led countries to borrow more from bankers and international lending agencies. Their indebtedness constrains economic growth as loan payments come at the expense of internal investment. In December 1976, foreign debt represented 18 percent of Gross Industrial Product in El Salvador and 10 percent in Guatemala. In Central America, public debt grew thirty-five-fold from 1960 to 1977. In Honduras, the 1987 budget of $965 million faced a $330 million deficit, or 34 percent. But in this multi-million-dollar budget, only 7 percent was earmarked for productive investment. However, 31 percent of the budget was slated to pay part of the public debt which in 1987 was about $2.3 billion. In 1985 alone, $100 million was paid in interest in Honduras.[71] Table 4-7 shows the dramatic growth in debt that continued into the 1980s.

Central American countries have turned to the IMF to help them finance trade deficits and public and private debt. The IMF in turn has made such financing contingent on state-enforced austerity programs which have brought economic hardship for these countries' workers. The so-called "IMF package" has included measures to reduce public spending and subsidies for social purposes and wages. The goal is to have countries maintain low levels of domestic spending and reduce import demands which have created trade imbalances as national export revenues fail to cover the total import bill. Another key element of the program is currency devaluation, designed to make exports more competitive in the international market. However, this IMF cure is as bad as the deficit disease itself. In fact, the IMF cure reinforces the disease as well as promoting the relations of dependency and all that entails.

Devaluation, by making imports cheaper, cuts into the living standards of workers. Governments also double their efforts to restrain labor in order to meet IMF guidelines and gain the private investment needed to provide taxes to pay off public debts. The IMF has also promoted the increase in export agriculture as a means of providing the capital necessary to alleviate the debt. Thus, the trade-debt cycle is completed, with exports fueling debt and debt fueling exports (and more debt incurred to pay off both original principal and accumulating interest payments).

The actual burden of the rising debt has been mediated by the Central American nations' attempts to renegotiate and restructure their debt. In 1986, the region allocated an average of 39 percent of its exports to *debt service,* as opposed to 11 percent in 1978 (according to a 1987 report in *Cepal Review).* In response, as countries have been unable to meet their external debt commitments, delays have occurred in the repayment of both principal and interest. In May 1986, Costa Rica informally suspended regular interest payments, equal to about 8 percent of Gross National Product.[72] But for countries like El Salvador, Guatemala and Honduras, the problems of debt have been partially ameliorated by U.S. aid.

Table 4-7: Debt as a % of GNP 1978 and 1983

	1978	1983
El Salvador	14.2	29.6
Guatemala	8.4	17.6
Honduras	41.4	59.9
Nicaragua	55.4	93.2

SOURCE: Debt Indicators of Selected Developing Countries, in United Nations Conference on Trade and Development, *Trade and Development Report,* (New York: United Nations, 1985), UNCTAD/TDR 15, p. 200.

4.4 Changing Relations of Dependency in the 1980s

The growing role of foreign lending, substantial increases in U.S. aid and capital flight have created what some observers have called "the changing relations of dependency" in Central America. Particularly in El Salvador, the relations of dependency with the United States have changed the pattern found in the 1960s and 1970s when multinational corporations were the preeminent actors. Carlos F. Diaz-Alejandro, a Latin American economist, observed a general trend for Latin America which bears directly on the Central American case:

> Since the late 1960s, a number of Latin American countries have borrowed extensively from private international banks; these flows have surpassed those for direct foreign investment and concessional finance.[73]

Table 4-8 shows the sporadic character of U.S. direct investment in El Salvador and its uneven growth in Honduras and Guatemala.[74] The data also show how private capital has fled from Nicaragua.

Table 4-8: U.S. Direct Investment Abroad in Central America
(in Millions of Dollars)

	El Salvador	Guatemala	Honduras	Nicaragua
1977	79	155	157	108
1978	98	147	164	119
1979	98	188	215	88
1980	105	229	288	89
1981	112	234	327	83
1982	96	233	247	20
1983	100	214	216	35
1984	94	240	288	39
1985	73	213	171	39
1986	NA	161	167	51
1987	51	159	203	93

NA: Not Available

SOURCE: *Survey of Current Business,* Vol. 64, No. 11, November 1984; Vol. 66, No. 8, August 1986; Vol. 68, No. 8, August 1988.

The growing importance of financial aid in sustaining the Central American military states can be traced to the impact which regional strife, guerrilla and contra activity, as well as militarization, have had on profitability and the stability of investments. By 1980, the average rate of profit on direct U.S. investment in Central America of about $1.1 billion was considerably lower than in the rest of Latin America.[75] Now, the U.S. government (through economic and military aid), and multilateral lending agencies and (to a lesser extent) U.S. private banks have become important forces shaping the economies of Central America. U.S. economic aid to the three military states has been growing steadily, supplemented by foreign bank lending (see Tables 4-9 and 4-10). Table 4-10 shows the increases in long-term foreign borrowing. The other side of the growing debt faced by Central American nations is the increased role which foreign banks and bilateral lending agencies, as well as the IMF and other multilateral agencies, have played in sustaining and reaping profit in Central American economies: "During the 1970s, Central America's debt to TNC banks increased twenty times to over $4 billion. TNC banks based in the United States accounted for about half of this commerical debt."[76]

Table 4-9: U.S. Economic Aid to Central America
(in Millions of Dollars)

FY	El Salvador	Guatemala	Honduras
1977	6.7	20.7	12.2
1978	11.0	10.7	17.1
1979	11.4	24.7	29.1
1980	58.3	13.0	53.1
1981	113.9	19.1	36.4
1982	182.2	15.5	80.7
1983	245.5	29.6	105.9
1984	215.9	20.3	95.0
1985	433.9	106.9	229.0
1986	322.6	116.7	136.6
1987	462.9	187.8	197.8

SOURCE: *U.S. Overseas Loans and Grants: Series Yearly Data, Volume II, Latin America and the Caribbean,* Obligations and Loan Authorizations, FY 1946 - FY 1985, Agency for International Development Washington, D.C.; *U.S. Overseas Loans and Grants and Assistance from International Organizations,* Obligations and Loan Authorizations, July 1, 1945-September 30, 1987, Office of Planning and Budgeting, Bureau for Program and Policy Coordination, Agency for International Development, Washington, D.C.

Table 4-10: Central Reserve Bank:
Long-term Foreign Borrowing in Local Currencies
(in Millions) *

	El Salvador	Guatemala	Honduras
1979	429	73.9	243.0
1980	651	129.9	287.3
1981	743	254.9	315.0
1982	816	312.9	333.1
1983	1,149	459.9	331.4
1984	1,158	543.6	359.0
1985	1,149	640.0	414.1

* Expressed in *Colones* for Central Reserve Bank in El Salvador, in *Quetzales* for Bank of Guatemala and in *Lempiras* for Central Bank in Honduras.

SOURCE: *International Financial Statistics,* Vol. 39, No. 11, November 1986.

In El Salvador, the repatriation of earnings by Salvadoran refugees living in the United States and revenues collected by the Christian Democratic-controlled state coffee monopoly have also become important forces in sustaining the political and economic system and have provided income and subsistence for the people who live under it. The Bank of America plays an important role as the only U.S. bank authorized to sell dollars in El Salvador. A large percentage of these dollars have ended up in the hands of the government which taxes these funds to finance the war and takes a profit after they are exchanged for the local currency.[77]

Growing debt has combined with the burdens of a war economy to create the new relations of dependency in Central America. The regional war has made foreign lending and U.S. assistance necessary to avert economic collapse. This is true particularly in El Salvador, where the war has brought capital flight in excess of a billion dollars, as well as tremendous infrastructure damage. As a result, El Salvador has increased its dependency on U.S. aid, which has totaled more than $1.8 billion since 1980.[78]

The war spending by the military states of Central America has brought its own contradictions, leading to cutbacks in social services and non-military government spending. The average annual rate of growth of military expenditures from 1977 to 1981 was 9.5 percent. However, for the period from 1981 to 1985, this figure increased to 14 percent.[79] Military spending is financed from three sources, the most important being foreign aid. In 1983, the military budgets of Costa Rica, Guatemala and Honduras amounted to an estimated $530 million, but U.S. security assistance was even greater, totaling $550 million. In fact, "U.S. military assistance to El Salvador in 1983 was equivalent to 55 percent of this country's national budget and 15 percent of its GDP."[80]

But military spending is not costless. In addition to direct U.S. aid, local taxes and foreign loans have financed military spending.[81] U.S. banks have acted as funders of the general government budgets of El Salvador, Guatemala and Honduras, acting as indirect supporters of the military economy. Domestic miltary spending has complicated IMF efforts to stabilize economies through restrictions on purchases. For example, in Honduras, strict wage freeze measures and restrictions on spending for goods and services have failed to reduce the growth of spending which rose by 12 percent in 1983. While higher interest payments were one factor explaining these developments, higher national defense spending also played a significant role, e.g., large military budgets create pockets of wealthy individuals who can pay for high-priced imports or lead to purchases to supply the military apparatus.[82]

The 1985 IMF report *El Salvador: Recent Economic Developments* stated that from 1979 to 1981, "the overall fiscal deficit increased sharply because of a rapid growth in public spending that was related mainly to the containment of the guerrilla activity, and it was financed mainly by domestic bank credit."[83] Given that domestic banks borrow substantial sums from foreign banks (see Table 5-10), this suggests another connection between U.S. banks and the repressive power of the Salvadoran government. While the Central American warfare state has grown in power, constraints on federal expenditures have come mainly as the result of a contracted welfare state:

> Mainly as a result of cutbacks in nondefense expenditure (particularly for investment), the overall deficit of the nonfinancial public sector (before foreign grants) declined from about 11 percent of GDP in 1981 to 8 percent in 1983, while public sector recourse to domestic bank credit was reduced considerably.[84]

The evidence is quite conclusive that foreign investment in Central America holds back the growth of industry, the production of food for domestic consumption, and national income. There is some evidence to suggest that Central American economies would be better off without foreign investment. For example, in Guatemala national planning authorities estimated that:

> in the absence of all foreign direct investment in the latter part of the 1960s and assuming that such investment had created (a) completely new activities (rather than acquiring or displacing existing national production) and (b) activities which could not have been undertaken by other forms of association with foreign factor suppliers, the

country's gross domestic product would have been lower by only 1 percent.[85]

Economic underdevelopment and political repression in the Central American military states have been mutually sustaining. Poverty has bred resistance, and resistance has been met with repression. On the other hand, repression has prevented land reform, the economic basis for income redistribution and the expanded growth through an internal market. Ultimately, equitable economic development rests on the development of cooperative forms of land ownership in which agro-exports are contracted and local food production is expanded. But, the full and equitable development of Central American economies will be impossible unless the masses of these nations are able to gain a larger share of the wealth generated by their labor. A graphic example of how wealth can be robbed from the peasantry even under societies with equitable land distribution and protectionist common markets is demonstrated in Table 4-11. The table illustrates the share of wealth generated for local producers in the world banana economy: "Whereas the gains of the domestic growers are about 11.5 percent, those of foreign enterprises are of the order of 88.5 percent."[86] Even less of this 11.5 percent can be expected to spill into the hands of *campesinos* at the bottom of the social ladder.

Political conflicts in Central America have prevented economic integration and the regional cooperation which is needed to expand markets based on economies of scale and economic specialization. The nationalistic economic approach is limited by a redundancy in economic institutions and overpopulation in certain nations. (El Salvador's population of more than five million is expected to reach about ten million by the year 2,000.[87]) Economic reform and growth depend on the development of democratic institutions "which incorporate the poor in decision-making regarding resource allocation in their communities and at the national level."[88] A liberalized U.S. trade and debt policy which favored native Central American industries and limited TNC ownership of Central American enterprises would also help promote equitable economic growth.[89]

Various political actors have presented obstacles to the development of a Central America freed from economic poverty and political repression. The oligarchy and business elite in Central America developed a partnership in which an inequitable social order is defended by death squads, attacks on trade unions and the forced removal of the peasantry from their means of livelihood in agriculture.

The U.S. warfare state has promoted the war economy by sustaining military states through lucrative economic aid. By supporting elite interests which oppose economic reform, warfare state military aid translates into economic underdevelopment. The TNCs have also encouraged economic stagnation and unequitable economic distribution by blocking land reform and

Table 4-11: Clairmonte's Model:
Illustrative Estimates of Main Cost Elements in the World Banana Economy in 1971

	% of Retail Unit Value	Retail Unit (USD per ton)
1. Reported production cost before harvesting	10.3	34
2. Harvesting and transport to packing plant	1.1	3
3. Producer gross margin	0.2	1
1-3. Estimated Gross Return to growers at packing plant	11.6	38
4. Packing	7.3	24
5. Transport to port	1.4	4
6. Loading and stevedoring	1.5	5
7. Export tax	0.8	2
8. Other charges	1.7	6
9. Exporters' margin	1.7	6
1-9. FOB Price	26.0	85
10. Freight and insurance	11.5	38
1-10. CIF price	37.5	123
11. Unloading and handing at port of discharge	4.8	16
12. Import duties	6.9	23
13. Importers' gross margin or commission	-0.1	-0.3
1-13. FOB selling price	49.1	161
14. Ripeners' gross margin	19.0	62
1-14. Ripeners' selling price	68.1	223
15. Retail Gross Margin	31.9	104
1-15. Retail price	100.0	327

SOURCE: UNCTAD, *The Marketing and Distribution System for Bananas,* TD/B/C.1/162, 1978 as cited in Frank F. Clairmonte and John Cavanagh, "Corporate power in selected food commodities," *Raw Materials Report,* Vol. 1, No. 3, 1982, p. 36 [Table 4].

reform governments, repatriating profits, exploiting national infrastructure expenditures while simultaneously providing minimal tax revenues, and helping to reproduce the agro-export economy. While some have debated whether transnationals or the colonial past bear the greater burden for underdevelopment, today the TNCs play an important political role in "rationalizing" the military states in Central America. The transnational corporations and banks have provided the economic "glue" for keeping in place a repressive social order.[30]

Theoretically, Central American states could turn to other countries or domestic entrepreneurs to develop industries. However, as noted earlier, many local businesses have been co-opted or displaced by foreign capital. The present military states of Central America are locked into a dependency on U.S. markets and the interests of foreign investors. As a result, this dependency of agriculture and industry on U.S. business interests has complicated efforts to provide employment and sustain industry without foreign capital.

The TNCs and the Central American economic elite stand together with the U.S. warfare state and the Central American military states as the major institutional actors behind underdevelopment in the region. We next examine the extent to which divestment actions can challenge these actors and weaken this "dependency" system.

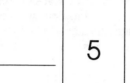

5

Towards Selective Divestment:
Using Corporate Pressure
Against the State

5.1 Confronting Corporate Complicity
in South Africa

What would a university-based movement challenging corporate support for interventionism mean? Would it involve the demand that companies withdraw their operations from Central American dictatorships? Would strategies which encourage U.S. capital to leave Central America prove beneficial to the Central American people? Are all U.S. companies equally condemnable? If a company invests in Central America, does this itself become grounds for a political organizing effort? More specifically, would organizing efforts which challenge the terms under which transnationals operate in Central America lead to severe economic hardship for the region's people?

To answer the questions posed above, it is useful to first look at the example of divestment from South Africa in order to lay out a possible rationale for a movement which challenges U.S. corporate ties to Central American military states. Second, we formally elaborate an argument for such a movement in the United States by considering both the economic and political repression that is linked to multinational investment in Central American countries. Third, we examine the limits of organizing a movement which, like the South African divestment campaign, attempts to pressure military states by demanding that companies cut off economic relations with them. Fourth, we explore the theory of "selective divestment" through "dual demands" which suggests that divestment from specific multinationals be contingent upon their policy towards trade union rights as well as political reforms by Central American governments. Fifth, we examine specific companies linked to Central America which could be pressured in a series of "corporate campaigns." Finally, we examine the limits of selective divestment and the necessity for challenging U.S. government support for repression by supplementary strategies which confront the war-making institutions of the military-industrial complex.

The practicality of a "selective divestment" strategy is contingent upon a number of factors which could limit its effectiveness. But while the ideas presented below might be considered "speculative," they build on the efforts of prior anti-corporate campaigns like the ones aimed at Dow Chemical, Coca-Cola and firms linked to apartheid in South Africa.

The previous chapters have linked terror and underdevelopment to the concentration of power, land and wealth among the rich and their partners in the military and death squads. However, in the process of building a popular movement to eliminate this concentration of power, opposition leaders attempt to gain concessions from the government, both to build political victories which legitimate their struggles and to alleviate the burdens faced on a daily basis. In this case, "reforms" take on a different meaning, i.e. they are "concessions from the state," and are a prerequisite for social actions attempting to eliminate the root causes of terror and underdevelopment by popular mobilization. On this political level, divestment actions might put additional pressure on the Central American military states to make such concessions. At the very least, such actions in the United States might provide the basis for developing larger networks to oppose intervention.

The South Africa divestment campaigns can teach us a great deal about the potential and ability of movements which use university investment port-folios to challenge repressive governments. The divestment movement grew out of a concern about U.S. economic support for the system of legalized racism in South Africa and the role that foreign investment plays in keeping the apartheid regime afloat. The international movement against corporate support for apartheid has included corporate shareholders' resolutions, bank with-drawal campaigns, product boycotts, local and national campaigns to divest public funds from companies linked to South Africa, and divestment efforts by churches and unions, as well as students and faculties pressuring their universities.[1]

In the late 1970s, students in Massachusetts, Wisconsin and Oregon demanded that their universities sell stock in firms with South African interests. Other institutions, such as the Universities of Illinois and Minnesota, agreed to join some church groups and unions in supporting shareholders' resolutions which would force U.S. firms to either oppose apartheid or close their South African operations.

The first university decision for divestiture occurred in September 1977; while students held a teach-in on South Africa, the University of Massachusetts trustees voted unanimously to sell stock in companies tied to South Africa. One of the most important early protests took place at Princeton University on April 14, 1978 when more than 200 divestment activists occupied a building on campus. The Princeton action encouraged protests at other schools such as Wesleyan University. In April 1985, several hundred Columbia students blockaded the front entrance to a main administration building, demanding that the university divest itself of $35 million in South African-related stocks. The protests at Columbia University, lasting months, together with similar actions at Berkeley, Rutgers, Tufts and Brown helped organize opposition to university support for apartheid on campuses across the United States. On October 12, 1985, thousands of protestors demonstrated at the White House and on college campuses across the country in what was "the largest coordinated protest against the United States investment in South Africa."[2] One of the greatest victories of the movement came in July 1986, when the University of California Board of Regents voted to divest itself of all $3.1 billion of its stock in companies active in South Africa.[3]

The divestment movement has been aided by the early efforts of progressive state legislators, such as Ernie Chambers in Omaha, Nebraska, and Mel King in Boston, Massachusetts, to push state governments to break their corporate ties to apartheid through public pension funds and other investments. One report in mid-1985, prior to the University of California decision to divest, noted the importance of state initiatives: "In the past year over twelve billion dollars has been divested from corporations operating in Southern Africa—and only $300 million of it has been by universities."[4] New York City and San Francisco have enacted phased divestment plans, a method which significantly reduces the transaction costs of portfolio sales. In August 1985, New Jersey's Governor Thomas H. Kean signed a major disinvestment bill that required the state pension system to sell about $2 billion in investments in companies with South African operations. State and local governments also have applied pressure by going beyond disinvestment and taking steps to stop purchasing goods from firms with holdings in South Africa.[5]

Prior to U.S. government-imposed sanctions passed in late 1986 (see below), one observer noted how the divestment movement has encouraged national government actions against U.S. corporate investment in apartheid: "As firms begin to feel the heat of political protest, they may favor government sanctions as a means of excluding all competitors from South Africa." A story in *The New York Times* on April 29, 1985 reported that corporate officials "acknowledge privately that the groundswell of university demonstrations, city council resolutions and congressional concern is taking a toll."[6]

Table 5-1: Selected List of U.S. College and University Divestment Action

Code	School	$ Amount Affected	Year
0	Amherst College	38,000,000	1978-86
2	Antioch College	NA	1978
1	Arizona State University	3,300,000	1985
0	Boston University	195,480	1985
0	Bowdoin College	1,800,000	1985
0	Brandeis University (1st)	350,000	1979
0	Brandeis University (2nd)	200,000	1986
1	Brandeis University (3rd)	1,600,000	1987
0	Brown University (1st)	4,600,000	1984
0	Brown University (2nd)	15,900,000	1988
0	Bryn Mawr	700,000	1986
1	Cal. State Univ./Northridge	2,300,000	1985
0	University of California (1st)	12,300,000	1986
1	University of California (2nd)	3,100,000,000	1986
0	Carleton College (1st)	295,000	1979
0	Carleton College (2nd)	3,300,000	1987
1	City University of New York	10,000,000	1984
0	Clark University	5,000,000	1986
0	Colby College (1st)	2,600,000	1978-84
2	Colby College (2nd)	6,500,000	1985
0	Colgate University	867,940	1979-85
0	Columbia University (1st)	2,700,000	1979
3	Columbia University (2nd)	29,000,000	1985
0	Connecticut College	6,000,000	1986
0	University of Connecticut (1st)	217,000	1986
0	University of Connecticut (2nd)	210,000	1988
0	Cornell College	NA	1985
0	Dartmouth College	2,000,000	1985
0	Drew University	50,000	1979-85
0	Duke University	12,500,000	1986
0	Earlham College	600,000	1984

Code	School	$ Amount Affected	Year
0	Eastern Michigan University	2,500,000	1980
2	Fairfield University	4,000,000	1985
1	Georgetown University	28,600,000	1986
0	Harvard University (1st)	50,900,000	1981
0	Harvard University (2nd)	1,000,000	1985
0	Harvard University (3rd)	2,800,000	1985
0	Harvard University (4th)	150,000,000	1986
1	University of Hawaii	2,300,000	1986
2	Howard University	8,000,000	1978
0	University of Illinois	3,300,000	1987
0	University of Indiana	543,000	1978-86
0	University of Iowa	2,250,000	1985
0	Iowa State University (1st)	130,000	1985
1	Iowa State University (2nd)	120,000	1985
0	Johns Hopkins University	3,900,000	1985
1	University of Kentucky	1,500,000	1985
1	University of Louisville	9,000,000	1985
2	University of Maine	3,000,000	1982
1	University of Massachusetts	600,000	1977
0	University of Miami	17,000,000	1985
2	Michigan State University	7,200,000	1978
2	Michigan State Univ. Foundation	500,000	1986
0	University of Michigan (1st)	306,117	1979
0	University of Michigan (2nd)	35,400,000	1984
0	University of Michigan (3rd)	5,800,000	1985
0	Middlebury College (1st)	1,500,000	1986
1	Middlebury College (2nd)	12,000,000	1986
0	University of Minnesota	35,000,000	1985
0	University of Minn. Foundation	5,000,000	1986
0	University of Missouri (1st)	5,000,000	1985
0	University of Missouri (2nd)	75,000,000	1988
0	University of New Hampshire (1st)	400,000	1985
0	University of New Hampshire (2nd)	5,000,000	1986
0	State University of New York (1st)	4,000,000	1985

Code	School	$ Amount Affected	Year
1	State University of New York (2nd)	11,000,000	1985
0	SUNY/Oneonta	80,000	1978
1	SUNY/Stonybrook	80,000	1985
0	Northeastern University (1st)	7,000,000	1985
1	Northeastern University (2nd)	14,000,000	1986
0	Northwestern University	3,500,000	1986
0	University of North Carolina	1,500,000	1985
0	Notre Dame	10,000,000	1985
0	Ohio State University (1st)	250,000	1978-79
2	Ohio State University (2nd)	10,800,000	1985
2	Ohio University	60,000	1978
0	Ohio Wesleyan University	850,000	1985
0	University of Pennsylvania	800,000	1983
0	Pennsylvania State University	700,000	1978-86
0	University of Pittsburgh	7,500,000	1986
0	Princeton University	295,000	1986
1	Univ. of Rhode Island Foundation	868,000	1985
0	Rutgers University (1st)	NA	1980
0	Rutgers University (2nd)	7,000,000	1985
1	Rutgers University (3rd)	7,500,000	1985
1	University of San Francisco	2,300,000	1985
2	Sarah Lawrence College	650,000	1985
1	Seattle University	2,500,000	1986
0	University of Southern California	35,000,000	1986
2	Spelman College	1,000,000	1986
0	Stanford University	350,000	1986
0	Swarthmore College (1st)	3,000,000	1981-85
0	Swarthmore College (2nd)	2,100,000	1986
1	Swarthmore College (3rd)	42,500,000	1986
0	Temple University (1st)	534,000	1985
1	Temple University (2nd)	1,960,000	1985
0	University of Tennessee	575,000	1985
0	Tufts University	100,000	1979
0	Vassar College	6,500,000	1978

Code	School	$ Amount Affected	Year
0	University of Vermont (1st)	2,100,000	1985
0	University of Vermont (2nd)	6,400,000	1986
0	University of Virginia	400,000	1986
0	University of Washington (1st)	800,000	1985
0	University of Washington (2nd)	4,500,000	1986
2	University of Washington (3rd)	6,400,000	1986
0	Wellesley College	2,900,000	1986
0	Wesleyan University (1st)	367,000	1980
0	Wesleyan University (2nd)	750,000	1985
0	Williams College (1st)	700,000	1980
0	Williams College (2nd)	672,000	1983
0	Williams College (3rd)	1,600,000	1986
2	University of Wisconsin	11,000,000	1978
1	University of Wyoming	1,450,000	1986
0	Yale University (1st)	1,600,000	1979
0	Yale University (2nd)	4,100,000	1984

CODE: 0-Partial Divestment (typically a variant of an Arthur D. Little ratings-based divestment policy).

1-Divestment of corporations with ownership operations in Southern Africa or of financial institutions whose loan/financing policies permit business practices with South Africa.

2-Total Divestment (outlined in the February 1987 Guidelines Update published by the Africa Fund in New York).

3-Columbia had pledged total divestment, but as of November 1986 had not divested of IBM, GM and Coke.

NA: Not available.

SOURCE: "Summary of U.S./Canadian College and University Divestment Action: Updated August 1988," ms., The Africa Fund, New York, NY, copyright 1988.

The divestment movement has also been successful in using corporations as "lobbyists" for government reforms in South Africa. For example, in December 1982, the Johannesburg-based U.S.-South Africa Chamber of Commerce asked the South African government not to pass a law that would have further inhibited the movement of blacks in South Africa. "The strength of the U.S. divestment movement at the state and local levels was stated as the reason, along with U.S. corporations' inability to 'contain' divestment pressure from spreading to the federal level if the law were passed." In February 1986, General Motors encouraged civil disobedience by offering to pay fines for any of its black employees who defied Port Elizabeth's beach segregation.[7]

On October 2, 1986, the Senate voted to override President Reagan's veto of legislation imposing sanctions on South Africa. This action put into place laws that would ban new investment by U.S. citizens in South African businesses, prohibit the import of products like steel and coal from South Africa, and cancelled landing rights in the United States for South African airlines.[8] However, some analysts argued that these sanctions would have a limited economic impact on South Africa. For example, in 1985, coal imports from South Africa totaled $43 million—a minor fraction of South Africa's total economic output that year of more than $50 billion. The same month that sanctions were approved, IBM and GM, two of the largest U.S. firms operating in South Africa, announced plans to withdraw their operations. While IBM cited deteriorating business and political conditions as factors motivating the decision, the company also said that it had felt the economic impact of pressure from U.S. groups opposed to corporate investment in apartheid. The GM and IBM departures were expected to lead many other firms to pull out of South Africa.[9]

The divestment movement provides much instruction for efforts dedicated to challenging U.S. corporate support for intervention in Central America. As can be seen in Table 5-1, numerous universities have divested themselves of stock in companies supporting apartheid. Such university actions, as well as campus protests, have clearly raised awareness of the problems of apartheid as well as providing leverage for national efforts to weaken apartheid by encouraging large-scale withdrawal by U.S. capital. The major force for capital flight from South Africa has been the growing wave of protests against apartheid by South Africans themselves; corporations are clearly wary of economic and political instability that threaten profits and economic planning. However, the actions and statements of corporations demonstrate that divestment protests have played a role in the transnationals' retreat from South Africa.

The divestment movement has also shown that universities may not suffer economically if they reorganize their portfolios in response to campus political pressures. Economic analysts have shown that divestiture can improve portfolio performance. Opponents of divestment such as trustees and investment bankers who manage pension funds and university endowments have maintained that "divestment will lower the return or increase the riskiness of institutional stock portfolios because divestment narrows the universe of possible stocks which portfolio managers can choose." However, several studies which evaluated the performance of South Africa-free funds found that "over a five to ten year span, South Africa-free funds have consistently outperformed the Standard & Poors (S&P) Index of 500 large companies." A 1985 *Business Week* survey of eighteen corporations which decided to divest part or all of their operations in South Africa showed that political and economic instability in South Africa made investments riskier and less profitable. All the companies cited declines ranging from 5-20 percent in the average return on their investments in South Africa.[10]

Divestment may actually improve a university's financial situation. In the case of Michigan State University, divestment led to a profit rather than a loss for the University.[11] On the other hand, university administrators such as Harvard's have maintained that divestment would compromise the university's academic freedom and lead to financial losses. Harvard president Derek Bok argued that divestment contravened the limited academic mission of the university and that universities lacked the necessary financial clout to influence corporations. In 1983, Harvard announced that it did not take ethical factors into consideration when deciding how to invest its endowment.[12]

Although Harvard sees divestment as having a negligible impact on corporate America, firms with ties to South Africa have struck back at colleges that divest. Some corporations subject to divestment protests have refused to contribute grants, scholarships and faculty bonuses to schools that have sold off shares of South Africa-related companies. A December 10, 1986 report in *The Wall Street Journal* explained university dependency on good political relations with corporations as follows:

> U.S. companies gave $1.57 billion to some 3,000 colleges and universities in 1984-85...And many of the biggest, most generous givers are the big-name concerns with high-profile units in South Africa.

One example of a corporation that has "struck back" is the Food Machinery Corporation (FMC). FMC ended $30,000 in grants to the University of Minnesota, failed to renew $24,000 in funds for four California universities and cut off grants to Michigan, Wisconsin and Arizona schools. While the aid embargo in this case may seem inconsequential, the potential impact of such actions is much greater. As an FMC spokesperson explained, "It removes [those colleges] from future consideration too... Right away, a whole flock of schools won't be eligible for donations."[13]

Corporate retaliation demonstrates the contradictory aspects of divestment. First, universities that have not yet divested often have substantial links to companies tied to South Africa. For example, MIT has failed to adopt aggressive divestment rules for an $800 million portfolio that includes $150 million in South Africa-related investments. John Deutch, provost at MIT, explains that a wholesale sell-off of South Africa-tied stocks by any school might prompt leading companies to "reevaluate their attitude toward that particular school and toward higher education generally."[14] The retaliatory moves by companies such as FMC, Mobil and Marathon Oil contradict the claims by educational leaders like Bok who argue that divestment has no impact on corporations tied to South Africa. Rather, academia's fear of a backlash reveals the political and economic constraints placed on universities by virtue of their extensive links to the corporate order.

The divestment movement must further contend with the ambiguity of what constitutes "divestment." More to the point, companies may attempt to conceal their ties to a repressive regime while stating that they have actually divested. For example, a 1986 report after the IBM and GM "divestment" decisions noted that:

> Both GM and IBM, like almost every other American company that has left South Africa in the last two years, will continue to sell their products and services there through licensing and distribution agreements.

GM also attempted to work out a buyback option under which it would be able to repurchase its South African business if the economic and political climate there improved.[15]

These challenges call for creative responses on the part of the divestment movement. Some anti-apartheid groups include in their divestment campaign demands that corporations change other practices and policies such as financing of nuclear power plants and the weapons industry.[16] In January 1986, a coalition of groups led by the AFL-CIO, United Mine Workers of America (UMW), the Free South Africa Movement and the National Organization for Women called for a boycott against Royal Dutch/Shell until the company and its subsidiaries withdraw from South Africa. Boycott organizers have argued that U.S. and South African workers have mutual interests in the downfall of the apartheid system. By taking advantage of lower labor standards and the abrogation of human rights in South Africa, TNCs like Shell have moved investments and jobs from developed countries to Third World nations where labor unions are subject to repression or cooptation by business interests.

In 1985, the management of the Rietspruit Opencast Services coal mine (where Shell-South Africa has a 50 percent interest) attacked 800 coal workers, using rubber bullets and tear gas. The workers had gone out on strike to protest management firings of union leaders. Rietspruit has an annual production output of six million tons and exports heavily overseas. Subsidized by the low wage rates enforced by apartheid, these exports undersell U.S. production in the international market. UMW organizers have linked contracted U.S. coal sales to layoffs of hundreds of coal workers in cities like Birmingham, Alabama. An April 1986 report in *The Multinational Monitor* described the already significant impact of the boycott by explaining how several of the 11,000 Shell stations nationwide had dropped gas prices below their competitors "in an attempt to offset negative publicity caused by the boycott."[17]

Other important innovations in divestment protest have occurred in California and Oregon. In California, the labor movement has played an important role in advancing divestment. In November 1984, the San Francisco-based International Longshoremen and Warehousemen's Union refused to handle South African goods. During the spring of 1985, members of the union marched to Berkeley to support student divestment actions. In Oregon, a local bank agreed to end all South African loans after local residents withdrew $300,000 in one day.[18]

A major victory for the international anti-apartheid movement occurred in November 1986 when Barclays of Great Britain pulled out of South Africa. The bank sold its 40.4 percent stake in its subsidiary, Barclays National Bank of South Africa (or "Barnat"), South Africa's second largest commercial bank. A primary motive for the sale was a campaign led by students to withdraw funds from the parent company in Great Britain. In explaining its actions, company representatives and British activists both pointed to the decline in Barclays' share of the student market. In 1983, the bank had a 27 percent share of the student market; by 1985, this had declined dramatically, to 17 percent.[19]

Another effective action targetting bank support for South Africa took place in the fall of 1986 in Baltimore. Students from Johns Hopkins University, anti-apartheid activists and local community leaders organized a campaign aimed at the investments of both the University and Maryland National Bank. To gain added leverage over the bank, they made links with community leaders, anti-apartheid activists and the Maryland Alliance for Responsible Investment. Together, the three groups sought to expose the bank's role in underdevelopment in the United States and to investigate laws, regarding socially responsible investment, that regulate U.S. banks.

By doing research, the coalition discovered that the Community Reinvestment Act of 1977 (CRA) allows the public to question whether bank mergers are in the best interests of neighborhoods. By filing a formal protest under the provisions of CRA, neighborhood groups can delay bank mergers, gaining leverage over banks by adding to their costs and giving them bad publicity. In August 1986, the Maryland National Bank announced plans to buy American Security Bank. The anti-apartheid coalition petitioned the Federal Reserve Board and alleged that the Maryland National Bank had engaged in redlining, an illegal practice in which banks systematically discriminate against low- and moderate-income areas, denying worthy borrowers access to credit and destroying the economic base of the community.

The combination of the CRA petition and student pickets of the two banks led Maryland National Bank to cut all ties with South Africa. The bank also agreed to lend at least $50 million to low- and moderate-income families, small businesses and housing developers over a five-year period.[20]

5.2 A Divestment Strategy for Central America?

Would a divestment movement similar to the campaign against South Africa be useful to Central America activists and the U.S. peace movement? There are four basic reasons for such a divestment movement. First, TNCs' operations in Central America contribute to repression in the region. Their presence there is partially based on an alliance with the ruling classes and the state which makes investment profitable by restraining workers' rights and power. TNCs have also destabilized reform governments and undermined popular opposition movements.

Second, divestment actions can represent a form of countervailing power on behalf of workers' struggles against the TNC as employer and as ally of the repressive state.

Third, an anti-corporate strategy would supplement current anti-intervention protests by 1) offering a context for protests against institutions more tractable than the U.S. warfare state and, 2) allowing for joint actions by protestors in North America on the one hand, and the opposition movements in Central America on the other hand. The corporate focus also provides a context for uniting groups in the United States as students, professors, church members, trade unionists, environmentalists and community activists have their own institutional link and particular grievances with target corporations.

Finally, an anti-corporate strategy could provide political leverage for movement protests by disrupting institutional support for the region's military states. A mobilization in universities would focus public attention on alternative views of these states and on university, corporate, congressional and executive branch support for repression in Central America.

The case for universities divesting themselves from companies tied to intervention in Central America begins with the connections already established between foreign investment and the repression of Central American workers (documented in our discussion of Coke, Bank of America and Castle & Cooke). However, such stories are not unconnected episodes but part of a larger system of repression based on the joint calculations of foreign investors and their state patrons. The economist Torres-Rivas argues that the repression of Central American workers is intrinsically linked to the drive to make investment more profitable. In nations like Guatemala and El Salvador, "State repression appears in order to reduce the costs of capital, and police repression grows at the same time in order to maintain low salaries."[21] Such repression by Third World governments is partially based on national policies which seek to promote agricultural exports: "Minimum wage laws for agricultural labourers are not enacted because they might make the country's exports 'uncompetitive.' "[22]

Corporations' desire to invest in the "low-skilled" nations of Latin America tends to be conditional on how much labor is restrained. A review of investment patterns in El Salvador helps bear this out:

> In the case of El Salvador it is indisputable that investor interest was contingent on the country being part of the [Central American Common Market]. Over half of all foreign investments in El Salvador during the twentieth century was made in the decade of the 1960s, and of these foreign investments over three-quarters was made between 1962-66. *The slackening of investor interest between 1966-68 reflects the big worker strikes of those years* [emphasis added].[23]

One UN official from the Third World has drawn out the links between foreign investment and the repression of labor as follows:

> The multinationals like to say they're contributing to development, but they come into our countries for one thing—cheap labor. If the labor stops being so cheap, they can move on. So how can you call that development? It depends on the people being poor and staying poor.[24]

Would corporations remain in Central America if workers' rights were protected? Would capital flee if movements pressured U.S. corporations to behave more responsibly towards their employees in the region? We have already seen in the Coca-Cola case that although operations were sold off, the Coke plant still was able to function economically after the pull-out. Similarly, although some companies withdrew from Nicaragua after a government more responsive to workers' interests took power, many multinationals have remained in the country.[25]

5.3 Limits to a Divestment Policy for Central America

The current terms under which foreign corporations and banks are linked to Central American economies through trade, agriculture, industry and foreign lending have brought few gains to the people of El Salvador, Guatemala and Honduras. On the other hand, a case has been made by various parties in Central American opposition movements that it is unwise to discourage foreign investment in Central America. It might also be argued that policies which attempt to encourage the severance of U.S. economic relations with Central America through opposition to bank loans, foreign investment or trade would most hurt workers and peasants. There are drawbacks to anti-corporate campaigns which attempt to provoke capital flight from the region.

The divestment policy advocated for South Africa-linked firms is based on the belief that any short-term damage done to the South African economy is outweighed by the terror inflicted on the black majority in South Africa. Divestment strategists argue that divestment pressure which encourages capital flight may hurt some workers in the short run. However, if the South African government can be brought down, then the possibilities for a restructured and more democratic society are well worth the costs imposed by capital flight. Some organizers argue that divestment is simply a moral movement against university complicity with repression in South Africa; they have no expectations about divestment leading to capital flight.

Unlike the South African case where the opposition movement has called for a divestment policy, the movement in Central America has not called for policies which *explicitly* encourage capital flight from Central America. A movement which calls for U.S. corporate divestment from Central America would also have to meet moral objections that some people's livelihoods depend on foreign investment or that such a movement would alienate constituencies dependent on foreign capital investment.

What are the constraints on the attempt to link divestment of foreign capital and strategies which could advance workers' interests? First, foreign firms provide jobs and thereby create constituencies who would oppose capital flight; workers employed by these companies might turn against the domestic political groups who encouraged their employer's flight. In the Coke controversy in Guatemala—where organized labor is critical to the national opposition movement—the battle was precisely over the economic repression of labor caused by capital flight. Even the Democratic Revolutionary Front (FDR) in El Salvador has expressed concern for the potential loss of jobs by coffee workers upon a mass exit of foreign capital from this sector.

In contrast to the argument that capital flight through divestment is justified by the repression found in Central American dictatorships, some scholars have argued that TNCs may be a pivotal force in political liberalization.[26] Diaz-Alejandro argued that although an open economy may provide trade to bolster a reactionary regime "under certain historical circumstances, a movement toward greater openness of the economy could strengthen progressive political forces and weaken local feudal and absolutist controls."[27]

In Diaz-Alejandro's view, the problem is not that an "open economy" or foreign investment *per se* is detrimental to economic development and democracy. Rather, the question becomes: under what conditions can nations favorably link up to the economies of the advanced capitalist nations?[28] Posing the question this way neglects the *political* role of the multinationals, but leaving such matters aside, it is important to examine the potential benefits of multinational investment. Foreign firms may contribute technologies and promote forms of industrial organization not available to or reproducible by local capitalists. Economist Stephen Hymer suggested that foreign direct investment takes place because corporations possess special skills or technologies which are not available to local entrepreneurs.[29] This view has been echoed by urban planning theorist Manuel Castells who argues that "it seems doubtful that Brazil, or any other country in the Third World, could develop its own technological base without relying on technology transfer from the multinationals."[30]

However, new technologies have not been assimilated by local entrepreneurs. Rather, as Torres-Rivas argues, they have merely administered businesses owned by foreigners. Some development economists argue that technology is emerging as a "significant and forceful instrument for maintaining existing dominance/dependence relations in the international economic and political system." Such critics of the uses of modern technology by Third World nations argue that technology should be acquired "on the initiative of developing countries," rather than left to the control and direction of the TNCs and economically developed nations.[31]

An "appropriate" technology policy could arise with cooperative relationships between the region and other nations and the expansion of learning institutions geared to developing emerging technologies responsive to popular needs like small-scale power-generating systems and integrated pest management programs which reduce dependency on agro-chemical pesticide imports. However, such a collective endeavor among Central American nations would require a progressive planning effort by governments less loyal to TNCs' interests as well as governments less likely to repress and destroy their universities. In short, links with advanced technologies from the advanced capitalist nations (or "socialist states") would have to be mediated by a more radical governments than now hold power in Guatemala, El Salvador or Honduras.

Nevertheless, multinationals have been increasingly welcomed by host governments in Third World nations because of the technology, capital and employment that they *do provide*. As a 1985 report noted, "even Nicaragua is drafting an investment code that will guarantee companies access to foreign exchange, in an attempt to lure foreign investment."[32] Thus, Diaz-Alejandro has argued that even socialist states have not *chosen* to "delink," i.e., voluntarily cut off trade and investment relationships with the advanced capitalist nations. Some advocates of delinking have referred to the historical examples of "self-reliance" following socialist revolutions:

> But the historical record of the immediate aftermath of important socialist revolutions such as those in the Soviet Union, China, and Cuba, while showing that indeed some species of delinking occurred during and immediately after those events, also indicate that delinking was not so much a choice of the revolutionary authorities but was imposed through blockages by the hegemonic capitalist countries.[33]

Nicaragua's ability to avoid wide-scale nationalizations of TNCs (and maintain good relations with a large segment of foreign capital) was facilitated by the concentration of Somoza-owned capital, later seized by the Sandinista government. The Somoza family fortune increased from around $60 million in the mid-1950s to about $400 to $500 million in the mid-1970s and included estates and agricultural enterprises, processing industries, industrial businesses, communications and banking and foreign investments.

Quite distinct from Nicaragua, however, is El Salvador, whose economy has suffered even more seriously than Nicaragua's from capital flight. Prior to and during the insurrection, Nicaragua lost about half a billion dollars in foreign investment. However, from 1979 to 1980 alone, $1.5 billion fled El Salvador.[34]

Having a base of investment may lessen the need for a TNC presence. However, both El Salvador and Nicaragua have become increasingly dependent on foreign economic investment (either through foreign aid or TNCs) because of economic damage caused by the regional war. Does the retention (or expansion) in foreign capital become important only after a progressive government takes power, as in Nicaragua? How does the Left in a country like El Salvador feel about political actions which lead to capital flight?

To a certain extent, the guerrilla movement in El Salvador supports a program of economic sabotage leading to capital flight. An example of the use of "economic sabotage" against the Salvadoran government was given in a report by *The New York Times* on January 10, 1986. The story noted attacks on local shops and the destruction of machinery at a local coffee processing plant, and concluded that such actions "sap the ailing economy" and "almost certainly weaken the Government's own standing."[35]

The economic sabotage campaign represents an important source of political leverage for the Left:

> Estimates of war-related damage and production losses from 1979 through 1983 range as high as $1.5 billion. Especially hard hit were rural buses and electrical transmission towers. Power outages resulting from sabotage cause refrigerated goods to spoil and interrupt production. Power was off in the port of La Unión for over 200 days in 1982.[36]

A 1986 report by the scholars of El Salvador's Central American University noted rebel propaganda claims that economic sabotage deprived the Duarte regime of resources for the war effort. The army is weakened as large numbers of soldiers are diverted from other tasks when they guard important economic targets. On the other hand, economic sabotage is used to undermine an important component of the counter-insurgency project—economic development. The FMLN seeks to discredit the notion that El Salvador can develop economically without radical structural change:

> The sabotage campaign is also based on the understanding that economic development might lead the masses to reject the FMLN if they were convinced that a Christian Democratic government could offer them improved living standards.[37]

In the past, the economic sabotage campaign even included transnational targets. The bombing of a McDonalds enterprise in the early 1980s led to the loss of thirty jobs; Alvis Glove closed its plant after workers seized the company president as a hostage for nine days as part of an effort to win wage demands.[38] However, it is critical to note that sabotage against the coffee oligarchy usually occurs after most of the value has been added to the product by coffee workers, i.e., after workers have been paid for producing the coffee and are less in danger of losing employment from economic sabotage.

Despite the use of economic sabotage, the Left's position does not explicitly provoke capital flight because, it is argued, capital flight can undermine a post-revolutionary reform-minded government attempting to build a mixed economy. Not only does capital flight aggravate employment and export problems in the short-run, but it also creates long-term economic difficulties. It is harder to get foreign capital to return to a country after it has relocated its managerial staff and/or broken its ties with local markets. If a reform government were to inherit a highly decapitalized economy, it might face pressures to limit civil liberties and restrain workers' demands for higher wages as it sought to combat demonstrations against shortages and encourage policies favorable to local businesses.[39] Indeed, the growing integration of the country into the world economic system would make a post-revolutionary regime highly vulnerable if it inherited a highly decapitalized economy. Philip L. Russell, author of *El Salvador in Crisis*, explains that "in the event of a rebel victory," the country would be "highly vulnerable to U.S. economic boycotts."[40]

Past capital flight makes remaining businesses all the more important. In addition, the consumption of local industrialists by TNCs and the destruction of subsistence farms in Central America have created obstacles which would make it difficult to replace foreign capital overnight with an economy geared to domestic needs. If capital flight leads to an exodus of managers, it will create serious economic problems for a revolutionary government. In fact, the economic and political changes introduced by revolutions increase the demand for managerial talent.[41]

In response to these dilemmas, the FDR/FMLN has sought to maintain the integrity of the coffee economy in order to maintain employment for a future reorganized mixed economy. As noted above, the primary targets of the guerrillas are now primarily economic infrastructure rather than TNCs. However, the resulting macroeconomic instability created by these attacks, as well as the political instability generated by strikes and the war, has helped encourage foreign capital to leave El Salvador. In a period when labor and urban community mobilization was less significant, the political leverage of the Left has been intrinsically bound up in efforts to weaken the economy of the government in power. As a result, economic sabotage, no matter how strategically planned or directed, has led to capital flight.

5.4 The Theory of Selective Divestment

The opposition movement has tried to take a middle road between actions which create political leverage (and also maintain the integrity of the economy) *and* actions which risk the departure of TNCs. While this policy is contradictory, the U.S. solidarity movement must also try to follow a middle road. The movement must develop leverage over the ruling interests in Central America by applying pressure on TNCs, while simultaneously giving TNCs specific options that would allow them to stay in Central America unsanctioned. One alternative for U.S. solidarity actions in this regard is "selective divestment."[42] Here, specific companies are selected as targets for political actions. They are encouraged to alter political support for their host government after observing the political pressure brought by solidarity activists and their allies on target companies' domestic operations. This "demonstration" effect leaves certain TNCs "untouched." It provides leverage over these companies, which may fear that they too could become targets of protest action.

By choosing a limited number of companies as targets of political mobilization, activists in the North would not be seen as abetting a process of full-scale capital flight. What demands should be made of the selected companies? Should demands be made that they abandon the military states or simply reform their actions? One option is for solidarity activists to demand that universities sell stock in corporations unless they offer documentation that they respect Central America's trade union rights and union organization. One problem with this demand is that many trade unions in Central America are controlled by the American Institute for Free Labor Development, an adjunct of the AFL-CIO and CIA. In El Salvador, the Institute has established unions which are parallel to existing labor organizations. The Salvadoran government has used these unions to break other unions which have challenged state policy.

In contrast to the AFL-CIO's policy of support for right-wing unions in El Salvador, progressive sectors of the U.S. labor movement have engaged in solidarity campaigns which could be broadened to support protests against particular corporations. In November 1986, 175 North Americans participated in a conference in El Salvador that was the largest single peace delegation ever to visit Central America. U.S. labor unionists who attended the conference sought to expand direct union-to-union ties to El Salvador by establishing "sister" locals (such as the one described in Chapter Two).

In El Salvador, TNCs are not a significant employer for workers represented by progressive trade unions. In some cases, TNCs have been willing to pay more than the government's informal cap on wages, designed to protect local capitalists from the TNC's higher pay scales. But some TNCs have offered their employees non-monetary incentives such as free use of doctors and exercise facilities or access to special wholesale price stores. Often, TNCs, such as Texas Instruments, have attempted to buy off workers and trade union leaders with such "incentives" as overtime.[43] Solidarity campaigns in the United States could pressure transnationals which attempted to subvert organizing efforts in old unions facing such cooptive measures or in new organizing campaigns where TNCs have resisted unionization.

Constraints on acts of repression against workers, community groups, human rights activists and the like would also facilitate workers' efforts to bargain for political power and higher wages from TNCs. Solidarity activists could demand that specific target companies cut off economic relations with Central America if the nations of El Salvador, Guatemala and Honduras failed to provide documentation that they abided by the United Nations' "Universal Declaration of Human Rights." Activists could demand that selected companies withdraw operations from El Salvador, Guatemala and Honduras, halt distribution of these nations' products (or exports of these nations' products from third countries), cease import purchases from these countries and end loans and technical support.

The Universal Declaration, adopted and proclaimed by General Assembly resolution 217 A (III) of December 10, 1948, could provide the framework for demands by anti-corporate protestors. Various articles in this resolution provide the language for demands that the state actively intervene to stop repression. The third article says that: "Everyone has the right to life, liberty and security of person." Article Five states that: "No one shall be subjected to torture or to cruel, inhuman or degrading treatment or punishment." Article Nine says, "No one shall be subjected to arbitrary arrest, detention or exile." Article 23, Section 4 says, "Everyone has the right to form and to join trade unions for the protection of his interests." Article 26 notes that "Everyone has the right to education."[44]

The Central American Peace Accord or "Arias Plan" was adopted by the governments of Costa Rica, El Salvador, Guatemala, Honduras and Nicaragua on August 7, 1987. This accord could also provide a mechanism for linking anti-corporate protests to state behavior. Article 3 of the Arias Plan outlines commitments made by the nations on "democratization." This Article begins as follows:

> The governments commit themselves to promote an authentic democratic, pluralist, and participatory process that includes the promotion of social justice, respect for Human Rights, [state] sovereignty, the territorial integrity of States, and the right of all nations to freely determine, without outside interference of any kind, its economic, political, and social model, and to carry out in a verifiable manner those measures leading to the establishment, or in their instances, the improvement of representative and pluralist democratic systems which would provide guarantees for the organization of political parties, effective popular participation in the decision making process, and to ensure free access to different currents of opinion to honest

electoral processes and newspapers based on the full exercise of citizens' rights.[45]

Nations that fail to uphold the Declaration and the Peace Accord should be subjected to selective divestment campaigns by solidarity activists. Activists could also demand that El Salvador not grant logistical support for the contra war and that Honduras and Costa Rica cease harboring contras, as well as U.S. armed forces and CIA personnel supporting the regional war against Nicaragua and the opposition movements. Article Six of the Arias Plan states that:

> The five countries which signed this document, reaffirm their commitment to prevent the use of their territory, and to neither render nor permit military or logistical support to persons, organizations, or groups attempting to destabilize the governments of the Central American countries.[46]

If human rights groups and the press failed to verify the expulsion of contras or U.S. troop withdrawals and base closures, then this too could be grounds for further protest actions against companies operating in or linked to Honduras and Costa Rica.

The component of the selective divestment strategy which seeks government reform depends on transnationals' ability to influence political changes. If a government's actions "threaten a region key to the transnational's operations, the threatening state may be disciplined with economic reprisals or 'destabilized,' its government replaced by a more amenable client regime."[47]

In a country like Guatemala where there are over 400 U.S. businesses which form "the backbone of the country's fragile economy," transnationals can use "the threat of withdrawal to press for change and augment the pleadings of the international human rights community."[48]

Corporations also have the power to coerce the state to make changes by threats to contract rather than expand operations, or by exploiting networks that lobby the state. After the 1954 coup in Guatemala, commercial interests organized themselves into a number of corporate associations to bring pressure on the government through general lobbying and other efforts designed to protect native and foreign investors against strikes and "permissive" labor legislation, among other activities. Such groups as the Associacion Comercio, and Camara de Industria "have come to expect the Guatemalan government to consult with them on all measures which might affect them and, in fact, on all important policy matters."[49]

Furthermore, TNCs have been known to apply leverage over the state by using the political weight of the native elite employed in high level corporate positions. Peter Evans, a political economist who studies Latin America, says that such employees are loyal to the TNCs:

Nationals working at the local level strive to absorb the cultural perspective of the organizations that provide their livelihood and their work environment. The ability to identify with the corporation as an organization and to acquire the cognitive and stylistic norms that prevail within it is an important prerequisite of executive success. The socialization of local elite personnel is reinforced by the employment of foreign personnel in key high-level positions.[50]

Certainly, what power the TNCs have is usually used to weaken or overthrow a progressive or reform regime before it has consolidated its control over a nation's military apparatus. However, some TNCs have accommodated themselves to socialist governments in Nicaragua and elsewhere. They have been willing to abandon right-wing or repressive regimes when the economic and political cost of supporting them became too high (as in South Africa). Political analysts also point to the development of a liberal policy strain among transnationals that seek expanded markets, high wages for Third World workers to bolster consumer demand, and a more tolerant attitude towards reform regimes that seek industrialization at the expense of oligarchic interests. This liberal policy strain is in conflict with right-wing state planners in the United States who support repressive and economically backward regimes. For example, certain transnationals opposed the U.S. embargo of Nicaragua.[51]

Can activists bring significant pressure on TNCs so that they will feel compelled to influence Central American governments to bring about positive structural change in Central America? Would the TNC-domestic ruling class alliance break down if corporations attempted to alter government policies or began to withdraw from Central American military states? Ultimately, if capital flight accelerated and exports from these states to the United States were seriously cut off, some constituencies in the state or the military would be forced to make political changes to bring greater economic stability.

Local employees of TNCs might be motivated to push governments for reforms if the failure to reform meant that they would lose their jobs because of capital flight linked to divestment, boycotts or economic sabotage. Even if the state failed to end support for death squad actions, the cost of this support would certainly be raised. The economic chaos that would occur if corporations *did* pull out of Central America (especially Honduras and Guatemala) could provide opposition movements with greater leverage in bargains with the state, perhaps accelerating the conditions necessary to bring down the military states through popular mobilization.

The criteria by which corporations should be "selected" as targets for popular mobilization could be identified by making links to trade union campaigns in Central America. In addition, selected companies should be those that would have the greatest leverage over Central American states if pressure were brought upon them. These are companies that are not likely to flee the region in the coming years. Companies such as banks or TNCs which are heavily dependent on Central America for their profits (like banana companies), would be less likely to cut off economic relations in Central America than industrial firms. These firms (described below) also have greater leverage over Central American nations than do the industrial firms because they act as conduits for certain high volume trade and state financing.

TNC export industries provide useful targets in pressuring Central American military states because of their high profit rates and alliances with associated industries. Development economists say that

> if the industry concerned is very profitable, the vested interest of the companies which are directly involved may exert pressure on the government to prevent a loss of earnings. Moreover, those engaged in other business activities which are, in one way or another, linked with or relevant to the export industry may also react to market losses. They include banks, insurance firms, transport companies, etc., which provide complementary services for export activities.

The selection of highly concentrated and large-scale industries such as banana firms and coffee producers also provides greater leverage because "for a given value of exports, the income losses [to the exporting nation] will be felt less seriously, the smaller is the size of exports involved in relation to the total exports and national income of the country."[52]

Industries like banking and petroleum exploration are always seeking to expand their markets or areas of penetration. Unlike the industrial firms that use little domestic labor and that can easily replace labor intensive activities with (non-Central American) Third World substitutes, the financial, resource processing and agricultural industries have a greater incentive to be loyal to a given locale. Other target companies needn't have direct operations in Central America at all, but market products of the three military states such as coffee. Pressure against companies which distribute agricultural products from these states could influence them because they depend on the processing, transportation and marketing capability of the TNCs.

Concentrating divestment actions against selected companies in Central America has several advantages. First, "selective divestment" less directly threatens industrial enterprises, i.e. the type of enterprise likely to be highly dependent on a wide range of foreign technology and harder to replace in a post-revolutionary or reformist regime needing consolidation by capital investments. Furthermore, the selective divestment strategy should target corporations that would be hesitant to respond to anti-corporate organizing efforts by cutting off imports and loans, or selling off operations. There are corporations (as has been shown in South Africa) that would prefer pressuring the state for reforms over relocating. The fact that political power in Central America is concentrated in very few companies means that corporate leverage over the state is significant.

This trajectory for the selective divestment movement would also counter objections that divestment would bring hardship on the Central American people or contradict FDR/FMLN policies which do not explicitly call for capital withdrawal by TNCs. Anti-corporate mobilization could assist the movement for equitable economic development in Central America by strengthening trade unions' attempts to redistribute wealth. Selective divestment campaigns could ultimately pressure TNCs to sell their Central American operations to holding companies or other financial entities controlled by the region's workers.[53]

The choice between a divestment strategy seeking corporate reforms and one explicitly aimed at capital withdrawal would be a subject for debate within the U.S. solidarity movement. It would also be part of a dialogue with opposition movements in Central America which could be carried out through the formal channels of a "divestment commission." This commission could exchange information with opposition and human rights groups in Central America, verify adherence to the Arias Plan and Universal Declaration and monitor the effects of U.S. anti-corporate protests on Central American workers and transnationals. Also, a selective divestment campaign, while narrowing its target, should expand its power base. Actions extended to pension divestments by local governments and unions, community boycotts of banks or portfolio divestments by churches would significantly bolster selective divestment campaigns.[54]

University-based divestment and protest actions alone may not prove sufficient to pressure corporations. However, universities may be the easiest institutions in which to *initiate* a divestment movement that would spread to other economic sectors and political groups. Unlike churches and unions where those controlling portfolios are less likely to be viewed as political "targets," university trustees are more easily identified as part of the corporate order. Union and church leadership will also be more willing to tackle the problem of Central America-related investments if a precedent has been set by university divestments. Some unions have limited control over their pension fund investments, although other unions have been both willing and able to divest themselves of South Africa-related stocks. Rank-and-file labor activists and progressive trade union leaders have already been active in pressuring the AFL-CIO to change its policies of support for the contras in Nicaragua, Duarte in El Salvador and conservative trade unionism in Central America. Local church activists have done extensive solidarity and anti-intervention work. National churches have carried out corporate shareholder actions against companies linked to repression in Central America.

On campus, divestment tactics could also include pressuring university trustees linked to target companies, protesting corporate recruitment, and campaigning against other institutions (such as banks and insurance companies) linked to the target firm. Further protests could be coordinated with boycotts by anti-apartheid divestment and trade union activists or actions against companies linked to nuclear power, pesticide abuse, or arms sales to the region (see Chapter Six).

The growing power of the Central American opposition movement and the softer Nicaragua policy of the Bush Administration may create space for the Central American Left to wage their political battles within existing governmental structures. If this should occur, then any arguments for provoking capital flight would clearly break down. But, if the liberalization implied by the Arias Plan should falter, then the risks of capital flight could appear more rational to opposition movements throughout the region.[55]

5.5 Possible Targets for Corporate Campaigns

Four specific kinds of transnational enterprises meet the criteria for providing leverage over El Salvador, Guatemala, Honduras and Costa Rica through corporate campaign and protest actions: the banana industry, the coffee industry, resource extraction enterprises such as oil and rubber, and banking enterprises.

Big Bananas

In the banana industry, three U.S. multinationals control 90 percent of Central America's banana trade, supplying 65 percent of the world market and

Table 5-2: Shares of the Multinationals in World Banana Trade

(in Thousands of Tons)

Year	United Brands	Castle & Cooke	Del Monte	Total
1966	1,807 34.0%	652 12.3%	58 1.1%	2,517 47.4%
1972	1,973 30.5%	1,168 18.0%	356 5.5%	3,497 54.0%
1980	1,966 28.7%	1,451 21.2%	1,053 15.4%	4,470 65.3%

SOURCE: FAO and Trade Sources as published in *The World Banana Economy, 1970-1984* (Rome: FAO, 1986), p. 8.

78 percent of the U.S. market. United Brands, Castle & Cooke and Del Monte (a subsidiary of RJR Nabisco) have also expanded into associated industries such as canning plants, pineapple farms, cattle ranches and shipping companies (see Table 5-2).[56]

The United States is the largest single market for bananas, making the Central American Common Market nations both economically dependent on the United States and vulnerable to boycott actions which cut into U.S. banana consumption. In 1984, the United States imported $860 million worth of bananas from the world market. Six countries—Colombia, Costa Rica, Ecuador, Guatemala, Honduras and Panama—account for 95 percent of all U.S. imports.[57] Furthermore, according to the FAO, in 1984 the approximate market share of Standard Fruit (owned by Castle & Cooke) in the United States was 29 percent; United Brands' share was also about 29, while Del Monte's share was 19 percent.[58] Meanwhile, banana companies are subject to the political and economic instability of their host countries. A 1985 corporate report by Castle & Cooke (C&C) shows that the transnationals are clearly conscious of the risks of doing business in regions like Central America:

> C&C's foreign operations are subject to risks of expropriation, civil disturbances, political unrest, burdensome increases in taxes, fluctuations of currency exchange rates and restrictive government policies. Loss of one or more of its significant foreign operations could have a material adverse affect on C&C's results of operations.[59]

While Castle & Cooke has shifted some imports to purchases from associate producers in Central America and can rely on banana production in Ecuador and elsewhere, it is still highly dependent on direct production in Central America. The other two leading transnationals are also dependent on their banana sales. For United Brands, bananas bring in five times as much profit as other food sales. For Del Monte's owner, RJ Reynolds (now RJR Nabisco), bananas represent only 7 percent of corporate sales *but 17 percent of profits.*[60] Tables 5-3 and 5-4 reveal how critical banana exports are to the economies of Honduras and Costa Rica. Guatemala also gets a substantial amount of export income from banana cultivation. The banana exports from Honduras and Costa Rica are largely in the hands of TNCs and these firms are able to exercise direct control over production in host nations through their ownership of large estates and businesses.

Banana companies such as Castle & Cooke can have extensive economic influence. A 1985 corporate report described the company's ownership through long-term leases of about 31,000 acres in Costa Rica. Central American bananas are shipped in chartered vessels and in nine company-owned-and-operated refrigerated vessels. Castle & Cooke also has an interest in the following properties in Honduras: a beer and soft drink bottling operation, a bottle and

Table 5-3: Total Country Exports:
Dollar Value of Exports of Bananas and Plantains [0573]

Year	Honduras	Costa Rica	Guatemala
1980	233,143,000	214,501,000	52,418,000
1981	201,457,000	229,128,000	58,476,000
1982	221,320,000	218,188,000	156,060,000
1983	199,573,000	286,177,000*	43,675,000
1984	234,595,000	295,385,000	63,744,000*
1985	323,872,000*	280,885,000*	72,973,000*
1986	285,258,000*	298,969,000*	46,552,000*

* Estimate

SOURCE: *1984 International Trade Statistics Yearbook*, Volume II (New York: United Nations, 1986), p. 314; *1986 International Trade Statistics Yearbook*, Volume II (New York: United Nations, 1988), p. 314.

Table 5-4: % Share of Export Companies in Total Banana Exports, 1984

Company	Costa Rica	Honduras
United Brands	25.3	62.0
Standard Fruit	34.7	37.5
Del Monte	38.4	0.5

SOURCE: *The World Banana Economy, 1970-1984* (Rome: FAO, 1986), pp. 22, 24.

carton facility for beverage-related products, a plastic injection facility (primarily for the manufacture of beer and soft drink plastic cases), a sugar mill, an edible oils refinery, a laundry soap factory and a palm oil plantation. The company also grows pineapples in Honduras. The fourth ranked Cerveceria Hondurena, a brewery owned by Castle & Cooke, had sales of $29.4 million in 1982.

United Brands is also involved in numerous palm oil and plastic manufacturing enterprises in Costa Rica and Honduras. The "Railroad" or Tela Railroad Company, owned by United Brands and involved in the banana business, was the first largest firm in Honduras in 1982. The company had sales that year of $114.3 million.[61]

The banana export economy provides significant tax revenues for the federal budgets of the military states. Table 5-5 shows the link between export income and tax financing for the government (and ultimately the military).

In 1983, the export price of bananas sold in Central America (taken as an average of Guatemala, Honduras and Costa Rica) was 30 percent of the retail price when sold in the United States (see also Table 4-11).[62] In September 1974, the governments of Colombia, Costa Rica, Guatemala, Honduras and Panama attempted to get a larger share of the profits in the banana business by forming the Union of Banana Exporting Countries (UPEB). In Costa Rica and Honduras, new laws cancelled contracts with the TNCs and revoked many concessions and "in general, greatly altered the freedom and stability which they had hitherto enjoyed."

However, the formation of UPEB and related national policies by the banana exporting nations changed the balance between the benefits and costs of direct production by the TNCs. By 1984, the banana area of Standard Fruit and Del Monte was about evenly split between their own land and that of

Table 5-5: Total Government Revenues from the Banana Export Tax, 1974-1984

(In millions of U.S. Dollars)

Year	Costa Rica	Guatemala	Honduras
1974	8.1	0.0	4.1
1975	22.5	0.4	5.7
1976	24.2	6.2	10.9
1977	23.9	6.1	12.2
1978	24.7	6.8	17.8
1979	23.9	5.9	24.6
1980	27.5	9.7	23.9
1981	50.6	9.9	21.4
1982	48.1	10.5	22.7
1983	50.1	5.9	18.0
1984	35.0	2.9	15.8
Total	338.6	64.3	177.1

SOURCE: UPEB, *Informe Mensual,* various issues, as published in *The World Banana Economy, 1970-1984* (Rome: FAO: 1986), p. 69.

independent growers. The instability of Central America, the formation of UPEB and more lucrative markets elsewhere have raised the specter of "capital flight" in the banana market (or a priority given to market other nations' exports). Nevertheless, there are reasons why banana companies stay involved in direct banana production (and maintain their interests in their overseas facilities):

> ...if strategies of withdrawal from direct production were put into motion, they would prove very difficult to reverse later, and would have a major impact on the capacity of governments to tax the banana sector in the future.[63]

Universities do not have extensive ties to banana multinationals so the campus may not be the most favorable organizing site. For example, Castle & Cooke has limited trustee on investment ties to universities (see Appendix One). One report on university endowment investments shows limited investments by colleges and universities in Castle & Cooke. However, the company has numerous subsidiaries distributed across North America which could become sites for local protest actions. These include: Castle & Cooke Foods of Canada, Ltd., Flexi-van Corporation of New York and E.T. Wall Corporation of California. Castle & Cooke also has had important banking relationships with Morgan Guaranty Trust Co. of New York and The First National Bank of Boston.[64]

The Burden of the Coffee Economy

The multinational coffee industry has also helped reproduce a system of agricultural underdevelopment in Central America. Coffee harvesting seasons differ from sugar cane and banana cultivating seasons. The variation in planting patterns allows for coffee to be marketed during the downturns in other crops. Coffee investment also allows investors to diversify their "portfolios." As a result, the coffee economy has stabilized business planning and economic expectations about investment.

The coffee economy is directly linked to the repressive state in Central America through the work relations that have developed on the coffee plantations and the subsidy which coffee provides to the armed forces in El Salvador and Guatemala. In coffee plantations in Guatemala, coffee workers are overworked and paid slave wages. Those with shelter live in a *galera* (roof without walls) with up to 300 people packed into a narrowly confined area. A Guatemalan coffee worker now living in exile in the United States describes life on the plantation:

> You work all day from 6 a.m. to 4 p.m. It is a very brutal job and you earn $1.50 a day to clear out the weeds around coffee plants. There is no such thing as overtime pay. Coffee pickers are transported to the *fincas* [plantations] in cattle trucks. Over a hundred people are packed

into these trucks like cattle...On the majority of *fincas,* there is no drinkable water. Everyone has to go to the river to wash clothes, bathe and get water to drink. There are no toilets...Many children die of worms, diarrhea and viruses. There is no health care on the plantation.

These conditions are enforced by an alliance between the military and plantation owners. Workers cannot complain about their low salaries "because complaining means death itself. In San Marcos, hundreds and thousands of workers have disappeared for claiming a better salary in order to live, or even, at least, eat a little better." The plantation owner pays the army $2,000 per week and also contributes money for military weapons:

> On many plantations, the army garrisons do not wear uniforms in the fields. The soldiers put their weapons in burlap bags and go into the fields dressed as peasants. They mix with the workers. That's the way they control the workers in the coffee fields.[65]

The work overseer is often a military commissioner. Workers who denounce the government or plantation owner can be reported by the overseer to the army and then "can be taken from their beds in the middle of the night and killed in some other place."[66] The coffee economy has provided major funding for the repressive state in Central America. On February 1, 1981, El Salvador's Minister of Trade told an American audience:

> Let me emphasize, that for El Salvador, coffee is the heart of the economy...coffee still means 60% of our foreign earnings, 15% of our gross national product, 20% of our fiscal income, and 25% of our labor force occupation.[67]

The Salvadoran government set up INCAFE as a national agency to buy, process, market and export Salvadoran coffee. The nationalization of coffee significantly reduced the margins for coffee growers. As a result, "the government of El Salvador has greatly increased government revenue to help finance the civil war."[68] The World Bank estimated that INCAFE earned $268 million in 1980. The Center of Documentation and Information of the Catholic University says that at least $128 million of these monies were used to finance the civil war and INCAFE's marketing operation.[69] In Guatemala, the coffee economy also helps sustain a repressive government. In 1980, Guatemala's coffee earnings totaled $463 million. About $155 million of this sum went directly to the Guatemalan government.[70]

While the coffee economy plays an important role in financing the war economies of El Salvador and Guatemala, it is difficult to directly link U.S. multinationals to coffee purchases from Central America. Part of the problem is that coffee multinationals do not directly own land in Central America. Companies which dominate the trade of coffee are different from companies which roast, pack and distribute coffee. The roasters purchase coffee beans from numerous importers, although a few traders dominate the business (on occasion a roaster may have its own importers, e.g. A&P). Companies frequently combine coffee beans from different countries into one blend of coffee.

The most likely target for political action would be these end users, the roasters and packers, for their size and political weight would give them more leverage over Central American states as well as exposure to universities through stock investments and trustee links. However, roasters are highly secretive about the coffee beans used in blending their coffee because such information is considered proprietary, a trade secret which would be useful to competitors. Another reason for corporate secrecy is that if traders knew how dependent specific companies were on beans from particular countries, they could then use this information against the roasters in bargaining with them. The leading coffee brands and the companies associated with them are listed in Table 5-6. According to *The Central America Fact Book,* General Foods, Nestle, Procter & Gamble, Consolidated Foods, Standard Brands (now part of RJR Nabisco) and Jacobs account for over 60 percent of the coffee roasting business.[71]

Multinationals market coffee produced by the local oligarchy, thereby supporting the interests of landed elites at home. One group of transnational

---

Table 5-6: Leading Coffee Brands in the U.S.A.

Roaster/Packer	Brand Name
General Foods Corp. (A)	Maxwell House, Sanka, Yuban, Maxim, Brim, Mellow Roast
Procter & Gamble, Inc. (A)(B)	Folger's, High Point
Hills Bros. Coffee, Inc.	Hills Bros., High Yield, Chase & Sanborn's, MJB
Coca-Cola Co. (A)(B)	Butternut, Maryland Club
A&P Coffee Division	Red Circle, Bokar, 8 O'Clock
CFS Continental, Inc.	Continental
Safeway Stores	Airway, Edwards
Chock Full O'Nuts Corp.	Chock Full O'Nuts
Wm. B. Reily & Co.	Luzianne, JFG
Tetley, Inc.	Martinson, Bustelo, Savarin, Medaglia d'Oro, Brown Gold, El Pico

(A) Indicates that these companies purchase Salvadoran coffee.
(B) Indicates that these companies purchase Guatemalan coffee.

SOURCE: *Ukers' International Tea & Coffee Buyers' Guide, Tea & Coffee Trade Journal,* 1986; *Central America Fact Book* (New York: Grove Press, 1986).

corporations, "multicommodity companies," purchases coffee from exporters in Central America and then sells it to other TNC roasters. Some of the corporations involved in the Central American coffee trade are: Procter & Gamble, Coca-Cola, General Foods and Nestle.[72] The coffee economy is critical in sustaining the economies of the military states of Central America. Coffee represents a large proportion of the total exports for the three Central American states: 52.8 percent for El Salvador, 30.5 percent for Guatemala, 24.4 percent for Honduras, and 24.2 percent for Costa Rica (as recorded for 1980).[73] Table 5-7 details the dollar value of Central American coffee exports.

In 1986, a drought in Brazil seriously damaged the coffee crop, leading many coffee importers to start purchasing beans from Central America instead of Brazil.[74] Furthermore, interviews with coffee traders reveal that almost all major roasters purchase coffee from Central America for their blends. One estimate by researchers affiliated with Northern California Interfaith Committee on Corporate Responsibility is that General Foods gets about 3 percent of its coffee beans from El Salvador. However, this information is not well documented.

At this stage, solidarity activists could use the information above as the basis for an information campaign, demanding that targeted companies divulge more information about their dealings in Central America. Objections about proprietary knowledge could be met with demands that the companies simply say whether or not they use *any* beans from Guatemala and El Salvador in their blends. Protests could also be directed against companies like General Foods,

Table 5-7: Total Country Exports:
Dollar Value of Exports of Coffee and Substitutes [071]

Year	El Salvador	Guatemala	Honduras	Costa Rica
1982	505,699,000	686,891,000	315,873,000	481,107,000
1983	393,432,000*	708,285,000	298,572,000	174,593,000*
1984	312,351,000*	345,257,000*	337,373,000	200,974,000*
1985	465,040,000*	374,388,000*	168,740,000*	246,550,000*
1986	564,386,000*	440,161,000*	326,249,000*	298,344,000*

* Estimates

SOURCE: *1988 International Trade Statistics Yearbook*, Volume II, (New York: United Nations, 1988), p. 61.

Coca-Cola and Procter & Gamble which "buy Salvadoran coffee but have no direct foreign investment in the country."[75] Nevertheless, even though this connection has been documented, the scale of company purchases is unknown. Monitoring a corporate embargo on Salvadoran coffee would be difficult given the secrecy of the coffee importers themselves, unless somehow the company could be trusted to provide an accurate account of this information.

Tire and Oil Companies: Resources for Repression

The anti-apartheid movement has made oil companies an important political target because of their strategic significance in aiding police and military forces. The Council of Unions of South Africa has called for international action against all oil companies that operate in South Africa. Likewise, in Central America crude petroleum plays an important role in fueling the war machine in Guatemala and El Salvador and is a strategically important commodity to Central American nations.

Table 5-8 shows Central America's dependency on crude petroleum. In Guatemala, Cia Distribuidora Guatemala Shell (also known as Compania Distribuidora Guatemala Shell), owned by Shell in the United Kingdom and The Netherlands, was the fourth largest company in 1982 with sales of $54 million. Shell also owns an oil refinery (Refineria Petrolera de Guate-Calif) and an agro-chemical firm (Shell Quimica de Guatemala) (see Chapter Three).

As noted earlier, Central American subsidiaries of Shell and Chevron are active in the pesticide trade. In Latin America, 48 percent of the petroleum used in agriculture is used for making fertilizer, 44 percent is used for motive power, and 8 percent for irrigation. The use of such petroleum-dependent technologies and chemicals results in higher yields per acre and per agricultural worker as

---

Table 5-8: Crude Petroleum as a Percent of Total Imports

Country	Percent
El Salvador	23.5 (a)
Guatemala	7.7 (b)
Honduras	5.9 (c)
Costa Rica	10.7 (a)

(a) 1982; (b) 1983; (c) 1984.

SOURCE: Author's calculations based on data on special imports C.I.F. of crude petroleum, etc. and total special imports as published in *1986 International Trade Statistics Yearbook*, Vol. 1 (New York: United Nations), pp. 286, 355, 457 and 482.[76]

well as increased agribusiness profits. But the import of oil from the major firms also contributes to increased foreign debt and dependency on TNCs, as seen in the data in Table 5-8. In the past, the Guatemalan government has received 55 percent of oil company revenues as a tax.[77] Such funding strengthens the state's power over civilian life and provides a subsidy for repression.

Texaco Guatemala owned by Texaco in the United States was the sixth ranked Guatemalan company in terms of sales in 1982. The subsidiary's sales (or turnover) were $31.5 million and it is engaged in the petroleum products business. The parent Texaco also has oil exploration (Getty Oil of Guatemala; Texaco Exploration Guatemala) and refinery operations (Texas Petroleum) in Guatemala. Esso Central America was the thirteenth ranked Guatemalan firm in 1982 with sales of $24 million. Exxon in the United States owns the company and has both a chemical products and petroleum business in the country.[78] In Guatemala, about one quarter of national consumption is met by domestic oil production of some 6,000 barrels per day. Although the rate of oil discovery has slowed, "for the last several years, U.S. government officials have regarded the country's supposed oil resources as the salvation of the economy."[79]

Another major TNC in Guatemala is Goodyear, owner of Fabrica Ginsa (also known as Gran Indus de Neumaticos or GINSA), a rubber plantation owner. In 1982, GINSA had sales of $24 million and was the twelfth largest company in the country. While GINSA serves as a tire manufacturer, a separate subsidiary, Plantaciones de Hule Goodyear, owns a rubber plantation. Goodyear has several rubber plantations which cover over 63,000 acres of land.[80] Table 5-9 details where the major oil companies have subsidiaries in Guatemala, El Salvador, Honduras and Costa Rica.

Table 5-9: TNC Oil Companies and Subsidiaries in Central America

Company	El Salvador	Guatemala	Honduras	Costa Rica
Exxon	Esso Standard Oil	Esso Standard Oil	Esso Standard Oil	Essochem de Centro America
	Essochem de Centro America	Essochem de Centro America	Essochem de Centro America	
	Refineria Petrolera Acajutla			
	RASA		*continued next page*	

Company	El Salvador	Guatemala	Honduras	Costa Rica
Texaco	Texaco Caribbean		Texaco Caribbean	Texaco Caribbean
		Texaco Guatemala	Refineria Texaco de Honduras	
		Texaco Exploration Guatemala		
		Texas Petroleum		
		Getty Oil (Guatemala)		
Chevron	Compania Petrola Chevron	Compania Petrola Chevron		Gulf Costa Rica
		Petroleos Gulf de Guatemala		Quimicas Ortho de California
Shell Oil	Refineria Petrolera Acajutla	Refineria Petrolera de Guate-Calif	Shell Honduras	Quimica Costar-ricense
	Shell El Salvador	Compania Distribuidora Guatemala Shell		
	Shell Quimica de El Salvador	Shell Quimica de Guatemala		
Mobil Oil		Mobil Oil	Mobil Oil	
		Superior Oil Guatemala	Mobil Exploration Honduras	
Occidental Petroleum Corporation			Occidental de Honduras	

SOURCE: Tom Barry and Deb Preusch, *The Central America Fact Book* (New York: Grove Press, 1986), Appendix II. A more recent source confirms each of the parent firms above as having operations in El Salvador, Costa Rica, Honduras and Guatemala as listed with these exceptions: Exxon is not listed as having operations in Costa Rica; Shell is not listed as having operations in any of the four countries and Mobil Oil is not listed as having operations in Guatemala. See *C/CAA's 1989 Caribbean and Central American Databook* (Washington, D.C.: Caribbean/Central American Action, 1988); *Who Owns Whom: International Directory of Corporate Affiliation 1988/89* (Wilmette, Illinois: National Register Publishing Company, Macmillan Directory Division, 1988), pp. 304-305.

Big Banks

Transnational banks have extensive ties to the nations of Central America, having substantial in-country operations as well as providing an important source of capital for loans which underwrite both the government and private bank debts and expenses. We have already discussed Bank of America's ties to repression in Guatemala (see Chapter Two). According to an estimate by the Northern California Interfaith Committee on Corporate Responsibility, the Bank of America held 13 percent of Guatemala's debt to banks of the industrialized nations. Citicorp and Chase Manhattan have important interests in the leading banks of Honduras. Demands that such banks close down Central American subsidiaries would provide limited leverage over the Central American nations because capital could always be lent from U.S.-based operations. Table 5-10 shows that the public sector in Central America has received a significant amount of assistance from the leading private banks, as have private borrowers in these nations. The data shows that private banks in the United States have loaned millions of dollars to El Salvador, Guatemala and Honduras.

U.S. banks also play an important role in the financial infrastructure of Central America. Table 5-11 indicates that the leading transnational banks have affiliate offices in Central America. These branch offices provide important financial services that would be difficult to coordinate from the United States, although consultants and other foreign banks could fill the void if these affiliates were to leave Central America.

Corporate campaigns could focus on transnational banks' loans to Central American nations. Corporate responsibility activists have argued that banks have an economic incentive to limit loans to countries marked by human rights abuses. They argue that countries with human rights abuses have responded to popular protest against poverty with repression; this repression brings instability which can threaten investments.[81] Given the complications of verifying which U.S. banks have made loans to Central America, an immediate demand might be that the major banks tied to Central America (listed in Table 5-11) withdraw their subsidiaries from the region subject to the dual demand criteria.

Campaigns against banks linked to investment in Central America could begin with the demand that universities divest from such banks (including endowment and direct university investments for transactions, e.g. use of bank accounts to pay employee salaries), students withdraw accounts from such banks and students pledge not to take out student loans from targeted banks. On the last point, it should be noted that student borrowing has grown dramatically since the early 1970s, rising from $1,015 million in 1970-71 to $8,288 million in 1985-86 for Guaranteed Student Loans. For National Direct Student loans, student borrowing increased from $240 million to $751 million during this same period.[82] Threats by students to bypass a bank for their student loans might provide significant leverage for banks already pressed by the possibility of massive defaults (or debt reschedulings) from Third World nations.

Table 5-10: Amounts Owed to U.S. Banks by Foreign Borrowers, by Form of Debtor

(in Millions of Dollars)

El Salvador	Total Amount Owed	Portion Owed By:		
		Banks	Public Borrowers	Private Nonbank Borrowers
Sept. 1988	83	33	28	22
June 1987	110	56	29	26
June 1986	115	89	17	8
June 1985	125.3	73.2	37.4	14.6
June 1984	123.4	58.9	46.2	18.3
Guatemala				
Sept. 1988	110	14	84	11
June 1987	68	14	43	11
June 1986	81	20	41	19
June 1985	142.2	31.4	62.3	48.4
June 1984	154.3	17.4	60.2	76.7
Honduras				
Sept. 1988	84	10	59	15
June 1987	174	26	112	36
June 1986	178	25	113	39
June 1985	144.3	14.2	77.5	52.5
June 1984	179.0	14.9	63.8	100.2

SOURCE: Table 2 in "Country Exposure Lending Survey," Federal Financial Institutions Examination Council, Releases of January 11, 1989; November 18, 1987; October 17, 1986; November 6, 1985 and October 15, 1984. Distributed by Federal Reserve Bank, Washington, D.C., Statistical Release E.16 (126).

Table 5-11: U.S. Transnational Banks:
Subsidiaries and Central American Connections*

U.S. Bank	El Salvador	Guatemala	Honduras	Costa Rica
Bank of Boston Corp.		Servicios Comerciales e Industriales (A)	Compania de Credito (A)(B)	Corporacion Intl de Boston (A)(B)
			First National Bank of Boston (A) [operations in country] (C)	Financiera de America (A) [operations in country] (C)
BankAmerica Corp.	[operations in country] (C)	Bank of America (A)	Bank of America (A)	Bank of America (A)
		[foreign offices and operations in country] (B)(C)		Financiera de America SA (92%) (B)
Chase Manhattan Corp.			Banco Atlantida, SA (A)(B)	
			Casa Propria (A)	
			Inversiones Atlantida,SA (A)(B) [operations in country] (C)	
Citicorp.	Citibank (A)(C)	Citibank (A)	Banco de Honduras SA (97%) (A)(B)	Citibank (A)
		Diners Club de Guatemala (A) [operations in country](C)	Diners Club de Honduras (A) [operations in country](C)	Citicorp, SA (B)(C)

* NOTE: The Southern Finance Project in Charlotte, North Carolina, has documented the North Carolina National Bank's links to both South Africa and Central America. In 1986, the bank had $73 million outstanding in loans to South Africa, of which 9.6 percent was to the public sector. The bank was also involved in Eximbank-supported loans to El Salvador and Guatemala. Pesca CA in Guatemala used such funding to finance helicopter equipment from Hughes Helicopter Inc. in California (through a $212,500 loan dated February 19, 1982).(D)

SOURCES: (A) Tom Barry and Deb Preusch, *The Central America Fact Book* (New York: Grove Press, 1986), Appendix II.

(B) *Who Owns What in World Banking*, Edited by Eileen Power, (London: Financial Times Business Information, 1986).

(C) *C/CAA's 1989 Caribbean and Central American Databook* (Washington, D.C.: Caribbean/Central American Action, 1988), pp. 96, 143, 179-181, 215-216. This source also lists the Banque de Paris as having operations in Costa Rica; Boston Overseas Financial Corporation as having operations in Guatemala; and American Express as having operations in Honduras.

(D) "Institutional Profile: NCNB Corporation [Excerpts]," *Southern Finance Project*, Charlotte, North Carolina, 1987.

5.6 Constraints on Selective Divestment: Geopolitics and the Warfare State

There are several constraints on the selective divestment strategy. Will corporations act as forces for constructive reform or force change on Central American states as capital pulls out of the country and U.S. markets are closed off in response to U.S. protests? What role will guerrilla, trade union and community opposition groups in Central America play in such protests? Will coordinated actions between the U.S. solidarity movement and the opposition in Central America develop against targeted companies? In South Africa, the call for divestment had the clear support of the opposition movement itself. The political clout of the opposition movement might be considered greater in South Africa than in Central America. Will U.S. protests amass the necessary political power to pressure corporations one way or another, i.e. to act as levers for political change in Central America?

The success of the international divestment movement against South Africa offers some room for optimism concerning the utility of corporate actions against Central America. The growth of solidarity actions in the United States and the opposition movement in Central America will make a selective divestment movement's goals easier to accomplish. Such a movement could also be aided if the Left in Latin America or the peace movement in Europe were to push their governments to impose sanctions on the Central American military states. International networks could be formed to increase the pressure on these nations to create a new political reality for the region. If such a movement gained ground in Europe, and among Third World nations, the United Nations might become a vehicle for imposing some form of trade sanctions on the Central American military states. Just raising the issue of sanctions would itself help expose the governments of El Salvador, Guatemala and Honduras.

Among advanced western nations, the United States is the premier trading partner with Central America. However, Europe's economic ties with Central America could create the foundation for expanding divestment/anti-corporate actions which could help isolate the Central American nations diplomatically. The constraints of protectionism (which have closed off U.S. markets) and overproduction of agro-exports have made the European market more critical to Central American nations. On December 29, 1986, Guatemala and Great Britain resumed diplomatic relations, after reaching a reconciliation over past disputes over Belize, formerly "British Honduras." Foreign Minister Mario Quinoez of Guatemala said that establishing relations with Great Britain was necessary because England "is a port of entry to Europe, and we need to increase our exports to the countries of the European Economic Community."[83]

Europe also imports a significant amount of Central American goods. In 1982, El Salvador exported $137.3 million worth of goods to West Germany, home of the Green movement. That same year, Guatemala exported $66.3 million to Italy, where the peace movement is now becoming a significant force. Direct actions might focus against subsidiaries of U.S. TNCs such as Ph. Astheimer & Solm, an affiliate of Castle & Cooke in Germany.[84] As in the international Coca-Cola actions, European activists could organize direct protest against European affiliates of U.S. TNCs and European parent TNCs in Central America (such as Shell). Actions could also focus on demands for economic sanctions or protests directed against imports from U.S. TNCs linked to Central America.

The most important allies for campaigns in the North that pressure TNCs in Central America could be the various trade union federations in El Salvador, Guatemala, Honduras and Costa Rica. As Costa Rica and Honduras withdraw their support for the contras, increasing attention should be paid to the labor practices of these nations. [85] A survey done in 1983 showed that the average hourly earnings or Costa Rican workers was $.787 per hour. A January 1986 report found that unskilled wages were about $4 per day.[86] In Honduras, where about 15 percent of the workforce is organized, minimum wages in 1985 ranged from $2.50 to $3.55 per day.[87] A 1988 estimate for the total monthly wage bill for 200 workers in an apparel manufacturing plant was only $23,718![88] The average daily wage in Guatemala was $2.15, according to a 1988 report.[89] In El Salvador, the daily minimum wage was about $3.50 in 1988.[90] These data show that campaigns in the United States to pressure TNCs to pay higher wages in Central America could be an important area for new solidarity campaigns.[91]

Ultimately, even if the logic of selective divestment were to break down due to corporate intransigence, corporate campaigns against the military states would make clearer the case against El Salvador, Guatemala and Honduras as pariah nations involved in genocide, terror and authoritarian rule. As these nations are increasingly viewed as outcasts, U.S. government efforts to aid these regimes will prove harder to sell in Congressional debates and administration aid requests.

However, there are other problems related to a selective divestment movement. The U.S. "warfare state"—not the U.S. corporate order—is the primary defender of the regimes in El Salvador, Guatemala and Honduras. The U.S. government is not primarily interested in supporting these regimes as preserves of profit but seeks to prevent the rise of governments politically independent of the United States, nations such as Nicaragua which provides a model for a different kind of society: "U.S. military and strategic interests are...more important in shaping policy than economic interests."[92]

Particular companies, like Castle & Cooke, have greater interests in "political stability" in Central America than the U.S. corporate order as a whole. However, the "new relations of dependency" in El Salvador described earlier, reveal that U.S. corporate investments can be replaced by U.S. government aid and foreign lending. On the other hand, a selective divestment movement would complicate U.S. government interests in maintaining the economic viability of the Central American military states. The most concrete manifestation of these interests has been the U.S. Caribbean Basin Initiative, designed to increase the agro-exports of the region. A selective divestment movement would also present a contradiction for the efforts of corporations mobilized under the leadership of groups such as Caribbean/Central American Action (see Chapter Two) to increase private investment in the region.[93]

Such anti-corporate actions must be supplemented by other political work which attempts to challenge the direct actions of the U.S. government in supporting repression. Ultimately, U.S. foreign policy is directed by a warfare state which is relatively independent from immediate corporate decision-making power and the calculus of profitability. Therefore, a selective divestment movement would have to join forces with other movements which make this warfare state the primary target of political change. The next chapter describes the rationale for targeting the universities themselves as part of actions designed to undermine the military-industrial alliance.

Part 3

6

The Warfare State and the University

6.1 The Warfare State and Intervention in Central America

Lying behind accelerated U.S. intervention in Central America and military actions against Libya, Lebanon and Grenada is the warfare state: the combined economic, political and military power centralized in the Pentagon, State Department, intelligence agencies and the armed forces. Intervention is part of a larger movement by the warfare state to acquire more and more power and authority at home and abroad.

In Honduras, the warfare state has extended its authority and control by war maneuvers that have turned the country into a military command post. Nicaragua has faced military and economic attacks organized and directed by U.S. war planners in the warfare state and their contract mercenaries, the contras. Throughout Central America, the centralized power of the U.S. government is used to manipulate the policies of nominally independent governments. Economic and military aid, as well as logistical military support, is used to extract concessions and organize government actions in the service of U.S. imperial interests.[1]

Domestically, we see the other side of interventionism in the rapid increase in defense spending, from more than $206 billion in FY 1980 to more than $302 billion in FY 1986 (figures in constant 1988 dollars). By increasing the number of people controlled, as evidenced in increased military procurement, Pentagon managers are able to hold greater authority and social power. These objectives are also met by using a military (as opposed to diplomatic) approach to current international political conflicts. In fact, spending on military intervention is a central part of the military budget. The Coalition for a New Foreign and Military Policy estimated in 1985 that 45 percent of the military budget was used for military intervention (this included funding for forces in the Persian Gulf, the Mediterranean and Latin America). Another report by the Council on Economic Priorities found that more than two-thirds of U.S. foreign aid now goes to military and other national security-related programs.[2]

Both the peace and solidarity movements have failed to address the link between interventionism and the centralized power of the warfare state. Ad hoc strategies such as pressuring the defeat of specific weapons systems, banning nuclear testing, material aid campaigns, defeat of contra aid bills, providing sanctuary for political refugees and national marches in Washington have been important defensive measures which have raised public awareness about militarism and intervention. However, in and of themselves, such actions leave intact and unchallenged the military bureaucracies which promote the arms race and keep in power military regimes in El Salvador, Guatemala, Chile and elsewhere.

In plotting an alternative course, it is essential to challenge the roots of imperial power and identify leverage points which would place constraints on the warfare state. In the earlier part of this century, colonial expansion and intervention reflected the immediate interests of corporations; corporate economic interests were directly translated into state policy. Since then, Central America has stood out as the premier economic colony of the United States where the dominant U.S. corporations have had "virtual free rein since the only other U.S. interests there are representatives of the national security bureaucracy—military attachés, AID advisers, and CIA agents." These regional representatives of the nation state knew "that their principal role" was to serve the corporations.[3]

However, the guiding force behind intervention has changed and is primarily rooted in the political directives of war planners who initiate military attacks on Third World states. Economic interests still provide a rationale for intervention. U.S. corporate holdings in the Caribbean Basin as a whole are substantial:

> Agriculture, manufacturing, mining, tourism, and commercial holdings account for $6.2 billion in productive investments, and another $16.9 billion is tied up in banking and financial operations in the Caribbean Basin. This constitutes about 9 percent of total U.S. investments abroad.[4]

But intervention based on such economic interests is derivative of the larger need to preserve foreign consumer and labor markets as a safe haven for U.S. investment. As Harry Magdoff, a radical economic scholar observes, "small Latin American countries that produce relatively little profit are important in United States policy making because control over all of Latin America is important."[5]

The need to keep vast regions in the Third World open to U.S. investment helps explain the development of institutions of intervention and the sabotage of independent regimes which seek economic justice for their people. However, these economic interests and the interventionary momentum have become internalized in a separate *political* logic that guides the national security agencies and war planners.

The United States has seized control of political life in Central America to ward off the "demonstration effect" of progressive regimes which show an economic alternative to the relations of dependency. George Shultz, U.S. Secretary of State under Reagan, best articulated this "danger" of the Nicaraguan example when he warned in March 1986 that if the Sandinistas "succeed in consolidating their power, *all* the countries in Latin America, who *all* face serious internal economic problems, will see radical forces emboldened to exploit these problems."[6] Similarly, ex-Secretary of State Alexander Haig, in testimony before the Bipartisan Commission on Central America chaired by Henry Kissinger, explained:

> Our problem in Central America is first and foremost global; second regional, with focus on Cuba, and third is local. If we fail to deal with these problems today in El Salvador, we may find them developing in other areas which are less ambiguous and far more dangerous.[7]

Haig's comments reflect the fact that regional and international economic interests are important in directing national security managers to extend their political power through intervention. But these economic motivations are becoming secondary to state planners in deciding how and when intervention is carried out. The increasing authority of the nation state in international affairs has relegated corporate interests to a secondary role in directing foreign policy and in triggering the U.S. military apparatus. As we have seen, the proximate interests of private capital in Central America are becoming less critical than the interest of "state capital." This follows a general pattern in the post-World War II era:

> The United States has sought to make U.S. corporations renounce their economic interest—free trade, unrestricted investment—to serve the interests of state capitalism. In the Third World it is U.S. government financing—World Bank, International Monetary Fund—that determines the investment patterns.[8]

The end result of U.S. foreign policy "has been to purchase political power, which includes the capability of waging economic warfare, at serious economic cost."[9]

In Vietnam and Central America, we see a general pattern where the quest for power outweighs the quest for profit in shaping the immediate causes of intervention. As foreign policy scholar Richard Barnet explains:

> Governments are willing to spend limitless sums to maintain control and to buy order even when the very social and political environment they are seeking to create is unlikely to yield any economic benefit remotely commensurate with the cost of creating it [sic].[10]

In Central America, Xabier Gorostiaga has underlined the greater importance of geopolitical interests in shaping our policy by defining just how great the economic costs of intervention really are. Noting the withdrawal of U.S. capital in response to the region's economic crisis, and that U.S. trade with Central America is only 2 percent of its trade with Latin America as a whole, he writes:

> On the one hand, the North American economic stake in the region is not high while, on the other, bailing out the region will prove extremely expensive. ECLA has estimated that more than US $20 billion would be required over the next five years to avoid regional economic and financial collapse. In short, Central America must be viewed as a net economic burden to the United States.

The importance of geopolitical concerns, such as the "protection" of the Panama Canal, "70 percent of whose traffic originates in or is destined for the United States," helps explain the "new relations of dependency" described in Chapter Four.[11]

Exploring the principal causes for increasing U.S. military and political control over Central America is necessary for informed political action. Many activists have an incomplete understanding of the institutions behind the U.S. war in Central America leading them to unworkable strategies.[12] One approach to limiting the scope of intervention rests on appeals to Congress. The defeat of a major contra aid package in the House on February 3, 1987 was an important victory for the anti-intervention movement. However, the institutions of intervention still held the power to destabilize Nicaragua. Nicaraguan President Daniel Ortega warned after the vote that as long as Reagan held power, an invasion of Central America by U.S. forces was still possible. In addition, many of the military forms of intervention are covert actions which have *de facto* Congressional support or occur without Congressional approval (legally or otherwise).

The Iran-contra arms scandal has demonstrated the importance of the "underground" government which carries out policies behind the backs of the North American people and Congress as well. As explained by former National Security Council operative, Lt. Col. Oliver North, the director of the CIA, William Casey, saw the diversion of funds to Iran:

as part of a more grandiose plan to use the Enterprise as a "stand-alone," "off-the-shelf," covert capacity that would act throughout the world while evading Congressional review.[13]

Arthur Liman, chief counsel of the Senate Committee investigating the scandal, explained the "Enterprise" and secret government in a memo to Senators Daniel Inouye and Warren Rudman before Congressional hearings began on May 7, 1987. He wrote that:

> After we establish that a policy decision was made at the highest levels to transfer responsibility for contra support to the NSC..., we favor examining how that decision was implemented...This is the part of the story that reveals the whole secret government-within-a-government, operated from the [Executive Office Building] by a Lt. Col., with its own army, air force, diplomatic agents, intelligence operatives and appropriations capacity.[14]

Even more sinister were plans described in a *Miami Herald* news story on July 5, 1987: "Lt. Col. Oliver North...helped draw up a controversial plan to suspend the Constitution in the event of a national crisis, such as nuclear war, violent and widespread internal dissent or national opposition to a U.S. military invasion abroad."[15]

The last finding in the *Herald* story is especially significant given the link some see between such resistance and the expansion of covert actions: "There is little doubt...that popular resistance has compelled the state to resort to indirect means to carry out its programs of terrorism and subversion in Central America, instead of sending military forces directly to achieve its ends."[16]

Military intervention abroad is in part the reflection of a drive by the state managers and the agencies of the warfare state to increase their power and authority. The power to carry out such military actions has shifted from the Congress to the executive branch. Planning for intervention overseas and the constraints of an economy geared to war production have created powerful and permanent war-making institutions in violation of the spirit behind the legal principles which guided the development of our country. In early discussions of the Constitution found in the *Federalist Papers,* Alexander Hamilton explained the requirement that Congress would be able to vote funds for military purposes every two years:

> The legislature of the United States will be *obliged,* by this provision, once at least in every two years, to deliberate upon the propriety of keeping a military force on foot; to come to a new resolution of the point; and to declare their sense of the matter, by a formal vote in the face of their constituents. They are not *at liberty* to vest in the executive department permanent funds for the support of an army, if they were even incautious enough to be willing to repose in it so improper a confidence...[17]

In contrast to this power of the purse which shapes Congressional power in foreign policy, the Executive Branch has been able to manipulate budgets to extract concessions from Congress. For example, in a contra aid vote at the close of 1987, House conferees accepted a catch-all appropriations bill that emerged out of negotiations with the Senate that provided $8.1 million in aid for the contras. Democratic leaders who opposed such aid compromised on the legislation before "direct and implicit threats" by the President:

> Lawmakers attributed the Administration's success in part to a White House message this weekend that President Reagan would not accept any spending resolution unless it contained some aid for the contras.[18]

Ignoring Hamilton's warning, Congress has sanctioned the development of permanent institutions of intervention which are extensions of the Executive Branch. Covert operations, not accountable to public debate or popular will, are still sanctioned by Congress despite the scandal revealed in the Iran-contra hearings. In a recent report on the betrayal of public trust, Congress declared:

> Because covert operations are secret by definition, they are of course not openly debated or publicly approved. So long as the policies which they further are known, and so long as they are conducted in accordance with law, covert operations are acceptable.[19]

This last sentence is especially revealing because the legal foundations of covert operations are most tenuous. As foreign policy scholar Robert Borosage observes, the CIA's charter "contains no explicit authority for either collection of intelligence or for covert action abroad."[20]

On the whole, Congress has been "the passive branch" in the development of foreign and domestic policies.[21] Occasionally, when political scandals have threatened the legitimacy of the American system, Congress has been motivated to resist executive infringements on its *decision-making power* in the implementation of covert operations. Congress has wanted a "piece of the action." But the legislature has never called for the abolition of agencies of intervention, although in the mid-1970s, the Senate's Church Committee "gave serious consideration to proposing a total ban on *all* forms of covert action."[22]

The Congressional desire to maintain its decision-making power has framed the legislative attempts to reform covert operations. The Ryan Amendment to the Foreign Assistance Act of 1961 provided that:

> ...no funds appropriated under any act may be expended by or on behalf of the Central Intelligence Agency for operations in foreign countries, other than activities intended solely for obtaining necessary intelligence, [unless the President finds that each such operation is] important to the national security [and] reports, in a timely fashion, a description [to the appropriate committees of Congress].[23]

The intent of such legislation was to make intelligence agencies more account-able to Congressional budgetary authority and provide advance notice for covert operations. However, these constraints have been rendered meaningless by Presidential delays in reporting on covert operations so that they become a *fait accompli*.[24] According to pronouncements found in President Reagan's State of the Union Address:

> Surely no issue is more important for peace in our own hemisphere, for the security of our frontiers, for the protection of our vital interests than to achieve democracy in Nicaragua.[25]

Because the Executive Branch's definition of "national security" is able to activate the covert operations trigger, absurd proclamations like this have had the force of law.

Other legislative reforms have also sanctioned U.S. political intervention. The new section 501 of the National Security Act of 1947, introduced as part of the Oversight Act of 1980, stated that the approval of the intelligence committees was not required for the initiation of a "significant anticipated intelligence activity" which would include any covert actions.[26]

As long as the *war-making institutions* are left intact and the legislature sanctions covert operations, the state managers will be able to intervene in Central America, Chile, South Korea or any other nation considered to be in the U.S. sphere of influence. This ability to project U.S. power suggests two central lessons of the Vietnam War. First, although the anti-war movement was able to speed the end of U.S. involvement there, it was unable to articulate a vision or amass the political power necessary to dismantle the war-making institutions. Second, although these institutions were not dismantled, the movement was able to limit the scope of U.S. intervention in Vietnam.

In his review of the Vietnam War and domestic opposition, political scientist Paul Joseph writes that "the anti-war movement did not end the Vietnam War but it limited the freedom of action available to decision-makers." Anti-war protests helped engender increased public dissatisfaction with the war and reduced the government's ability to mobilize domestic support. Escalation was blocked by the fear that protestors would turn to more radical actions, or that expanded involvement would increase public anti-war sentiment and the number of peace protestors. As Admiral Thomas Moorer, Chief of Naval Operations, testified before Congress, "*If domestic restraints were relaxed,* the U.S. would have the option of bombing Haiphong harbor in North Vietnam and landing amphibious assaults behind North Vietnamese lines."[27]

Despite the success of efforts which, as in Vietnam, have focussed on the specific role of one regional intervention, there is a need to expand current strategies in order to dismantle the war-making institutions. A repeat of the strategy used against intervention in Vietnam may prove ineffective no matter how disruptive anti-war demonstrations become.

Under current war policies, the U.S. warfare state is able to inflict heavy damage upon Third World opponents without deploying the ground troops that would trigger the massive opposition of the Vietnam War era. For U.S. state managers,

> the lesson of Vietnam was not that more intervention by the USA would have won, but rather that the resort to direct intervention, from 1965 to 1973, was mistaken as a whole, and could not have attained victory even if it had been carried out with greater numbers and determination. The political problem posed within the USA would, in these terms, be not that of gradually winning support for direct intervention, but rather of consolidating long-run support—in Congress, the public, the military and the government for [low-intensity conflict] involvements.[28]

Military intervention in Central America rests on massive arms sales and the use of "low-intensity conflict," including U.S. support for right-wing guerrillas in Nicaragua and counter-insurgency in El Salvador, Guatemala and Honduras. In the future, the use of military proxies could be supplemented by Navy shelling and air strikes similar to recent attacks against Lebanon and Libya. Such intervention rests on maintaining a consensus in support of intervention in public and civilian institutions. Not only the president, national security agencies and Congress, but also the media, universities and trade unions play a role in shaping this consensus.

At this writing, the combined domestic opposition to administration policies and whatever satisfaction the Right has gleaned from covert actions (both legal and illegal) against Nicaragua and counter-insurgency efforts elsewhere have not tipped the scales towards large-scale U.S. ground troop deployment. If such troops are committed, it is likely that the heavy losses they would suffer (in combination with heightened domestic political opposition) would lead to their withdrawal. However, even under the current political stalemate, Central American countries continue to suffer immense losses—not just economically and politically, but in human terms; slaughter and torture still are everyday realities for civilians in Central America.

For the peace and solidarity movements, the current "stalemate" represents an inability to project the political power necessary to either significantly raise the cost of current policies to the administration or to develop coalitions with other social groups which have an interest in dissipating the size, scope and power of the warfare state. While some hope to recreate the direct action (and not so civil disobedience) of the anti-Vietnam War movement, it seems unlikely that a radical politics of confrontation would emerge without a large-scale U.S. invasion. But a political strategy that depends on *reacting*, i.e. waiting for the bombs to drop or the invasion to begin, leaves unchallenged the source of state military power and will ultimately prove ineffective at combatting U.S.-sponsored slaughter abroad.

Militant actions or ad hoc campaigns which do not seek to restructure the war-making institutions are reformist undertakings (see Chapter Eight). The basis for state military power lies in those institutions which help create the consensus for intervention and includes the military bureaucracies, national security agencies, military and media corporations and universities as central actors. A shared ideological consensus of anti-communism and domination of Third World resources and nation states unites the Congress and the Executive in the interventionary project. In order to confront the concentrated bureaucratic power and ideological consensus that lies behind intervention, it is necessary to constrict the territorial scope of the warfare state, provide alternatives to its hegemonic manipulation of public discussion and plan for the disarmament of covert and other war operations.

Political action in the university can play two critical roles in advancing this agenda. First, if the university becomes "politicized" it can function as a support for an anti-interventionary ideology. Second, the universities currently provide resources for the warfare state. The Pentagon and its affiliated agencies, the National Aeronautics and Space Administration (NASA) and the Department of Energy (DOE), function as controllers of research and other agendas of universities and military-serving corporations. By challenging university and corporate involvement in the warfare state, we can begin the process of weakening its supporting pillars.[29]

Disarming the warfare state requires a national movement which develops legal constraints on the rule of force, budgetary alternatives to the sponsorship of genocide overseas and a popular awareness of the dangers of an interventionary and permanent warfare state to domestic liberties. Political action against universities' ties to intervention can become one institutional lever for limiting the influence of the warfare state. The transformation of university curriculum and research can make universities part of an overall process of converting our war economy and ideology to a peaceful alternative. Before analyzing the strategies used to carry out this goal, we review the place of the university in the development of the warfare state. Here, the central issues are: How do universities enhance military power? How does academia legitimate war thinking and planning? And finally, how does universities' dependency on the military organize academia as a political constituency in support of warfare state budgets?

6.2 Universities and the Creation of the Warfare State

The Pentagon's need for technological information to run its war machine laid the basis for university-military cooperation. In the 1960s, Michael T. Klare, a researcher on defense issues, dubbed this relationship: "The University-Military Complex." Klare wrote that, without the support of the universities, "The United States would not have acquired the intercontinental ballistic missile, and would not have developed a counterinsurgency strategy for intervention in Vietnam." Defense Department sponsorship of university research has also spurred a host of other technological developments. The expansion of the military sector has depended on a vast network of scientific researchers and laboratories which have pursued the Research and Development (R&D) needs of the Pentagon:

> Since the only reservoir of trained scientific manpower available for such work is the university campus, it was thus inevitable that the Pentagon should call upon the universities to collaborate in the foundation of a military research network.[30]

As a result, the university has become a major think tank for the Pentagon. During World War II, military research was carried out through the Office of Scientific Research and Development (OSRD). This civilian agency's directors "tended to favor the large established institutions from which they themselves hailed, where, they believed, their work could be done most expeditiously."[31] Such favoritism encouraged a concentration evident even before the war broke out, partly due to links between elite universities and leading industrialists and corporations. During the war, the elite universities (such as MIT, California Institute of Technology, Columbia and Harvard) received the largest military contracts, worth millions of dollars. Military largesse gave these universities a taste for power which they were not prepared to relinquish. As historian Daniel Kelves explains:

> the War effort had given professors the heady taste of doing research with few financial restraints. Typically the young physicists at the MIT radiation laboratory had grown accustomed to signing an order for a new instrument whose cost would have deadlocked a faculty before the War.[32]

These incentives helped create the predecessors to today's alliance between the military and the universities:

> Long before Hiroshima, it was widely acknowledged in government circles that the maintenance of a strong national defense in the post-

war world would require the ongoing participation of civilian scientists and engineers in military research and development.[33]

After World War II, there arose a serious shortage of science professors, in part due to "frenetic recruitment" by armaments industries. This shortage led the major universities to approve "an increasing flow of military contracts" which enabled such institutions to inflate salaries and thereby attract the more qualified scientists. Given the concentration of military contracts in elite institutions, this process helped foster the dominance of these military-linked schools over smaller colleges. It is worth noting that during World War II, proposals for "nationalizing" the war industries and drafting necessary technical and scientific personnel were considered but rejected in favor of the military contract system.[34]

In the 1940s, business leaders discussed how to continue the government subsidy of industry and selected universities which had occurred during World War II through military expenditure. One of the first public pronouncements of the value of a permanent war economy occurred at a January 1944 meeting of the "Army Ordnance Association" which gathered high Army and Navy officers as well as leading industrialists. In a speech before the Association's annual dinner, Charles E. Wilson, executive vice chairman of the War Production Board, declared:

> What is more natural and logical than that we should henceforth mount our national policy upon the solid fact of an industrial capacity for war, and *a research capacity for war* that is also 'in being'? It seems to me that anything less is foolhardy [emphasis added].

Wilson observed that industry's cooperation with the Army and Navy during the last two years had made a "very effective combination" which should be extended into the postwar period.

Wilson advocated the integration of political, military and industrial life in order to promote U.S. world power. Essential to this scheme was keeping the United States "scientifically and technologically ready for war" by continuing the defense research capacity of government agencies and armed services as well as industry. The integration of civilian research with the permanent war economy could occur by naming civilian administrators to institutional committees that could maintain a liaison with industry and government laboratories. Wilson called for the chairs of such committees, together with ranking Navy and Army officers, to create a general organization for continuing postwar research and development.[35]

Many business leaders chose to adjust to the postwar decrease in demand for war materiel by favoring this state-guaranteed market for technological production. In each major military build-up in the postwar period—the Korean War budget expansion in the early 1950s, the Kennedy military build-up, and the last two Reagan administration budgets—"there was concern over domestic economic stagnation." As Noam Chomsky explains:

> For a variety of reasons, the device that best serves the needs of existing power and privilege is what is sometimes called "military Keynesianism": the creation of a state-guaranteed market for high technology rapidly-obsolescing waste production, meaning armaments.[36]

The corporations and universities played a role in supporting military Keynesianism and war planning as two central agents in the cycle of military production beginning with research and development, leading to prototypes and actual production of military technologies. Wilson's proposals were carried forward in a reorganization plan carried out by General Dwight D. Eisenhower as Army Chief of Staff in 1946. Eisenhower issued a memorandum on "Scientific and Technological Resources as Military Assets," which Pentagon critic Seymour Melman later called the "birth certificate" of the military-industrial complex.[37] It is worth taking a fuller look at this remarkable document which details the desires of war planners to combine and integrate the military and the university:

> ...It is our job to take the initiative to promote the development of new resources, if our national security indicates the need. It is our duty to support broad research programs in educational institutions, in industry, and in whatever field might be of importance to the Army. Close integration of military and civilian resources will not only directly benefit the Army, but indirectly contribute to the nation's security, as civilians are prepared for their role in an emergency by the experience gained in time of peace. The association of military and civilians in educational institutions and industry will level barriers, engender mutual understanding, and lead to the cultivation of friendships invaluable for future cooperation...In the interest of cultivating to the utmost the integration of civilian and military resources and of securing the most effective unified direction of our research and development activities, this responsibility is being consolidated in a separate section on the highest War Department level...[38]

The Eisenhower plans were given fuller expression in the Armed Services Procurement Act of 1947. This legislation authorized the military services to contract with industries and universities through advertising and bidding. However, a policy of "negotiating" contracts was introduced through a number of exceptions to these more competitive forms of business practice.

As early as 1947 the Steelman Report noted the influence of universities in advisory committees which shaped the contracting process. These committees:

> ...are influential in awarding contracts commonly negotiated without competitive bidding. Since the outstanding scientists of the country are frequently associated with the largest industries and universities, insti-

tutions engaged in or attempting to secure contract work often have officers or employees who sit upon the program-planning and evaluative committees.

These advisory committees became the most visible way in which the goals of corporations and military planners became integrated. But, as Robert Borosage explains, "the basic method of integration was the development of interlocking managerial positions." Thus, by 1961 the Hebert Congressional subcommittee revealed that 261 generals and admirals and 485 retirees above the rank of colonel and Navy captain were employed by companies that had garnered 80 percent of the nation's military contracts. These connections helped ensure that corporations linked to defense work would receive a "steady and continuous flow of military contracts."[39]

One of the first organized expressions of the new alliance among universities, industry and government took shape in the Office of Naval Research (ONR). Historian Kelves has called the ONR "the greatest peacetime cooperative undertaking between the academic world and government." As historian David Noble writes:

> By 1949, the ONR was sponsoring 1200 research projects at 200 universities, involving 3000 scientists and nearly as many graduate students...By 1948, the Department of Defense research activities accounted for 62 percent of all federal research and development expenditures, including 60 percent of federal grants to universities for research outside of agriculture. By 1960, that figure had risen to 80 percent.[40]

Kelves and Noble describe a system in which forces promoting increased university and Pentagon ties are not the simple reflection of economic interests but correspond to a drive by universities and academics to increase their influence and power. Research for the military, through the provision of large sums of capital and subsidization of scientific equipments and facilities, has enhanced the status and prestige of professors and university alike. Military advisory boards have also provided access to the centers of power in the Pentagon for the university presidents and academics who, in turn, have provided technical and political advice to the state managers.

The universities are further tied to corporations through trustees who are also corporate directors, and by their investments in arms manufacturers, including those that make weapons ending up in El Salvador, Guatemala and Honduras (see below). Military industry executives also can be found on the boards of trustees of research institutes, think tanks and universities. These economic ties and political affiliations have strengthened the alliance among war corporations, universities and the state—an alliance which reached maturity in the postwar era.

6.3 Research in the Service of War

Universities have provided the infrastructure of intervention in the Third World by advancing military research and development which has served the warfare state, enlarging its power domestically and overseas. This logistical support for war-making and war-thinking has extended even into the "soft" social sciences. As James Ridgeway, author of the *Closed Corporation*, wrote in 1968:

> George Washington and American Universities in Washington, D.C., run two of the Army's centers which deal in different aspects of psychological warfare. George Washington's Human Resources Research Office (HumRRO) is concerned with teaching combat soldiers to kill more efficiently, while American University's Center for Research in Social Systems (CRESS) collects intelligence on countries of the third world and tries to build systems which will manipulate their policies so that communists can be kept out of power.[41]

How critical are universities to the defense establishment? Is the research they perform peripheral to the needs of the military-serving agencies in the Defense Department, Department of Energy and NASA? Table 6-1 indicates that while universities' applied research activities might be peripheral to the institutions, the warfare state is *highly dependent* on the universities in the area of basic research. National Science Foundation estimates for 1987 show that universities carried out a little more than half a billion dollars worth of research and development work for the Defense Department alone, an extraordinarily high figure considering that much of this activity is labor-intensive. A recently

Table 6-1: University Commitments to the Military for Basic and Applied Research in 1987

(in Thousands of Dollars)

	Basic Research			Applied Research		
	University Share	Total	% of Total	University Share	Total	% of Total
DOD	476,160	907,599	52.5	204,878	2,439,957	8.4
DOE	248,224	1,068,465	23.2	123,467	1,029,386	12.0
NASA	220,060	1,013,717	21.7	42,964	1,255,530	3.4

SOURCE: Federal Funds for Research and Development, Detailed Historical Tables: Fiscal Years 1955-1989, National Science Foundation, Washington, D.C.

released report by the Defense Department shows a steady progression in the percentage of their obligations for basic research (so called "6.1.-funded research") going to academic institutions, suggesting that the Pentagon is growing more dependent on the universities for this basic research. In 1981, 39.8 percent of Defense Department obligations for basic research went to academic institutions. In 1982, this rose to 43.8 percent, and by 1986 it had risen still further to 54.5 percent.[42]

There are now more than 250 universities and colleges involved in military activities. Table 6-2, listing university military contractors, shows that military-supported research is concentrated in a handful of major universities. In FY 1983, the top ten university military contractors received 73.3 percent of the Pentagon's $942 million in university research funds. However, in the past, the Defense Department has attempted to "spread the wealth" and thereby extend its authority over an even larger number of educational institutions. Under Project Themis, begun in 1967-68, fifty research contracts were awarded to fifty different institutions. The plan arose as Pentagon managers were concerned that "smaller colleges and universities had been getting small shares or no funds at all from the main federal research-supporting agencies, those in the Department of Defense orbit."[43]

Universities are tied to the Defense Department through research and applied work carried out under contract by Defense Department-linked institutes. The two forms of university ties to the military, contractual and institutional, tend to overlap as defense contracts ascend in scale. Viewing university relations with the Pentagon and other military agencies as mere "contracts" tends to conceal the degree to which university research functions as an institutional form. Universities renew their contracts with the military year after year so that Pentagon research often becomes a structural component of academia. This pattern is especially true of those universities with the largest Defense Department contracts.

Pentagon contracts are granted for research, development, testing and evaluation. But what do the line item figures in Table 6-2 really mean? Do university-military contracts serve the benign function of furthering scientific innovation and technological development which is not necessarily exploited for military purposes? In 1974, researchers Stanton A. Glantz and Norm Albers examined Defense Department research at Stanford University and concluded that military research on campus was largely mission-oriented:

> There are non-military applications of much DOD sponsored R&D, but when one assesses the nature of DOD research in the university, this random "spillover" must be contrasted with the systematically organized program to develop military technology that underlies every decision to fund or not to fund a proposal.[44]

Table 6-2: Fiscal Year 1987:
A Selective Listing of University Contracts for Research, Development, Test and Evaluation with the Defense Department
(in Thousands of Dollars)

University	Contract Amount
Amherst College	119
Arizona State University	1,726
Auburn University	5,445
Boston College	511
Boston University	3,604
Brandeis University	52
Brown University	3,593
California Institute of Technology	6,660
California State University	2,707
Carnegie Mellon University	41,516
Case Western Reserve	3,476
Catholic University of America	1,395
City University of New York	708
Clark University	207
Colorado State University	2,941
Columbia University	7,907
Cornell University	11,196
Dartmouth College	1,421
Drexel University	1,183
Duke University	2,306
Educational Testing Service	665
Emory University	419
George Washington University	1,530
Georgetown University	1,083
Georgia Institute of Technology	33,293
Harvard College	5,928
Howard University	130
Johns Hopkins University	354,925
Lawrence Livermore Laboratory	6,764
Mass. Institute of Technology	407,640
Michigan State University	807
New Mexico State University	13,229
New York University	3,518
Northwestern University	2,283
Oregon State University	5,443
Pennsylvania State University	38,994
Princeton University	5,559

Purdue University	8,628
Rice University	1,935
Rutgers, The State University	1,429
San Diego State University, Foundation	1,796
San Jose State University	361
Spelman College	84
Stanford Leland Jr. University	37,021
State University of New York	4,994
Syracuse University	4,172
Tufts University	370
University of Arizona	6,447
University of California	33,085
University of Chicago	1,568
University of Colorado	4,282
University of Connecticut	2,159
University of Florida	7,854
University of Hawaii	1,422
University of Illinois	18,017
University of Iowa	2,923
University of Maryland	13,652
University of Massachusetts	9,935
University of Michigan	6,731
University of Minnesota	2,557
University of New Mexico	11,355
University of North Carolina	3,162
University of Notre Dame	579
University of Oregon	1,700
University of Pennsylvania	6,035
University of Pittsburgh	3,097
University of Rhode Island	1,859
University of Rochester	6,098
University of San Francisco	137
University of Southern California	32,813
University of Texas	39,049
University of Virginia	2,378
University of Washington	19,626
University of Wisconsin	4,416
Washington State University	815
Wayne State University	416
Washington University	2,075
Wesleyan University	48
Yale University	8,051

SOURCE: *Educational and Nonprofit Institutions Receiving Prime Contract Awards for RDT&E, Fiscal Year 1987* (Washington, D.C.: Directorate for Information, Operations and Reports, the Pentagon, 1988).

The Defense Department's Science and Technology Program is most likely to fund pure or "basic" research. Yet, its main objective is "to increase capabilities in weapons, mobility, command and control, and other important military functions." A division of labor among Pentagon research projects conceals the military applications of "unclassified" basic research:

> Work which might be classified, and thus less attractive to campus researchers, can be fragmented into many separate projects, some of which can remain unclassified, and seemingly basic. When the research is completed, the central agency, either a private firm or a DOD laboratory, assembles all the parts into whatever system was originally desired. Only the central agency has access to the details of the entire system.[45]

Other data suggest that military-funded R&D leads to development with little use for civilian enterprise. The link between *national* military R&D funding and military applications has been discussed repeatedly by critics of the military-industrial complex who have described the limits to the amount of civilian "spinoffs" generated by military-funded technology. Citing one report, Seymour Melman wrote that "a formal inquiry into the possible percentage of spinoff effect from military research expenditures has found that perhaps 5 percent, but not more than 10 percent, of spinoff for each military research dollar may have occurred."[46]

The Defense Department-funded scientific disciplines in "basic research" include physics, radiation science, astronomy, astrophysics, electronics, chemistry, mathematics, computer sciences, mechanics, energy conversion, aeronautical sciences, oceanography, terrestrial sciences and atmospheric sciences, as well as biological and medical sciences. Most important of these is fundamental research in the physical sciences, the largest and most diverse area of the Defense Department research program. A Defense Department report on the Pentagon's "Basic Research Program" says:

> The physical sciences are basic to the whole range of military science and technology; some examples are the phenomena of photoemission (for night vision), molecular kinetics (in combustion and explosives), and solid-state effects (upon which electronic devices depend). In a sense, physics is the parent of the other physical sciences, and its military applications are extremely diverse.

The "Chemical/Biological defense" program has been central to providing "fundamental information and new concepts in support of new or improved defensive systems against the chemical and biological...warfare threat and a sound deterrence system of chemical munitions." In biology and medicine, the Pentagon recently has been concerned with "the physiological demands imposed by developmental systems and modern doctrine. These demands approach and may exceed the limits of human tolerance, thus making man [sic] the limiting factor in modern systems design." In mathematics and computer sciences, applied analysis is used to develop the military's C^3I system of command, control, communications and intelligence. The Mathematics Research Center at the University of Wisconsin is supported by the Army Research Office.[47] Nor are the behavioral and social sciences free from military funding:

> In 1967, a Committee of the National Academy of Sciences advised the Department of Defense to increase its support for, and use of, research in the fields of the social and behavioral sciences. The National Academy study group argued that the Department of Defense "must now wage not only warfare but 'peacefare' as well," and that "pacification, assistance and the battle of ideas are major segments of the DOD responsibility..."[48]

More recently, the Pentagon explained its interest in these two fields by calling human beings "devices":

> The arena in which the armed forces must function is becoming increasingly complex. Weapon systems are more sophisticated, the speed of battle has increased, and the demands on the individual are mounting. Even the pressures of changes in our social system during peacetime are being felt by the military. Therefore, the DOD supports research in the behavioral sciences that aims at fuller understanding of the most complex device of all, the human being.

The Pentagon's research interests extend to intergroup relations:

> research aimed at improving our understanding of how individuals with diverse ethnic and cultural backgrounds can be merged into effective teams, crews, and units (conditions of close confinements such as on board ship are of particular interest; the effects of integrating women into the military continue to be a major area of emphasis).[49]

In recent years the Pentagon has supported a number of large-scale research programs at universities designed to provide weapons technologies superior to our "adversaries" overseas. In addition to the Strategic Defense Initiative (described in Chapter Seven), the Strategic Computing Initiative (SCI) has been a major resource program for organizing universities' science capacity in service of the warfare state. In FY 1985, the SCI granted 47.5 percent of its funds to industry (or $32.4 million), followed by 40.7 percent (or $27.8 million) to universities.

SCI is being promoted as a means of automating war-fighting. As the military explains:

> instead of fielding simple guided missiles or remotely piloted vehicles, we might launch completely autonomous land, sea, and air vehicles

capable of complex, far-ranging reconnaissance and attack missions.

The military is increasingly looking to computers to wage war because "improvements in the speed and range of weapons have increased the rate at which battles unfold." The SCI also funds Artificial Intelligence research at universities in order to develop guidance systems for the "autonomous" vehicles. Among the forces propelling SCI are the military's wish to develop robotics for automated military production systems which reduce the armed forces' reliance on blue-collar labor.

Among the university participants in the SCI in 1985 were the University of Maryland (which worked on Vision Based Navigation for the Autonomous Land Vehicle); Carnegie Mellon University and MIT (which helped develop systems for the Navy's program) and Los Alamos National Laboratory of the University of California (which participated in the AirLand Battle Management program).[50]

Universities have also played a role in the resurgence of Chemical Biological Warfare research. From 1980 to 1984, total federal support for research in the life sciences declined by 1.2 percent although Defense Department funding increased by 50.3 percent. In 1981, the Defense Advanced Research Projects Agency, which serves to transfer technology from industry and university laboratories to the military, created a new program aimed at emerging biotechnologies. Partially as a response to recommendations made by the Defense Science Board in the mid-1970s regarding Soviet and U.S. chemical warfare capabilities, the Defense Department claimed that the United States had major deficiencies in its ability to fight a chemical war. Such perceptions were used to generate support for increased chemical warfare spending, particularly for a new generation of chemical weapons called the "binaries."

Recent reports by *The New York Times* and student researchers pointed to MIT as a major recipient of Army research into biological warfare. In particular, the Institute's program has focussed on the toxicity of mycotoxins, "a poison typically produced in nature by living organisms like fungi, and used as an agent of biological/chemical warfare." A report in the progressive student newspaper *The Thistle* stated:

> Careful scrutiny of the "MIT Report of the Office of Sponsored Programs" for 1985 revealed that approximately $1,550,000 has been provided by the Army to support a mycotoxin research program at MIT over the three year period from 9/82-7/85. This averages to $515,000 per year. In 1986 this figure increased to $737,000, a 43% increase.[51]

6.4 The Deadly Connection: Universities and the Nuclear Umbrella for Intervention

Universities are an essential institution for the propagation of nuclear weaponry and the escalation of the arms race. They have provided two critical services for advancing nuclear politics at home and abroad. First, universities have contributed to the development and refinement of nuclear weapons through their research and development work for the military. Second, universities have provided political sanctions for the managed escalation of the arms race through their delineation of the ideology of "arms control." By advancing nuclear weaponry, universities have extended the political power of the American military machine, giving it greater leverage to intervene in the affairs of Third World nations as well as controlling the destinies of millions of Europeans under the U.S. nuclear umbrella.[52]

What are the connections between nuclear capabilities and intervention in the Third World? As explained to Congress by President Carter's Secretary of Defense Harold Brown, with U.S. strategic nuclear capabilities, "our other forces become meaningful instruments of military and political power." Checks on U.S. intervention and aggression by the conventional forces of other powers are limited by the U.S. nuclear forces.

Although the United States lost a conventional war in Vietnam and was routed in Lebanon by guerrilla and "terrorist" attacks, it repeatedly has threatened to use its nuclear arsenal. For example, from 1969 to 1972, President Nixon contemplated the use of nuclear weapons in Vietnam. After the Soviet invasion of Afghanistan, President Carter threatened to use "any means necessary, including military force" against a further Soviet move in the Persian Gulf region. An extensive military study of the Persian Gulf warned, "that the American forces could not stop a Soviet thrust into northern Iran and that the United States should therefore consider using 'tactical' nuclear weapons in any conflict there."[53] Such threats to use nuclear weapons take on the force of reality once it is remembered that the United States actually did use nuclear weapons, twice, against Japan at the close of World War II.

The technological development and refinements in nuclear technology have increased the political power of the United States and Soviet Union over other nations. Both superpowers account for about 85 percent of the world total expenditure on military R&D. Without such a capability there would be neither new production of major weapons nor significant improvements of existing weapons. As a result, "the arms race, at least in the qualitative sense, would grind to a halt, even though the size of arsenals may increase and the arsenals of smaller powers may be brought technologically closer to those of the great powers by global arms trade."[54]

Towards the top of the hierarchy of military-serving universities is the University of California's Department of Energy-linked laboratories which have branches in Berkeley and Los Alamos. The Los Alamos laboratory has designed and built hydrogen bombs. The University of California is the principal contractor of the Lawrence Radiation Laboratory in Berkeley, California, with 9,783 employees; the Los Alamos National Laboratory in Los Alamos, New Mexico has 7,368 employees. Most nuclear weapons research on design, weapons applications, safeguards and isotope separation is conducted at Los Alamos Laboratory and Lawrence Livermore, in Livermore, California.

Other Department of Energy-sponsored laboratories linked to universities include the Argonne National Laboratory in Chicago and the Idaho National Engineering Laboratory in Idaho Falls. The University of Chicago is a principal contractor of these two labs. In the 1960s, MIT and Johns Hopkins ran centers which designed missiles, and half of the MIT budget and three-quarters of Johns Hopkins' budget came from running defense labs. These universities are still major bases for military research and have been among the top 100 Department of Defense contractors year after year (see Table 6-2).[55]

One estimate suggests that about "half of the total employment at the main nuclear weapons laboratories is directly weapons related." However, "much of the balance of the service and support workers indirectly depend on weapons contracts for their jobs." The university nuclear laboratories are part of "the nuclear weapons production complex" which is managed and owned by the Department of Energy. This complex begins with basic research in the university-linked laboratories and extends into "nuclear weapons material production facilities, the weapons fabrication facilities, the nuclear weapons test sites, and the treatment, storage and disposal of radioactive wastes."[56]

Advances in military electronics have made a nuclear war more probable by improving the accuracy and reliability of strategic missiles and antisubmarine warfare techniques. Also dangerous in this regard are the development of space-based navigational aids and technologies which seek to destroy enemy ballistic warheads and enemy satellites in space.

Beyond their contributions to the material chain of nuclear production, universities have assisted in the propagation of arms control ideology and negotiations. The theory of arms control emerged from a 1960 seminar funded by "the Rockefeller Foundation and was co-sponsored by the Center for International Affairs and MIT's Center for International Studies." A recent formulation of arms control was given by one of its principle architects, Thomas Schelling, a Professor of Political Economy at Harvard. He wrote that: "If people really believed that zero is the ultimate goal it is easy to see that downward is the direction they should go. But hardly anyone believes that zero is the goal."

Arms control has been one of *the* central ideologies which has provided a rationale for keeping nuclear weaponry in stock, supplying a logic for the use of nuclear weapons in theoretical mystifications such as "deterrence," "counter-force," and other notions which assume a "balance of terror." As peace scholar Robert Krinsky explains:

> The equivocal term "arms control" even leaves honest supporters of reversal of the arms race confounded. "Control" can mean upward, downward, or constant. Thus far it has been upward.[57]

An early accounting in 1961 by Seymour Melman discerned that arms control had become the major ideological weapon used to keep nuclear stockpiles in place:

> A few years ago, arms control meant arms limitation, the first steps of a disarming process. Today, arms control is a series of schemes for international military deterrence...the new arms controllers see themselves as managers of a world system of deterrence by means of military balances, deciding for the great powers what is "actually desirable" militarily. This is part of the continuing effort to treat the international relations of American society as a military strategy problem.

To stop the arms race requires a "freezing of military technological advances," i.e., the conversion or disbanding of university weapons labs and a freeze on all weapons production.[58] Yet, a review of arms control research performed by universities will reveal almost no discussion of such economic conversion or disarmament itself. Such academic research is not a benign, pragmatic search for a "way out" but an instrumental part of the warfare state.

Arms control academics embellish the language and theater of arms control negotiations to provide a palliative to public fears of destruction wherein the superpowers agree to maintain their most deadly weapons in exchange for throwing out their obsolete ones. Despite all the talk and sanctification of arms control negotiations, the theory that deterrence is a substitute for disarmament has plainly failed. The total firepower used during World War II was three megatons. Today, the firepower in existing nuclear-weapon arsenals is 18,000 megatons. Even at the height of arms control talks, the weapons build-up continues without restraint. As a 1978 paper by political scientist Robert Johansen explained:

> The most intense recent negotiations to control the arms race have been the Strategic Arms Limitation Talks (SALT) between the United States and the Soviet Union. During the period of time from the opening of the talks until one year after the Vladivostok Accord (1969-75), the number of deployed strategic launch vehicles increased by one-third.[59]

The Reagan administration's INF treaty leading to the reduction of intermediate-range nuclear forces in Europe only *confirms* the failures of arms control. Critics have suggested that the treaty "might be used to rationalize the development and deployment of new weapons, which would be used to 'fill in the gaps' left by an 'imperfect' treaty." At best the treaty is expected to reduce the size of superpower arsenals by only 5 percent. The treaty was also linked to a decline in public support for the peace movement by Paul Boyer, Professor of History at the University of Wisconsin: "An arms control treaty could assuage public opinion and take the wind out of the sails of the peace movement."[60] Thus, the peace movement's own adoption of the rhetoric and language of arms control and piecemeal disarmament has set the stage for the current situation where the population is satisfied with crumbs.

Universities are also trying to spread the mystification of arms control under the misleading label of "Peace Studies." As the President of Tufts University, Jean Mayer, explained to *The New York Times* in a story about a new "worldwide curriculum for peace": "The best chance to stop the arms race is to have an informed public opinion that sees arms control as an element of national security." Among those institutions backing this program are Harvard, Yale, Stanford and the University of Pennsylvania. The objective of the program, the *Times* explained, was "to increase the number of people who understand the issues of arms control from the thousands to the hundreds of thousands." The disturbing character of such "peace" studies was made evident, however, during a planned meeting on the world peace curriculum when university presidents would "not take a position on disarmament."[61]

Arms control has in fact been regarded as a substitute for disarmament, a step-by-step process which aims at the gradual elimination of nuclear and large-scale conventional weapons. Disarmament is based on a phased *elimination* of weapons through national treaties that rely on verification arrangements and citizen participation in monitoring each nation's adherence to treaty provisions. However, the view that arms control could stand alone as a means of bringing peace runs contrary to the early formulations of the United States Arms Control and Disarmament Agency. In a 1962 publication, *Toward A World Without War: A Summary of United States Disarmament Efforts—Past and Present,* complete with a preface by President John F. Kennedy, the Agency declared:

> Arms reduction—classic "disarmament"—is simply not enough. It is equally important that the major powers *do something now* to cut the risks of war, while at the same time working for agreement on arms reduction plans. So the concept of "arms control"—controlling, in the sense of calming, the military situation—was evolved. Arms control means measures, other than arms reduction itself, which lessen the risk of war. "Arms control" is a twin to "arms reduction"—*not* a substitute for it. Arms control measures are *not* intended to replace arms reductions but to accompany them.[62]

Universities across the country have propagated arms control ideology, thereby rationalizing and extending the military's power over domestic and international affairs. Political science, international relations and "Peace" departments have helped construct this science of war. They have contributed to the dominance of military approaches to international relations and by extension the use of force as a substitute for diplomacy and international law.

6.5 From Pentagon Consultant to Trenchcoat Academic

The political and scientific consultant boards that involved university personnel which arose in the postwar era have developed into a number of military advisory boards and include the Defense Science Board, the Army Science Board, the Naval Research Advisory Committee, the Air Force Scientific Advisory Board, the SDI advisory group and the Defense Department think tank, Jason (see Appendix Two).

The Defense Science Board was established more than twenty-five years ago to provide "objective scientific advice to the Defense Department's highest echelons." Military advisory boards have also been set up to advise the Army, Navy and Air Force. The recommendations of these boards have been far-reaching and have affected government policy decisions on weapons systems and other outlays costing billions of dollars.

Similarly, the Naval Research Advisory Committee (NRAC), established to advise the U.S. Navy on R&D problems and other issues, has been tied to universities through faculty participation on its panels. Also, "administrative support for NRAC operations and membership to NRAC panels are provided through a contract with Catholic University." John Beusch, affiliated with the MIT Lincoln Laboratory, has been a member of the NRAC's panel on the "Anti-Jamming Naval Tactical Communication System Options for VHF/VMF Voice and Data." The Congressional Committee on Government Operations' report on military advisory committees suggested that Beusch had financial interests, based on his salary, which could be affected by the VHF/VMF panel's recommendations.

The Air Force Scientific Advisory Board (SAB) advises the U.S. Air Force. Daniel DeBra, a member of the "Air Force Manufacturing Technology Program," is affiliated with Stanford University. The Government Operations' report suggested that he had financial interests, based on his salary, which could be affected by the Manufacturing Technology Committee's recommendations. Another member of this committee, Ira Hendrick, also had possible conflicts of interest based on salary from (and stock in) Grumman Aerospace and stock in

General Electric. Other panel members had ties to defense-based firms such as Raytheon, the Fairchild Republic Corporation, Martin-Marietta, Hughes Aircraft and Lockheed.[63]

The Jason organization comprises a team of forty-four academics across the country who meet each summer to study military products for the Defense Department, the CIA and the Department of Energy (see Appendix Two). The organization was created in 1960 to reunite the military and academia, both of which suffered from the shock of the Soviet Union's successful launching of the Sputnik spacecraft in 1957. During the Vietnam War, Jason devised the "electronic" or "automated" battlefield, an anti-infiltration system which was criticized as leading to the deaths of thousands of civilians. The Red Cross deplored this invention as a violation of international law because it did not discriminate between soldiers and civilians. Jason's more recent efforts have concentrated on the development of new nuclear weapons and anti-submarine warfare.[64]

In addition to the military advisory boards, academics and university graduates alike have delivered their services to the warfare state through their work for elite foreign policy groups like the Trilateral Commission and the Council on Foreign Relations (CFR). A 1984 report noted that some 360 faculty served in some consulting capacity with the CFR, which advises the State Department on military and international policy. Columbia University students found five current or former CFR members among faculty at Columbia's School of International Affairs and three CFR members on the School's Board of Trustees.[65] The 1985 North American membership list of the Trilateral Commission listed eight university-affiliated members including professors at Johns Hopkins, Georgetown University, Columbia University, the University of Chicago and Harvard as well as the president of the University of Notre Dame.[66]

The various military branches also recruit university faculty on their leave time. In the winter of 1980, the research director at the Naval Research Laboratory reported that "at any given time we have about 200 tenured faculty who are spending their summer vacations with us or their sabbatical leaves with us."[67]

The most publicized connections involving faculty consulting for the warfare state centers around the CIA. Established in 1947, the CIA is part of the larger "National Security State," which envelops military-industrial firms, the universities and the Pentagon.[68] The Agency's Congressional charter created the CIA as a central authority to coordinate, correlate and evaluate intelligence for the National Security Council. The CIA was also designated to carry out clandestine activities abroad. However, it has extended its scope to spy on domestic institutions, partially under the rationale that the activities of foreigners in the United States fall within its domain. More importantly, the Agency has sought to expand its base of information to include foreign affairs specialists working for a variety of domestic institutions. As a result, the CIA, like the Defense Department, has enjoyed a long-standing relationship with the academic community. Its predecessor agency, the Office of Strategic Services, employed numerous social scientists in interdisciplinary studies of various nations.

The CIA's many activities on campus have included spying on students and faculty, as well as recruiting from these groups for spies. CIA agents have "routinely approached professors and students who received grants for foreign travel or research with requests to moonlight as intelligence agents during their study abroad."[69] The CIA financed the Center for International Studies at MIT, from its founding in 1951 until 1965. "The Center served as a source of research and analysis, and a training institute for future CIA analysts." During the early 1960s, "the CIA used Michigan State University's police training program as a cover for CIA agents and activities."[70] The CIA also has sponsored student organizations within the United States:

> Between 1952 and 1966 the National Student Association (NSA) received an estimated $3,300,000 in funding from the CIA which, during certain years, amounted to as much as 80 percent of NSA's entire budget. This subvention resulted in the cooperation of "witting" NSA officials and representatives who influenced the policies of the organization in directions favored by the Agency.[71]

Numerous protests against the CIA in the 1960s, together with Congressional investigations in the mid-1970s, helped distance the CIA from academia. Despite these attacks, intelligence agencies never completely left the universities. In October of 1979, Princeton University hosted a conference on the Middle East which included CIA personnel. In 1981, the related Defense Intelligence Agency (created in 1961 to coordinate intelligence-gathering Defense Department activities) "approached at least four African-studies centers about the prospect of developing a 'relationship.' "[72] More recently, the CIA has expanded on-campus recruitment and worked to restore links to academics in order to get more advice on questions pertaining to foreign policy and international relations. This trend has its roots in the Carter administration, although the effort to solicit help from "the best minds in the country" was accelerated under President Reagan's tenure. Failed U.S. objectives, in Iran and elsewhere, have led the CIA to diversify its sources of intelligence. In 1986, Robert Gates, Deputy Director of Intelligence for the CIA, told *The New York Times* that about one-fourth of the Agency's estimates are reviewed in draft form by professors or other outside experts. In previous years, only "minuscule" amounts of the Agency's research was reviewed in this fashion. Since 1982, the CIA has sponsored seventy-five conferences a year (up from three to four in previous years) in which Agency personnel met with professors and experts outside government.[73]

A new CIA program, launched in 1987, placed CIA agents on university faculties as visiting scholars. The "Officer-in-Residence Program" was described by one Agency official as an effort to "enhance CIA's recruiting efforts by providing an opportunity for experienced officers to serve as role models, [and] to counsel interested students on career opportunities with the CIA." In this program the Agency both selects and pays the salary of the agent; the university provides an academic appointment. The University of California, Santa Barbara, the Georgetown University School of Foreign Service and the Lyndon B. Johnson School of Public Affairs at the University of Texas, Austin, have participated in the program. Other schools, such as Harvard's John F. Kennedy School of Government, have also been linked to this new CIA recruitment effort.[74]

A scandal, in the fall of 1985, drew national attention to CIA links to academia. Nadav Safran, director of Harvard University's Center for Middle Eastern Studies (CMES), received $107,430 from the CIA to help him publish a book on Saudi Arabia. He also got another $45,700 from the CIA for a conference on "Islam and Politics in the Contemporary Muslim World." An investigation by Harvard's Dean of Arts and Sciences into the case found that Safran had violated the University's guidelines by not disclosing the CIA's sponsorship of the Middle East conference and failing to let participants know of the Agency's role. Critics called these findings a "whitewash," although the scandal led to Safran's resignation as head of CMES and the disbanding of its Executive Committee.[75]

The Safran case illustrates the ways the warfare state dominates aspects of university functioning, but more telling is a 1985 exposé of the CIA's connections to Tufts University alumni, faculty, administration and trustees. John Roosa, a Tufts graduate, revealed that Tufts' Fletcher School of Law and Diplomacy, the nation's oldest graduate school of diplomacy, has been an important training center for future U.S. Foreign Service officers. In a Fletcher alumni book, Roosa found nineteen graduates who openly acknowledged currently holding positions at the CIA. Over the years, the Fletcher School not only has made a concerted effort to send students to work at the CIA, but the CIA has returned the favor by encouraging undergraduate students to attend Fletcher. Tufts faculty have been linked to the CIA as Agency personnel, employees at CIA-linked think tanks and in jobs related to the intelligence field. CIA documents released under the Freedom of Information Act have confirmed that several Tufts political scientists had consulting relationships with the Agency during the mid-1970s. Several trustees, administrators and advisors to Tufts academic programs have either worked for the CIA (such as former CIA Deputy Director Bobby Inman) or have associations with people close to the Agency. Fletcher has also taken money from foundations active in "publicly promoting the need for a strong CIA," such as the Scaife and Smith Richardson Foundations.[76]

An even more direct tie, between the universities and repression in Central America was discovered in 1986. That year, the Institute for Policy Studies found that three alleged members of El Salvador's early-1980s death squads were learning counterterrorism techniques from Northwestern University professors. These included El Salvador's Chief of Intelligence Jose Adolfo Medrano, Chief of Administration Baltazar Lopez Cortez and Chief of Staff Jose Dionison Hernandez. With fifteen other officials, the three were enrolled in the University's "Traffic Institute," founded in 1936 to "conduct training and research in traffic safety and accident prevention" but later expanded to give instruction in broader "law enforcement" areas.

In 1985, the Traffic Institute joined the State Department as the sole university participant in the State Department's Anti-Terrorist Assistance Program (ATAP). One course in the ATAP program, the "Senior Officer Law Enforcement and Counterterrorism Seminar," required that the Salvadorans attend three weeks of classes outside Washington, D.C. and work as interns with off-duty police in Phoenix, Arizona for a week.[77]

6.6 Organizing Cannonfodder and Labor for Repression

In addition to military contract work and consulting, the educational system serves the military labor market by assisting in conscription and training of military personnel and technical employees for defense contractors. The revival of the draft has once again made universities and high schools the allies of the armed forces in enlisting soldiers for intervention overseas. Charley Maresca of the National Interreligious Service Board for Conscientious Objectors has warned that, "To restore induction authority, rather than actual inductions, I believe the conditions are now right...Congress might see it as an expedient means of sending a message to somebody, like the Sandinista government." The Selective Service has purchased lists of licensed drivers from most states and compared these lists to the registration rolls to check up on the 400,000 men who have failed to register. Those suspected of not registering have received a series of warning letters before their names are sent to the Justice Department for prosecution.[78]

The Solomon Amendment is a 1982 law which forbids college students who fail to register for the draft from receiving financial assistance. Critics charged that the law unfairly discriminated against the poor and middle class, groups dependent on financial aid. On July 5, 1984, the U.S. Supreme Court defended the law against challenges that this amendment was unconstitutional.[79]

The Amendment is only one step away from a new contractual system whereby university attendance depends upon military service. At the annual meeting of the National Association of State Universities and Land-Grant Colleges, David S. Saxon proposed such a "national service." In the MIT Chairman's program, American youth would be compelled to perform some form of military or civilian work in exchange for college benefits, such as those of the GI Bill of Rights. Recent formulations of such service would provide an alternative to economic conscription (see Chapter Eight).[80]

The militarization of education has extended into the nation's high school system. Recruiters, by law, have *carte blanche* access to high school directory information on students. In January 1984, the Selective Service tested a program in western states which sought "the aid of high schools in publicizing the registration law." High schools set up publicity displays, made in-school announcements, hosted Selective Service speakers, and provided mailing lists of students. A critical summary of the program concluded, "Schools will not only be used to publicize registration but to *conduct it.* Selective Service speakers who go to the schools to publicize registration will also register students there." James Feldman, staff attorney for the Central Committee for Conscientious Objectors, a military and draft counseling group in Philadelphia, describes "recruiters" who "are ever present in our schools...In Atlanta, Georgia's 22 public high schools...military recruiters made more than 500 visits last year. And Atlanta is by no means an isolated case."

The military's Junior Reserve Office Training Corps (JROTC), a program aimed at high school students, involved a record 227,000 teenagers at more than 1,500 schools nationwide in 1986.[81] In the United States, the Armed Services Vocational Aptitude Battery tests are pre-enlistment surveys given in high schools "under the guise of vocational counseling."[82]

One dramatic example of the military's free rein in our nation's high schools occurred in Tennessee in 1987. A surprise raid by six camouflaged soldiers fired M-16s into a crowd of screaming students watching a film at the high school auditorium. The gunplay ended almost immediately and the students were informed by a sergeant in the Tennessee Army National Guard that the soldiers were shooting blanks. While the exercise may have seemed a publicity stunt to the military, the ardent nationalism lying behind it appears much more sinister. The demonstration had been staged in at least fifteen schools and "was intended to make pupils realize what could happen if they did not live in a free country." Following the incident, the sergeant gave a brief speech after which students were asked "to raise their fists and shout 'Hurrah!' if they loved America."[83]

The Pentagon's use of the universities as training grounds for military technicians is another way of tying militarism to the educational system. The Pentagon has used science fellowships and the Reserve Office Training Corps program (ROTC) to provide increasing numbers of scientific and engineering officers with four-year service commitments to meet its internal demand for research personnel.[84] About 70 to 75 percent of the active-duty officers in the armed forces are from ROTC. This includes both the commanders of U.S. troops in Central America and the upper echelons of the military hierarchy. The ROTC program helps instill militarism through courses which teach marching and drilling as well making students economically dependent on the military through scholarships. Students on ROTC scholarship cannot drop out of the program after their first year. If they refuse to report for duty after graduation, they go to jail.[85]

The ROTC program attempts to attract the poor and the unemployed with its offers of scholarships and financial aid. A U.S. Navy brochure boasts:

> Everything from high school courses to college degrees can be yours at little or no cost in the Navy. A program called Navy Campus offers all kinds of educational opportunities. Included are educational counseling, free testing services, certificate/degree programs, and even college classes taught at sea by civilian professors. Navy Campus can help you get the education you want. You can also start a personal education fund. For every $1 you invest, the Navy will add $2. After three years the total of your contributions and the Navy's could reach $8,100. You can start using your education fund after completing your first enlistment period and up to ten years after leaving the Navy. Education is a big part of the Navy adventure.[86]

Such advertisements are part of the military's more than $500 million a year effort (about $3000 per recruit) to entice young people to enlist. The military has specifically aimed recruitment efforts at black youth:

> A scan through the special engineering issue of the "Black Collegian Magazine" of January, 1983 reveals an ad section almost totally subsidized by the weapons and defense industry, the C.I.A., and armed forces...[87]

The end-product of these efforts and worsening economic conditions for the inner-city poor is an "all-volunteer" Army that is 33 percent black, a proportion almost three times greater than that of blacks in the U.S. population. The present conscription system reinforces the trend where the poor continue to volunteer or re-enlist because economic opportunities outside the military are limited.[88]

While the military advertises itself as a mecca of opportunity, the data show that in-service opportunities are limited. In FY 1984, blacks represented 27.5 percent of the Army's overall forces, but held 45.2 percent of the positions in food service. On the other hand, they were assigned to 17.3 percent of military intelligence and 23.2 percent of engineering jobs, both of which are higher-skilled categories.[89] That same year, blacks made up 23.3 percent of the army infantry but only 9.8 percent of commissioned officers. One Congressional study found that 90 percent of enlistees who had been promised access to college courses by recruiters were turned down by their unit commanders.[90]

Women also face problems with the "new Army of opportunity." The number of women in the Army jumped from 2.1 percent in FY 1972 to 9.9 percent in FY 1984. Three-fourths of the Army women responding to an August 1981 poll said they had been sexually harassed in the past twelve months. In FY 1984, 50.9 percent of female soldiers reported some form of sexual harassment. Military sexism is also widespread in its civilian institutions. Although the Military Selective Service Act says that "no person shall be denied membership on any local board...on account of sex," most draft boards are comprised of four men and one woman.[91]

Financial incentives are not only aimed at luring women and people of color. A 1985 Defense Department report said that its basic research program supported about 4,000 graduate students each year. The Pentagon also instituted a series of graduate fellowships in the early 1980s. In 1984, such fellowships and assistantships supported almost 200 students.[92] Among the graduate fellowships sponsored by the University Research Initiative are the Navy's Office of Naval Research Graduate Program, offering stipends of $13,000 to $15,000 annually, and the Air Force's Laboratory Graduate Fellowship Program, providing similar stipends and funding of students' tuition and fees. The Los Alamos National Laboratory offers even more generous funding for postdoctoral fellows, with annual stipends of $45,480. Among the many awards for academics sponsored by the Defense Department is the ONR's Young Investigator Program. It was created "to establish strong long-term ties between DOD and outstanding academics," where "base funding is $50,000 per year for three years."[93]

The Defense Department and its related agencies are not short of funds to carry out their objective of forging closer ties between academia and the Pentagon. This financial power is also shared by numerous defense contractors. For example, Hughes Aircraft Company, now owned by General Motors, describes the full range of its educational programs in a prospectus designed for college students with the seductive title: "All about engineering and computers and you and electronics at Hughes." While passing over Hughes's high level of economic dependency on the Defense Department, the brochure explains that:

> You and Hughes can do great things for each other. Your training and ability can earn you many different kinds of rewards, if you can help us keep innovating, keep showing the way, in the field where we excel: *High-technology electronics.*[94]

The rewards are extensive: each year several hundred "Hughes people" carry on graduate-level studies with the help of fellowships awarded by the company. Employees can apply for a renewable stipend plus full academic expenses at an approved university for a nine-month academic year. If an employee is offered a fellowship and accepts, he or she follows the military pattern of dedicated service to the company: "You will work full-time at Hughes before you begin study." Hughes offers Master's Fellowships, Engineer Fellowships and Doctoral Fellowships, each a vehicle for extending the military's reach into academia.[95] General Electric, the company whose weapons have ended up in the hands of Central American dictatorships, offers a less enticing tuition refund program for employees to attend work-related courses.[96]

In the 1985 study "On the Number of Engineers and Scientists Serving the Defense Sector," Warren F. Davis estimated that at least 27.8 percent of scientists and engineers enter defense employment annually. The estimate was based on survey data collected from placement offices at twenty-four institutions which collectively graduated 15,013 engineers and scientists per year.

However, this number represents the lower range of the actual number of scientists and engineers engaged in defense work. First, many companies perform services or manufacture products for both the commercial and defense market. These firms might not have been characterized as defense firms by placement officers responding to the Davis survey. Second, companies like Digital Equipment Corporation which sell many products to the military are not considered defense-related. Finally, much defense-related work is done through non-Defense Department funding; placement officers do not list students taking positions with NASA or DOE (or the companies under contract to them) as entering military employment.[97]

6.7 Arms Contractors: Tracing Corporate Complicity in Arms Sales to Central America

One of the most explicit links of U.S. universities to intervention in Central America is their connections to arms contractors supplying the military states of El Salvador, Guatemala and Honduras. Universities allow recruitment by such firms on campus and have endowment investments in them as well. Many university trustees sit as directors of these arms contractors, some of the largest corporations in the United States.

In the *American Arms Supermarket*, Michael T. Klare examines the growing importance of foreign arms sales to the U.S. economy. In the pages that follow, we review some of his work in order to provide a framework for analyzing corporate—and university—complicity in arms shipments to Central America.

There are two primary channels for U.S. arms shipments abroad: the Commercial Sales (CS) program governs private sales by U.S. corporations and the Foreign Military Sales (FMS) program directs government-to-government sales by U.S. agencies. Generally, the large military contractors work on FMS projects as part of their ongoing Defense Department work. The thousands of smaller firms receive some FMS orders but mainly depend on the CS program for their export sales.[98]

The distinctions between the CS and FMS program become important in organizing campaigns against university ties to arms contractors. University officials or corporate targets themselves could argue that weapons ending up in the hands of Central American governments were sent by the U.S. government, i.e. the companies are not responsible for the arms shipments. Such claims could not be made for CS-associated weapons transfers because "normally, commercial sales transactions are initiated by private firms and come to the government's notice only when the company involved applies to the Office of Munitions Control (OMC) for a license to export the items in question."[99] However, government complicity still exists in such cases because licenses can be denied.

U.S. legislation and executive policies have occasionally blocked arms transfers to Central America under the FMS program. The 503B provision of the Foreign Assistance Act of 1978 made El Salvador and Guatemala ineligible for FMS arms credits.[100] The Carter administration blocked the sale of F-5ES airplanes to Guatemala, following a policy which banned the export of sophisticated weapons to certain nations.[101] Corporations are not without responsibility in the FMS program; although the government is "empowered to initiate arms transactions on its own," it still must "contract with private companies to produce munitions which it then resells to foreign governments."[102]

However, the contractor/company role becomes blurred when the U.S. government exports arms from existing stockpiles. For example, companies can claim that weapons destined for use by the U.S. Army or supplied to general government arsenals were later transferred to Central American nations independent of their authority and direction. There are also cases where contractors act as *sales agents*, often initiating an FMS sale to beat out a competitor: "U.S. firms engage in a wide range of overseas promotional activities designed to persuade a potential customer to ask for its products by 'brand name' when approaching the U.S. government to supply a particular system." The overseas lobbying effort by companies has included everything from advertising to bribery in an effort to "win" a share of U.S. government contracts for supplying foreign nations. U.S. producers also attempt to attract weapons buyers abroad by going on demonstration tours overseas and bringing potential customers to U.S. factories for visits of production facilities. Klare concludes that corporate initiated efforts "tend to create a momentum behind a particular sale that is very hard to reverse once the formal decision-making process begins."[103]

Whether weapons are sent to Central America under CS or FMS programs, arms contractors cannot hide behind the rationale that they are supplying purely defensive weapons. The arms supplied to Honduras, and to a lesser extent Guatemala and El Salvador, have been used to protect the contras and promote a regional war of intimidation directed against Nicaragua. In addition, the "defensive" cast of these weapons breaks down when considering systems like tear gas, riot gear and certain armed personnel carriers. The goal of controlling a civilian population is *designed* into these weapons even before a sale is initiated. These weapons are most useful for internal repression rather than the defense of national boundaries. Many companies export a large share of their production of such weapons overseas and view export sales as integral to their balance sheets.[104]

In fact, a third channel for arms shipments, the Military Assistance Program (MAP) was designed to subsidize forces responsible for "internal security" overseas. The expansion of the MAP program was an integral part of the development of U.S. counter-insurgency strategy. Even *before* the U.S. defeat in Vietnam, the U.S. experience there in the early 1960s convinced war planners of the utility of funding foreign military proxies through MAP from 1963 onwards.[105]

A final political argument can be raised against the arms contractors supplying Central America. Whether riot gear or long distance bombers are supplied, these products could be and often have been used to repress the domestic populations. In addition, this production fuels both militarism in Central America and the U.S. permanent war economy, which has brought human misery, resource depletion and industrial decline at home and abroad. All weapons shipments to the Pentagon increase the U.S. capability for intervention overseas, although some systems, such as ship production for the rapid deployment force, are more linked to this capability than others. In conclusion, any weapons supplied to the Pentagon, whether destined for use by Central American or U.S. forces, are weapons of repression and tools of militarism.

The connection between "internal repression" in El Salvador, Guatemala and Honduras and U.S. military shipments becomes clearer after a re-examination of these shipments. What weapons are sent? Who receives them? What do the recipients do with these weapons? These are the three critical questions. U.S. military shipments of police and security gear to the three military states demonstrate that weapons shipments are not neutral but shape political repression in Central America.

In El Salvador, the Treasury Police, after receiving U.S. police aid, "became the base for death squads that killed some 10,000 Salvadorans, including political, labor and religious leaders without a single prosecution of an officer in the security forces." In Guatemala, the police forces "failed to prevent, failed to investigate, and in fact participated in the worst blood-baths in the region's history."[106] According to a report by the U.S. Congress Arms Control and Foreign Policy Caucus, "During the state of siege in 1970 and 1971, 7,000 civilian opponents of the security forces 'disappeared,' followed by another 8,000 in 1972 and 1973."[107]

The CS program facilitates many of the weapons sales to "security" or police forces in Central America (see Table 6-3).[108] Under this program, corporations are directly involved in the sale of firearms, tear gas, revolvers and other weapons in licensed corporate-to-country transfers. All sales of so-called "Munitions List"[109] items to police and intelligence operations overseas are carried out through the CS program. In FY 1985, El Salvador received $2,196,000 worth of commercial exports licensed under the Arms Control Export Act. Guatemala got $135,000 and Honduras $1,167,000. Table 6-4 lists some of the companies which have been involved in such direct Commercial Sales arms transfers.

The use of weapons shipments to Central America as tools of internal repression can also be seen in how such FMS shipments have supported the air war in El Salvador (described in Chapter Two) as well as the Salvadoran armed forces. Shipments under the FMS program include infantry weapons such as small arms, jeeps, radios and the like, which can be used for either internal or external security. In addition, weapons used for internal security, such as armored cars, tear gas grenades and counter-insurgency planes, are also sent under the FMS program.[110] Much of the equipment sent to El Salvador and Honduras has been through the Foreign Military Sales program. In FY 1985, El Salvador received $112,335,000 in FMS deliveries. Guatemala got $1,077,000 and Honduras $26,822.[111]

Planes used for counter-insurgency operations in the Third World, such as the Cessna A-37B Dragonfly, have been sent overseas under the FMS program and the Military Assistance Program, a plan of military grants to selected countries. A 1984 study by Tom Gervasi, author of *The Arsenal of Democracy III*, found that Guatemala had eight of these planes and Honduras four. A 1985

Table 6-3: U.S. Arms Sales to Central American Police Forces: September 1976-May 1979

	Gas grenades, projectiles	Gas guns	Rifles, carbines, submachine guns	Pistols, revolvers	Ammunition (1,000 rds)
El Salvador	852	4	—	173	—
Guatemala	5,000	—	65	1,006	6,763
Honduras	1,700	—	—	59	418

SOURCE: Michael T. Klare and Cynthia Arnson, *Supplying Repression* (Washington, D.C.: Institute for Policy Studies, 1981).

Table 6-4: Companies Selling Weapons to Police Forces in Costa Rica, El Salvador, Guatemala and Honduras: September 1976-May 1979

AAI Corporation, Baltimore, Maryland

5,000 gas grenades (licensed in 1978) to National Police and Federacion National de Tiro in Guatemala.

Jonas Aircraft and Arms Co., New York, New York [1]

200,000 rounds of ammunition (licensed in 1976 and 1977) for police use and for National Police in Guatemala.

Colt Industries, New York, New York [2]

28 pistols and revolvers to Security Services for Freund, S.A. de C.V. (licensed in 1978) in El Salvador.

675 revolvers to National Police (licensed in 1977) in Guatemala.

85 revolvers and pistols to Federación National de Tiro (licensed in 1979) in Guatemala.

Smith and Wesson, Springfield, Massachusetts

300 CN gas projectiles; 552 CS gas projectiles and 4 37-mm. shoulder gas guns to Police (licensed in 1976) in El Salvador.

24 revolvers to Federacion Nacional de Tiro (licensed in 1976) in Guatemala.

418,000 rounds of ammunition to Honduran Police and Government (licensed in 1976) in Honduras.

continued next page

study by NARMIC, National Action/Research on the Military Industrial Complex of the American Friends Service Committee, found that El Salvador had nine of these planes, and that both Guatemala and Honduras had increased their fleet to ten A-37s each.[112]

Table 6-5 documents the use of such counter-insurgency planes as support vehicles for the Salvadoran air war against civilians in rural zones. Planes supplied by U.S. manufacturers have become the direct tools of slaughter and intimidation.

The use of FMS weapons as tools of internal repression strengthens the case of activists, highlighting the corporate role in the supply of these systems to both the Pentagon and Central America. Troop-carrying helicopters, such as the Bell/Textron UH-1 Iroquois, or "Huey," and armored cars, like the Cadillac-

1,400 gas discharge grenades; 300 CS & CN gas projectiles and 230 quarts CS & CN gas formula to Public Security Forces to Public Security Forces (licensed in 1977) in Honduras.

4,000 rounds of ammunition to Costa Rican police (licensed in 1977) in Costa Rica.

12 gas masks to Banco Central de Costa Rica (licensed in 1978) in Costa Rica.

150 gas grenades and projectiles and 8,000 rounds .38 ammunition to Ministry of Public Security, Adaptacion Social (licensed in 1978) in Costa Rica.

Winchester International, New Haven, Connecticut [3]

167,500 rounds of ammunition and 65 rifles to Federacion Nacional de Trio con Armas de Caza (licensed in 1977) in Guatemala.

345,400 rounds of ammunition to Federacion Nacional de Tiro (licensed in 1979) in Guatemala.

[1] Not a publicly traded company.

[2] For an update on the status of Colt Industries, see Alison Leigh Cowan, "Colt to Go Private for $660 Million," The New York Times, March 11, 1988.

[3] In 1981, U.S. Repeating Arms Co., based in New Haven, took over Winchester International's firearms and small weapons production facilities. Olin Corporation, the prior owner of Winchester International, maintained control of Winchester's ammunition production division. While U.S. Repeating Arms is a privately held company today, it retains Olin to distribute its weapons to all countries outside the United States and Canada. Olin purchases U.S. Repeating Arms' products and distributes them in Europe and elsewhere. (Phone interview with Tom Krajewski, Director of Administration, U.S. Repeating Arms Corporation, July 21, 1987).

SOURCE: Michael T. Klare and Cynthia Arnson, Supplying Repression (Washington, D.C.: Institute for Policy Studies, 1981).

Gage V-150 Commando, have been sold to Third World FMS customers and "are primarily intended for rural counterinsurgency warfare or, in the case of the V-150, for urban security operations."[113] Gervasi's 1984 study found that both El Salvador and Guatemala each had six UH-1D helicopters.[114] NARMIC found that El Salvador had fifty-one UH-1 helicopters and four UH-1H in its possession, Guatemala had nine Bell UH-1D/H helicopters and Honduras eleven UH-1B helicopters and ten Bell UH-1H helicopters.[115] NARMIC found that Guatemala owned seven of the V-150 armored cars produced by the Cadillac Gage Company. Gervasi also found that South Africa owned 100 of these vehicles.[116]

Table 6-5: Corporations and the Air War in Central America

Cessna Aircraft Co., Wichita, KS
(Subsidiary of General Dynamics, St. Louis, MO)

The A-37 Dragonfly, a converted twin-engine Cessna training jet, is custom-made for bombing in a mountainous and densely-populated country like El Salvador. Father Jose Rutilio Sanchez linked bombings, killing at least seven people on August 8, 1984, to a flight by four A-37 planes that day. (A)

Flying time for A-37s increased from thirty-one to fifty-two hours per month between July 1983 and February 1984; during this same period, bombing raids rose from an average of 16.5 to 25 per month and over 100,000 civilians were displaced from rural areas of conflict. (B)

A U.S. Defense Department panel of military experts recommended against the A-37 in El Salvador because of mounting criticism of the civilian casualties it inflicts. (C)

In April 1985, Dr. Roberto Castillo described the A-37 air force planes in El Salvador: "In 1982 they introduced the A-37 which is better at strafing [than the Fouga Magister]...It shoots an astonishing number of bullets at once, and they're harder to get away from than the old Fouga Magister strafings." (D)

On February 15, 1985, the villages of Guaycume, Piedra Labrada, Santa Barbara, Los Laureles and Colonia San Jose Las Flores in Cuscatlan province suffered bombing and strafing attacks by two A-37s. (E)

On November 21, 1986, Christina Courtright of Medical Aid for El Salvador reported an attack on the residents of the Guazapa foothills, a civilian region where rebels exercise control: "Three A-37s appeared one after the other, each dropping nose-first in a screaming dive, then pulling up and over, leaving a huge BOOM on the ridge just beyond us. Again and again, taking turns until each had dropped its payload of six. There were four of us in the half-open "tatu" [shelter] I dove into...We counted 24 bombs dropped—another plane must have joined the first three..." (F)

Grumman, Bethpage, NY & Lockheed, Calabasas, CA

The Lockheed C-130 airplane is used with the A-37 and the OV-1 "Mohawk" plane as part of a counter-insurgency effort in El Salvador.

Dr. Eliseo Duran reported in June 1985: "At night, a slow airplane like a C-130 or a 'tattletale' will pass over. The first thing it does is drop Bengal lights. This is a 15-inch aluminum capsule filled with burning luminous powder that falls slowly, on a little parachute, producing a bright light as if it were day. This light can illuminate up to a kilometer of land for up to three minutes at a time. This same observation plane can then circle back and drop an incendiary bomb on the illuminated area, or else it is followed by an A-37 which drops bombs." (G)

A report by *The New York Times* on May 24, 1983 noted the basing of four AC-130 reconnaissance planes at the Pentagon's Howard Air Force Base, in Panama: "The four aircraft, which are Lockheed C-130 cargo planes that have been modified to carry electronic surveillance equipment and small weapons, including 40-millimeter cannon, have been used in a clandestine effort to monitor guerrilla activities in El Salvador..." (H)

Beginning in early 1984, U.S. pilots began to fly daily reconnaissance missions over the Salvadoran countryside from a secret military airfield in Palmerola, Honduras. They used an OV-1 "Mohawk" plane, manufactured by Grumman, which is equipped with infrared sights that can distinguish between human heat patterns at night, "but cannot distinguish between civilians and armed rebels." The Mohawks are complemented by C-130 surveillance planes flown from Panama. (I)

The information gathered by the Mohawks is passed on to the Salvadoran military, primarily to assist in aerial attacks, but also to provide information for ground operations. During the initial years of U.S. involvement in Vietnam, this plane was equipped with napalm, fragmentation bombs, rockets and rapid-fire machine guns. "Presumably those Mohawks in use in El Salvador could be armed at any time..." (J)

Hughes Helicopters
(Subsidiary of McDonnell-Douglas, St. Louis, MO)

The Hughes 500 helicopters can fire 5,000 to 6,000 bullets per minute and are used to sweep contested areas of the civilian population in El Salvador. The February 15, 1985 attack described in Note (E) above involved four helicopters "of which three were purportedly Hughes 500."

McDonnell-Douglas, St. Louis, MO

A McDonnell-Douglas produced C-47 was involved in the attack described in Note (E) above.

Christina Courtright documented the use of McDonnell Douglas-produced AC-47's in the strafing and reconnaissance flights in Note (F) above.

In 1985 *The New York Times* reported that AC-47 gunships were commonly deployed against guerrilla units by the Salvadoran Air Force. (K)

SOURCES:

(A)-Quoted in Christina Courtright, *Notes on the Air War in El Salvador,* Medical Aid for El Salvador, Los Angeles, California, Updated July 10, 1985, p. 4.

(B)-"U.S. Aid to El Salvador: an evaluation of the past, a proposal for the future," Senators Hatfield and Leahy, Rep. Miller, February 1985; Courtright, *op. cit.,* p. 4.

(C)-"Panel Wary on U.S. role in Salvador," *Sun,* June 1, 1984; Courtright, *ibid.,* p. 5.

(D)-Quoted in Courtright, *ibid.,* p. 6.

(E)-*Ibid.,* p. 7.

(F)-Christina Courtright, *Prelude to Operation Phoenix, ms.,* Medical Aid for El Salvador, Los Angeles, California, 1986.

(G)-Courtright, *Notes, op. cit.,* p. 3.

(H)-Philip Taubman, "Role in Panama of U.S. Military Causing Strains," *The New York Times,* May 24, 1983, p. A1, A7.

(I)-"U.S. Pilots Fly Spotter Missions," *Los Angeles Times,* March 12, 1984; "U.S. Said Planning More Exercises for Latin America," *Washington Post,* October 25, 1984; Courtright, *Notes, op. cit.,* p. 4.

(J)-David Raymond, *Grumman Corporation: OV-1 Mohawk Reconnaissance Plane,* ms., Berkeley, California, 1985-1986. See also Tom Gervasi, *The Arsenal of Democracy III,* (New York: Grove Press, 1984), p. 144.

(K)-James LeMoyne, "Salvador Air Role in War Increases," *The New York Times,* July 18, 1985.

6.8 Gaining Leverage on Arms Exports Abroad: From the Israeli Connection to Socially Responsible Investing

U.S. universities have invested in the arms contractors whose weapons have supplied the air war and companies which in the past, through their subsidiaries, have sold weapons to the internal security forces of the three Central American military states. Appendix One provides a comprehensive list of recent arms shipments to Central America, the companies involved and the university trustee ties and endowment investments in such companies. Such university connections could provide the basis for an organized effort in which university complicity in repression in Central America is documented and challenged.

However, two important points might be raised that question the usefulness of such an effort. First, several other countries, besides the United States have supplied weapons to the Central American military states and the contras. It might be argued that such third country shipments would render efforts aimed at academic-military-industrial links useless in stopping the flow of weapons to Central America. Second, many will argue that U.S. arms contractors are not the central actors initiating and projecting arms sales to Central America. Instead, the U.S. Congress, the President and the collected agencies and interests represented by the warfare state are believed to be most responsible for the arms flow to Central America, i.e. arms contractors are the wrong target.

Prior to World War II, most of the weapons shipments to Latin America did not come from the United States but the major European powers: France, Germany and Great Britain. Today, while the United States stands as a major bankroller of weapons shipments to Central America, other nations have sent a great deal of munitions to the region. From 1976 to 1980, the United States supplied only five of thirty million dollars worth of total arms transfers to El Salvador and ten of fifty million dollars worth of weapons going to both Guatemala and Honduras. Argentina and Brazil have become major producers of arms; they have begun to sell their weapons, mostly small arms and counter-insurgency equipment, to other nations in Latin America.[117]

The nations supplying Central America with weapons are numerous. For example, "since 1975 Guatemala has received arms from the United States, Israel, France, Switzerland, Taiwan, Italy, Belgium, and Yugoslavia." A newscast on Israeli state television in 1982 also identified South Africa as another arms supplier.[118] Brazil is also a supplier of weapons to Central American military states.[119]

Aside from the United States, the most important supplier of weapons to Central America has been the Israeli government and its arms contractors. Israel has been ready and willing to supply weapons to the states of El Salvador, Guatemala and Honduras as well as the contras when domestic political constraints prevented the United States from doing so:

> When U.S. military assistance programs were suspended to Somoza's Nicaragua, to the governments of El Salvador and Guatemala in the late 1970s and early 1980s and, more recently, to the Nicaraguan rebels, Israel filled the gap. Israel stepped in to support police forces in Costa Rica, Guatemala and El Salvador when the U.S. Congress banned such aid between 1974 and 1985.[120]

By 1984, Israeli arms sales in Central America had reached $22 million. Israeli Knesset member Mattiyahu Peled explained his country's role in 1985 by writing, "In Central America Israel is the 'dirty work' contractor for the U.S. Administration."[121]

In 1973, Israel signed its first major military agreement with El Salvador and pledged to make its air force the best in Central America. Israel agreed to sell El Salvador forty-nine planes, which were delivered by 1975; these included eighteen 1950s French Ouragans—the first jet fighters in Central America.[122] In his book *The Israeli Connection,* Dr. Benjamin Beit-Hallahmi, a professor at the University of Haifa, wrote:

> During 1977-1979, when Israel was most active [in El Salvador], it was also training counterinsurgency teams—less elegantly known as death squads. Francisco Guerra y Guerra, an undersecretary of the interior in the Salvadoran government in 1979, reported in an interview that Israeli intelligence advisers, stationed in El Salvador permanently, were working with the notorious ANSESAL death squads.[123]

The Stockholm International Peace Research Institute reported that 83 percent of El Salvador's defense imports between 1975 and 1979 were from Israel.[124] After the United States resumed sales in 1980, Israel became the second largest weapons supplier. However, in 1981, Israel agreed to give El Salvador $21 million in aid which was to be refunded by the United States.[125]

In Guatemala the "Israeli connection" also runs deep. Israel became the country's largest arms supplier in the mid-1970s; between 1975 and 1979, 39 percent of Guatemala's weapons imports came from Israel.[126] Beit-Hallahmi reports that "over the years, representatives of Israeli government corporations and private firms involved in arms sales have achieved positions of power and influence in Guatemala."[127] In 1983, Israel sold its "obsolete" Mauser rifles to Guatemala, some of which "were used to arm members of the civil patrol system (PAC), which involved the rural populace in coerced paramilitary service." Others ended up in Honduras, to be used in basic training by the contras.[128]

The Israeli government and corporations have also been linked to support for the counter-insurgency war and other forms of support for the organized system of internal repression in Guatemala: "Israeli advisers—some official, others private—helped Guatemalan internal security agents to hunt underground rebel groups."[129] The Israelis have supplied the Guatemalans with sophisticated computer technology that has been a central weapon of the Guatemalan police and military in their campaign of domestic repression: "The Army Transmission and Electronics School, inaugurated by President Romeo Lucas Garcia in 1981, was 'designed, staffed and funded by Israelis.' " The officer in charge of the school reported that "teaching methods, the teaching teams, the technical instruments, books, and even the custom furniture were designed and built by the Israeli company DEGEM systems."[130]

In Honduras, the Israelis have assisted the air force by training pilots and supplying rebuilt French Dassault Super-Mystère B2 jets equipped with American engines—the first supersonic jet fighters in the region. Israeli Galil rifles and Uzi submachine guns have supplied Honduran ground forces. Both the Honduran ground forces and air force have Israeli advisers.[131] Israel has also been critical in assisting the contras and first supplied them with arms in July 1983.[132] News reports in 1984, using U.S. government and contra sources, said that Israel had supplied the contras with just under $5 million in covert aid.[133] *Time* magazine reported in 1984 that "Israeli intelligence experts helped the CIA train the contras and retired or reserve Israeli army commandos have been hired by shadowy private firms to assist the rebels..."[134]

The framework for Israeli actions as a proxy for U.S. policy objectives in Central America was outlined in the Memorandum of Understanding on "strategic cooperation" signed by U.S. Secretary of Defense Caspar Weinberger and Israeli Minister of Defense Ariel Sharon on November 30, 1981. The agreement, soon suspended and then revived in 1983, allowed the United States to "grant third countries permission to spend part of their U.S. military credits in Israel."[135]

Do Israeli arms shipments to Central America *simply* reflect U.S. policy objectives or does the Israeli Government have its own independent political objectives in the region? This question is of more than academic interest because its answer provides a clue to a more important one: Can pressure on U.S. government policy in Central America translate directly into a vehicle for ending Israeli support for military assistance? Beit-Hallahmi writes that "numerous reports from Israeli sources mention either joint planning by the United States and Israel, or American pressure on Israel to support the contras."[136] But more complex interests than U.S. pressure have pushed Israel into becoming a major arms supplier.

Israel, a nation of only four million people, has become one of the top ten arms exporters in the world; a report in *The New York Times* noted that "Israeli businessmen are among the world's leading arms merchants."[137] Arms exports have been encouraged because weapons manufactured for the Israeli Defense Forces become cheaper when manufactured in large quantities. Those weapons which represent a surplus to the domestic military have been sold abroad. Dependency on arms exports is encouraged because the vast diversion of resources represented by the Israeli military economy has made the Israelis increasingly competent at military production at the expense of civilian production.

An estimate published in 1986 suggested that "as many as 140,000 Israelis—10 percent of the work force—are involved in manufacturing or selling military hardware." Arms exports have become such a big business that Israeli Aircraft Industries "got about 60 percent of its business from exports" in 1985.[138] A 1985 paper by Professors Alex Mintz and Daniel Maman found that "the Israeli military-industrial sector employs about one-fourth of the industrial labor force in Israel" and "produces about one-fourth of the country's industrial exports." Data published by the Stockholm International Peace Research Institute stated that the estimated share of arms exports in conventional arms production was 55 percent and that such arms transfers represented 17 percent of total exports in 1984.[139]

In addition to the arms export economy, Israel has also supported Central American military states in order to find political allies for its international disputes in the United Nations and other forums. Another troubling motivation, documented by Beit-Hallahmi and others, is that many Israeli military officials have increasingly identified themselves with the region's military, seeing the state under siege in Guatemala (and elsewhere) as a reflection of their own situation at home.[140]

But despite the economic and political considerations that help project Israeli arms sales to Central America, there is reason to believe that political mobilization in the United States (within the context of anti-corporate protest) could slow or prevent Israeli arms shipments to Central America. Political actions in the United States can help shape Israeli arms shipments policy because the political and economic links between Israel and the United States act as one political lever shaping Israeli government decisions.

The Israelis are heavily dependent on U.S. economic and military aid: in 1986, they received $4.5 billion from the United States, making them "the world's largest per capita recipient of U.S. foreign aid."[141] United States military credits helped the Israelis to develop their first battle tank, the Merkava.[142] The Israeli government also depends on U.S. technology, research and development, and data exchange agreements for its military industries. According to researcher Sheila Ryan, the expansion of Israel's military economy "has made Israel more dependent upon the United States than ever before to underwrite its major industrial institutions, with all the political ramifications that entails."[143]

The economic links between Israel's economy and U.S. corporations could theoretically provide political leverage in pressuring the Israeli government to cease its arms shipments to Central American states.

One connection is U.S. ownership of Israeli military contractors. For example, GTE, Inc. owns 22 percent of Tadiran, Israel's largest private-sector firm, which established a weapons factory in Coban, Alta Verapaz, a northern province in Guatemala.[144] Table 6-6 outlines U.S. ownership of some Israeli military companies in data collected by Ryan. Another connection linking Israel to the U.S.

Table 6-6: U.S. Corporate Stake in the Israeli Military Economy*

U.S. Corporation	Israeli Corporation	Financial Relationship
AEL Industries, Inc.	Elisra Electronic Systems, Ltd.	AEL owns 58 percent of Elisra.
Astronautics Corp. of America (ACA)	Astronautics CA Ltd.	Subsidiary of ACA
Control Data Corp.	Elbit Computers, Ltd.	Elbit USA, which seeks joint ventures and markets for Elbit in the U.S. and the French and German affiliates of Elbit are wholly owned subsidiaries of Control Data.
GTE, Inc.	Tadiran Israel Electronics Industries, Ltd.	GTE owns 22 percent of Tadiran.
Gerber Scientific, Inc.	Beta Engineering and Development, Inc.	Through Gerber Venture Capital Corp., a wholly owned subsidiary, Gerber Scientific owns 35 percent of Beta Engineering.
Intel Corporation	Intel Israel, Ltd.	Wholly owned subsidiary
Motorola, Inc.	Motorola Israel, Ltd.	Wholly owned subsidiary
United Technologies, Inc.	Bet Shemesh Engines Ltd.	UT bought 40 percent of the Israeli government's shares of BSE in 1984.

* A separate compilation in 1985 identified General Dynamics and McDonnell-Douglas as investing or operating in Israel. See Figure 1 in Alex Mintz and Daniel Maman, "Center vs. Periphery in Israel's Military-Industrial Sector: Implications for Civil-Military Relations," paper presented at the "Section on Military Studies/ISA" meetings, Urbana, Illinois, November 7-9, 1985.

SOURCE: Table II: U.S. Corporate Ownership of Some Israeli Military Industries, in Sheila Ryan, "US Military Contractors in Israel," *Middle East Report*, January-February 1987, p. 21.

economy exists in Israeli companies traded on Wall Street; these include military industries offered publicly over the American Stock Exchange, New York Stock Exchange and over the counter. Table 6-7 lists Israeli companies traded on Wall Street and identifies which are military-linked firms.

A campaign of protest against investment in Israeli corporations and U.S. companies owning Israeli military firms could begin to apply significant pressure that would help raise the costs of current Israeli military policy in Central America. Such actions could call for the divestment from Israeli war corporations, pressure on their U.S. parents and/or a boycott of Israeli stocks if the Israeli government does not cease providing weapons and logistical support for the contras and military states in the region. The Israeli government should also be encouraged to set up an economic conversion commission to study how Israel can escape from dependency on military production. Such efforts could link up with American Jews, organizations concerned with Israel's human rights violations and others seeking to advance a just and equitable solution to the Middle East conflict.[145]

The U.S. government stands as the central actor in projecting arms transfers to Central America; even in the case of Israel, arms shipments are to a certain extent underwritten by the United States. Third countries could also replace Israel as a supplier of weapons to Central America, but if significant pressure arose to change U.S. government policies, it is possible that third countries would be less likely to supply arms to the region. Some of them, like

Table 6-7: Israeli Companies on Wall Street: 1987 Listing

Company and Symbol	Market	Defense Firm
Alliance Tire (ATRA)	A	
American Israeli Paper (AIP)	A	
Ampal-American Israel A (AISA)	A	
Bank Leumi (BKLMV)	O	
Bio-Technology General (BTGC)	O	
ECI Telecom (ECILF)	O	Yes
Elbit Computers (ELBTF)	O	Yes
Elron Electronics (ELRNF)	O	Yes
Elscint (ELT)	N	
Etz Lavud (ETZ)	A	Yes
Fibronics (FBRX)	O	
Haganah Ltd. (units) (HGNHU)	O	Yes
IDB Bankholding (IDBBY)	O	
I.I.S. Intell. Info. (IISLF)	O	

continued on next page

Brazil, have their own connections to U.S. arms makers (see Note 119). Again, it is worth noting that corporate connections to arms shipments provide levers for activists in Europe and Latin America concerned with *their own* nations' complicity in repression against the Central American people.

Still, it could be argued that it is wiser to pressure the U.S. government directly to stop arms sales to Central America. For example, a 1987 vote in the Western Hemispheric Affairs Subcommittee of the House Foreign Affairs Committee defeated a proposed sale of Northrop F-5 fighter planes to Honduras worth $74 million. The sale was blocked by a six-to-six vote and arguments that the introduction of such an advanced fighter to Honduras could provide an excuse for the Nicaraguans to purchase advanced MiG-fighters from the Soviet Union.[146] At issue in this case was a particular technology; the question of whether military aid of any sort should be provided to Central American military states did not hang in the balance.

Withdrawal of military aid, as suggested earlier, rests on larger political and economic forces than twelve Congressional representatives. It depends on a calculus which weighs the costs and benefits to political decision-makers on voting for particular arms sales and supporting administration policies. Divestment campaigns and anti-corporate protests could begin to raise the costs of existing administration policy in the region and create constituencies to influence Congressional decisions regarding Central America on a district-by-district level. In addition, such constituencies could be strengthened by links with conversion coalitions on a state-by-state basis (see Chapter Eight).

Company and Symbol	Market	Defense Firm
InterPharm Labs (IPLLF)	O	
Israel Investors (IICR)	O	
Isramco (units) (ISRLU)	O	
Laser Industries (LAS)	A	
Obtrotech (OPTKF)	O	
PEC Israel Economic (IEC)	A	
Rada Electronics (units) (RADUF)	O	Yes
Scitex (SCIXF)	O	
Suspens. & Parts Indus. (SPILF)	O	Yes
Taro-Vit (TAROF)	O	
Teva Pharmaceutical (TEVIY)	O	

LEGEND: N=New York Stock Exchange
A=American Stock Exchange
O=Over-the-Counter

SOURCE: Identification of firms as Israeli military businesses traded on stock market from: Sheila Ryan, "US Military Contractors in Israel," *Middle East Report*, January-February 1987. List of Companies from: "Israeli Companies On Wall Street," Government of Israel Investment Authority, New York, NY, 1987.

Divestment organizing against defense firms could include faculty actions as well. A report in the Fall 1984 issue of the journal *Thought and Action* noted how university *faculty* investments were also tied to the military:

> university financial practices and retirement funds tie faculty to the military through corporate investments. The College Retirement Equities Fund, which is perhaps the major annuity fund for college faculty, held stocks or notes in 73 of the 100 largest defense contractors in the country in 1983.[147]

University investments in companies tied to the supply of weapons to Central America are extensive. However, as is the case of investment in South Africa-linked corporations, there are alternatives to university policies which promote the work of corporations tied to military repression in El Salvador, Guatemala and Honduras. An example of the lesson that profits alone do not explain university support for repression can be found in research on so-called "social investment" funds. Defense contractors are compared with non-defense-dependent companies to test whether it was possible to invest profitably in non-military corporations in the May/June 1985 issue of *Good Money: The Newsletter of Social Investing and Inventing*. In an article entitled "Investing to Avoid Defense Work," the editors picked ten of the best known large and smaller defense contractors. They constructed a war-work portfolio by purchasing 100 shares each in these companies (including Raytheon, Rockwell, Lockheed and Grumman) at the 1974 average stock price (then the last big market bottom). They then examined the performance of this portfolio by the end of 1984, for capital gains achieved and increased number of shares due to stock dividends and splits. They found that a non-war portfolio (including companies such as the Washington Post Co., Subaru of America, Hershey Foods and Computervision) of ten non-defense companies had surpassed the defense contractors portfolio for the same period of time. By the end of 1984, the original 1,000 non-war shares had grown to over 4,000, and their total value had increased 1,244 percent. While the war-work portfolio had a ten-year capital gain of $125,244, the non-war portfolio gained $152,910, or 22 percent better.[148]

In addition to the theoretical exercise above, there are practical alternatives for universities. The Pax World Fund, a diversified mutual fund, was the first social responsibility fund to stress investments in non-war-related industries. The fund does not invest in securities of companies appearing on the Defense Department's 100 largest contractors list or companies contracting with the Defense Department which had 5 percent or more of their gross sales for their prior fiscal year derived from such contracts. Pax World Fund performance similarly shows that investing in non-war-related industries can be profitable. For the ten years ended in 1984, Pax achieved an average total return of 14.1 percent. The July 1985 *Consumer Reports* found that the fund was one of only forty-four stocks funds that outperformed the Standard & Poor's 500 Stock Index "in at least three of the past five years" i.e. 1980-1985. Among investors in Pax are colleges, churches and corporations.[149]

Concern for a more "diversified" portfolio, as described in Chapter Five, may keep universities from investing more extensively in social investment funds like Pax. Or, academia may be concerned that such funds are not profitable *enough*. In any case, these two examples do illustrate that universities could conceivably reap "profits" without supporting the arms trade. However, the extensive trustee, faculty and investment ties that bind the universities to the military-industrial complex would make the divestment of university stocks from war companies tied to intervention in Central America a difficult undertaking in many instances. Nevertheless, the examples of alternative investment possibilities are useful, if only at the level of raising questions to university officials and combatting their propaganda. The extensive connections between the military and the university also suggest that in order to challenge the militarization of academia supplemental strategies to divestment are needed. Such alternatives are addressed in Chapter Eight.

7

Growing Pentagon Hegemony Over Universities:
Military Dependency and Labor Under the Warfare State

7.1 The Militarization of University Research and Development

Universities, professors and students, as well as youth kept out of the university by income and race barriers, have all become more dependent on the military as a source of employment. The military's growing power over these groups has broadened the warfare state's constituency.

This chapter will examine the economic and political forces lying behind this growing dependency, in an effort to answer a crucial strategic question: How can we deny the universities' resources to the military?

The academic establishment and the Pentagon have in recent years expanded a long-standing alliance. In a major report in 1982, "the Pentagon Defense Science Board told Congress that cooperation of the universities was an essential ingredient of the nation's rearmament programme."[1] Leading the academic stampede toward the Pentagon, the Association of American Universities "claimed that obsolete research facilities and a shortage of graduate students in key scientific disciplines posed a threat to national security."[2] The Pentagon echoed this claim, citing data showing that, between 1968 and 1980, R&D funds as a portion of the federal budget declined by 36 percent and as a portion of the gross national product by 19 percent.[3]

However, the *military* slice of the federal R&D pie has increased dramatically. According to a report by the Federation of American Scientists, the military share of federal R&D increased from 55 percent in 1980 to 65 percent in 1985. The Carter and Reagan administrations have brought us the "re-militarization" of national research and development expenditures:

> Federal outlays for military R&D fell from a peak of about 1.5 percent of GNP in the mid-1960s to a low of around 0.6 percent in the late 1970s, and...They have now "recovered" to a level of around 0.8 percent. The Federal outlays for nonmilitary R&D, by contrast, have been in a more or less steady decline, from around 0.7 percent in the mid-sixties to about 0.4 percent [in 1986].[4]

Other data show an increasing university dependency on the military. Appendix Three shows the share of university obligations for both basic and applied research governed by the various military serving agencies: the Department of Defense, NASA and the DOE. Federally funded basic research coming from military-linked national agencies has increased from 18 percent in 1975

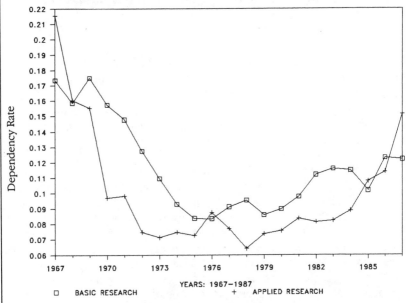

Figure 7-1: University Military Dependency:
Defense Department Share of Total Federal Obligations
To Universities from Government Agencies

SOURCE: Derived from data on federal obligations for Basic and Applied Research by University and College Performers for the Department of Defense published by the National Science Foundation, Washington, D.C., 1986-1987.

(the last year of direct U.S. involvement in the Vietnam War), to 20 percent in 1987. Similarly, the share of federally funded applied research coming from military-linked agencies has increased from the mid-1970s (see Appendix Three). Figure 7-1 uses a more conservative estimate showing the percent of federal money for basic and applied research coming from just one agency, the Department of Defense.

Estimates suggest that 50 to 90 percent of NASA's R&D spending is military-related. P.B. Stares, in *The Militarization of Space*, writes that "space has been an integral part of the superpower arms race for over 25 years."[5] The militarization of space began with the launch of military satellites in 1958. "By the end of 1985, 2314 military satellites had been launched. This constitutes about 75 percent of all satellites orbited," launched mainly by the United States and USSR, and are "the essential eyes, ears and nerves of the fighting forces of today." The second phase of space militarization began with the development of weapons to destroy these satellites, which, although not yet deployed, will soon be introduced "under the guise of defensive systems."[6]

The Strategic Defense Initiative (SDI), or the "Star Wars" anti-missile defense program, is accelerating the militarization of space. As Italian peace scholar Mario Pianta explains, "The largest contracts for missile defense have gone to the same companies that are major producers of U.S. nuclear weapons."

> It is hard to imagine how companies with a major interest in the production of nuclear (attack) weapons could be the agent of a strategic transformation that would make such weapons, in President Reagan's words, "impotent and obsolete." Rather, such a concentration of the current SDI research in the institutions and companies of the US "military-industrial complex" is further evidence that Star Wars is essentially an extension into space of the current arms race.[7]

The first objective of the Space Shuttle program under the Reagan administration was to "strengthen the security of the United States." Therefore, the Defense Department gets the first rights to shuttle launches and is their largest user: "Fully 34% of shuttle payloads through 1994 will be military, with many of the missions scheduled to deliver and test hardware for the Strategic Defense Initiative."[8]

Like NASA, the DOE—and to a lesser extent its predecessor agencies: the Atomic Energy Commission and the Energy Research and Development Administration—is also a military-serving agency. The DOE administers about 280 nuclear weapons facilities. "With over $24 billion in physical assets, DOE's bomb program would rank in the top tier of the 'Fortune 500' corporations."[9] The DOE likes to make a distinction between its primary orientation and the defense research it funds at universities. For example, out of $365.9 million spent by DOE for university R&D in FY 1985, its "defense program office" funded just $8.4 million.[10] However, part of the civilian energy budget must be considered military-oriented because of the nuclear radiation waste cycle, i.e. waste by-products of certain nuclear power plants can be used to arm nuclear weapons.[11] DOE is also working to develop high-powered outer space reactors to be used for military purposes.[12]

During President Reagan's tenure, the DOE nuclear weapons budget rose from $3.6 billion in FY 1981 to $7.6 billion in FY 1987 (in 1987 dollars). In the same period, atomic defense rose from 38 to 61 percent. Military programs, such as nuclear warheads and research on a "Star Wars" X-ray laser device that would be powered by a nuclear detonation, represented about 65 percent of the Energy Department's budget.[13] After considering the military character of DOD, DOE and NASA-sponsored research, Professor Lloyd J. Dumas at the University of Texas concluded that "the military's fraction of total R&D performed at universities and colleges and the federally-funded research and development centers they administer would be slightly over 30 percent" in 1980.[14]

Another indicator of increased dependency on military spending is evident in growing Defense Department support for individual branches of

Table 7-1: Defense Department Support for University R&D in Selected Fields

Field	Defense Department Support for University R&D (in Millions of 1985 Dollars)		DOD share of all federal support for University R&D	
	FY 1980	FY 1986	FY 1980	FY 1986
Physics	44.9	59.0	13.8%	14.0%
Mathematics	21.3	34.5	32.9%	35.3%
Computer Sciences	25.0	59.6	45.8%	53.9%
Materials Sciences	29.4	49.7	38.7%	48.4%
Aeronautics/ Astronautics	39.2	36.7	65.6%	56.0%
Electrical Engineering	68.0	83.5	66.5%	59.8%
Mechanical Engineering	19.8	34.8	45.5%	48.1%

SOURCE: Table VIII, in John P. Holdren and Bailey F. Green, "Military Spending, The SDI, and Government Support of Research and Development: Effects on the Economy and the Health of American Science," *FAS Public Interest Report*, Vol. 39, No. 7, September 1986.

science. Table 7-1 documents how a variety of fields of study have become more dependent on Defense Department contracts as a share of total federal support. Each of these research areas includes departments, faculty, students and administrators who are now more dependent on military spending and thus more strongly tied to the larger military system. What might this mean for political activists on campus trying to oppose the warfare state? Increased military dependency will strengthen the ties of the university to the military. Political interests between both parties will grow closer, leading to greater legitimacy and support for Defense Department objectives. Table 7-2 shows how many leading universities have received increased levels of funding from the Defense Department in real terms.

Such an assessment of declining dissent from military objectives is well founded. For example, in 1987, MIT's biology department, distressed by the increasing reliance of their field of research on Pentagon monies, voted to refuse Pentagon funds entirely. However, the MIT administration, directing depart-

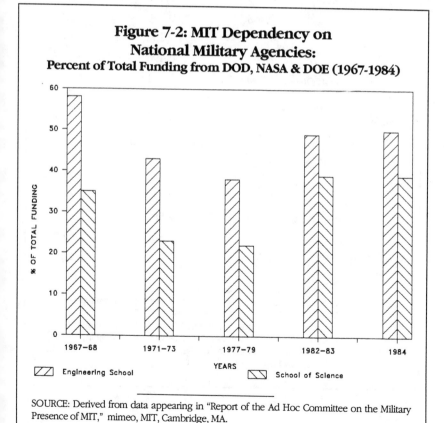

Figure 7-2: MIT Dependency on National Military Agencies:
Percent of Total Funding from DOD, NASA & DOE (1967-1984)

SOURCE: Derived from data appearing in "Report of the Ad Hoc Committee on the Military Presence of MIT," mimeo, MIT, Cambridge, MA.

Table 7-2: Defense Department Spending at Twenty Universities

(In Thousands of 1982 Dollars)

School	1982	1986	% Change
MIT	216,562	317,284	+47
Johns Hopkins	235,517	276,226	+17
Stanford	22,763	32,886	+44
U of WA, Seattle	10,388	17,420	+68
U of IL	8,957	13,117	+46
Princeton	2,855	6,530	+129
U of CA, Berkeley	8,627	6,496	-25
Columbia	5,468	9,056	+66
Cornell	4,872	8,262	+70
UCLA	4,546	6,496	+43
U of MI, Ann Arbor	3,980	5,571	+40
Yale University	4,264	3,895	-9
U of WI	4,611	4,702	+2
U of PA	3,790	5,335	+41
Harvard University	2,736	7,013	+156
Brown	1,942	5,340	+175
Northwestern	1,916	2,558	+34
New York University	1,896	2,581	+36
U of CO, Boulder	1,757	2,880	+64
U of CT	1,241	1,395	+12

SOURCE: Author's calculations based on *Educational and Non Profit Institutions Receiving Prime Contract Awards for R.D.T.&E.*, Fiscal Years 1982, 1986, Department of Defense, Directorate for Information Operations & Reports; "Table 7.17: Fixed-Weighted Price Indexes for National Defense Purchases of Goods and Services, 1982 Weights," *Survey of Current Business*, U.S. Department of Commerce, Washington, D.C., Vol. 66, No. 7, July 1986, and Vol. 67, No. 5, May 1987.

ments which are highly dependent on military funding (see Table 7-3 and Figure 7-2), challenged the biology department's decision:

> To defend the cozy relationship, the administrators threatened to cut off the biology department's in-house funding if the biologists turned down the military money. Squeezed, the biologists reversed their decision and once again allowed Pentagon funding.

In another case, a science writer for the University-Industry Research Program at the University of Wisconsin, was dismissed from his job for disclosing his university's efforts to increase its program of biological warfare research.[15]

In sum, the military's impact on the universities is far greater than the line items representing Defense Department-funded university research. The military's presence is widely felt and its political influence can be considerable. Scientists, for example, are frequently pressured to take money from sources that can fund unusually costly research projects. As Table 7-1 indicates, for many branches of science, defense monies are likely to provide such funds. Accepting defense money becomes the *sine qua non* of life for many academics. As Richard De Veaux, an Assistant Professor in the Program in Statistics and Operations Research at Princeton University, explains:

> It is certainly true that the military provides a substantial amount of funding in the area of statistics and operations research. If I had a strong enough position so that I didn't accept military funding for any basic research the only problems that would cause is that now I've limited myself to one quarter of the available funds. These funds are very competitive to get regardless of the source...[they] are an important aspect in the tenure decision, your ability to provide funds for your research and to support your students...[16]

In addition, as professors and students become more dependent on military-serving agencies, there will be a greater tendency for them to fall in step behind the military's objectives in science policy. This results from the strategy employed by faculty and graduate students to think in terms of research that would be of interest to, hence funded by, the Defense Department. Such dependency could also shape the political orientation of faculty, affecting what questions they ask and do not ask of their benefactors.

The connection between political orientation and dependency on military R&D was best explained by Under Secretary of Defense Donald Hicks who told *Science* magazine on April 25, 1986 that:

> I am not particularly interested in seeing department money going to someplace where an individual is outspoken in his rejection of department aims, even for basic research.[17]

Such veiled threats help define the informal social regulations which govern the academic scientist. Steve Slaby, Professor of Civil Engineering at Princeton University, argues that defense sponsorship of university research has a direct impact on the political stances taken by academic scientists:

> As far as I'm concerned there are strings attached. Maybe very subtle strings, psychological strings. Strings that affect peoples' political outlooks, peoples' political views, peoples' political action...in the past I have known people during the Vietnam War, some of my colleagues who would not sign anti-Vietnam War petitions, yet they would say, "I agree with you Steve but I can't sign because as you know I get Defense Department research monies"...

Similarly, Terry Matilsky, an Astrophysicist at Rutgers University, found that such self-regulation has also limited faculty resistance to Star Wars:

> There's a nation-wide petition against Star Wars signed by thousands upon thousands of scientists...You can see the institutions that are highest on the list of signatories. You find that the people who are not accepting too much Defense Department contracts are signing it at the rate of 80 to 90 percent and the places that do have a lot of military research on campus such as MIT, that is hovering at around 50 percent...Even within disciplines the same thing is happening. If you look in the Chemistry Department you have a much higher percentage of signatories than say in the Physics Department or Engineering Department.[18]

But the political obedience inherent in military dependency is not just the reflection of what overt political stands military-sponsored scientists take on war and peace. Rather, military-dependency determines what kind of science is taught and what kind of science is practiced by graduating students. On the first point there is a close relationship between science and engineering curriculum and the sponsors of faculty research. As Carl Barus, Professor Emeritus of Engineering at Swarthmore College reflected:

> Professors teach what they know. They write textbooks about what they teach. What they know that is new comes mainly from their own research. It is hardly surprising, then, that military research in the university leads to military-centered undergraduate curricula.

Such links have also had a more organized expression. For example, in 1968, the American Society for Engineering Education (ASEE) published its Final Report on the *Goals of Engineering Education*. A section entitled "The Engineer in Future Society," summarizes a report by the military-linked RAND Corporation which forecasted the world in 1984 and in 2000. "These forecasts suggest that...development will continue...of space programs and design of more efficient and humane [sic] military defense systems." The self-fulfilling prophecy is completed when the report claims that "within this context" the report "has attempted to point the way toward the development of engineering education in the decades ahead."[19]

If professors teach what they know, and what they know becomes more and more a reflection of military-sponsored university research, then this is bound to affect the career choices of students after they leave the university: "they will find themselves drawn into careers in military work, not just dissertations, because the narrow and highly applied character of their graduate work leaves them few other choices."[20] The narrowing of the scope of scientific inquiry inherent in the militarization of science can be seen in the decreasing applicability of military-sponsored research to civilian needs (see Section 7.5).[21]

7.2 The Forces of Destructive Production: Explaining the Militarization of University Research

The deepening of Pentagon control over the universities has appeared against the backdrop of an increase in demand for university scientific labor and an accompanying subsidization of that labor by the State. The military seeks more and more of the university's resources and the federal government has financed increased Pentagon control (although budgetary legislation in the Gramm-Rudman law and increased budget deficits may slow the acceleration of university militarization). Beyond such immediate causes, Pentagon control has grown in response to a drive by the military to increase the size and scope of its influence. Supporting these efforts is a perpetual cycle of military intervention, project innovation, militaristic rhetoric and jingoism.

Seymour Melman has explained the increasing control of the military over civilian life as a central force propelling the "state managers" of the Pentagon:

> As in managerialism generally, the extension of managerial control, the acquisition of more power and higher status, is a first priority of the state-managed military economy. As in other managements, an increase in the number of people controlled is both a persistent objective and a conclusive test of managerial success.[22]

This drive for power and control over increased numbers of workers, seen in expanding military budgets and growing Pentagon funding for university research, helps explain the expansion of the Pentagon's control over academia.

There is evidence of this power drive in the military's own proclamations. The universities have provided a logistical base for the recent arms build-up; the expansion in defense spending has depended on the universities. Jimmie R. Suttle, assistant director for research at the Defense Department, explained the relationship as follows: "There's a movement now to re-establish our commitment with the universities because we need them." This need is rooted in the universities' role as technological innovators, explained earlier: "one of our strongest bases for resources and people for the development of basic research is the university system. Since the [Defense Department] is one of the major users of technology, we have to take advantage of research capability where we can find it," said Suttle.[23]

Leo Young, the director of Research and Laboratory Management, Office of the Under-Secretary of Defense for Research and Engineering, explained the Pentagon's use of universities as a source of political power as follows:

> Research and graduate education go hand in hand in this country and they make a powerful team that has enabled the United States to assume world leadership, both in performing research and in training research workers for industrial and government laboratories."[24]

Similarly, former Secretary of Defense Caspar Weinberger in a 1986 address praising the glory of West Virginia's software valley and military-backed software declared:

> ...true national security rests not only on our deployed military strength...But also on our political will as a nation, our underlying economic strength, and our scientific and technological creativity. By bringing together, in an entrepreneurial spirit, participants from academia, the computer hardware and software industry, and government, software valley is as great an investment in our national security as an aircraft manufacturing plant or a shipyard.[25]

The need to project U.S. power across the globe, to enhance the power of the United States with respect to the Soviet Union, the Third World and Western European allies as well, has helped drive the expansion in Pentagon funding of and control over universities. The renewed cycle of intervention has created a climate of jingoism and militarism which has helped restore the legitimacy of military-serving work that was largely lost at the height of protest against our involvement in Vietnam. Since the end of the Vietnam War, monies that once went to direct weapons production have been freed up for R&D.[26]

The most recent wave of interventionism, and the expansion of military R&D, have their roots in the Carter administration; it did not begin with Reagan. President Carter seized the initiative with the collapse of the anti-War movement and the political revolutions in Iran and Nicaragua. Carter was also forced to respond to leftist electoral triumphs in Dominica, St. Lucia and St. Kitts, as well as the spread of guerrilla movements in El Salvador and Guatemala. In June 1979, "at a high-level White House meeting, the Pentagon, the CIA and the National Security Council proposed resuming aid to the right-wing governments in El Salvador and Guatemala."[27] That October, President Carter announced the establishment of the "full-time Caribbean Joint Task Force headquarters," expanded military maneuvers in the region, and increased surveillance of Cuba.[28] Carter also launched the new wave of Pentagon contracts for universities:

> the Pentagon has been trying for several years to support more academic research and restore its friendship with universities, which was almost destroyed by the antagonisms of the Vietnam war. The Carter Administration encouraged the reconciliation, and its budgets almost doubled the Defense Department's expenditure on academic science.[29]

As fear of the Soviets and imagined Sandinista enemies diminishes, new rationales are invented to prop up the military economy and the benefits it brings academic and industrial constituents. Academics tied to the Pentagon have encouraged a greater role by the Pentagon in economic planning. The increasing dependency of U.S. defense contractors on foreign suppliers has helped create this political opening. Experts now call for the Pentagon to have a greater say on policies governing taxes, trade, education and the environment.[30]

Concurrent with aggression toward the Third World has been the expansion of high-technology-based weapons systems. These weapons have made the military even more dependent on the technological information of research organizations. In part, recent R&D spending has increased so dramatically because the Pentagon is replacing labor with capital in the military budget:

> With military hardware costs reaching astronomical levels, the armed services understandably seek doctrinal breakthroughs enabling them to get more combat power out of the arsenals they already have—or more "bang for the buck," in military lingo.[31]

University-developed advances in military technologies, propelled by increased military R&D, are an integral part of the military's attempt to gain the upper hand against guerrilla opposition movements in the Third World:

> There has been a shift in U.S. military strategy from massive retaliation to the use of limited war as the Soviet 'threat' has declined and the 'threat' of third world nationalism has increased. As nationalists increasingly engage in guerrilla warfare (as in Vietnam and Guatemala) the Defense Department is forced to rely on sophisticated technology to readjust the balance of power. It is the role of the university to provide the technological weaponry.[32]

The increased demand for engineers and scientists by universities is explained partially by an elaboration of the military procurement process, described in Mary Kaldor's book, *The Baroque Arsenal.* Because U.S. military doctrine calls for military superiority, state planners call upon military supplying firms to come up with state of the art weapons systems or sacrifice contracts. This approach leads to planned obsolescence, as manufacturers' weapons systems must be updated to keep pace with real or imagined capabilities of the enemy or with offerings from military salesmen only too ready to produce new and improved versions of existing tanks, planes or missile systems. The arms makers encourage this circulation of capital, for the military planners see the development of bigger and better weapons systems as the key to the growth and stability of U.S. global power. War planners' expectations of larger and more destructive weapons are readily met by military blueprints. As one corporate vice-president said, the government "depends on companies like ours to tell them what they need."

The rapid turnover of capital in the military economy, led by the injunction "design or die," has forced the high demand for engineers to beat-out the competition. Firms seek to develop the most sophisticated and destructive weapons, meet complicated Pentagon requirements, or merely warehouse large numbers of engineers in offices or factories in order to impress Pentagon planners of their high-tech competence and superior skills. For example in the aircraft industry:

> Superior performance expressed in higher speeds, greater ceilings, heavier loads and longer ranges wins contracts. To stay in business, manufacturers soon learned that they must maintain engineering staffs capable of exploiting the latest findings in aeronautical science, translating theory into practical designs.[33]

This oxymoronic process of destructive construction, has led to greater numbers of engineering and technical personnel per production worker employed in military firms when they are compared to civilian industry. As economist Ann Markusen explains: "The higher level of sophistication of military products, together with the constant product innovation in military industry, leads to the large numbers of scientists and technicians employed by military suppliers."[34] Whereas engineers represent 11 percent of aircraft, 15 percent of communications equipment, and 31 percent of guided missiles workforces (all high-tech sectors linked to defense), in manufacturing as a whole they represent only 3 percent.[35] The increasing R&D-intensity of high-tech weapons systems, such as SDI, will raise the demand for technical personnel supplied by the universities: "the R and D input per unit of output value is some 20 times higher for military than for civilian goods, and the disparity is doubtless growing with the increased sophistication of weapons systems."[36] In fact, a report published in 1987 found that "since 1981, military research and development has grown twice as fast as overall Pentagon spending."[37]

In sum, the military's demand for university labor is fueled in part by a need to acquire the scientific talents of students and professors. This demand also explains why vast numbers of engineers and scientists are hired by military contractors. But demand does not create its own supply. What are some of the factors luring students into defense work? How is the military able to channel university graduates into jobs servicing the Pentagon, DOE and NASA? One answer is money. Firms which have government contracts because of the cost-plus system described below offer salaries which are substantially higher than are available at civilian firms. Students are also attracted to the opportunities which defense-serving employment offers to work advancing "state-of-the-art technologies not available, often as a consequence of secrecy in the name of national security, in the commercial sector." Defense work based on the cost-plus system also "gives the engineer privileged access to materials and facilities beyond reach in commercial product development." The cost-plus system also gives them a significant financial advantage over non-defense counterparts in recruitment campaigns at universities.[38]

7.3 From Star Wars to Regional Military Complex: The Universities and the Military Economy

In the recent period, the SDI program has been advanced by military planners as a way for the U.S. government to subsidize development of many of the advanced technologies designed to give the United States a military and economic edge over our "rivals." According to President Reagan, SDI "holds the promise of changing the course of human history" by rendering "nuclear weapons impotent and obsolete." The Star Wars project involves the use of beam weapons against Soviet Inter-Continental Ballistic Missiles (ICBMs), bombers and air-launched short-range missiles.[39]

SDI also serves to increase U.S. political and economic power over our allies. Mario Pianta describes the use of the program in this regard as a "Technological Star Wars" strategy in which U.S. sponsorship of military-linked technologies in Europe and Japan co-opts foreign enterprise into those economic sectors where Americans have the comparative advantage: "With limited resources for R&D and innovation, participation in Star Wars will mean a reduced European effort to develop new commercial technologies in other fields." Once SDI is accepted as the grounds for future technological competition, "European industry can hardly hope of being more successful than its established U.S. competitors."[40]

The use of Star Wars as an economic strategy has been explored by Harvard industrial policy economist Robert Reich. He notes that SDI "has been touted in Congressional hearings as a path to competitiveness in advanced technologies." While the policy of government subsidy for technological development represented by SDI repeats a familiar pattern, Reich argues that the program has intensified Pentagon control over technological development:

"never before have we entrusted so much technological development to the Pentagon in so short a time".[41] A study by John Pike, affiliated with the Federation of American Scientists, estimated the potential cost of SDI development as follows:

> if SDI encounters the cost overruns and schedule delays that are typical of high risk, high technology products such as the ASAT anti-satellite system, the Teal Ruby space-based infrared sensor, the AMRAAM advanced air-to-air missile and the VHSIC very high speed integrated circuit computer program, it could become a twenty year, 225 billion dollar development effort.[42]

Former Secretary of Defense James Schlesinger estimated that, after deployment, the program could end up costing as much as $1 trillion.

The Reagan administration's vision of the program sought to turn SDI into "the largest single research programme ever developed by a Western government." Actual SDI budget authority from 1984 to 1987 amounted to $9.4 billion dollars. From 1984 to 1987, SDI budget authority represented 6.3 percent of national research monies and SDI growth was 41.9 percent of national research growth.[43] SDI contracts to universities from 1983 to 1986 came to $180 million. The major program areas being funded in universities include: ultra-high speed computing, new space-based power sources, novel laser concepts and new types of optic sensors.[44] The fiscal pressures facing the Bush administration have led to pronouncements by Defense Secretary Dick Cheney that SDI was "oversold" during the Reagan administration as a leak-proof umbrella against nuclear attacks. Cheney also has called for cutbacks in funding. In April 1989, he announced that "instead of spending $40 billion over the next five years on SDI, we'll spend about $33 billion."[45]

In addition to the financial links which bind the Pentagon to the universities under the SDI,[46] a distinct "politics of Star Wars" has emerged on university campuses in which the Pentagon has attempted to exercise greater authority over academia. While only 5 to 10 percent of the SDI budget has been slated for university research, university support has been critical in building a political case for SDI. When asked why Strategic Defense Initiative Organization's office of Innovative Science and Technology was soliciting proposals for FY 1986 far in advance of congressional budget decisions, Star Wars director James A. Ionson told *Science* magazine:

> It's probably something that's never been done, but this office is trying to sell something to Congress. If we can say that this fellow at MIT will get money to do such and such research, it's something real to sell. That in itself is innovative.[47]

Ionson's comments reveal how the Pentagon has attempted to use its sponsorship of university research as a tool to legitimate the power of the warfare state, its right to usurp and control resources. A letter published on May 14, 1985 in MIT's student newspaper, *The Tech,* noted that 25 percent of the research at Lincoln Laboratory was then funded by SDI. The author, reflecting on the goals of SDI, argued that increasing university dependency on the program served to co-opt the universities as lobbyists for the military:

> DOD knows that the influence of thousands of missile and aircraft employees has swayed many weapons procurement votes in Congress...It is clear that DOD intends that the researchers and administrators at MIT serve as a similar constituency for SDI.[48]

A major instrument in increasing the military's influence through SDI is the use of secrecy to control the actions of faculty and their student assistants. Several federal departments have clauses written into their contracts which give the government the right to review research findings before they are published. The web of censorship is easily extended to basic research, if military personnel feel that it has some practical application. As John Shattuck, Harvard's vice-president for government, community and public affairs, explained:

> If it looked like what I was studying was going to become a key part of the 'Star Wars' defense system, the Defense Department could turn around and classify it...[49]

The problem of censorship may be limited at major research universities by prohibitions against classified research which arose in response to the anti-war movement of the Vietnam era. But the problems associated with increased secrecy, such as the attempted regulation of faculty behavior in service of the military, persist. The commander of an Army Corps of Engineers laboratory at the University of Illinois at Urbana-Champaign threatened to sever relations with scientists who opposed President Reagan's Star Wars program. The threats were issued in a memorandum authored by Col. Paul J. Theuer, commander and director of the army's Construction and Engineering Research Laboratory. Theuer instructed the laboratory's technical director to discontinue "projects or official relationships" with those university researchers who said they would refuse to conduct SDI research. Although Theuer apologized for the memo, the controversy led the University's chancellor to issue a statement disassociating his institution from a position favored by fifty faculty members and seventy graduate students who signed an anti-SDI petition.[50]

The problem of defense censorship of academic research is not new. An illustrative example occurred in August of 1982 when the Defense Department blocked the presentation of about 100 technical papers just before they were to have been delivered at an international convention on optical engineering. As a report in *The New York Times* on the incident noted: "The action disrupted the 26th annual international technical symposium of the Society of Photo-Optical Instrumentation Engineers by eliminating about one of every six papers scheduled to be presented."[51]

The expansion of weapons systems relying heavily on research and development inputs has contributed to the furtherance of a series of "regional" military-industrial complexes. The Star Wars program will accelerate this trend. In the period from 1984 to 1990, U.S. high-tech industries will have received a $30 billion subsidy in research funds from the SDI program. In 1984, while spending on defense electronics was estimated to exceed $40 billion, consumer electronics spending was only $30 billion.[52]

Universities have proven instrumental in the development of high-technology industries and have intricate links with high technology companies, many of them defense related. At Stanford and in Boston, "there is crossing over between military-industrial and university posts." Of the top twenty manufacturing sectors characterized as defense-dependent by the Bureau of Industrial Economics, only two sectors were not listed as high-technology: ship-building repair and miscellaneous nonferrous foundries.[53] Numerous science parks, linking universities to R&D companies, have arisen since the first one was established in Cambridge, Massachusetts, in 1973.

Many university personnel also have started their own high-tech firms. Several federal initiatives have encouraged university links to high-technology firms: tax incentives have been granted to those manufacturers of scientific instruments willing to donate these to universities; patent legislation also has been revised so that small businesses as well as universities can profit through patenting inventions deriving from federal funds. Industry and university collaboration also has been furthered by "revised anti-trust guidelines, so that collaboration of market competitors in a joint programme of research will no longer carry the danger of prosecution under anti-trust law."[54]

The growth of the defense-linked high-technology sector has created an additional complex of political interests on the regional level wedded to Pentagon revenue. Such examples exist in high-technology councils which seek to further the aims of university-linked military contractors in Massachusetts and Michigan. In Massachusetts, the "Military Affairs Council" was established in March of 1985. The Council includes some of the state's largest military contractors (including Raytheon, GTE, Northrop and MIT's Lincoln Labs). One of the initiators of the Council says that its goal is to "maintain and preserve the presence and long term power" of the state's defense industry by lobbying public officials and through campaigns designed to improve the public's perception of the military. By the close of 1985, the Council had lined up more than 100 corporate members.[55]

A "High Tech Task Force" was created in Michigan in 1981 to study high-technology economic development strategies for the state. The Task Force was comprised of the president of the University of Michigan, Harold Shapiro; Herbert H. Dow, secretary of the Dow Chemical Corporation (who has served as a trustee of MIT); Ted Doan, former president of Dow Chemical Company; Paul McCracken, University of Michigan economist and a director of Dow Chemical and William N. Hubbard, president of Upjohn who has served as a trustee of Columbia University.

A July 1981 report of the Task Force recommended that Michigan concentrate on the development and expansion of robotics and industrial biology. A Task Force plan in the early 1980s called for the University of Michigan to serve as a magnet for "high-technology" investment. Part of the strategy for funding high technology development has been to apply to the Department of Defense for R&D funds. In August 1981, the Governor of Michigan set up a high technology R&D Procurement Panel to attract Defense Department contracts to Michigan.[56]

Region-specific military-industrial complexes have emerged through the concentration of military spending in areas like the Route 128 hub surrounding Boston. The Pentagon has actively encouraged the development of such local economies which help integrate universities into the military. A 1985 report published by the Academy for State and Local Government, *Planning A Government Procurement Outreach Center* states that "the Federal government and specifically the Department of Defense has a commitment to enhance small business participation in defense production." The Pentagon's Office of Economic Adjustment (OEA) has propelled local defense economies through the Defense Procurement and Economic Development Project. A manual drafted by the Project in 1983 explains how businesses and local governments can profit from defense funding:

> The rising levels of defense spending suggest new opportunities for local economic growth. Most analyses of defense requirements project annual increases of defense spending of as much as seven to ten percent after allowance for inflation. The increases are concentrated in the purchases of goods and services, which will grow much faster than personal expenditures. Community leaders therefore see defense contracts as an important market for local industry.[57]

The OEA has promoted the local defense economy through the development of "procurement outreach centers" which are publicly funded projects "organized to generate employment in a locality by assisting firms in attracting defense (and other government) contracts." Among the contributors to such centers are the Defense Department, state and local governments and private foundations. The Defense Department has also encouraged small businesses to solicit proposals under another program, Small Business Innovation Research (SBIR) which was initiated by Congress. The Defense Department variant of SBIR is designed to:

> stimulate technological innovation in the private sector, strengthening

the role of small business in meeting D.O.D. research and development needs, fostering and encouraging participation by minority and disadvantaged persons in technological innovation, and increasing the commercial application of D.O.D.-supported research or research and development results.

By extending the scope of the military, these local initiatives close off the range of civilian channels in which academic research can operate. SBIR provides an illustrative example of this process. Since money in this program will have Pentagon ties, university researchers (in their role as "R&D entrepreneurs") will become attracted to the program. At Columbia, the *Office of Projects and Grants Newsletter* explained the faculty role as follows: "Small businesses...are not really equipped to plan and submit research proposals for SBIR monies and they have relied on their university friends with either formal subcontract arrangements or with individual consulting agreements."[58]

7.4 Fiscal Crisis/Financial Squeeze: Channeling Students and Faculty in the Service of the Military

The increase in military R&D going to universities in the Star Wars era has made academia as defense dependent as it was in 1968, at the height of the Vietnam War. The expansion in military-sponsored R&D is one side of the coin. The other is the contraction of alternative sources of federal funding and other financial pressures which make the military look more and more attractive as a source of sponsorship of research and funds for facilities and laboratory equipment. While civilian R&D money is shrinking, the military accounted for about two-thirds of the government's proposed 1986 R&D spending.[59] Universities which used to get National Science Foundation (NSF) funding have been told by the government to go to the SDIO (Strategic Defense Initiative Organization), the government arm of Star Wars. Robert L. Park, Executive Director of the Washington Office of the American Physical Society, has stated that researchers in fields like plasma physics may see SDI funding as the only way to continue their research projects. In fact, "if D.O.D. funding to off-campus affiliates like MIT's Lincoln Laboratory is taken into account, the Pentagon is now outspending N.S.F. on university research."[60]

The university elite has rationalized increased ties to the Defense Department as necessary to cope with its own financial crisis and manpower shortages. Concurrently, the economy is caught between a military induced "brain drain" and diversion of productive resources to arms production on the one hand, and an expanding demand for high technology products (represented by advanced systems of automation, telecommunications, computerization and information processing) on the other hand. However, many universities have faced constraints in training students in state of the art technology and finding faculty (many drained-off into their own or big business defense firms) to engage in research in support of such technological development. For example, a 1982 report by the Massachusetts High-Technology Council showed a shortfall of 1,000 engineers a year for firms clustered around the defense-dependent "Route 128." Financial problems plague universities trying to pay for competitive salaries, the subsidization of inflated tuitions, and the costs of increasingly capital-intensive training equipment in technical scientific branches, such as electrical engineering and computer science.

The financial shortfall results from a fiscal crisis linked to federal funding cutbacks and generated by inflationary increases "which have escalated campus costs at rates exceeding any budgetary increases." At private institutions, endowments have been "decimated" by inflation. At public institutions, decreased non-defense government funding has created similar difficulties. From FY1979-1980 to FY1981-1982, total state government allocations decreased in real dollars by 4 percent. Some states faced budget reductions as great as 17 percent.[61]

These problems have been aggravated by decreases in national aid to education. In the mid-1970s, federal support for basic research had fallen by 15 percent in constant dollars from 1968 to 1976. Between 1980 and 1984, the non-military share of Federal R&D funding fell by 30 percent. A 1981 NSF report noted that universities have not been provided with funds for basic infrastructure expenses, such as bricks and mortar, since the mid-1960s.[62] The university fiscal crisis has made the universities ever more dependent on the military. At the same time, the deterioration of those "have not" universities left out of the military trough (or without large endowments) strengthens the power and academic standing of those universities which maintain or increase their dependency on the Pentagon.

To better understand how these relationships encourage increased reliance on the military, we examine the case of a highly defense-dependent university (MIT) on the one hand, and a university struggling to increase its dependency on the other hand (University of Michigan). Dubbed "the second Pentagon" in the 1960s, MIT today still lives up to its former reputation as a major center for military research. Table 7-2 shows that from 1982 to 1986, Department of Defense contracts increased at MIT by 47 percent. A recent report prepared by a faculty-led committee at MIT gives us a rare look at how military spending has increased on a department-by-department basis at one of the country's top military-serving institutions (see Table 7-3). The consistent and heavy reliance of MIT on the three defense-serving agencies is also depicted in Figure 7-2. It shows the average annual share of support at the schools of science and engineering from these three national agencies.

Table 7-3: 1983 DOD Contracts at MIT

Dept. or Laboratory	Total Sponsored Expenditures	DOD Sponsored Expenditures	% DOD
Architecture	$1,345,130	$1,002,963	74.6
Aero-Astro (General)	$3,260	$3,249	99.7
Aero Physics Lab.	$4,729,891	$1,896,540	40.1
Chemistry	$8,798,428	$911,499	10.4
Earth & Planetary Science	$8,431,128	$1,468,987	17.4
Electrical Engineering	$2,549,445	$1,259,874	49.4
Mechanical Engineering	$5,882,507	$963,904	16.4
Material Sci. & Engineering	$6,288,759	$1,007,781	16.0
Ocean Engineering	$1,829,740	$942,697	51.5
Artificial Intelligence Lab.	$5,836,816	$4,544,097	77.9
Lab. for Information and Decision Systems	$1,931,106	$1,161,128	60.1
Computer Science Lab.	$7,420,259	$5,500,197	74.1
Mat. Processing Center	$2,972,771	$1,117,348	37.6
National Magnet Lab.	$8,776,574	$1,045,205	11.9
Research Lab. for Electronics	$10,505,804	$4,846,690	46.1
TOTAL	$77,241,618	$27,671,159	35.8

SOURCE: Ad Hoc Committee on the Military Presence at MIT, Massachusetts Institute of Technology, Cambridge, MA.

The central institution linking MIT to the military is Lincoln Laboratory, which was established in 1951 at the request of the Air Force. The Laboratory was called upon to develop the concepts and components that would become part of an integrated Continental Air Defense System. War planners sought such a system "to counter the threat posed by the development of the Soviet A-bomb." An FY 1985 budget at Lincoln Laboratory of $240 million was divided as follows: Air Force 43.5 percent, Army 30.4 percent, Defense Advanced Research Projects Agency 17.5 percent, Navy 4.3 percent, Federal Aviation Administration 3.9 percent and other organizations such as NASA .3 percent. Lincoln is responsible for projects researching strategic offense and defense, military satellite communications, space surveillance, high energy laser technology, sensors and communications, and advanced electronics. Lincoln Laboratory is connected to the larger university community through its financial support of faculty, students and research assistants and its subsidization of university-wide functions: "In addition to its overhead payments for services in *direct* support of its activities, Lincoln's payments for support services on campus (libraries, Medical Department, employee benefits, etc.) and for administrative costs were about $5.5 [million] in 1985."[63]

These payments reveal one of the many ways universities can become hooked on the military economy. The rise of large scale "research universities," like MIT, in part reflects the needs of large transnational corporations and the military for centers of basic research. At the same time, universities have grown in size and complexity, reflecting the expansion in secondary education, a projected need for detailed record and administrative control systems, and the expansion in advanced scientific laboratories and equipment. This expansion in the post-War era has led to increased administrative costs (or overhead) for universities.[64] While these costs may have stabilized in recent years, they represent a constant source of expenditures that must be met with revenues. By meeting overhead expenses for laboratories, equipment and general research and development, military contracts help universities meet these costs.[65] Universities become hooked on the military to meet their budgetary obligations.[66]

The Lincoln Laboratory example also illustrates the role which university military research plays in supporting direct military production of Pentagon weapons: "Its activities lie along a continuum that stretches from basic research, at one end, to consultation with manufacturers about the design of production prototypes, at the other."[67] This function is not unique to MIT. As a recent Defense Department report notes, one of the basic purposes of Pentagon sponsorship of universities is to "assist in transferring new technologies emerging from university research into industrial applications for both military and civilian uses."[68]

Like MIT, the University of Michigan (U of M) is attempting to broker technological expertise into Pentagon contracts. From 1982 to 1986, Defense expenditures at the University of Michigan at Ann Arbor rose by 40 percent (see Table 7-2). The impact and origins of such accelerated military spending were examined by the Committee for Non-Violent Research, based in Ann Arbor, Michigan. They undertook a detailed study of U of M's ties to the military-industrial complex. Their report, *Going for Broke: The University and the Military Industrial Complex*, provides many useful examples of how university relations with the Pentagon have developed in the 1980s. The University has attempted to use its technological expertise as the basis for a new entrepreneurial strategy. U of M is setting up new research institutes, linking it to military and corporate R&D programs. "Administrators are hacking chunks of money out of programs with little or no potential for attracting funds from military or industrial sponsors."[69] As part of this strategy the University hired George Gamota, former head of research administration at the Department of Defense, to direct the Institute of Science and Technology. The Geography Department was phased out and targets for budget cuts included the Institute of Labor Relations, the interdisciplinary Women's Studies program and the School of Art, Education and Natural Resources. U of M directed its funding towards engineering, business, economics and computer science departments, as well as the new Center for Robotics and Integrated Manufacturing (CRIM).[70]

Both CRIM and the Michigan Research Corporation (see Table 3-5) are examples of the University's attempts to expand its ties with the military-industrial system. In 1982, CRIM sought out a $7.2 million grant from the Air Force. In FY 1983, the Air Force sought to develop a $215.2 million program for manufacturing technology designed to increase productivity in defense industries and provide more managerial control of the workplace. The Air Force is trying to automate bomber and missile production. It is also interested in artificial intelligence to guide missiles and bombers. These technologies can be developed at robotics centers like CRIM and at off-campus research corporations such as Ann Arbor's Environmental Research Institute in Michigan (ERIM). ERIM is a leader in the development of artificial intelligence for military applications. "Some key ERIM personnel, including Chief Scientist Emmit Leith, hold faculty appointments at the University."[71]

Going for Broke also gives us an idea of the specific projects which faculty work on in military research contracts and their links to Pentagon war needs. One professor, George Haddad, performed computer simulation tests on various electronic device designs utilizing "diodes." According to his contract, the diodes were destined for use in missile guidance systems. Professor Thomas Senior and his assistants "use model airplanes covered with silver paint and a specially constructed chamber to simulate the electromagnetic conditions anticipated during a nuclear war."[72] This research is then turned over to the Air Force Weapons Laboratory at Kirtland Air Force Base. Professor Michael Parsons, Chairman of Naval Architecture & Marine Engineering, designed new control systems for "hunter-killer" attack submarines. Other faculty worked on sensing technology for the Navy's "Project Squid."[73] Table 7-4 lists Defense Department research projects at the University of Michigan in the twelve months preceding October 1981.

Concurrently, universities' fiscal crises and labor shortages further propel academia towards the Pentagon. First, the absence of military dollars might lead to a cyclical process of collapse for a university department. If there are no defense funds to keep faculty salaries competitive with industry (assuming the

Table 7-4: University of Michigan Defense Contracts: 1980-81 (a)

Rank	Department	Total No. of Projects	Total $ Value
1	Electrical & Computer Engineering	19	1,131,000
2	Aerospace Engineering	9	412,000
3	Industrial & Operations Engineering	9	236,000
4	Mechanical Engineering	5	231,000
5	Business School	5	223,000
6	Material Engineering	4	225,000
7	Architecture & Urban Planning	4	354,000
8	Institute of Social Research	4	305,000
9	Chemistry	4	189,000
10	Naval Architecture	3	43,000
11	Medical School	3	80,000
12	Engineering Administration	2	697,000 (b)
13	Mathematics	2	42,000
14	Physics	2	98,000
15	Natural Resources	1	50,000

(a) The table above ranks University of Michigan Departments by the number of Department of Defense Research projects received in the twelve-month period preceding October 1981.

(b) The Engineering Administration did not carry out research and development with these funds; rather, they coordinated the "Materials Research Council" for the Defense Advanced Research Projects Agency (DARPA).

SOURCE: *Going For Broke*, (Ann Arbor, MI: Committee for Non-Violent Research, 1982); University of Michigan Division of Research Development and Administration.

absence of large private endowments), a downward spiral would be expected in engineering education:

> A shrinking number of faculty members means fewer projects to sustain graduate students, and fewer graduate students means fewer faculty. As the number of people declines, a secondary spiral is touched off: research also declines. As research winds down, so do funds to support it; and as funds are withdrawn, research withers further.[74]

Meanwhile at MIT, a large recipient of defense funds, one might expect to see a reverse image of the negative feedback loop suggested above:

> Research instrumentation has grown sophisticated and research costs have risen sharply while there has been a severe and prolonged erosion in the condition of many university laboratories. As a result, quality research efforts have shifted to a limited number of superior laboratories which have sources of funding enabling them to keep up.[75]

Here, access to Pentagon dollars, together with sizeable real estate investments and the like, help reinforce the Institute's power and status. Those who get Pentagon dollars become "quality" institutions and as a result continue to get funding from the Defense Department or private industry.

7.5 No Bread, Just Bombs: The Economics of Conscription

Like the financial squeeze that has made military funds more attractive to academic researchers, economic pressures have also affected students pressed by the rising cost of education and limited civilian-linked funds to cover these costs. This pressure has made military scholarships and programs like the ROTC and Junior ROTC more attractive to students seeking to attend colleges and universities. In addition, institutional racism and class barriers keeping people of color caught in the "secondary labor market," low wage jobs or permanent un- or under-employment have combined with this financial squeeze to push blacks into military service.[76]

In August of 1985, the College Board released a report which showed that the cost of going to college was rising at nearly twice the estimated rate of inflation.[77] A later report published by the Board found that the cost of attending a private four-year college *as a percent of disposable income per capita* rose from 65.4 percent in the period 1980-81 to an estimated 71.9 percent for the 1984-85 period. For public four-year colleges the increase was less dramatic, a rise of 30.1 percent to an estimated 32.2 percent.[78]

The rising costs of higher education represent a problem for poor and middle class alike. But the divergence between the costliness of attending private versus public universities also suggests one means by which the poor and people of color are kept out of elite institutions or must look to other vehicles for escaping their low-income status. Decreasing income levels for blacks and Latinos have also raised the cost barrier of attending college (from 1979 to 1984 the mean income of black families with children decreased by 8.2 percent; for Latinos the corresponding figure was 8.9 percent).[79] Some universities have attempted to increase the financial aid available for such groups, but on the whole the *kinds* of aid that have become available in recent years have discouraged enrollment by the disenfranchised.

Note the percent change in total available aid from 1980-81 to 1984-85: grants decreased by 24.1 percent, work aid decreased by 20.03 percent but loan availability increased by 12.16 percent.[80] In fact, loans increased from 40.7 percent to an estimated 50.2 percent as a percent of total aid between these two time spans.[81] A comprehensive examination of federal student aid funding by the American Council on Education found that total student aid decreased by 12 percent from FY 1980 to 1987.[82]

How have these changes affected people of color and the poor? The growth of the civil rights movement and expansion in federal social welfare programs during the 1960s and early 1970s created strong incentives that encouraged participation by blacks in higher education. A report by the U.S. Department of Education found that:

> by 1975, the percent of Black high school graduates who enrolled in college was the same as that for whites (although high school graduation rates were still lower for Blacks than whites).

Also, during the first half of the 1970s, 10 percent of full-time undergraduates were black, "about the same proportion as they comprised of all high school graduates 18 to 24 years old."

However, during the last half of the 1970s the number of blacks enrolled in college remained about the same although the number of black youths eligible for college increased by about 20 percent. By 1980, many of the favorable trends of increasing black enrollment had reversed (see Table 7-5).[83]

The reversal depicted here stems in large part from the changing political climate which has made attending college increasingly burdensome for the poor. An August 1985 report in *The Chronicle of Higher Education* explained that one reason for the decline in the proportion of black high-school graduates was that "the amount of federal student aid available has fluctuated, and limitations have been placed on who can apply for aid, even as college tuitions have increased substantially."[84] Cutbacks in aid and tuition inflation have also made attendance at historically black colleges increasingly difficult.[85]

Table 7-5: Changing College Enrollment Patterns in the 1970s
Blacks Aged 18-24 Enrolled in College

Year	Number	% of Black high school graduates
1970	416,000	26
1975	665,000	32
1980	688,000	28

NOTE: The percent of white high school graduates aged eighteen to twenty-four enrolled in college remained at 32 percent in 1970, 1975 and 1980.

SOURCE: U.S. Department of Commerce, Bureau of the Census, Current Population Reports, *School Enrollment - Social and Economic Characteristics of Students*, Series P-20, Nos. 222, 303 and 362, as cited by Susan T. Hill, "Participation of Black Students in Higher Education: A Statistical Profile from 1970-71 to 1980-81," *Integrated Education*, Vol. 22, Nos. 1-3, Winter 1984.

Such changing economic patterns have diverse roots, but federal policies have encouraged students to rely more heavily on the military as a job ladder as well as a source of education and employment. A news story in 1981 reported:

> Although the federal government has reduced the number of grants and loans given to college students by the Department of Education, more money will be available to students participating in the Reserve Officer Training Corps this fall.

In exchange for an eight-year commitment to ROTC, participants in the program receive army scholarships, the majority for the two final years of college, that cover tuition, books and a subsistence stipend of $1,000 a year. By 1987, the Army ROTC had become increasingly competitive in commissioning new officers and calling them to active duty:

> The competition for choice active duty assignments results from a combination of fewer places in the Army for younger officers and an increase in applications for ROTC scholarships as the cost of education rises and the reservoir of financial aid shrinks.

In 1981, 8,500 ROTC scholarships were awarded, 2,000 more than the year before. In 1980, Congress approved doubling the ceiling on army scholarships, from 6,500 to 12,000. The number of Navy and Air Force ROTC scholarships was also increased.[86] Figure 7-3 depicts the fall in Senior ROTC enrollment by the early 1970s, and a slow but steady increase since then. As seen in Figure

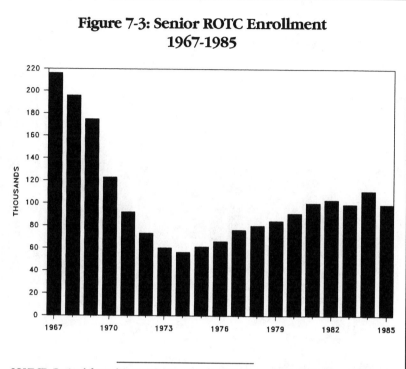

Figure 7-3: Senior ROTC Enrollment 1967-1985

SOURCE: Derived from data in U.S. Department of Defense, *Selected Manpower Statistics*, annual; and *Military Manpower Statistics*, monthly, as published in U.S. Bureau of the Census, *Statistical Abstract of the United States*, various years, Washington, D.C.

7-4, Junior ROTC enrollment has experienced a steady rise since the late 1960s, increasing most rapidly in the early 1980s.[87]

In addition to the rising costs of education and decreased parental income levels, high levels of unemployment among poor and predominantly Latino and black youth have made the military an attractive proposition. Data from the Bureau of Labor Statistics show that the unemployment rate for black males aged 16 to 24 has consistently been greater than 20 percent throughout the 1980s.[88] At the same time, the turn of the decade and the early 1980s saw an acceleration in the already rapid growth of the percent of blacks in the armed forces (see Figure 7-5). The increasing participation rates of blacks in the military threaten to repeat the pattern by which the poor serve as cannon fodder for the Pentagon planners and the warfare state.[89]

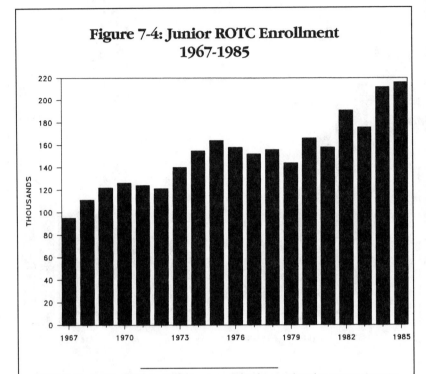

Figure 7-4: Junior ROTC Enrollment 1967-1985

SOURCE: Derived from data in U.S. Department of Defense, *Selected Manpower Statistics*, annual; and *Military Manpower Statistics*, monthly, as published in U.S. Bureau of the Census, *Statistical Abstract of the United States*, various years, Washington, D.C.

7.6 The University Military Lobby: Academia's Political Commitment to the War Economy

The leading defense-dependent universities are not neutral parties which sit back and let Pentagon money fall on them from above; they are not passive actors, mere victims of the Pentagon assault to increase its managerial power, authority and control over institutions of higher learning. A complex pattern has emerged in which dependency on the military has brought its own rewards, rewards described by historians such as David Noble who point to the incentive structure which emerged in World War II. The universities have not been shy about asking the Pentagon for more money. Senator Stennis put the matter bluntly in 1969: "at some of our Appropriations Committee hearings, we see where these universities come down here fighting tooth and nail to get that

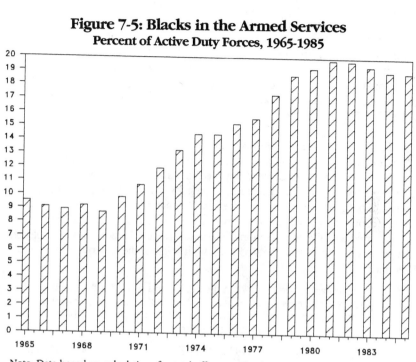

Figure 7-5: Blacks in the Armed Services
Percent of Active Duty Forces, 1965-1985

Note: Data based on calculations for total officers and enlisted personnel. Calculations for 1979 and 1980 based on male population only.

SOURCE: Derived from data in the U.S. Department of Commerce, U.S. Bureau of the Census, Statistical Abstract of the United States, 1970, 1974, 1976, 1979, 1982, 1986, U.S. Department of Commerce, Washington, D.C.

money."[90] As discussed earlier, the universities seek to increase their social power and control by amassing technical resources and research capital. Insofar as they are able to get such capital, the war academics take their share of the spoils and complacently fill their niche in the military division of labor.

The institutions behind the current face of the university-military alliance are based in part on these incentives of money and power which Pentagon largess brings, as well as long historical patterns of defense contracts and associations connecting the Pentagon, national security planners, directors of defense firms and university trustees. The DOD-University Forum grew out of Defense Science Board (see Section 6.5 above) recommendations that there was a need to restore a "healthier and more vital relationship between D.O.D. and the university community." The Forum was established to "allow periodic consultations between senior university representatives and D.O.D. officials on the full range of research-related needs and issues that affect the Department's ties with universities." The organization of the Forum reveals the full extent to which the academic establishment is locked in to the interests of Pentagon planners. The Forum is jointly sponsored by the Defense Department and three higher education associations: the Association of American Universities, the National Association of State Universities and Land Grant Colleges, and the American Council on Education. Forum members are drawn equally from the Defense Department and the university community (see Appendix Four).

In recent years the Forum has been concerned with the deterioration of the engineering and scientific capabilities of the United States and has recommended the "development of university programs in Defense-related technologies," the expansion of new appropriations for scientific instruments and laboratories as well as increased funding by the Defense Department and civilian programs for university research. Given the military's large influence in the economy as a whole, it is not surprising that the Pentagon should be concerned with the deterioration of the infrastructure. Thus, the Forum's official reports reflect the Pentagon's concern with shaping the destiny of the civilian economy:

> DOD has an important stake in the quality and supply of the national pool of engineers and scientists. Since DOD exerts a substantial influence over the entire system, it has a leadership responsibility to address the current crisis in engineering and science education.[91]

A counterpart to the DOD-University Forum is the work of the University Research Initiative (URI). URI participants include the Army, Navy, Air Force and the Defense Advanced Research Projects Agency (DARPA). URI also is concerned with the shortage of faculty qualified to teach certain "state-of-the-art technologies," obsolete research instrumentation, and the declining number of American citizens pursuing science and engineering graduate degrees. In seeking to address these problems, URI works to improve the:

> quality of research performed at universities to meet defense needs; to strengthen multidisciplinary research which supports selected key defense technologies; to provide expanded opportunities for interactions between universities and the DOD research and engineering community, particularly the laboratories of the three services.

The URI also promotes the military control of the physical and labor resources needed to advance defense technologies by supporting fellowships and investments in major pieces of research equipment at universities.

The URI provides yet another example of the extension of Pentagon managerialism into the university. It also indicates the desperation of universities for Pentagon money. A report in the July 1986 issue of *Science* described a Defense Department announcement of receipt of 963 proposals for research under the new program. If the Pentagon had accepted all of them, it would have cost about $6 billion. However, a still considerable sum of $110 million *was* to be distributed by defense scientists for eighty-six projects at seventy universities in the program's first year.[92] The value of the requests was roughly sixty times the value of those receiving aid. In other words, many more scientists are thinking about and shaped by defense funding than actually get it. For those who don't get defense funding there may be pressures to re-orient their research so that it better meets Pentagon requirements the next time around.[93]

The Defense Department's concern for the deterioration of U.S. engineering capacity, labor shortages and the quality of high schools might be considered admirable by some. However, it is the greatest irony that the military has chosen to take a leadership role in confronting these problems. If any one institution could be singled out for its role in the deterioration of U.S. industrial competence and the brain-drain in U.S. universities, it would be the Department of Defense. But even if the Pentagon were to "rescue" the universities, this act would not promise renewal for the economy as a whole. It is important to explore the shortcomings of Pentagon "industrial policy" in order to put to rest the myth that economic benefits of Pentagon aid for the universities outweighs its costs.

Military-dependent academics have evolved several rationales to justify their connections to the military. A first line of defense is the claim that their work is important to the "national interest." In reality this has meant that the role of such academics in the military division of labor has made them accessories in the expansion of the warfare state and has helped legitimate its power and authority. When this political appeal begins to falter, as it did during the Vietnam War, the economic case is made that military-sponsored R&D helps aid technological development and the nation's industrial base. The belief that military research is justified by its fostering of spinoffs, useful technologies for the civilian economy, is one of the key ideological claims made by military-dependent academia. But this claim is belied on the whole by the limited number of commercial spinoffs generated by such military research. Military-serving R&D has retarded the civilian economy by diverting resources, narrowing the scope of scientific inquiry and distorting the development of technology.[94]

On the most elementary level the bloated defense budget explains what happened to monies which might have gone to laboratories, teaching facilities and equipment, higher salaries for instructors, increased fellowships for scientists and their students. Scientists and engineers employed by the Pentagon and its supporting enterprises are offered salaries and conditions of work often unmatched by the rest of the civilian economy. This has helped draw large numbers away from industry and academia.[95] As noted earlier, 65 percent of Federal R&D is sponsored by the military; this represents a vast diversion of resources which could enhance civilian industrial productivity as well as increase our capacity to address social problems such as the inequitable distribution of housing, health care and educational resources.

More subtle is the limiting effect the Defense Department has on the development of scientific knowledge. First, talent is funneled into research investigations which have as their first priority narrow military objectives. By rewarding investigations of limited scope, the Pentagon helps encourage "over-specialization." Government secrecy and this narrow scope of investigation "retard the process of inquiry and distort engineering applications to such an extent that civilian uses of the research are limited," hence an insignificant number of spinoffs for civilian industry result.[96]

Other factors help explain the limited number of such spinoffs. The applicability of military funded research to civilian research needs declines each step up the research and development ladder, from basic research all the way up to engineering development. This hierarchy is apparent in the vertical organization of RDT&E, the Research, Development, Test and Evaluation program of the military:

> Many of the concepts enter the system at the Basic Research (6.1) level, where fundamental investigations into the nature of Basic Research processes are conducted. Successful completion of a 6.1 program frequently leads to Exploratory Development (6.2) in which the proven concept is used in or applied to some device having potential military application. This is sometimes called the "breadboard stage." The Advanced Development (6.3) stage follows, during which a prototype or "brassboard" of a specific system or subsystem is built and tested as a confirmation of the successful 6.1 and 6.2 research. Finally, Engineering Development (6.4) reconfigures the successful prototype in preparation for production, should circumstances require it.[97]

Each step up this ladder leads to inquiries or product ideas likely to be of less utility to the civilian economy as the research program becomes increasingly wedded to the requirements of military production: scientific inquiry is narrowed, other questions are not asked. With this in mind, two questions emerge: First, how much does the Pentagon allocate its resources to the lower rungs of the ladder? Second, how have commitments to the lower versus higher rungs of the ladder changed over time? On the first point, Berkeley economist Jay Stowsky observes that:

> only about 2 percent of the Pentagon's R&D money is slated for basic research, and less than 20 percent will go to research and development of base technologies most likely to produce commercial spinoffs that could enhance U.S. competitiveness in world markets.[98]

On the second question, Robert Krinsky has found that university commitments to the higher rungs of the ladder have *increased* in recent years (see Appendix Five).[99]

Military-dependent academics will still argue that military research and development has led to important discoveries like radar. But current trends suggest a growing divergence between military and commercial applications of defense-sponsored research. For example, in laser technology sponsored by the military, the commercial applications are constricted: "Nearly all of SDI's X-ray laser research aims at extremely high-powered, application-specific uses; indeed, the typical Star Wars laser must be powered by a nuclear explosion."[100] If such research areas are pursued (and funded) specifically with civilian applications in mind, they are more likely to produce commercial applications. In the case of lasers, the Japanese are doing just this, funding private commercial research into lasers with immediate civilian uses, e.g. semiconductor diode lasers that can power compact-disc players.[101]

The secrecy of Pentagon research also places constraints on the diffusion of basic research into the world of commercial applications. Firms are less likely to produce civilian products suggested by academic research as a significant number of engineers and the nation's production capacity have become wedded to the military economy.[102]

On many occasions, the Pentagon has had a direct regressive effect on commercial development and/or use of a new technology. For example, numerically-controlled machine tools (a computer-based technology for automating industrial production developed by the Air Force and MIT scientists in the post-War era) were made less accessible to the commercial world. David Noble shows that military influence in the development of numerical control made it virtually inaccessible to firms engaged in cost-minimizing activities,[103] i.e., firms not supported by government subsidies that must drive-down their expenses to remain competitive. Among the array of possible developments in numerical control technology, an alliance of interests promoted those designs which were of such high price and cost as to make them unaffordable to most firms. This technological catastrophe was encouraged by an electrical engineering department at MIT which wanted to advance technologies whose complexity increased its authority and prestige. MIT was joined by large U.S. machine tool firms which sought major war-related orders that stabilized short-run production and Air Force Generals who preferred technologies better suited to weapons production than civilian needs. These narrow economic and political interests retarded the American development and diffusion of a major cost-saving technology.

Military influence also places an "exaggerated emphasis on capital intensive methods and automation" that accounts for decreases in the reliability of industrial systems and also eliminates "irreplaceable human skills."[104] Recent research by Earl Yang at Columbia's Department of Industrial Engineering and Operations Research has shown that in the thirty years since the late 1940s, both military spending and federal expenditures on R&D (which are dominated by defense outlays) have been *negatively correlated* with a measure of productivity relating changes in capital and labor output.[105] One could infer from Yang's research that increased military funding for university research will not halt the U.S. productivity decline.

Progress in civilian technology should lead to more capital being deployed per worker. Together with a supporting system of cost minimization, the extension of capital investments should raise both capital and labor productivity through the development of production techniques which utilize resources more efficiently.[106] However, the military operates on a system of cost maximization which slows down U.S. productivity.

The military firm operates under a cost-plus system in which payment by the Pentagon to military contractors is based on a guaranteed profit rate. An accompanying system of subsidy maximization, in which government funds are transferred to defense firms, also removes competitive pressure on firms by allowing them to pay higher prices for inputs. As a result, the firm has little or no incentive to depress costs. As Lloyd J. Dumas explains, "to the extent that the firm wants to increase sales revenue, it will have a very powerful incentive to run its costs up in order to achieve the highest possible payment for its product."[107] This cost maximizing system is not self-contained within the military but has spread like a cancer throughout industry. The Pentagon has provided a blank check and guaranteed market for military production. As a result, the military firm is able to pay inflated rates for material and labor resources. Dumas also argues that this collapse of competition also bids up costs which *other* firms pay for scientists, machine tools and the like.[108]

Cost and subsidy maximization, together with the "brain drain," which funnels leading scientists and engineers into the military, have helped keep the United States behind nations like West Germany and Japan in measures of capital and labor productivity. A study appearing in a 1986 issue of the *Lloyds Bank Review* reinforces these conclusions by noting that both Britain and the United States, which over the years have spent much more than other nations on military research, also have a tendency to score low in a measure of economic competitiveness developed by the Organization for Economic Cooperation and Development.[109] Therefore, the university's contribution to the military will *contribute* to the economic decline of the United States by fostering the military-economy.

The military's efforts to renew on-campus projects, such as ROTC and CIA activity, have met less resistance since the collapse of the student and faculty anti-war protests after the Vietnam War. In recent years, renewed campus activism has begun to change this, providing some obstacles to the expansion of universities' links to the military. In response to student protests against university complicity in the Vietnam War effort, many military research centers severed their ties to universities; they created off-campus autonomous research organizations.[110] For example, the Riverside Research Institute, which designs nuclear weapons in New York City, once was part of Columbia University. The Environmental Research Institute of Michigan (ERIM), a mainstay in the Pentagon's Electronic Warfare program, split off from the University of Michigan in 1972. In some university towns, more research is conducted by such off-campus research institutes than by the university itself.[111] The Columbia University student strike of 1968 made the University's ties to the military and CIA a major issue. The strike, together with growing illegitimacy of the Vietnam War, pressured University officials to sever some of their ties to military projects. In 1972, after five years of organizing, peace activists at the University of Michigan forced that university's regents to ban all research which might lead to the destruction of human life.[112]

The Pentagon's renewed interest in on-campus military research is based partially on the belief that universities are no longer centers of radical agitation. A Pentagon Defense Science Board report in 1981 stated this view:

> Fortunately the universities' attitudes today are different from those of the Vietnam era. The tensions between the Defense Department and the universities, which characterized that era, have diminished and the universities are receptive to positive actions to restore the strength of that relationship and to augment their research capabilities.[113]

ROTC programs also expanded with the decline of the anti-war movement in 1975. A Pentagon report in 1981 glowed over the revival of ROTC on campuses since the end of the Vietnam War. Lt. Col. James P. Hunt, a coordinator of Army ROTC programs, argued that the "overriding" reason for the enrollment increase was a decline in antiwar sentiments among students since the Vietnam War era. "Many of these kids don't remember Vietnam," he said. "We're getting Vietnam behind us, and we're getting a more patriotic group of kids that want to serve."[114] According to a February 1984 report in *The Progressive,* "the CIA is enjoying a remarkable renaissance in American college campuses. Gone is the militant protest, gone is the stigma." A CIA officer, knowledgeable about recruitment efforts, noted that "students seem to be more responsive" than they were even five years ago, "and more are applying, certainly." The Agency now recruits openly on 300 campuses. Like the ROTC, the CIA links its new fortunes to an "increased" level of patriotism. Said the CIA officer, "I've gotten an awful lot of that," and added that "the anti-CIA demonstrations on campus have dramatically declined."[115] All this enthusiasm for growing patriotism came before a dramatic rise in radical student activism, which hit campuses in the Spring of 1985.

8

A Disarmament Strategy for the University

8.1 Challenging the Academic-Military-Industrial Complex: A Movement Begins

The previous chapters have discussed how transnational and state actors, supported by university resources, project militarism and underdevelopment at home and abroad. Corporate campaigns represent an organizing strategy designed to gain leverage on *transnational* actors linked to intervention in Central America. A separate strategy is needed to weaken universities' ties to the *state* militarist system. This strategy must address the various ways in which the university community and youth outside academia become conscripted or co-opted into service of the warfare state.

The anti-intervention movement has attempted to challenge the specific regional intervention in Central America primarily through general public education, lobbying campaigns aimed at Congress, national demonstrations and direct actions designed to raise the cost of maintaining current state policy. However, this political program has thus far failed to challenge the institutional bases of intervention and underdevelopment. As a result, the institutions (and causal system) which lie behind the imperial order continue operating unchallenged and unimpeded.

To successfully challenge the war-making institutions requires political campaigns which address the supporting pillars of the larger system. In order to deny the military machine the resources of the university (and other defense contractors) some form of planning or "counter-planning" is needed. Before elaborating how such a strategy could evolve, we review some of the recent history of student and faculty resistance to the encroachment of military power on campus.

The growing movement against intervention in Central America has encouraged several waves of protests against CIA recruitment on campus. One of the first protests took place in March 1984 when nineteen students were detained and one non-student was arrested at Cornell University. A later demonstration at Tufts University in October gained national attention. About fifteen students lined up in front of the recruiter, placing themselves between him and other students. In response to administration attempts to punish the protestors, Tufts students organized a collective defense and distributed literature which defended their actions as justified in light of the CIA's use of repression abroad. Their efforts led to a mass meeting of students at a disciplinary hearing for the original CIA protestors. The protestors got the Tufts administration to agree that they would place an "injunction on CIA recruitment" before an official policy on recruitment was decided. This concession came at a heavy price to the administration; the Associated Press and local media picked up the story and suggested that student protests had forced the University to stop CIA recruitment. Later statements made by Tufts president Jean Mayer that the CIA was never actually barred did not effectively counter the press' original version.

By November, the CIA anti-recruitment effort was a strong force at Brown University. Students there disrupted an appearance by CIA recruiters by attempting to put them under citizens' arrest. The Brown action, like the one at Tufts, was picked up by the national media and helped to spread the protests to other schools. Brown had also gained national attention with a student vote which asked the University to stock suicide pills, in the event of nuclear war.

The student actions at Cornell, Tufts and Brown helped generate a cycle of protest at other universities, taking anti-CIA demonstrations to the University of Michigan at Ann Arbor, University of Massachusetts at Amherst, Grinnell in Iowa and other schools. More actions occured in 1986. At a 1986 demonstration at the University of Colorado about 125 police officers in riot gear used mace, clubs and German shepherds to battle some 300 students protesting CIA recruitment.[1]

The expansive Star Wars program has also led to efforts, by students and faculty, to oppose military-directed activities on campus. The program has provoked widespread opposition among physicists who feel it is ill-conceived, unfeasible and dangerous. Opponents of SDI include fifteen Nobel laureates who contend that the impenetrable defense against ballistic missiles, as described by President Reagan in March 1983, is technically impossible.[2] A central focus of organizing efforts against Star Wars has been the circulation of a petition in universities across the nation asking scientists eligible to receive funds "neither to solicit nor accept SDI support."

A report on Star Wars opposition in the May 21, 1986 issue of *The*

Chronicle of Higher Education noted that over 6,500 scientists, engineers and graduate students had signed the pledge since it was launched in the summer of 1985. The SDI boycott has spread to over 110 research institutions in forty-one states. The *Chronicle* report noted that the pledge's signers included 57 percent of the faculty at the nation's twenty top-ranked physics departments. Professor Zellman Warshaft, an electrical engineer at Cornell University, observed that scientists and engineers have never organized so extensively to boycott the development of a specific weapons system.[3]

The pledge has helped weaken a campaign by the Pentagon to use universities to broaden political support for SDI in Congress and the public at large. Mike Weissman, a physicist at the University of Illinois and original drafter of the pledge, notes how the tables have been turned on the Pentagon:

> What we *have* done is we've turned it around. With such a large number of scientists opposing the project, we have generated a tremendous amount of negative advertising. I think that we have been very successful in reaching the general public. I know we are reaching Congress.[4]

However, despite the success represented by the SDI boycott, there are a number of problems with the campaign. As stated in "A Status Report on the Boycott of Star Wars Research by Academic Scientists and Engineers," authored by four of the pledge's originators:

> The pledge of non-participation is an individual statement by researchers not to participate in Star Wars research. In particular, it does not request university administrators to impose a blanket ban on Star Wars research.

Oscar Hernandez, who was a leader in the boycott at Harvard, has observed that "the natural step of working for a complete boycott of all SDI research on campus is being avoided."[5] According to a poll taken at Cornell University in 1986, of 111 faculty members in twelve departments who signed the pledge, 52 percent have received, currently receive or are looking for research funding from the Defense Department.[6]

In contrast to the pledge, a more comprehensive stand against the military's influence in the university was taken by national science groups during the height of opposition to the Vietnam War. In 1968, the Federation of American Scientists adopted a resolution which declared:

> Except in time of national emergency, the university should not be a part of the military establishment and should not directly or indirectly take part in military operations or participate in the collection of military intelligence. The university should not enter into any contract supporting research the specific purpose of which is the development of weapons or devices designed to destroy human life or to incapaci-

tate human beings, nor should it provide administrative services for
government weapons laboratories. For example, it is inappropriate for
the University of California to lend its name and implicit endorsement
to the weapons laboratories at Livermore and Los Alamos.[7]

This statement has lost neither its urgency nor relevancy today. It serves as a
standard for any current efforts designed to weaken academia's links to the
warfare state.

The opposition to the spread of Star Wars-related research in the university
and anti-CIA protests, like the movements for divestment and against institutional racism, hold open the possibility of a larger effort to challenge university
links to interventionism and the warfare state. Together with increased military
research funding on campus, these movements have helped rekindle an interest
in university ties to the war machine. This interest has been broadened by
student and faculty conferences examining the military's role on campus. At
MIT, student and faculty efforts led to a report examining the extent to which
military-linked funding had changed the character of the university's research.[8]

Movements like the campus CIA and SDI protests have been a concern
to national leaders concerned with political stability in an era of increasingly
militarized universities. At Congressional hearings in 1982 which examined
proposed increases in defense spending for university-military contracts, the
question of student reaction still lingered in Congressman Courter's mind. He
asked then University of California president David Saxon (now Chair of MIT)
whether:

> in view of the fact that there is a growing debate in the United States
> as to the proper role of this government vis-à-vis El Salvador, if
> [Department of Defense] money is sent to universities for research and
> development, do you anticipate any type of student involvement or
> university involvement by way of activities against universities par-
> ticipating in research and development?[9]

Saxon's reply was that students of today are different than the students of the
1960s.

Courter's concern has been matched by campus administrators' attempts
to resist political disruption which has challenged warfare state policy. In the
New Left period, police were deployed against protestors challenging
universities' military links at Columbia University, the University of Wisconsin
and other campuses.[10] More recently, over 100 university lawyers and administrators met in a conference on "Universities and South Africa: Divestment and
Campus Disruption" in Washington, D.C. held in September 1985. The gather-
ing, sponsored by the National Association of College and University Attorneys,
included officials from South Africa, the U.S. State Department and Mobil Oil.
One topic discussed was how to block anti-apartheid sit-ins and shanty towns.
An attorney representing Virginia State University suggested that legal maneu-

vers based on the university's property rights would be useful to get around students' "free speech protections." Other lawyers said that campus regulations and disciplinary procedures did not require "due process" and should be used against activist students.[11]

However, despite the optimism of university leaders like Saxon, students have begun to make explicit links between universities and the role which corporations play in shaping U.S. relations with Central America. In February 1986, about 100 students at the University of California at Berkeley successfully disrupted recruitment efforts by military contractors tied to the supply of weapons used by the Salvadoran military. In January 1987, students at Columbia University handed out mock-recruitment flyers when the W.R. Grace Company came to recruit at their school. The flyers described Grace's efforts in assisting the contras and detailed the the contras' role in terrorizing Nicaragua.[12]

8.2 Movement Strategy and the War-Making Institutions

The peace and anti-intervention movements face the dual burden of constricting the power of the warfare state and military economy on the one hand, and on the other providing their participants with a strategy in which some short-term victories are possible.

Operationally, the anti-intervention movement has been organized around such short-term goals as winning specific military aid votes or stopping the warfare state's particular regional intervention in Central America. The short-term nature of the movement is not limited to the problem of adjusting actions to Congressional timetables. An additional problem is that the particular focus on the U.S. government's intervention in the region has come at the cost of a qualitatively different educational effort which is necessary to successfully challenge the warfare state. The same could be said of the narrow focus found in the protests against CIA recruitment and Star Wars research.

Certainly, a movement that directly attacks the warfare state is bound to breed cynicism and despair if it is not linked to more modest targets or activities which make people conscious of their political power. In another context, peace activist Lisa Peatie has explained the necessity of short-term actions:

> To put an end to the nuclear arms race requires much more basic changes than putting an end to the Vietnam war, and some of the peace movement's current state of deflation may well be the outcome of the massive efforts at public education which have gone before. People realize what they are up against, and turn away at the enormity of the project. If one cannot see what to do, it is not unreasonable to do nothing...

Peatie rightly asserts that "movements need victories or they die." As a result, "the peace movement has to find specific victories it can win."[13]

On the other hand, short-term actions can easily let the larger political institutions, such as the various components of the warfare state, off the hook. By failing to attack the system which lies behind the immediate targets, the anti-intervention movement also risks defeatism by shlepping activists through a series of protests that leave centralized power intact:

> Even a series of successes in unlinked short-term operations can leave the war-making institutions with their decision power intact: their budgets, their organization, and especially the ideological support system. Recall that the test-ban treaty was accompanied by agreements with the Joint Chiefs of Staff to make available more funds, more manpower for nuclear weapons development. So *after* the partial (atmospheric) test-ban treaty was signed, there was more nuclear weapons testing than ever before.[14]

This problem is not limited to the anti-nuclear movement. As discussed in Chapter Six, reliance on particular piecemeal legislation to slow the tide of intervention against Nicaragua has proven contradictory. Even with the first legislative victory against contra aid, covert assistance to the contras continued as did massive military maneuvers in the Caribbean which maintain Honduras as a garrison state.

Some political organizations on the Left have operated a cottage industry based on selling "the lessons of the 1960s." But most have missed this major shortfall of the New Left and the movement against the Vietnam War: a limited ability to link short-term actions to an overall strategy designed to diminish the size and scope of the warfare state. Thus, one pamphlet circulated prior to mass demonstrations in Washington and San Francisco in April 1987 explained that:

> The strategy that has worked most effectively in the past to end or reverse bad government policies has been the continuous mobilization of thousands of people in the streets protesting in an organized and disciplined manner.[15]

National demonstrations were powerful tools against the War in Vietnam. However, they did not eliminate, permanently weaken or transform the institutions that supported the War. In 1971, Norman Fruchter, a movement activist explained that while increasing numbers of protestors provided political leverage, the centralized power of the state was still left unchallenged. In view of the romanticism and revisionism applied to these demonstrations, it is worth quoting his comments at length:

> Instead of confronting the question of power, we have continued to play out a series of strategies which are actually attempts to persuade power to change its mind, through demonstrations of our numbers or

the intensity of our convictions. What we have done, for six years, amounts to different forms of petitioning. The mass demonstration is a way of saying, to the executive as well as to the nation via the mass media, that all these numbers of people want the war to end: it is a way of indicating the strength of opposition through a show of numbers. That is why the numbers game *feels* so crucial in every mass demonstration, for the real meaning of the event lies only in attendance...Individual acts of resistance, group acts of resistance, like burning draft cards or draft files, even the destruction of government or corporate property are all symbolic protest which indicate, to power, the intensity of conviction and increasing cost, in terms of social stability, of continuing the war. Power still makes the choice, and always chooses new forms of repression against the symbolic protestors...All of our tactics, developed over the past six years, have actually been different attempts to use our numbers or the intensity of our convictions as a way to persuade power to withdraw.[16]

The New Left student movement *was* successful in weakening universities' links to the military in the 1960s and 70s.[17] Scientists were freer to express their political views and devote their knowledge to peaceful purposes. But the regional military complexes which now surround elite technical universities across the country are a serious reminder that a broader strategy is needed to confront the Pentagon, involving not only students but faculty, community supporters and perhaps administrators on campus as well.

The point is not to dismiss all protests which have a narrow objective. Rather, what is required for an effective anti-intervention and peace movement today is the combination of short-term actions that are part of a long-run process that pares back the power of the warfare state. Thus, short-run actions must build the base for a political movement with larger objectives. As Seymour Melman argues, the gains from short-term campaigns:

> are not consolidated because the various peace organizations do not usually accompany action on single issues with background analysis of the origins of the issues, and explanation of linkage to further actions and their relation to the power-wielding of the war-making institutions.[18]

Similarly, Noam Chomsky observes that popular opposition to the arms race, and the anti-intervention and related movements are

> typically spontaneous, decentralized, rising and declining rapidly, oriented towards specific issues. Invariably, dissidence begins from no organized base and leaves no lasting structure within which the public can become informed and active.[19]

8.3 Conversion and Disarmament Coalitions: Broadening the Base of the Anti-Intervention Movement

Coalition efforts which link disarmament and anti-intervention activity to movements for economic justice, development and redistribution represent an alternative to the fragile political culture represented by the movement activities Chomsky describes. The creation of these coalitions depends nationally on greater public support for economic conversion, planning for disarmament of the covert operation infrastructure and a political program which links alternative national budgetary priorities to the civilian development of military defense laboratories, bases, training institutions and industrial establishments.

Economic conversion is the political, economic and technical process for assuring an orderly transformation of labor, machinery and other resources now being used for military-oriented purposes to alternative civilian uses.[20] By mobilizing in support of conversion and raising questions about how an alternative national budget could provide civilian alternatives to the warfare state, traditional peace and anti-intervention activists can build bridges to labor, community and professional groups. These groups are often disenfranchised by the military economy and would benefit from the conversion of military resources. Political actions in universities and other local institutions with investment or political ties to intervention will also help create the political space required to sustain movement activities. This is one hope for an expanded focus on university complicity in intervention *and* production for the warfare state.

Why is the university a useful starting point for both anti-intervention and conversion efforts? Organizing in the universities can provide political leverage over larger social institutions, as seen by the role that university disarmament campaigns played in building the strength of the larger anti-Vietnam War movement. Such leverage creates the objective basis for victories needed to convince movement participants of their own power. The universities are also a natural base for organizing given the large number of progressive academics and students in the anti-intervention movement itself. There is a natural logic to mobilizations that build upon the groups and networks created by institutions such as schools, trade union halls, churches and more informal meeting grounds such as dormitories and bars.

A few radical sociologists and historians have explored how "free institutional space" has played "a central role in emerging group consciousness among oppressed groups."[21] Central among these theorists is peace activist and historian E.P. Thompson who has written about "the semi-autonomous working-class structures in which workers could experiment with new ideas and form a new sense of themselves."[22] The university has become politicized in the past[23] partly because it has generated this political space. For example, in the New Left student movement, protestors seeking political leverage through disruption looked to the university:

> The exigencies of mass action are such that they were constrained to act out their defiance within the universities where they were physically located and could thus act collectively, and where they played a role on which an institution depended, so that their defiance mattered.[24]

Such locally-based actions translated into direct leverage on the warfare state by helping break down the consensus for U.S. participation in Vietnam. On the other hand, as suggested by critics like Chomsky and Melman, these forms of protest can often encourage the provincial and limited political focus which precludes long-term strategies such as conversion and public education about the warfare state. Thus, protests which focus solely on recruitment and investment policies are likely to leave the university's military research capability intact. A successful action, when it is completed, should be the starting point for a direct attack on the support systems of the warfare state.

University-based campaigns are uniquely placed to challenge other manifestations of the warfare state which may be spatially concentrated in the university itself, e.g., the propagation of arms control ideology, the basic research capacity for the military and the provision of labor for the military machine. University-corporate connections can be used by campus activists to reach out to church groups, opposition movements in Central America and campaigns to divest municipal funds from TNCs sending weapons to Central America. Many of the companies linked to intervention in Central America also support apartheid through their investments in South Africa (see Appendix One). Common action against these corporations can help link the anti-apartheid movement and Central America solidarity activists. A university conversion effort can also be used to mobilize students, faculty and local communities in support of broader state and national conversion legislation.

The conversion of the military economy is central to anti-intervention objectives. Conversion can help reduce the scope of the military budget and associated economic and political institutions which make military intervention more likely. By contracting the military economy through conversion, legislators, trade unions and businesses can become less wedded to the militaristic rhetoric and politics that help promote intervention. The economic dependency of local regions on the defense budget helps explain why ninety-seven of the House members who voted for a nuclear freeze in Congress, also voted for the MX missile program.[25] As each constituency group finds economic alternatives to military capital (through economic conversion), they are less likely to support the warfare economy.

Conversion planning could contribute to a process whereby the U.S. economy becomes less reliant on exploitative economic relations with the Third World. By freeing up resources from the military economy, conversion can assist in the renewal of the technological and productive base of the domestic economy. If local establishments become more competent in producing the many goods now supplied by foreign businesses, more domestic jobs will be created and TNCs will become less reliant on cheap labor abroad. This will make relations of dependency between the U.S. and the Third World less important because TNCs will have less need for maintaining repressive regimes that keep wages low. In addition, by expanding the base of domestic employment (through a U.S. "import substitution") the spending power of U.S. workers will increase. Conversion, then, is part of a "domestic reflation" strategy, making overseas markets less important, and thereby weakening corporate incentive for overseas intervention.[26]

8.4 Economic Conversion: An Alternative to Academic Dependency on the Military

The growing reliance of universities, faculty and students on military research and development, and the conscription of teenagers and young adults into military service explains how economic dependency on the warfare state co-opts human resources for militarism. Recent economic research also shows an increased military dependency among regions and defense contractors, thereby limiting the demand for civilian R&D. In addition, some trade unions also appear to be growing more dependent on the military as basic civilian industries close and the share of their dues paying members working at military plants increases.[27] These forces have broadened the warfare state's constituency among these groups. It has made it *potentially* more difficult to enlist their support in efforts to weaken the military's stranglehold on the economy and society.

The need to provide faculty, students and youth outside academia with economic alternatives to the military requires changes in university, state and federal budgetary policies. But strategies which simply call for cutting defense budgets and throwing the military off campus are not an adequate response to the realities confronting military-dependent communities. These communities have often argued that they have no other choice, i.e., they do not have an alternative economic base of income or capital to do their research or find meaningful employment. Such an alternative base of support can be provided through economic conversion and a new federal commitment to civilian R&D.[28]

The successful conversion of military-dependent university laboratories and the provision of civilian alternatives for scientists depends on a three-tiered strategy with political participation on the university, regional and national levels. At the university level, past efforts have included the documentation of work opportunities in alternative energy production. In 1978, the University of California Nuclear Weapons Labs Conversion Project studied the possibilities of converting the Lawrence Livermore National Laboratory to alternative production in the energy field. The Project requested and received a detailed computer print-out of every employee's job category and salary at the Laboratory. After drawing up an inventory of skills and research expertise among university scientists, conversion planners matched them with an alternative agenda for peaceful research.[29]

Following the example of the University of California Nuclear Weapons Labs Conversion project, a full-scale conversion program for universities could begin with an inventory and review of academic departments, the funders of university research and the number of faculty and students dependent on military-serving research. This approach would be of most use in those scientific programs where a military orientation is built into research budgets and staffing of laboratories. An inventory of faculty and student skills could be matched with proposals for peaceful research.[30] The criteria for such research could be developed in consultation with organizations of scientists, engineers and other professional associations; economic, peace and environmental think tanks and experts in government and academia itself.[31]

The formal organization of conversion planning requires the creation of alternative-use committees in military-dependent universities throughout the country. Such committees could draw on the technical knowledge of scientific laborers and the management skills and political connections of administrators; these committees would be evenly divided between administrators and researchers. These two groups would negotiate and plan the development of alternative research programs in military-dependent departments throughout the nation.

In the schools of biology and agricultural science, there are alternatives to military- and TNC-sponsored biotechnology. Changes in consumer preferences and rising health consciousness have created incentives for a transformation of these scientific areas. Agricultural industries have been hurt by a shift in demand from beef and canned products to poultry and fresh fruits and vegetables. These changes open up new research areas:

> The research capabilities of the University system can be utilized to conform food commodities to dietary standards and consumer preferences, to invent or develop new processing technologies for foods, and even to create new food products which are amenable to current lifestyles.

An expansion in U.S. programs investigating Integrated Pest Management (IPM) can also provide alternatives to biotechnology programs. Pesticide toxicity, the pollution of acquifers and water supplies by pesticides, plant nutrients and soil additives require research into alternative methods of commodity production which would reduce dependence on agro-chemicals.[32] Programs examining solutions to the AIDS crisis and other health hazards can also provide a civilian alternative for biologists and medical researchers.

Scientific and engineering experts could turn their attention away from military production and toward research of renewable energy resources such as solar power, hydro-electricity, co-generation and alcohol fuels from biomass. Alternative energy research, together with alternative medical and IPM research, can be shared with Third World nations seeking solutions to their own scientific problems. The Japanese are developing a comprehensive alternative to SDI through the "Human Frontiers Science Program." While the program relies on "big science," and all the dangers of centralization that entails, the program plans to study "energy conversion from light (photosynthesis) and other sources to electrical, chemical and kinetic energy."[33]

8.5 Confronting Obstacles to Conversion Planning

Several obstacles will emerge in attempts to convert the universities towards civilian research and development. Faculty and administrators may claim that alternative research programs represent a threat to academic freedom. Another problem will grow out of the political and economic links that tie universities to TNCs, the regional military-industrial complex and national defense agencies. The political control of universities by corporate boards of trustees and the centralization of administrative power in trustees and university presidents can also create obstacles to conversion planning. While conversion represents an alternative to military dependency, those organizing for university conversion will still face the claim that the university has no choice but to do military-serving research, i.e., there are no alternative markets or funders to support a large scale alternative research program. Such objections and resistance could well be expected in light of many universities' growing dependence on military-serving agencies.

The response to these objections can be summarized by two questions: First, how can students and faculty gain political leverage to effect conversion of the universities? Second, how can universities, which are pushed to (or are already sympathetic with) conversion, finance planning and alternative research programs?

Objectively, future cuts in defense spending will create incentives among defense-dependent groups to decrease their reliance on the military economy.

The broader coalitions needed to mobilize support for conversion planning in the university are increasingly possible as large military cuts are on the horizon. The Washington summit bringing together President Reagan and General Secretary Gorbachev at the signing of the INF treaty symbolized the growing commitment of elites in the United States and Soviet Union to cut national military spending as a way to cope with domestic economic problems. One symbol of a new tendency to speak in terms of arms reductions was former Secretary of Defense Frank C. Carlucci's announcement at the close of 1987 that the military services were instructed to cut $33 billion from the coming year's budget in what was portrayed as a reduction of more than 10 percent.[34]

Such military "cuts," together with growing budget deficits, threaten the Strategic Defense Initiative and other large-scale programs which have pumped millions of dollars into university science departments across the country. The articulation of alternatives to military research programs through conversion plans would provide universities with a concrete option to scrambling over a shrinking or finite pool of Pentagon funding. In 1970, federal defense cuts led *The New York Times* to declare that a "research emergency" was at hand:

> The Pentagon has never failed to impress the political leaders with its dependence on the creativity of the ablest minds on campus; it would be a devastating commentary on the nation's values if history were to record that the military establishment was the only dependable patron of American research and scholarship, and that when military support was cut off, scientific research withered and died.[35]

This declaration helped define the *potential* constituency for conversion planning as encompassing the executive officers of universities themselves because ultimately the contradictory ebbs and flows in military spending have proven an illusory safety net for scientists depending on federal research funds. The new "research crisis," combined with organizing by advocates for peaceful science, may push university administrators and faculty to use their national lobbying networks for peace rather than war. Administration support is most likely to come from those universities on the periphery of the military economy, outside the universities which garner most military contracts (see Table 6-2).

Two examples illustrate that the growing defense-dependency of research institutions has created a new interest in the expansion of alternative civilian research spending. In a January 1988 briefing, the Los Alamos National Laboratory, whose nuclear weapons technology program made up half of funding that year, declared an interest in furthering "research in support of technological competitiveness." The Laboratory claimed that it was "working hard to establish a growing role" for itself "in environmental research and development." A different example relates to Columbia University president Michael Sovern. At a January 18, 1989 conference, he told journalists covering the Bush administration to monitor whether the President calls for a modest shift from applied military research to basic research. Sovern said such a shift "would be more productive in general and probably enhance our national security." [36]

The idea that universities can band together in order to mobilize their collective resources for the alternative management of our nation's research and development resources may strike many as naive and utopian. However, history has given us the fortunate example of such an attempt in the mid-to-late 1970s. At that time, several Southwestern universities attempted to create a consortium that would replace the University of California as managers of the Los Alamos Scientific Laboratory in Los Alamos, New Mexico. The twelve schools had attempted to break a pattern whereby "competitive proposals had never been sought in selecting a contractor to manage a major weapons laboratory."[37]

The foundation for putting together such a coalition of universities was laid when opposition grew to the management of these labs in California and when the Los Alamos Laboratories began encroaching on the resources of the regional universities. The Regents of the University of California came within a narrow margin of voting to sever ties with their atomic laboratories on several occasions during the period from 1975 to 1978. When national budgets for nuclear weapons research began to contract, Los Alamos began to "diversify" into the civilian energy sector by "pirating" neighboring university researchers, offering them large salaries to help them set up new energy programs.

The failure of this alternative management effort came when attempts "to get the universities' congressional delegations to intervene in ERDA's [Energy Research Development Administration] contract renewal negotiations with the University of California 'just never got off the ground.' "[38] In addition, the military-wing of ERDA successfully mobilized against the encroachment on its authority. While the proposed new management plan was not specifically aimed at conversion, it did try to provide an alternative to the usurpation of university resources by federal agencies.[39] The mobilization by this university coalition is also instructive of how liberal universities can work to provide greater political leverage to shape federal R&D policies.

The consortium stands as a model for how universities *could* pool their resources in pursuit of the conversion of university weapons labs to peaceful uses. Faculty and students must make links to constituencies outside the university if they hope to gain leverage on the disposition of university resources. These allies are essential in lobbying for new federal civilian R&D spending. Without such allies, there is no way to develop a countervailing source of leverage to the academic-military-industrial alliance.

New allies can be found in the different occupational groups which have suffered from the current diversion of military resources. This country's decaying infrastructure, homelessness and factory closures have made whole classes of professions and social groups potential beneficiaries of a national conversion program. The industrial decay rooted in the diversion of scientific and engineering talents suggests that workers in coalitions against plant shutdowns could become allies in a new program to revitalize the civilian economy through new civilian R&D spending.[40]

University scientists and engineers can play a pivotal role in reversing this process and rebuilding the economy by lending their talents to economic development projects as diverse as designing pre-manufactured housing components for the homeless to high-speed energy efficient mass transit construction. They can also help retrain their counterparts in the military sector whose socialization to the patterns of military-serving research has created a trained incapacity for alternative civilian work.[41]

The conversion of universities also depends on the participation of campus-based and progressive coalitions in local and national efforts to convert the economy and university. Peace, environmental, labor groups, movements and associations representing women, people of color, the working class and the poor each have a stake in what universities do and the organization of the nation's research and development program. These groups can apply (and have applied) pressure on the universities to expand research programs such as Women's Studies, Black and African-American Studies and peace research.

If industries make more civilian products and fewer military ones, there will be a greater demand for civilian R&D. Markets will emerge to support civilian R&D and professional associations and some business interests tied to such an alternative R&D policy could be part of university, regional or national conversion movements.[42] These movements should also establish links with the civilian R&D bureaucracy which might lobby for increased dollars for the non-military programs they administer.[43]

The economic literature on the military economy and the growing dependence of domestic institutions on Pentagon capital indicates that many universities, like prime military contractors, will resist conversion unless they are forced by legal and political means. The necessary planning is defined by a 1989 bill in Congress, HR 101, introduced into the House of Representatives by New York Representative Ted Weiss. The Defense Economic Adjustment Act would establish "alternative use" committees at every military base and industrial facility, including university research laboratories, employing at least 100 people that receive defense contracts.

The Weiss Bill would require (as a condition of receiving military funds) universities and other defense contractors to pay into an economic adjustment fund an amount equal to one and one-fourth percent per year of the value of the contractor's gross revenue on military sales. Thus, in response to university claims that they can not afford conversion planning, the Weiss Bill allows university conversion to be self-financing through military contracts. In 1989, Congressman Weiss was joined by Congressmen Sam Gejdenson (D-Connecticut) and Nicholas Mavroules (D-Massachusetts) in proposing a joint conversion bill that was supported by Congresswoman Mary Rose Oakar (D-Ohio) and House Speaker Jim Wright (D-Texas). The legislation has gained the attention of Congressional leaders confronted with a host of budgetary problems and social issues that cannot be addressed unless new resources are diverted from defense towards productive civilian activity.[44]

Legislative alternatives also have developed to confront the twin problems of economic conscription and the marginalization of the working class and people of color in higher education. In Massachusetts, Mel King, a founder of the Rainbow Coalition, is leading efforts to create a "Future Corps." This program would help finance college educations for youth in exchange for participation in public service work. The Future Corps proposal is designed to provide an alternative to military service by providing these opportunities as well as financial aid, tuition subsidies and funding for student living expenses. Unlike King's education-centered proposal, other programs are primarily job creation measures. In California, the roots of such an alternative youth service can be seen in the East Bay Conservation Corps (EBCC). This program has provided an alternative for black youth in areas such as Oakland and Richmond where unemployment rates approach 50 percent. By 1986, EBCC had served over 700 East Bay youth in a program combining educational training, employment, environmental activism and community service. In addition to a law in California, state-wide activity supporting a youth service has occurred in Minnesota and Massachusetts.[45]

8.6 Towards Comprehensive Disarmament of Covert Action Institutions

Conversion represents a vehicle for diminishing the power of the warfare state by reducing the scope of its corporate submanagerial components, the defense contractors. However, a distinct national strategy is needed to constrain the covert action institutions associated with the Pentagon and CIA. A link must be made between campus-based campaigns and national legislative efforts.

The power of covert action agencies is rooted in secrecy, the command of financial and human resources and the sanction of a widely embraced anti-communist ideology which masks the pillage of the Third World. These forces project U.S. military power and create a gap in the ability of conversion legislation to immediately constrain U.S. intervention. However, the economic approach of conversion is still relevant: an alternative to the bureaucratic power behind intervention lies in strategies which constrict the finances of war-making institutions like the CIA by cutting their budgets and planning for the retraining of their personnel. In addition, an antidote to the poisioning of democracy found in secret state initiatives which violate popular will would be to develop a system where bureaucratic functionaries and private sector intervention operatives are accountable to the rule of law. Finally, a counterweight to the force of anti-communist interventionary ideology in defining public debate on covert operations lies in campaigns directed at media institutions and universities.

A starting point for challenging the promulgation of ideologies which service intervention and the warfare state would be to review university curricula. Student and faculty committees could jointly examine how various aspects of university curricula address problems dealing with sexism, racism, the warfare system and/or contain an historical bias, e.g., history courses on the Vietnam War which inaccurately portray the conflict there as a "civil war."[46]

If arms control represents the theology which lies behind the managed escalation of the arms race, then peace studies can become the "conversion of arms control," an alternative project to replace this theology. Unlike the proposed "peace studies" programs discussed earlier, peace studies programs should make the discussion of disarmament a central concern. The process of converting the curriculum of the social sciences can begin with reviews of course catalogues and reading lists of courses which address problems in international affairs, political science, economics, economic development and the Third World. A review in 1972 found that:

> No textbook, for all the discussion about economic utility, recognizes that military goods and services, whatever their worth other than economic, yield no economic utility in the ordinary sense of contributing to consumer goods or services, or to capability for further production.[47]

Peace studies curricula could provide an alternative framework to warfare state ideology if they included a discussion of the impact of the war economy and the need for General and Complete Disarmament (GCD). A program of deep military cuts and large scale conversion of military serving institutions requires such comprehensive disarmament. Fear of the Soviet Union and other military states requires a political plan through which the superpowers can initiate mutual and verifiable arms reductions. Such reductions require mutual commitments to scale back both nuclear and conventional weapons.

A comprehensive disarmament treaty can provide the planning vehicle for these reductions through mechanisms of verification and inspection of military production and distribution sites, the phase-by-phase elimination of conventional and nuclear stockpiles. Marcus Raskin, at the Institute for Policy Studies (IPS), has proposed such an initiative, "The Draft Treaty for a Comprehensive Program for Common Security and General Disarmament." This treaty proposes the disarmament of all nuclear and conventional armed forces (except those needed for "internal order") in three five-year phases. National organizing could push forward such proposals through the development of accompanying national disarmament legislation or Senate treaties.[48]

At the university level, curricula that embrace the comprehensive disarmament approach found in the Raskin Treaty would represent an alternative to arms control ideology. IPS and the Network of Educators' Committees on Central America (both located in Washington, D.C.) have developed specific curricular alternatives that challenge established foreign policy thinking.[49]

The secrecy which protects covert operations abroad represents a direct threat to popular and democratic control of foreign policy at home. Therefore, a full program to restore openness in government and the free flow of information is essential to the disarmament of our covert operations. This program could include several components, such as: granting both Congress and the press full and timely access to U.S. military operations, stronger enforcement of the Freedom of Information Act and limitations on the classification of government documents on the ground of national security.[50]

The Congressional committees investigating the Iran-contra scandal found that the underground and illegal supply of weapons to the contras was motivated in part by a desire to escape Congressional and popular control.[51] But until there are criminal sanctions against actions that violate international and domestic law, criminal activity by covert operatives will continue. For this reason, Congressman John Conyers introduced the "Official Accountability Act of 1987," HR 3665 into the House of Representatives on November 20, 1987. His bill establishes a code of legal responsibility for civilian or military officials charged with the operation of national security policy. It makes criminal covert operations which violate any statute or Executive Order in force or international agreements to which the United States is a party. The bill also establishes an institutional mechanism for the investigation and prosecution of violations of those laws.[52]

Ultimately, "a bill to prohibit covert paramilitary operations would prevent the United States from engaging in any paramilitary operation until the policy is openly acknowledged, publicly debated, and approved by a joint resolution of Congress." But although Congress has "the constitutional authority and the statutory means to prohibit the use or support of covert paramilitary operations," it lacks "the political will" to do so.[53] In 1989, the Center for National Security Studies in Washington, D.C. began a campaign to develop a network backing comprehensive legislation limiting covert operations. Proposals by the Center would make Presidential authorization for paramilitary activity contingent on Congressional approval. In addition, the government would "be prohibited from such things as engaging in assassinations, overthrowing democratically elected governments, interfering in elections through secret or illegal means, and engaging in propaganda disinformation."[54]

To challenge Congress to seriously constrain the power of the intelligence agencies would require a movement of major proportions. This movement could begin by organizing four key constituencies. First, the traditional anti-intervention and peace community could be appealed to on moral and political grounds to support legislation that attempted to regulate covert operations. A second constituency lies in the groups suggested by conversion coalitions. Those groups which become disenfranchised by the war budget can gain resources by diverting them from the CIA. And as implied above, there is a need for an *international* conversion movement. The Israelis, for example, need economic conversion as much as we need it in the United States.[55] The links between intervention in the Third World and the risk of triggering a nuclear confrontation suggests that anti-nuclear groups could become part of larger anti-intervention coalitions. Finally, the civil liberties and progressive legal community should be another important ally.

Unfortunately, there has been a serious geographical and political gap between the grassroots anti-intervention community and the Washington, D.C. community of legal reformers. Until the former organizes behind comprehensive national legislation governing covert operations, the latter will be forced to support limited piecemeal measures. But the Conyers Bill and the Center for National Security Studies' proposals do at least give both parties a place to start serious political education regarding intervention.

The media, arms contractors and other groups tied to the warfare state represent powerful forces opposed to disarmament and anti-intervention policies. But the power of such forces should not be cause for cynicism regarding the chances for comprehensive disarmament and a progressive realignment of our relations with Central America and the Third World as a whole. Precisely because the forces supporting intervention are so diffuse, they exist in institutions which can be shaped and influenced by their local constituencies.

The terror in Central America takes place against the backdrop of a revolution in the economic structure of the global economy and the role technology plays in shaping the military, economic and political relationship among states. The revolution in microelectronics has also brought us the promise of ever deadlier weapons systems. Advances in biotechnology under corporate stewardship will lead to ever greater pillage of the Third World.

But such technological revolutions have made research institutions even more pivotal in the global assembly line which leads to underdevelopment and militarism. As technology expands its role in world agriculture and arms manufacturing (as weapons become more important than people), knowledge is becoming one of the main sources of power. Universities are one of the sources of this knowledge and the political debate over how such knowledge is applied should become a central question for the years ahead. The pillage by the corporate order and warfare state then is the other side of the choice intellectuals make when they work silently for a machine which has its own dependency in their actions. This need not be an empty existential formulation. Rather, concrete planning is needed to show where choices exist in new curricula, new research policies and alternative forms of organization and investment in the university and the nation.

Appendix 1

Transnationals Linked to Intervention in Central America

This Appendix provides a detailed list of the trustee and investment connections of various corporations discussed throughout the text. It is not an exhaustive listing of either university trustee affiliations or university investments.

Church, union, local government, and selected private and non-profit organizations' investments are listed as well as those of two university-linked investment agents: The First Wachovia Corporation and the College Retirement Equities Fund (CREF). According to First Wachovia's 1987 Annual Report, "First Wachovia Student Financial Services, Inc., is one of the largest processors of student loan accounts in the country." Universities across the country contract out student billing to First Wachovia. CREF and its university ties are described below. The affiliation of banking companies as "bank custodians" for universities has been identified by the National Association of College and University Business Officers.

The Appendix also lists participation of defense contractors in the nuclear production industry and arms sales to Central America. This information supplements previous tables which identified companies linked to police sales and the air war in El Salvador.

In some cases a prior history of arm sales or trade with a particular Central American nation could be used as the basis of inquiry as to what a company's future plans are vis-à-vis arms shipments or pesticide production. Where particular information indicating direct (or continuing) corporate culpability is lacking, the links already established could be used as an aid for such information campaigns.

The connections established regarding South African affiliates were the latest available as this study was being completed. Further updates on South African investment patterns are available from the American Committee On Africa (ACOA), New York, New York.

Inquiries to university administrators or these corporations could follow the recommendations made in the appropriate chapters of this book. Churches could also be contacted to assist in preparing formal presentations along the lines of "corporate responsibility" resolutions directed at shareholders. For information about shareholder resolutions to these companies, contact the Interfaith Center for Corporate Responsibility (ICCR), New York, New York. All legends and additional sources can be found on page 293-294.

AAI Corporation, Coceysville, Maryland (subsidiary of United Industrial Corporation, New York, New York)

Links to Central America:

Arms Sales:
See Table 6-4.

Selected Institutional Owners
(survey of United Industrial Corporation):

Name	Shares Held	Filing Date
College Retirement Equities	90,315	[3]
CA State Teachers Retirement	72,971	[3]
University of MI	9,000	[5]

American Cyanamid Inc., Wayne, New Jersey

Links to South Africa:

Has direct investment in South Africa including these subsidiaries/affiliates: S.A. Cyanamid (Pty.) Ltd.; Shulton Africa Ltd.; Shulton SA (Pty.) Ltd.; Lederle Labs. (Pty.) Ltd. (F1)

Links to Central America:

See Table 3-2; Table 3-4.

Affiliations of Corporate Directors:

Arnold J. Levine is chairman of the Department of Molecular Biology and Harry C. Weiss Professor of Molecular Biology at Princeton University.

Paul W. MacAvoy is dean of the William E. Simon School of Business Administration at the University of Rochester.

Alexander M. Schmidt is Professor of Health Policy and Social Medicine at the Institute of Public and Government Affairs, University of Illinois, Chicago.

Selected Institutional Owners:

Name	Shares Held	Filing Date
College Retirement Equities	1,054,800	[3]
NY State Common Retirement	610,000	[3]
CO Public Employee Retirement	517,000	[3]
NY State Teachers Retirement	472,300	[3]
CA State Teachers Retirement	331,924	[3]
Harvard College	122,000	[3]
Howard Hughes Medical Institute	120,000	[3]
Aid Association for Lutherans	88,000	[3]
MD State Retirment	70,400	[1]
OH School Employee Retirement	49,800	[3]
First Wachovia Corporation	39,395	[3]
Mineworkers Pension Scheme	30,286	[3]
Bucknell University	30,000	[5]
University of MN-14	20,000	[5]
Lehigh University	14,000	[5]
MI State Treasurer	5,300	[3]
Depauw University	4,800	[5]
Albright College	3,000	[5]

SOURCE: *Proxy Statement for Annual Meeting of Stockholders,* April 18, 1988, dated March 7, 1988, American Cyanamid, Inc.

BankAmerica Corporation, San Francisco, California

Links to Central America:

See Section 2.4; Table 2-1; Section 5.5; Table 5-11.

Affiliations of Corporate Directors:

Andrew F. Brimmer serves as chairman of the board of trustees of Tuskegee University, as a trustee of the College Retirement Equities Fund, and as an overseer of Harvard College. He is also a member of the Council on Foreign Relations.

A. W. Clausen is a member of the Harvard Business School board of directors of the associates, the board of trustees of Carthage College and the advisory board of the University of California, Berkeley, Business School.

Kathleen Feldstein is a trustee of Simmons College.

Philip Metschan Hawley is a trustee of the California Institute of Technology and the University of Notre Dame. He serves as a board of directors associate of the Harvard University Graduate School of Business Administration; on the advisory council of the Stanford University Graduate School of Business and on the visiting committee of the UCLA Graduate School of Management.

David Sloan Lewis, Jr. is a trustee of Washington University, St. Louis.

Ignacio E. Lozano, former American Ambassador to El Salvador 1976-77, is a trustee of the University of Notre Dame.

Ruben Frederick Mettler is chairman of the board of trustees of the California Institute of Technology.

Selected Institutional Owners:

Name	Shares Held	Filing Date
College Retirement Equities	1,323,700	[3]
NY State Common Retirement	845,000	[3]
CA State Teachers Retirement	565,333	[3]
NY State Teachers Retirement	425,400	[3]
TX Teacher Retirement System	396,800	[3]
Harvard College	361,100	[3]
University of TX System	300,000	[6]
MD State Retirement	228,500	[1]
FL State Board/Administration	200,000	[2]
University of VA	49,700	[5]
First Wachovia Corporation	37,029	[3]
CO Public Employee Retirement	30,900	[3]
Duke Endowment	30,000	[3]
Georgetown University-19	20,900	[5]
Lehigh University	18,000	[5]
MI State Treasurer	8,900	[3]

Colleges/Universities using Bank of America as a Custodian:

Harvey Mudd College, Pomona College, Pitzer College, Scripps College.

SOURCE: *Notice of the Annual Meeting of Stockholders and Proxy Statement,* May 26, 1988 dated April 15, 1988, BankAmerica Corporation; *Notice of Annual Meeting* and *Proxy Statement,* dated March 18, 1988, E.I. Du Pont de Nemours and Company; *Who's Who in America, 45th Edition, 1988-89* (Wilmette, Illinois: MacMillan Directory Division, 1988); Cambridge Associates, *1988 NACUBO Endowment Study* (Washington, D.C.: National Association of College and University Business Officers, 1989).

Bank of Boston Corporation, Boston, Massachusetts

Links to Central America:

See Section 5.5; Table 5-11.

Affiliations of Corporate Directors:

Alice F. Emerson is president of Wheaton College.

Ira Stepanian is a trustee of Tufts University.

Stephen D. Hassenfeld is a trustee of Johns Hopkins University.

Joe M. Henson is active in the governance of the Massachusetts board of regents of higher education.

Samuel Huntington is a professor at Harvard University.

Donald F. McHenry is University Research Professor of Diplomacy and International Relations at Georgetown University.

Colman Michael Mockler, Jr. is chairman of the corporation, Simmons College.

J. Donald Monan is president of Boston College.

Selected Institutional Owners:

Name	Shares Held	Filing Date
College Retirement Equities	983,926	[3]
NY State Common Retirement	480,500	[3]
CA State Teachers Retirement	363,689	[3]
NY State Teachers Retirement	360,711	[3]
General Electric Master Retirement	359,800	[2]
University of PA	212,725	[2]
Putnam Management Co. Inc.	202,453	[3]
FL State Board/Administration	120,011	[2]
First Wachovia Corporation	119,506	[3]
OH School Employee Retirement	47,400	[3]
Knights of Columbus	40,500	[3]
MD State Retirement	33,700	[1]
University of TX System	80,800	[6]
Harvard College	32,400	[3]
University of MI	15,750	[5]
University of WI	12,900	[5]
CO Public Employee Retirement	12,300	[3]
MI State Treasurer	3,700	[3]
University of CO	3,300	[5]

Colleges/Universities using Bank of Boston as a Custodian:

Boston College, MIT, Tufts University.

SOURCE: *Notice of Annual Meeting of Stockholders*, March 31, 1988, *Proxy Statement*, February 25, 1988; Cambridge Associates, *Who's Who in America, 45th Edition, 1988-89* (Wilmette, Illinois: MacMillan Directory Division, 1988). *1988 NACUBO Endowment Study* (Washington, D.C.: National Association of College and University Business Officers, 1989).

Bayer AG, Leverkusen, West Germany (principal U.S. subsidiary: Rhinechem Corporation)

Links to South Affrica:

The U.S. subsidiary Miles Laboratories ceased operations in South Africa. Bayer AG has other subsidiaries in South Africa, but ownership does not go through the United States. (F1)

Bayer has a 74 percent interest in Bayer-South Africa (Pty.) Ltd. Johannesburg, South Africa. (F2)

Bayer-Miles (Pty.) Ltd. is in Johannesburg, South Africa. (F2)

Links to Central America:

See Table 3-2; Table 3-4.

Selected Institutional Owners:

Name	Shares Held	Filing Date
Tulane University	5,000	[5]
Williams College	3,000	[5]
Boston University	2,000	[5]

Bell Helicopter, Ft. Worth, Texas (subsidiary of Textron, Inc., Providence, Rhode Island)

Links to Central America:

Arms Sales:

Bell UH-1 Iroquois Helicopter	El Salvador (6)/(A); (51)/(B3)
	Guatemala (6)/(A)
Bell UH-1H Helicopter	El Salvador (4)/(B3)
	Honduras (10)/(B3)
Bell UH-1D/H Helicopter	Guatemala (9)/(B3)
Bell UH-1B Helicopter	Honduras (11)/(B3)
Bell 206B Helicopter	Guatemala (5)/(B3)
Bell 206L1 Helicopter	Guatemala (4)/(B3)
Bell 212 Helicopter	Guatemala (1)/(B3)
Bell 412 Helicopter	Guatemala (6)/(B3)

Recent Transactions:

El Salvador (20 additional) *UH-1s* sent in 1985/(C), report confirmed of fifteen or more delivered in February 1985/(D3), additional order of six reported in July 1985. (D5)

Other April 1986 reports of (6) *UH-1Hs* and (12) *UH-1N* helicopters destined for El Salvador. (D8)

The Bell Helicopter Division in Fort Worth, Texas was involved in a $13.4 million arms deal with Honduras in December 1985 for five *Bell 412* helicopters. The Honduran Air Force has an option for five more helicopters. (C, D7)

Honduras received seven Bell 412 *Helicopters* in December 1986. (D10)

Affiliations of Corporate Directors (Textron):

William A. Anders is a member of the Defense Science Board and is currently a Major General in the U.S. Air Force Reserve.

R. Stuart Dickson is a trustee of Davidson College and the University of North Carolina at Charlotte.

William M. Ellinghaus is chairman of WNET-TV, Channel 13 (New York).

Amos A. Jordan, Jr. is vice chairman of the board of the Center for Strategic and International Studies and a member of the Council on Foreign Relations and the Institute for Strategic Studies (London).

Barbara Scott Preiskel is a successor trustee of the Yale Corporation.

J. Paul Sticht a trustee of Grove City College, a trustee of Rockefeller University, and a member of the Board of Visitors, Duke University Graduate School of Business Administration. He also is a member of the Council on Foreign Relations.

Selected Institutional Owners (survey of Textron):

Name	Shares Held	Filing Date
College Retirement Equities	758,100	[3]
NY State Common Retirement	730,800	[3]
NY State Teachers Retirement	342,400	[3]
Lutheran Brotherhood	100,000	[3]
Harvard College	87,000	[3]
OH School Employee Retirement	59,200	[3]
MD State Retirement	54,100	[1]
Tulane University	34,000	[5]
First Wachovia Corporation	25,720	[3]
University of Rochester	20,000	[3]
CO Public Employee Retirement	16,800	[3]

Bowdoin College	16,000	[5]
University of MI	14,000	[5]
Scripps College	14,000	[5]
MI State Treasurer	5,000	[3]

SOURCE: *Notice of Annual Meeting,* April 27, 1988 and *Proxy Statement,* dated March 15, 1988, Textron; *Who's Who in America, 45th Edition, 1988-89* (Wilmette, Illinois: MacMillan Directory Division, 1988).

Castle & Cooke, Inc., Los Angeles, California

Links to Central America:
See Section 2.4; Table 3-2; Table 5-2; Table 5-4; Section 5.5.

Affiliations of Corporate Directors:
James F. Gary is a trustee of Linfield College; on the board of managers of Haverford College and a member of the University of Hawaii Board of Regents.

Selected Institutional Owners:

Name	Shares Held	Filing Date
CA State Teachers Retirement	309,893	[3]
College Retirement Equities	197,384	[3]
NY State Common Retirement	90,000	[3]
University of TX System	3,000	[6]
MI State University	7,000	[5]
Columbia University	3,333	[5]

SOURCE: *Notice of Annual Meeting of Stockholders,* May 26, 1988, and *Proxy Statement,* Castle & Cooke, April 11, 1988.

Chase Manhattan Corporation, New York, New York

Links to Central America:
See Section 5.5; Table 5-11.

Affiliations of Corporate Directors:
James L. Ferguson is a trustee of Hamilton College.

Edward S. Finkelstein is a member of the advisory board of the Yale School of Organization and Management and on the board of directors of the advisory board, Harvard Business School.

Robert E. Flowerree is a member of the board of administrators of Tulane University and a life trustee of Lewis and Clark College.

Laurance Fuller is a trustee of Northwestern University.

Thomas G. Labrecque is a trustee of Villanova University and Marymount College and a member of the Board of Visitors of Duke University's Fuqua School of Business.

John D. Macomber is chairman of the visiting committee of the Yale University School of Management and is a trustee of the Whitehead Institute, MIT.

John H. McArthur is dean of the Harvard Graduate School of Business Administration.

David T. McLaughlin, former president of Dartmouth College (1981-1987), is chairman of the Aspen Institute for Humanistic Studies.

Edmund T. Pratt is a trustee of Duke University and is on the board of overseers, Wharton School of Commerce and Finance, University of Pennsylvania.

Henry B. Schacht is a trustee of the Yale Corporation and a member of the associates of the Harvard Business School.

Kay R. Whitmore is a trustee of the University of Rochester.

Selected Institutional Owners:

Name	Shares Held	Filing Date
MI State Treasurer	4,269,800	[3]
College Retirement Equities	1,850,722	[3]
TX Teacher Retirement System	1,061,948	[3]
NY State Common Retirement	874,000	[3]
NY State Teachers Retirement	651,847	[3]
CA State Teachers Retirement	557,527	[3]
First Wachovia Corporation	348,549	[3]
University of TX System	153,600	[6]
OH School Employee Retirement	44,600	[3]
MD State Retirement	41,500	[1]
University of VA	40,000	[5]
Columbia University	38,200	[5]
Harvard College	31,500	[3]
Cornell University	26,175	[6]
Mt. Holyoke College	16,200	[5]
CO Public Employee Retirement	15,900	[3]
University of CO	4,100	[5]

Colleges/Universities using Chase Manhattan as a Custodian:

Clarkson University, Fordham University, Georgetown University, Middlebury College, College of New Rochelle, Oregon State System of Higher Education, Rockefeller University, Stanford University.

SOURCE: *Notice of the Annual Meeting of Stockholders,* April 19, 1988, dated March 8, 1988, Chase Manhattan Bank; *Notice of 1988 Annual Meeting and Proxy Statement,* April 27, 1988, dated March 14, 1988, Westinghouse Electric Corporation; *Who's Who in America, 45th Edition, 1988-89* (Wilmette, Illinois: MacMillan Directory Division, 1988). Cambridge Associates, *1988 NACUBO Endowment Study* (Washington, D.C.: National Association of College and University Business Officers, 1989).

Chevron Corporation, San Francisco, California

Links to South Africa:

Chevron has a 50 percent interest in Caltex Petroleum, its U.S. subsidiary whose affiliate in South Africa is Caltex Oil (Pty.) Ltd. Chevron is also tied to South African Oil Refining Co. (Pty.) Ltd. (F1)

Links To Central America:

See Table 3-2; Table 3-4; Table 5-9.

Affiliations of Corporate Directors:

Kenneth T. Derr is a trustee of Cornell University.

Sam L. Ginn is a trustee of Mills College.

George P. Shultz was Secretary of State (1982-89).

James N. Sullivan is a member of the board of regents of St. Mary's College.

Selected Institutional Owners:

Name	Shares Held	Filing Date
NY State Common Retirement	4,416,000	[3]

College Retirement Equities	2,588,800	[3]
TX Teacher Retirement System	1,793,860	[3]
NY State Teachers Retirement	1,575,900	[3]
CA State Teachers Retirement	1,573,310	[3]
MI State Treasurer	1,310,100	[3]
OH State Teachers Retirement	1,292,100	[3]
CO Public Employee Retirement	654,600	[3]
University of TX System	463,700	[6]
First Wachovia Corporation	411,335	[3]
MD State Retirement	261,700	[1]
Ford Foundation	250,000	[3]
Rice, William Marsh University	234,946	[3]
OH School Employee Retirement	233,900	[3]
Young Men's Christian Association	104,000	[3]
Rockefeller University	99,100	[3]
Columbia University	81,512	[5]
Lutheran Brotherhood	50,000	[3]
Lehigh University	14,000	[5]
University of TN	14,000	[5]
Tulane University	12,600	[5]
Boston University	9,000	[5]
Duke Endowment	6,000	[3]
Scripps College	5,000	[5]
University of MN-14	5,000	[5]
University of Houston	4,000	[5]
University of VA	2,500	[5]

SOURCE: *Notice of the Annual Meeting of Stockholders,* May 2, 1989 and *Proxy Statement,* March 20, 1989, Chevron.

Ciba-Geigy, Basel, Switzerland (principal U.S. subsidiary: Ciba-Geigy Corporation, Ardsley, New York)

Links to South Africa:
Ciba-Geigy (Pty.) Ltd. in Isando, South Africa. (F2)
Links to Central America:
See Table 3-2; Table 3-4.

Citicorp, New York, New York
Links to South Africa:
Citibank maintains "correspondent" banking ties with its former South African subsidiary, First National Bank. Citicorp is a depository institution for American Depository Receipts, a vehicle for purchasing shares in South African companies. The Citicorp subsidiary, Diners Club Inc., continues to franchise its former South African subsidiary. (F1)
Links To Central America:
See Section 5.5; Table 5-11.
Affiliations of Corporate Directors:
Kenneth T. Derr (see Chevron above).

John M. Deutch is provost at MIT.

James H. Evans is a trustee of the University of Chicago.

Lawrence E. Fouraker, professor emeritus, Graduate School of Business Administration, Harvard University.

Juanita M. Kreps is James B. Duke Professor of Economics and vice president emeritus, Duke University.

Edgar S. Woolard, Jr. is vice chairman of the United Negro College Fund of Delaware and a trustee of North Carolina State University.

Selected Institutional Owners:

Name	Shares Held	Filing Date
MI State Treasurer	11,431,700	[3]
College Retirement Equities	4,773,200	[3]
NY State Common Retirement	3,400,300	[3]
CA State Teachers Retirement	2,462,208	[3]
TX Teacher Retirement System	2,086,900	[3]
NY State Teachers Retirement	1,579,800	[3]
University of PA	1,532,147	[2]
OH State Teachers Retirement	1,311,000	[3]
CO Public Employee Retirement	1,299,800	[3]
MD State Retirement	292,200	[1]
First Wachovia Corporation	248,980	[3]
FL State Board/Administration	248,600	[2]
University of TX System	178,900	[6]
Harvard College	117,500	[3]
University of VA	105,000	[5]
OH School Employee Retirement	89,200	[3]
Cornell University	47,850	[6]
University of Delaware	37,800	[3]
Boston University	36,600	[5]
Duke Endowment	20,000	[3]
Alma College	20,000	[5]
Georgetown University-17	16,000	[5]
Mineworkers Pension Scheme	14,680	[3]
University of Alabama	13,600	[5]
Grinnell College	10,000	[5]
Williams College	8,400	[5]
Colby College-4	7,600	[5]
Depauw University-3	6,600	[5]
OH State University-1	6,200	[5]
University of CO	4,000	[5]
Drew University	2,400	[5]

SOURCE: *Notice of Annual Meeting* and *Proxy Statement*, dated March 18, 1988, E.I. Du Pont de Nemours and Company; *Who's Who in America, 45th Edition, 1988-89* (Wilmette, Illinois: MacMillan Directory Division, 1988).

Coca-Cola Company, Atlanta, Georgia

Links to South Africa:

Coca-Cola continues to sell syrup to and have a licensing agreement with its former South African subsidiary, National Beverage Industries. (F1)

Links to Central America:

See Section 2.4; Section 5.5; Table 5-6.

Affiliations of Corporate Directors:

Charles W. Duncan, Jr. served as Deputy Secretary of the United States Department of Defense from 1977 to 1979 and as Secretary of the Department of Energy from 1979 to 1981.

Richard J. Flamson, III is a trustee of Claremont Men's College.

James T. Laney is president of Emory University.

Donald F. McHenry (see Bank of Boston above).

James B. Williams is a trustee of Emory University and on the board of visitors of Berry College.

Selected Institutional Owners:

Name	Shares Held	Filing Date
University of California	4,342,795	[3]
First Wachovia Corporation	3,274,086	[3]
NY State Common Retirement	2,744,100	[3]
College Retirement Equities	2,675,900	[3]
CA State Teachers Retirement	1,907,976	[3]
NY State Teachers Retirement	1,813,300	[3]
TX Teacher Retirement System	1,150,800	[3]
CO Public Employee Retirement	670,400	[3]
OH State Teachers Retirement	461,300	[3]
Rice, William Marsh University	422,130	[3]
MD State Retirement	288,400	[1]
University of TX System	247,200	[6]
Harvard College	136,800	[3]
OH School Employee Retirement	122,500	[3]
Aid Association for Lutherans	116,000	[3]
University of Delaware	105,300	[3]
Lutheran Brotherhood	100,000	[3]
Columbia University	79,500	[5]
University of VA	58,200	[5]
University of Rochester	54,100	[3]
University of MN-14	49,500	[5]
Colgate University	27,000	[5]
Mineworkers Pension Scheme	25,713	[3]
Wellesley College	24,000	[5]
Williams College	23,800	[5]
MI State Treasurer	22,100	[3]
Carleton College	18,000	[5]
Case Western Reserve	13,800	[5]
University of Houston	10,500	[5]
OH State University-1	8,000	[5]
Duke Endowment	7,000	[3]
Bowdoin College	1,200	[5]

SOURCE: *Proxy Statement for Annual Meeting of Shareholders,* April 20, 1988, dated March 9, 1988, The Coca-Cola Company; *Who's Who in America, 45th Edition, 1988-89* (Wilmette, Illinois: MacMillan Directory Division, 1988).

College Retirement Equities Fund, New York, New York

The College Retirement Equities Fund (CREF) was formed to aid and assist non-profit educational and research organizations by providing retirement benefits and financial security to faculty and other employees of these organizations. CREF is the "companion organization" of the Teachers Insurance and Annuity Association of America which "offers fixed annuities and insurance benefits suited to the needs of the types of institutions and employees served by CREF." In addition to the investments described in this Appendix, CREF investments are listed in "Financial Statements (Unaudited), College Retirement Equities Fund, June 30, 1988."

University and Academic Linked Members and Trustees of CREF:

Irma Adelman, professor of Economics and professor of agricultural and resource economics, University of California at Berkeley, is a trustee of CREF.

Robert H. Atwell, president of the American Council on Education, is a member of CREF.

Elizabeth E. Bailey, dean, Graduate School of Industrial Administration, Carnegie Mellon University, is a trustee of CREF.

Andrew F. Brimmer (see BankAmerica Corporation above) is a trustee of CREF.

James F. Brinkerhoff, vice president and Chief Financial Officer and professor of business administration, the University of Michigan, is a trustee of CREF.

Nancy L. Jacob, dean and professor of finance, School and Graduate School of business administration, University of Washington, is a trustee of CREF.

Marjorie Fine Knowles, dean and professor of law, Georgia State University, College of Law, is a trustee of CREF.

Juanita M. Kreps (see Citibank above) is a member of CREF.

Stephen A. Ross, Sterling professor of economics and finance, Yale University, is a trustee of CREF.

Harry K. Spindler, Senior vice chancellor, Division of Administrative Affairs, State University of New York, is a trustee of CREF.

SOURCE: "Prospectus, Individual Tax-Deferred Variable Annuity Certificates," Issued by College Retirement Equities Fund, New York, New York, April 1, 1988; "Variable Annuity Certificates Issued Persuant to a Master Group Contract," Offered by College Retirement Equities Fund, Statement of Additional Information, New York, New York, April 1, 1988.

Colt Industries (subsidiary of Colt Holdings, Inc.), New York, New York

Links to Central America:

Arms Sales:

The M-16 rifle produced by Colt has been sent to El Salvador in September of 1981, in December of 1982 and March of 1983. The rifle was also sent to Honduras in May of 1981 and in 1982. (B2) A September 1987 "Letter of Offer" for M-16 rifles destined for El Salvador was reported in February 1988. (D13) In October 1988, 20,000 M-16A2 5.56mm rifles (worth $13.8 million) were ordered by Guatemala. (D16)

See also Table 6-4.

According to a 1988 report, the Colt Industries group was listed as having operations in Guatemala.

Affiliations of Corporate Directors:

Robert A. Alberty is professor of chemistry, MIT, School of Science.

Paul W. MacAvoy (see American Cyanamid, Inc. above).

NOTE: On June 10, 1988, Colt Industries Inc. became a privately held company and no longer has any publicly held common stock. Aberty and MacAvoy are still associated with Colt Industries as directors according to a 1989 report.

SOURCE: *Notice of Annual Meeting of Shareholders*, May 7, 1987, and *Proxy Statement*, Colt Industries, dated March 26, 1987; Letter from John Ennis, Assistant Treasurer, Colt Industries, dated December 2, 1988; Colt operations in Guatemala listed in *C/CAA's 1989 Caribbean and Central American Databook* (Washington, D.C.: Caribbean/Central American Action, 1988), p. 180. Update on directors' status from *Standard & Poor's Register of Corporations, Directors and Executives*, Vol. 1 (New York: Standard & Poor's Corp., 1989), p. 624.

Coors, Golden, Colorado
Links to Central America:

The Coors Foundation has funded the right-wing student group, Students for a Better America (SBA), which has red-baited solidarity organizations like CISPES. Joseph Coors, vice chairman of Coors, and associated family interests have supported two right-wing aid groups that have supported the contras: the U.S. Council for World Freedom and the Nicaragua Refugee Fund. The Council has served as a major source of funds and supplies for the contras and a 1985 report in the *Miami Herald* suggested that this group gave as much as $500,000 a month to the contras. The Fund is a sponsor of Americares, a "humanitarian" aid group which has provided logistical support to and raised money for the contras. Joseph Coors is a Member of the Council for National Policy which has acted as a fundraising network for the contras and covert action entrepreneur, Maj. General John K. Singlaub. The Adolph Coors Company and the Adolph Coors Foundation have provided financial assistance to the Heritage Foundation, which has advocated overthrowing the Nicaraguan government, support for the contras and conservative forces in Nicaragua. Joseph Coors is also a trustee of the Foundation. The Congress reported in 1987 that during the years 1985 and 1986 Joseph Coors had given $65,000 to the Enterprise, the illegal government organization headed by former Lt. Col. Oliver North to assist the contras.

Selected Institutional Owners:

Name	Shares Held	Filing Date
NY State Common Retirement	500,000	[3]
College Retirement Equities	374,800	[3]
NY State Teachers Retirement	195,000	[3]
CA State Teachers Retirement	130,054	[3]
University of TX System	25,000	[6]
OH School Employee Retirement	22,800	[3]
WI Investment Board	20,000	[3]
MD State Retirement	17,300	[1]
Harvard College	10,000	[3]
Georgetown University-17	10,000	[5]
CO Public Employee Retirement	6,700	[3]
MI State Treasurer	2,100	[3]

SOURCE: Sara Diamond, "New Right's Student Shock Troops Target CISPES," *Guardian*, April 17, 1985; Philip J. Meranto et al., *Guarding the Ivory Tower* (Denver: Lucha Publications, 1985); Tom Barry, Deb Preusch and Beth Sims, *The New Right Humanitarians* (Albuquerque: Inter-Hemispheric Resource Center, 1986); *The Heritage Foundation*, Washington, D.C., Annual Report, 1985; *Report of the Congressional Committees Investigating the Iran-Contra Affair*, S. Rept. No. 100-216; H. Report No. 100-433, 100th Congress, 1st Session (Washington, D.C.: U.S. Government Printing Office: 1987), pp. 335-336.

Del Monte (subsidiary of RJR Nabisco, Inc., Atlanta, GA)

Links to South Africa:

Del Monte Corporation has direct ownership in South Africa through South African Preserving Co. (Pty.) Ltd. and Rooihoogte Suid Farm (Pty.) Ltd. RJR Nabisco has additional ownership ties through Royal Beech-Nut, Ltd. and Huntley and Palmers (Pty.) Ltd. (F1)

Links to Central America:

See Table 5-2; Table 5-4; Section 5.5.

Affiliations Of Corporate Directors (RJR Nabisco):

Charles E. Hugel is chairman of the board of trustees of Lafayette College.

Vernon E. Jordan is former president of the Urban League and a trustee of Clark College.

Juanita M. Kreps (see Citibank above).

John D. Macomber (see Chase Manhattan Bank above).

John G. Medlin, Jr. is a trustee at Wake Forest University and chief executive officer of the First Wachovia Corporation.

J. Paul Sticht (see Bell Helicopter/Textron above).

Selected Institutional Owners (survey of RJR Nabisco):

Name	Shares Held	Filing Date
First Wachovia Corporation	5,703,207	[3]
College Retirement Equities	1,850,525	[3]
NY State Common Retirement	1,790,000	[3]
NY State Teachers Retirement	1,132,650	[3]
TX Teacher Retirement System	1,059,032	[3]
CA State Teachers Retirement	899,006	[3]
CO Public Employee Retirement	592,800	[3]
Kentucky Teachers Retirement	250,000	[3]
University of TX System	210,600	[6]
MD State Retirement	191,481	[1]
WI Investment Board	187,800	[3]
Rice, William Marsh University	116,050	[3]
Harvard College	87,552	[3]
OH School Employee Retirement	71,650	[3]
Lehigh University	15,672	[5]
MI State Treasurer	14,400	[3]
Boston University	10,000	[5]
Smith College-4	9,507	[5]
Williams College	9,500	[5]
University of ID	9,000	[5]
Colby College	8,230	[5]
Bowdoin College	675	[5]

SOURCE: *Who's Who in America, 45th Edition, 1988-89* (Wilmette, Illinois: MacMillan Directory Division, 1988); *1987 Annual Report*, First Wachovia Corporation, Winston-Salem, North Carolina, February 12, 1988.

Dow Chemical Corporation, Midland, Michigan

Links to Central America:

See Table 3-2; Table 3-4.

Links to South Africa:

Dow Corning Corporation, a joint venture between Dow Chemical Corporation and Corning Glass Works, has a South African subsidiary, Dow Corning Africa Silicones. (F1)

Affiliations of Corporate Directors:

Herbert H. Dow is a member of the MIT Corporation.

Barbara H. Franklin, senior fellow at the Wharton School of the University of Pennsylvania, is a director of the Wharton Government and Business Program and serves on the board of visitors of the Defense Systems Management College.

William N. Lipscomb, Jr. is professor of chemistry at Harvard University.

Keith R. McKennon is a trustee at the Institute for Health Policy Analysis at Georgetown University.

Harold T. Shapiro is president of Princeton University.

Selected Institutional Owners:

Name	Shares Held	Filing Date
University of California	2,315,308	[3]
NY State Common Retirement	1,484,500	[3]
College Retirement Equities	1,374,500	[3]
NY State Teachers Retirement	955,200	[3]
TX Teacher Retirement System	677,000	[3]
CA State Teachers Retirement	672,841	[3]
Harvard College	320,800	[3]
Ford Foundation	315,000	[3]
First Wachovia Corporation	275,944	[3]
CO Public Employee Retirement	235,800	[3]
MD State Retirement	147,100	[1]
Rice, William Marsh University	121,600	[6]
KY Teachers Retirement	100,000	[3]
University of TX System	93,550	[6]
OH School Employee Retirement	77,200	[3]
University of MN-14	45,000	[5]
Columbia University	39,200	[5]
Aid Association for Lutherans	30,000	[3]
Wooster College	19,136	[5]
Simmons College	14,000	[5]
MA Institute of Technology	12,750	[5]
Colby College	12,500	[5]
Carleton College	11,400	[5]
Cornell University	11,325	[6]
MI State Treasurer	11,200	[3]
Cornell University	10,325	[3]
Mineworkers Pension Scheme	10,000	[3]
Tulane University	10,000	[5]
Duke Endowment	9,000	[3]
Georgetown University-17	4,500	[5]
University of MI	1,302	[5]

SOURCE: *The Dow Chemical Company, Notice of the 1987 Annual Meeting,* May 12, 1988, and *Proxy Statement,* dated March 23, 1988, Dow Chemical Company; *Notice of 1988 Annual Meeting and Proxy Statement,* April 27, 1988, dated March 14, 1988, Westinghouse Electric Corporation; *Who's Who in America, 45th Edition, 1988-89* (Wilmette, Illinois: MacMillan Directory Division, 1988).

Remington Arms Company, Inc., Wilmington, Delaware
(subsidiary of E.I. Du Pont de Nemours & Co., Wilmington, Delaware) and Du Pont Family Connections
Links to Central America:

Arms Sales:

A September 1987 "Letter of Offer" for Remington shotguns destined for El Salvador was reported in February 1988. (D13)

NARMIC has identified Remington Arms Co. as a past supplier of ammunition to Guatemala. (B1)

The Du Pont family also has ties to clandestine weapons shipments to the contras through Richard C. Du Pont, owner of Summit Aviation. Gerald Colby, author of a book on the Du Pont family details how Summit Aviation worked hand in hand with the CIA, in supplying military converted Cessna 404 aircraft to the Nicaraguan terrorists of the Revolutionary Democratic Alliance. Colby cites one source who told him that "automatic weapons were also being shipped out of Summit Airport to Somoza's Nicaragua." The Company also has ties to other regimes: "A visit to Summit in August 1983 found the company still outfitting planes for at least one Latin American regime, probably Guatemala." Summit has also converted Cessna and Piper airplanes into sophisticated warplanes and sold them to the military states of Haiti, Honduras and Guatemala. See Gerald Colby, *Du Pont Dynasty* (Secaucus, New Jersey: Lyle Stuart Inc., 1984).

E.I. Du Pont de Nemours & Co., Wilmington, Delaware
Links to South Africa:

Du Pont has direct investment in South Africa through Du Pont de Nemours International, Soc. Anon. (F1)

See Table 3-2; Table 3-4.

Affiliations of Corporate Directors (Du Pont):

David Kennedy Barnes is on the board of trustees of Olivet College.

Elwood P. Blanchard, Jr. is a member of the national advisory board of the Georgia Institute of Technology.

Andrew F. Brimmer (see BankAmerica Corporation above).

Edgar M. Bronfman is president of the World Jewish Congress and a director of the Weizmann Institute of Science and the School of International and Public Affairs of Columbia University.

Charles L. Brown is vice chairman of the Institute of Advanced Study.

Irenee Du Pont, Jr. is a life member of the MIT Corporation and is a trustee of Wilmington College, Inc.

Richard E. Heckert is a member of the dean's associate business advisory council, Miami University School of Business Administration. He is also a trustee of Tuskegee University.

Edward G. Jefferson is vice chairman of the board of trustees of the University of Delaware.

Howard W. Johnson is honorary chairman and a former chairman (1971-1983) of the MIT Corporation.

Edward R. Kane is a member of the MIT Corporation.

H. Rodney Sharp, III is a trustee of St. Augustine's College.

Constantine Stavros Nicandros is a member of the International Institute for Strategic Studies and a trustee of the Baylor College of Medicine, the University of Houston Foundation.

John Livingston Weinberg is a member of the advisory council, Stanford Graduate School of Business, Governor and member of the Executive Committee of the New York Hospital—Cornell Medical Center, charter trustee of Princeton University, and member of the Council on Foreign Relations.

Edgard S. Woolard, Jr. (see Citicorp above).

Selected Institutional Owners (survey of Du Pont):

Name	Shares Held	Filing Date
NY State Common Retirement	2,115,500	[3]
University of California	1,505,200	[3]
College Retirement Equities	1,441,087	[3]
NY State Teachers Retirement	1,143,000	[3]
CA State Teachers Retirement	847,401	[3]
TX Teacher Retirement System	542,900	[3]
First Wachovia Corporation	311,288	[3]
MD State Retirement	186,600	[1]
CO Public Employee Retirement	175,100	[3]
Kentucky Teachers Retirement	150,000	[3]
Harvard College	108,335	[3]
University of TX System	106,600	[6]
OH School Employee Retirement	98,700	[3]
Rice, William Marsh University	82,600	[3]
University of Chicago	59,780	[3]
University of Delaware	56,750	[3]
Lutheran Brotherhood	50,000	[3]
Young Men's Christian Association	35,000	[3]
Columbia University	30,700	[5]
Bucknell University	22,500	[5]
MI State Treasurer	14,000	[3]
University of MN-14	14,000	[5]
Case Western Reserve	16,500	[5]
Lehigh University	7,000	[5]
Carleton College	6,000	[5]
Tufts University	5,580	[5]
Georgetown University-17	4,500	[5]
Wooster College	3,000	[5]
MA Institute of Technology	2,861	[5]
University of CO	1,200	[5]

SOURCE: *Notice of Annual Meeting* and *Proxy Statement,* dated March 18, 1988, E.I. Du Pont de Nemours and Company; *Who's Who in America, 45th Edition, 1988-89* (Wilmette, Illinois: MacMillan Directory Division, 1988).

E-Systems, Dallas, Texas

Links to Central America:

Arms Sales:

In December 1984, a $3.4 million arms deal was transacted with El Salvador for the supply to El Salvador of five C47/DC-3 Aircraft modified to airborne support platform cofiguration data. (C)

Affiliations of Corporate Directors:

S. Lee Kling is a member of the executive committee, Caribbean/Central American Action and co-chairman of the Coalition for Enactment of the Caribbean Basin Initiative.

Francine I. Neff is a trustee of Cottey College and a member of the advisory council, Management Development Center, Robert O. Anderson Graduate School of Business and Administrative Sciences, University of New Mexico.

William F. Raborn is a former director of the CIA (1965-1966).

Selected Institutional Owners:

Name	Shares Held	Filing Date
OH State Teachers Retirement	1,417,400	[3]
WI Investment Board	363,500	[3]
College Retirement Equities	266,700	[3]
NY State Common Retirement	204,500	[3]
NY State Teachers Retirement	191,000	[3]
CA State Teachers Retirement	130,381	[3]
University of TX System	88,900	[6]
Harvard College	41,100	[3]
MD State Retirement	20,700	[1]
Bates College	12,000	[5]
OH School Employee Retirement	10,400	[3]
TX Teacher Retirement System	9,100	[3]
First Wachovia Corporation	7,022	[3]
CO Public Employee Retirement	5,800	[3]
MI State Treasurer	1,800	[3]

SOURCE: *Notice of Annual Meeting of Stockholders to be held April 26, 1988* and *Proxy Statement,* dated March 14, 1988; *Who's Who in America, 45th Edition, 1988-89* (Wilmette, Illinois: MacMillan Directory Division, 1988).

Elbit Computers Ltd. (subsidiary of Elron Electronics Industries Ltd., Haifa, Israel)

Links to Central America:
See Table 6-6; Table 6-7.

Selected Institutional Owners:

Name	Shares Held	Filing Date
Columbia University	1,000	[5]

Exxon Corporation, New York, New York

Links to South Africa:
Exxon continues licensing and technical agreements with former subsidiaries/affiliates. (F1)

Links to Central America:
See Section 5.5; Table 5-9.

Affiliations of Corporate Directors:
Jack F. Bennett is a member of the Harvard Graduate Society Council, Joint Council on Economic Education and the Council on Foreign Relations.

Randolph W. Bromery, Commonwealth professor of Geophysics at the University of Massachusetts at Amherst, is a trustee of the Johns Hopkins University, Mount Holyoke College and Talladega College. He is a member of the Council on Foreign Relations.

Jess Hay is on the board of regents of the University of Texas System.

Philip E. Lippincott is on the board of overseers of the Wharton School, the University of Pennsylvania and the Dartmouth Institute.

Margaret L. A. MacVicar is dean of undergraduate education, professor of physical science, and Cecil and Ida Green professor of Education, MIT. She is also a member of the corporation of the Charles S. Draper Laboratory.

Lawrence G. Rawl is on the College of Engineering board of visitors, the University of Oklahoma and is a member of the Council on Foreign Relations.

Charles R. Sitter is a member of the board of visitors, Fletcher School of Law and Diplomacy, Tufts University; on the board of overseers, Hoover Institution on War, Revolution and Peace, and on the board of administrators, Tulane University.

Selected Institutional Owners:

Name	Shares Held	Filing Date
College Retirement Equities	14,508,400	[3]
NY State Common Retirement	11,282,800	[3]
NY State Teachers Retirement	6,850,800	[3]
TX Teacher Retirement System	5,828,480	[3]
CA State Teachers Retirement	5,587,478	[3]
University of California	4,735,973	[3]
First Wachovia Corporation	2,305,006	[3]
OH State Teachers Retirement	1,899,600	[3]
FL State Board/Administration	1,290,000	[2]
MD State Retirement	1,091,100	[1]
CO Public Employee Retirement	897,000	[3]
Harvard College	628,730	[3]
OH School Employee Retirement	609,200	[3]
Rice, William Marsh University	433,584	[3]
Ford Foundation	400,000	[3]
University of Chicago	268,516	[3]
Howard Hughes Medical Institute	200,000	[3]
Young Men's Christian Association	200,000	[3]
Kentucky Teachers Retirement	195,000	[3]
University of Delaware	149,824	[3]
Knights of Columbus	142,072	[3]
Mineworkers Pension Scheme	109,560	[3]
MI State Treasurer	81,000	[3]
University of TX System	70,008	[5]
Lutheran Brotherhood	50,000	[3]
Rockefeller University	50,000	[3]
Bucknell University	40,000	[5]
University of MI	30,800	[5]
Grinnell College	28,400	[5]
MA Institute of Technology	21,410	[5]
University of Rochester	11,400	[3]
Depauw University-3	10,536	[5]
Boston University	9,050	[5]

SOURCE: *Notice of the Annual Meeting,* May 19, 1988, and *Proxy Statement,* Exxon Corporation, dated March 28, 1988; *Who's Who in America, 45th Edition, 1988-89* (Wilmette, Illinois: MacMillan Directory Division, 1988).

Fairchild Industries, Inc., Chantilly, Virginia

Links to South Africa:

Fairchild Industries may have a distribution agreement with the South African company Hestico (Pty.) Ltd. for plastic molding tooling and die-casting. (F1)

Links to Central America:

Arms Sales:

Fairchild C-123 Provider	El Salvador (3)/(B3)
Fairchild Hiller FH-1100 Helicopter	El Salvador (1)/(A); (1)/(B3)

Affiliations of Corporate Directors:

Thomas H. Moorer is senior advisor at the Center for Strategic and International Studies.

Selected Institutional Owners:

Name	Shares Held	Filing Date
College Retirement Equities	69,000	[3]
CA State Teachers Retirement	47,356	[3]

SOURCE: *Notice of Annual Meeting of Stockholders*, April 27, 1988, and Proxy Statement, Fairchild Industries, dated March 21, 1988; *Who's Who in America, 45th Edition, 1988-89* (Wilmette, Illinois: MacMillan Directory Division, 1988).

FMC Corporation, Chicago, Illinois

Links to South Africa:

FMC believed to have licensing/distribution with its former subsidiary FMC South Africa (Pty.) Limited. (F1)

Links to Central America:

See Table 3-2; Table 3-4.

Arms Sales:

M113A1 Armored Personnel Carriers	Guatemala (32)/(A)
M113-A2 Armored Personnel Carrier	Costa Rica (3)/(E)

Affiliations of Corporate Directors:

Bernard Adolphus Bridgewater, Jr. is a trustee of Washington University, St. Louis.

John J. Cardwell is a trustees of Northwestern University.

Paul L. Davies, Jr. is a regent of the University of the Pacific.

Robert H. Malott is on the board of directors of the associates of Harvard Business School; the board of overseers of the Hoover Institution (vice chairman); the board of governors of Argonne National Laboratory; and a trustee of the American Enterprise Institute and the University of Chicago.

General Edward C. Meyer, international consultant and former chief of staff, United States Army, serves on the visiting committee for the University of Miami School of Business Administration.

William J. Perry, former Undersecretary of Defense for Research and Engineering from 1977-1981, is a trustee of Rockefeller University, MITRE Corporation and the Carnegie Endowment for International Peace.

Raymond C. Tower is a trustee of Illinois Institute of Technology and an associate of Northwestern University.

Selected Institutional Owners:

Name	Shares Held	Filing Date
College Retirement Equities	419,167	[3]

NY State Teachers Retirement	363,900	[3]
NY State Common Retirement	312,200	[3]
CA State Teachers Retirement	246,786	[3]
Knights of Columbus	31,200	[3]
OH School Employee Retirement	16,600	[3]
Harvard College	14,500	[3]
Depauw University-3	10,700	[5]
First Wachovia Corporation	8,160	[3]
CO Public Employee Retirement	6,400	[3]
University of MI	5,000	[5]
University of CO	3,500	[5]
MI State Treasurer	2,600	[3]

SOURCE: *Notice of Annual Meeting of Stockholders,* April 24, 1988 and *Proxy Statement,* dated March 21, 1988; *Who's Who in America, 45th Edition, 1988-89* (Wilmette, Illinois: MacMillan Directory Division, 1988).

GTE Corporation, Stamford, Connecticut

Links to South Africa:
GTE maintains licensing and sales agreements with its former South African subsidiary, Valenite-Modco. (F1)

Links to Central America:
See Section 6.8; Table 6-6.

Links to the Nuclear Weapons Industry:
GTE has worked on the MX missile program, the Minuteman missile project, ballistic missile defense, and Project ELF (a communications system that the U.S. Navy wanted to develop for communication with ballistic missile submarines). (G)

Affiliations of Corporate Directors:
James R. Barker is a member of the business advisory committee of the Transportation Center at Northwestern University, the board of visitors of Columbia University, and the board of directors of the associates of Harvard Business School.

James L. Broadhead is a member of the Cornell University Council and the Cornell Engineering College Advisory Council.

George V. Grune is a trustee of Duke University.

James L. Ketelsen is a trustee of Northwestern University.

Sandra O. Moose is a member of the board of trustees of Wheaton College.

Russell E. Palmer is dean of the Wharton School, University of Pennsylvania.

Roger W. Stone is a member of the board of overseers of the Wharton School, the University of Pennsylvania, an associate of Northwestern University, and a member of the advisory board of the J.L. Kellogg Graduate School of Management of Northwestern.

Robert D. Storey has served as an overseer of Harvard University.

Selected Institutional Owners:

Name	Shares Held	Filing Date
University of California	5,089,606	[3]
NY State Common Retirement	2,892,250	[3]
MI State Treasurer	2,550,050	[3]
TX Teacher Retirement System	2,295,950	[3]
College Retirement Equities	1,759,150	[3]
NY State Teachers Retirement	1,547,850	[3]

CA State Teachers Retirement	1,502,602	[3]
OH State Teachers Retirement	637,500	[3]
First Wachovia Corporation	256,887	[3]
MD State Retirement	252,450	[1]
University of TX System	173,200	[6]
University of Chicago	167,781	[3]
FL State Board/Administration	149,200	[2]
Mineworkers Pension Scheme	138,032	[3]
Rockefeller University	135,000	[3]
Harvard College	121,300	[3]
OH School Employee Retirement	109,950	[3]
CO Public Employee Retirement	61,500	[3]
Georgetown University-19	35,550	[5]
Simmons College	34,500	[5]
Williams College	17,800	[5]
Duke Endowment	15,000	[3]
Mt. Holyoke College	15,000	[5]
University of MI	13,800	[5]
University of WI	9,300	[5]
Drew University	9,150	[5]
University of ID	8,000	[5]
University of CO	2,800	[5]

SOURCE: *Notice of Annual Meeting of Shareholders* and *Proxy Statement*, April 20, 1988, dated March 3, 1988, GTE Corporation.

Cessna, Witchita, Kansas (subsidiary of General Dynamics Corporation, St. Louis, Missouri)

Links To Central America:

Arms Sales:

*Cessna A-37B Dragonfly**
El Salvador (9)/(B3)
Guatemala (8)/(A);(10)/(B3)
Honduras (4)/(A);(10)/(B3)

* A report on the shipment of six of these planes to Honduras in 1984 does not identify them as likely candidates for shipments delivered from U.S. government stocks. (E)

Cessna Model 337; Super Skymaster/0-2 & 02A El Salvador (2)/(A);(11)/(B3)
Honduras (5)/(B3)
Nicaraguan contras (3)/(A)

Cessna Model 185; Skywagon/U-17 Costa Rica (7)/(A)
El Salvador CE-185 (1)/(B3)
Honduras (3)/(A); [CE 180/185] (4)/(B3)

Cessna Model 207 Guatemala (4)/(A)
Cessna Model 180 Skywagon El Salvador (7)/(B3)
Guatemala (3)/(A); (2-3)/(B3)
Honduras (1)/(A)

Cessna CE-182 El Salvador (1)/(B3)
Cessna Model 150/A 150 Aerobat Guatemala (6)/(A)
Cessna Model T-41 Mescalero El Salvador (6)/(B3)
Guatemala (12)/(B3)

Cessna Model 177 Cardinal/V206C	Honduras (5)/(A); (5-7)/(B3)
Cessna CE-170A/B	Guatemala (2)/(A)
Cessna CE-172K Skyhawk	Guatemala (4-6)/(B3)
Cessna CE-310	Guatemala (8)/(B3)
Cessna CE-V-206C Stationair	Guatemala (1)/(B3)
Cessna T-37C Tweety Bird	Guatemala (2)/(B3)
	Guatemala (3)/(B3)

Recent Transactions:

El Salvador (3) additional *A-37s* delivered in January of 1985. (C,D2) Other April 1986 reports of (1) *A-37* to be sent to El Salvador. (D8)

Costa Rica, transfer reported of (2) *T-41* Aircraft in January 1985. (D3)

Costa Rica (2) *Cessna 206* aircraft delivered in July 1985. (D5)

See also Table 6-5; Table 6-6.

Links to the Nuclear Weapons Industry:

Since the 1950s, General Dynamics has been a leader in the production of nuclear weapons delivery systems and launch platforms. General Dynamics' Electric Boat Division is the sole producer of the Trident submarine, "a 560 foot underwater platform" that can launch twenty-four strategic nuclear missiles. General Dynamics has also worked on the design and development of cruise missiles and the nuclear-capable F-16 "Falcon." (G)

Affiliations of Corporate Directors (General Dynamics):

Lester Crown a trustee of Northwestern University and chairman of the board of overseers, the Jewish Theological Seminary in New York City.

David S. Lewis, Jr. (see Bank America above).

Cyrus R. Vance was Secretary of State in the Carter Administration.

Selected Institutional Owners (survey of General Dynamics):

Name	Shares Held	Filing Date
College Retirement Equities	502,000	[4]
NY State Common Retirement	289,000	[4]
CA State Teachers Retirement	226,000	[3]
NY State Teachers Retirement	133,000	[4]
University of TX System	99,000	[4]
FL State Board/Administration	50,000	[4]
MD State Retirement	33,000	[1]
OH School Employee Retirement	28,000	[4]
First Wachovia Corporation	16,000	[4]
University of MI	15,400	[5]
Harvard College	11,000	[4]
CO Public Employee Retirement	7,000	[4]
University of WI	5,300	[5]
University of CO	5,200	[5]
MI State University	3,200	[5]
University of TN	3,000	[5]
MI State Treasurer	2,000	[4]

SOURCE: *Notice of Annual Meeting of Shareholders,* May 4, 1988, and *Proxy Statement,* dated March 29, 1988, General Dynamics; *Who's Who in America, 45th Edition, 1988-89* (Wilmette, Illinois: MacMillan Directory Division, 1988).

General Electric Company, Fairfield, Connecticut

Links to South Africa:

General Electric has ties to South Africa through licensing and sales and may have a distribution agreement with the South African firm Electronic Building Elements (Pty.) Ltd. (F1)

Links to Central America:

Arms Sales:

El Salvador and Honduras both have received shipments of GE's minigun machinegun. (B2)

Recent Transactions:

The Armament and Electrical Systems Department, in Burlington, Vermont sent $5.0 million worth of military-related items to Honduras for five *SEA-GATT-20* (small naval anti-aircraft systems) and spare parts production equipment, technical manuals, in-country instructions and in-country, technical support to Honduras in March 1985. (C)

Links to the Nuclear Weapons Industry:

General Electric manufactures electronic components for nuclear weapons systems at the government-owned Pinellas plant in St. Petersburg, Florida. Pinellas now constructs highly complex, miniaturized, neutron generators and electrical assemblies and specialty neutron generation and measurement devices for nuclear weapons testing, among other products. GE has also produced re-entry vehicles for several U.S. ICBMs, including the Titan II and Minuteman III, "the mainstays of the current land-based ICBM force." The company contributes to the nation's submarine and missile program, making fire control systems for the Poseidon and Trident I. GE is also a major producer of propulsion systems for nuclear-powered submarines.

Affiliations of Corporate Directors:

Charles D. Dickey, Jr. is a trustee of the University of Pennsylavania.

Lawrence E. Fouraker is a fellow of the John F. Kennedy School of Government, Harvard University.

Gertrude G. Michelson is a trustee of Columbia University and Spelman College.

Barbara Scott Preiskel (see Bell Helicopter/Textron above).

Lewis T. Preston is a trustee of New York University.

Frank H. T. Rhodes, president of Cornell University, has been a director since 1984. He is chair of the board of directors of the American Council of Education.

William French Smith is trustee of Claremont McKenna College and a member of the visiting committee, Center for International Affairs, Harvard University.

Selected Institutional Owners:

Name	Shares Held	Filing Date
NY State Common Retirement	7,692,600	[3]
University of California	7,215,774	[3]
College Retirement Equities	7,044,500	[3]
TX Teacher Retirement System	4,892,300	[3]
MI State Treasurer	4,794,600	[3]
NY State Teachers Retirement	4,489,400	[3]
CA State Teachers Retirement	3,833,062	[3]
OH State Teachers Retirement	2,698,600	[3]
First Wachovia Corporation	1,823,948	[3]
Ford Foundation	1,050,000	[3]
FL State Board/Administration	1,008,000	[2]
CO Public Employee Retirement	795,600	[3]
Harvard College	735,356	[3]
MD State Retirement	699,200	[1]
Kentucky Teachers Retirement	510,000	[3]

University of TX System	545,300	[3]
Rice, William Marsh Univ	447,022	[3]
OH School Employee Retirement	314,200	[3]
WI Investment Board	260,000	[3]
Mineworkers Pension Scheme	178,920	[3]
University of Chicago	177,402	[3]
Rockefeller University	140,000	[3]
Lutheran Brotherhood	130,000	[3]
University of MN-14	95,000	[5]
Columbia University	71,800	[5]
Lehigh University	54,000	[5]
Aid Association for Lutherans	48,000	[3]
University of Rochester	46,600	[3]
Mt. Holyoke College	36,362	[5]
Duke Endowment	30,700	[3]
Bucknell University	30,000	[5]
Colgate University	28,600	[5]
Carleton College	26,300	[5]
OH State University-3	25,000	[5]
Bowdoin College	24,400	[5]
Simmons College	21,680	[5]
Boston University	19,522	[5]
University of TN	17,000	[5]
Case Western Reserve	14,600	[5]
Wehaton College	14,000	[5]
Clark University-2	14,000	[5]
Georgetown University-18	12,000	[5]
Bates College	10,130	[5]
Tulane University	10,000	[5]
University of MI	10,000	[5]
Williams College	7,552	[5]
University of Delaware	5,600	[3]
OH State University-1	5,500	[5]
Wooster College	5,000	[5]

SOURCE: General Electric; *Notice of 1988 Annual Meeting and Proxy Statement,* April 27, 1988, dated March 8, 1988, General Electric; *Who's Who in America, 45th Edition, 1988-89* (Wilmette, Illinois: MacMillan Directory Division, 1988).

General Foods Corporation, White Plains, New York
(subsidiary of Philip Morris Companies, Inc., New York, New York)

Links To South Africa:
The parent of General Foods, Philip Morris, is believed to have licensing and distribution links to South Africa. (F1)

Links to Central America:
See Section 5.5; Table 5-6.

Affiliations of Corporate Directors (Philip Morris):
Thomas F. Ahrensfeld is a member of the board of visitors of Columbia Law School.

Harold Brown, former U.S. Secretary of Defense (1977-1981), is Chairman of the Foreign Policy Institute, School of Advanced International Studies, Johns Hopkins University.

T. Justin Moore, Jr. is a trustee of the Virginia Foundation for Independent Colleges.

John A. Murphy is a trustee of Marquette University and Alverno College.

William Murray is a trustee of Polytechnic University.

John S. Reed is a member of the MIT Corporation.

Frank E. Resnik is on the board of associates of the University of Richmond and is on the board of directors of Saint Vincent College.

William P. Tavoulareas is a member of the board of governors of St. Johns University.

Selected Institutional Owners (survey of Philip Morris):

Name	Shares Held	Filing Date
Harvard College	329,506	[5]
Rice, William Marsh University	286,500	[5]
University of TX System	173,830	[6]
University of VA	38,000	[5]
University of MI	31,500	[5]
Mt. Holyoke College	28,300	[5]
Willliams College	20,100	[5]
Wellesley College	17,900	[5]
Harvey Mudd College	16,500	[5]
Carleton College	15,975	[5]
University of Rochester	14,600	[5]
Colgate University	12,000	[5]
Tulane Universsity	12,000	[5]
Depauw University-3	10,400	[5]
Bates College	10,050	[5]
Georgetown University-19	10,000	[5]
University of MN-14	10,000	[5]
Boston University	6,500	[5]
University of WI	6,000	[5]

SOURCE: *Notice of Annual Meeting of Shareholders,* April 28, 1988 and *Proxy Statement,* March 9, 1988, General Foods.

General Motors Corporation, Detroit, Michigan

Links to South Africa:

General Motors continues to provide designs and parts to its former subsidiary, renamed Delta Motors Corporation. (F1)

Links to Central America:

Arms Sales:

General Motors Corporation, Allison Gas Turbine Operations, Indiana, in July 1986 provided $5.7 million for engineering services for the T-56 engine applicable to the Component Improvement program which supports the C-130 aircraft to Honduras and 19 other countries. (C)

Affiliations of Corporate Directors:

Anne L. Armstrong, chairman of the President's Foreign Intelligence Advisory Board (in 1988), is chairman of the Center for Strategic and International Studies in Washington, D.C. She is also a member of the board of overseers of the Hoover Institution.

Donald J. Atwood, is a member of the executive committee of MIT. He is also a director of Charles Stark Draper Laboratory, Inc.

James H. Evans (see Citicorp above).

Walter A. Fallon is a trustee of the University of Rochester.

Marvin L. Goldberger, former president of the California Institute of Technology, is presently director of the Institute for Advanced Study, Princeton, New Jersey and a member of the Council on Foreign Relations.

Elmer W. Johnson is a trustee of the University of Chicago.

Edmund T. Pratt (see Chase Manhattan Bank above).

Lloyd E. Reuss is a trustee of the Lawrence Institute of Technology, Louisville Presbyterian Theological Seminary and Vanderbilt University.

John G. Smale is a director of the United Negro College Fund and a trustee of Kenyon College.

Roger B. Smith is a trustee of the California Institute of Technology.

Robert C. Stempel is a trustee of the Worcester Polytechnic Institute.

Leon H. Sullivan is pastor of the Zion Baptist Church of Philadelphia.

Thomas H. Wyman is chairman of the board of trustees of Amherst College, a faculty fellow at the Yale School of Organization and Management and a member of the Council on Foreign Relations.

Selected Institutional Owners:

Name	Shares Held	Filing Date
MI State Treasurer	4,424,200	[3]
NY State Common Retirement	2,314,600	[3]
CA State Teachers Retirement	1,647,355	[3]
College Retirement Equities	1,518,700	[3]
NY State Teachers Retirement	1,491,858	[3]
TX Teacher Retirement System	973,140	[3]
University of Pennsylvania	450,095	[5]
FL State Board/Administration	390,000	[2]
OH State Teachers Retirement	385,000	[3]
CO Public Employee Retirement	358,500	[3]
University of TX System	296,890	[6]
MD State Retirement	241,800	[1]
WI Investment Board	231,200	[3]
Harvard College	212,950	[3]
First Wachovia Corporation	205,894	[3]
Ford Foundation	125,000	[3]
OH School Employee Retirement	101,300	[3]
Lutheran Brotherhood	50,000	[3]
University of MN-14	43,500	[5]
Kentucky Teachers Retirement	40,000	[3]
Knights of Columbus	35,375	[3]
Columbia University	24,520	[5]
Georgetown University-19	24,500	[5]
Wellesley College	20,000	[5]
University of VA	18,960	[5]
University of Rochester	18,000	[3]
Williams College	16,500	[5]
University of MI	16,300	[5]
Grinnell College	15,900	[5]
Tulane University	14,500	[5]
Lehigh University	10,000	[5]
MA Institute of Technology	9,028	[5]
Georgetown University-17	7,500	[5]
Duke Endowment	6,300	[3]
Boston University	2,200	[5]
University of CO	1,400	[5]

SOURCE: *Notice of Annual Meeting of Stockholders,* May 20, 1988, and *Proxy Statement,* dated April 15, 1988, General Motors; *Who's Who in America,* 45th Edition, 1988-89 (Wilmette, Illinois: MacMillan Directory Division, 1988).

Goodyear Tire & Rubber Co., Akron, Ohio

Links to South Africa:
Goodyear owns Goodyear Tyre & Rubber Co., SA (Pty.) Ltd. and Kelly-Springfield Tyre Co., SA (Pty.) Ltd. (F1)

Links to Central America:
See Section 5.5.

Links to the Nuclear Weapons Industry:
The Goodyear Atomic Corporation employed 3,200 Workers at its Portsmouth Gas Diffusion Plant, a nuclear materials production facility, during 1985 in Piketon, Ohio. (G)

Affiliations of Corporate Directors:
Thomas H. Cruikshank is a member of the board of governors of Rice University, Houston.
Gertrude G. Michelson (see General Electric above).
Steven A. Minter is a trustee of the College of Wooster.
Agnar Pytee is president of Case Western Reserve University.
William C. Turner is a member of the board of governors of the Lauder Institute of Management and International Studies of the University of Pennsylvania.

Selected Institutional Owners:

Name	Shares Held	Filing Date
College Retirement Equities	690,776	[3]
NY State Common Retirement	662,776	[3]
OH State Teachers Retirement	529,121	[3]
TX Teacher Retirement System	328,669	[3]
NY State Teachers Retirement	234,738	[3]
CA State Teachers Retirement	203,887	[3]
University of Alabama	50,000	[5]
MD State Retirement	43,500	[1]
OH School Employee Retirement	34,183	[3]
University of TX System	30,100	[5]
Simmons College	25,000	[5]
Harvard College	23,900	[3]
FL State Board/Administration	20,000	[2]
Mt. Holyoke College	14,900	[5]
First Wachovia Corporation	13,597	[3]
CO Public Employee Retirement	10,800	[3]
Duke Endowment	9,000	[3]
Boston College	5,500	[5]
MI State Treasurer	3,300	[3]

SOURCE: *Notice of 1988 Annual Meeting of Shareholders and Proxy Statement,* April 11, 1988, dated February 22, 1988, Goodyear Tire & Rubber.

Grumman Corporation, Bethpage, New York

Links to Central America:
See Table 6-5.

Affiliations of Corporate Directors:
Lucy Wilson Benson is a trustee of Lafayette College. She is also a member of the Council on Foreign Relations.

Renso L. Caporali is a trustee of Clarkson University.

Victor Hao Li, who has been a consultant for the U.S. Senate Foreign Relations Committee, is president of the East-West Center, in Honolulu, Hawaii, a public, non-profit corporation established by the U.S. Congress as an educational institution.

John O'Brien serves on the council of overseers for the Faculty of Business, Public Administration and Accountancy at C.W. Post College.

Ellis L. Phillips, Jr. is president of the Ellis L. Phillips Foundation and former president of Ithaca College from 1970 to 1975.

Selected Institutional Owners:

Name	Shares Held	Filing Date
NY State Teachers Retirement	297,000	[3]
College Retirement Equities	285,800	[3]
NY State Common Retirement	234,000	[3]
CA State Teachers Retirement	112,356	[3]
Harvard College	54,500	[3]
University of MI	18,300	[5]
OH School Employee Retirement	10,000	[3]
CO Public Employee Retirement	6,200	[3]
MI State Treasurer	1,900	[3]

SOURCE: *Notice of Annual Meeting of Shareholders,* dated April 21, 1988 and *Proxy Statement,* dated March 11, 1988, Grumman Corporation; *Who's Who in America, 45th Edition, 1988-89* (Wilmette, Illinois: MacMillan Directory Division, 1988).

Hercules Incorporated, Wilmington, Delaware

Links to Central America:
See Table 3-2.

Affiliations of Corporate Directors:
Stuart E. Eizenstat, a former member of the White House Staffs of both Presidents Johnson and Carter, is an adjunct lecturer at the John F. Kennedy School of Government at Harvard University.

Robert G. Jahn has been professor of aerospace sciences since 1967 at Princeton University.

Selected Institutional Owners:

Name	Shares Held	Filing Date
University of California	2,046,941	[3]
College Retirement Equities	671,500	[3]
NY State Common Retirement	506,000	[3]
NY State Teachers Retirement	390,500	[3]
University of TX System	255,700	[6]
CA State Teachers Retirement	219,236	[3]
First Wachovia Corporation	37,291	[3]

Columbia University	37,200	[5]
MD State Retirement	30,000	[1]
Harvard College	21,300	[3]
Tulane University	19,000	[5]
OH School Employee Retirement	17,200	[3]
CO Public Employee Retirement	9,200	[3]
Bates College	8,000	[5]
MI State Treasurer	3,200	[3]
Albright College	3,000	[5]

SOURCE: *Notice of Annual Meeting of Stockholders,* March 22, 1988 and *Proxy Statement,* dated February 15, 1988, Hercules, Inc.; *Who's Who in America, 45th Edition, 1988-89* (Wilmette, Illinois: MacMillan Directory Division, 1988).

Hoechst, AG, Frankfurt, West Germany (principal U.S. subsidiary: Hoechst Celanese Corporation, Somerville, New Jersey)

Links to Central America:
See Table 3-2; Table 3-4.

Selected Institutional Owners:

Name	Shares Held	Filing Date
Tulane University	8,000	[5]

ICI Americas Inc., Wilmington, Delaware (subsidiary of Imperial Chemical Industries, PLC, London, United Kingdom)

Links to Central America:

Arms Sales:
NARMIC has identified ICI Americas, Inc. as a firm whose ammunition supplies are used by Guatemala. (B1)

Selected Institutional Owners (survey of Imperial Chemical Industries, PLC):

Name	Shares Held	Filing Date
Alma College	13,000	[5]
Wellesley College	12,200	[5]
University of VA	10,000	[5]
Boston University	5,000	[5]
Wooster College	5,000	[5]
Carleton College	300	[5]

Jonas Aircraft and Arms Co., New York, New York

Links to Central America:
See Table 6-4.

Litton Systems, Inc., Beverly Hills, California (subsidiary of Litton Industries, Inc., Beverly Hills, California)

Links to South Africa:

Litton may have a distribution agreement with Tedelex in South Africa. (F1)

Links to Central America:

Arms Sales:

Litton Systems, Inc., Tempe, Arizona, was involved in a $6.2 million arms deal for image intensification devices MX-9916 and MX-9644 to El Salvador and another country in May 1986. (C)

Links to the Nuclear Weapons Industry:

Litton Industries has received contracts for work on electronic countermeasures for the B-52 bomber. In programs for the Navy's nuclear missiles, Litton has worked with Lockheed to develop an "advanced re-entry vehicle" i.e. "the part of the ballistic missile that carries the warhead to the target." Litton has also been heavily involved in developing cruise missile guidance systems (receiving a $1 billion contract to build 5,500 in 1979). The company has also developed jamming systems for nuclear-capable planes. (G)

Selected Institutional Owners (survey of Litton Industries):

Name	Shares Held	Filing Date
NY State Common Retirement	398,000	[3]
College Retirement Equities	322,594	[3]
CA State Teachers Retirement	291,595	[3]
FL State Board/Administration	60,000	[2]
NY State Teachers Retirement	27,770	[3]
OH School Employee Retirement	21,406	[3]
MD State Retirement	19,800	[1]
University of MI	11,800	[5]
Harvard College	11,600	[3]
University of TX System	8,500	[3]
University of WI	5,300	[5]
CO Public Employee Retirement	4,800	[3]
Georgetown-17	2,800	[5]
Depauw University-3	2,500	[5]
MI State University	2,346	[5]
MI State Treasurer	1,500	[3]

Lockheed Corporation, Calabasas, California

Links to Central America:

Arms Sales:

Lockheed T-33A Trainer; T-33A Shooting Star	Guatemala (5)/(A); (5)/(B3)
	Honduras (3)/(A); (3)/(B3)
Lockheed L-188 Electra	Honduras (1)/(B3)

Links to the Nuclear Weapons Industry:

Lockheed has received millions of dollars for work on military space systems and has been active in the development of the Navy's Submarine Launched Ballistic Missile (SLBM) project. Some specific nuclear weapons-linked projects have included: the Trident C-4 and D-5 missiles, U-2 reconnaissance aircraft maintenance, the Space Shuttle and the Tomahawk cruise missile. (G)

Affiliations of Corporate Directors:

Warren Christopher served as U.S. Deputy Secretary of State from 1977 to 1981.

Houston I. Flournoy is professor of public administration and Special Assistant to the president for governmental affairs, University of Southern California, Sacramento, California.

Robert A. Fuhrman is a member of the advisory board of the College of Engineering at the University of Michigan. He is also a member of the advisory board, University of Santa Clara.

James F. Gibbons is dean of the School of Engineering, Stanford University, Stanford, California.

John E. Swearingen is a member of the advisory board of the Hoover Institution on War, Revolution and Peace (since 1967). He has been a trustee of Carnegie Mellon University since 1960.

Selected Institutional Owners:

Name	Shares Held	Filing Date
WI Investment Board	1,706,900	[3]
NY State Common Retirement	1,018,600	[3]
College Retirement Equities	781,300	[3]
CA State Teachers Retirement	471,312	[3]
NY State Teachers Retirement	218,000	[3]
Harvard College	89,100	[3]
MD State Retirement	50,500	[1]
University of TX System	26,900	[6]
University of WI	26,500	[5]
University of MI	13,700	[5]
Tulane University	12,000	[5]
CO Public Employee Retirement	11,600	[3]
Alma College	8,000	[5]
Depauw University-3	6,300	[5]
Bates College	6,000	[5]
Lehigh University	4,900	[5]
MI State Treasurer	3,800	[3]
MI State University	3,100	[5]
University of CO	2,300	[5]

SOURCE: *Notice of Annual Meeting of Shareholders,* May 10, 1988 and *Proxy Statement,* dated April 4, 1988, Lockheed Corporation; *Who's Who in America, 45th Edition, 1988-89* (Wilmette, Illinois: MacMillan Directory Division, 1988).

Magnavox Government & Industrial Electronics, Co., Ft. Wayne, Indiana (subsidiary of North American Philips Corporation and the ultimate parent firm, Philips International B.V., Eindhoven, The Netherlands)

Links to Central America:

Arms Sales:

Magnavox Electronic Systems Co., Fort Wayne, Indiana, in January 1987 was involved in a $3.6 arms deal for receiver transmitters and controls applicable to AC-164(V) UHF radios used on various aircraft to El Salvador and thirteen other countries. (C)

Affiliations of Corporate Directors (North American Philips, Corporation):

Scott C. Lea is a trustee of Johnson C. Smith University, Charlotte, North Carolina.

Selected Institutional Owners (survey of North American Philips):

Name	Shares Held	Filing Date
Columbia University	39,200	[5]
University of MI	12,700	[5]
University of WI	9,700	[5]
MI State University	5,100	[5]

SOURCE: *Who's Who in America, 45th Edition, 1988-89* (Wilmette, Illinois: MacMillan Directory Division, 1988).

Hughes Helicopters, now McDonnell-Douglas Helicopter Co., Culver City, California (subsidiary of McDonnell-Douglas, St. Louis, Missouri)

Links to South Africa:
The former Hughes Helicopters has business ties to Comair Sales (Pty.) Ltd. in South Africa. (F1)

Links to Central America:

Arms Sales:

Hughes 500 Helicopter	El Salvador (6)/B3
Hughes TH-55A Helicopter	Honduras (4)/B3

Recent Transactions:
In 1985, El Salvador received at least four Hughes 500 MD defenders. (C) A report that ten Hughes 500 helicopters were to be sent to El Salvador was confirmed in May of 1985. (D4) A report by the IRRC on the 1985 order of (4) model 500MD Defender scout helicopters to be sent to El Salvador did not identify this transaction as likely being delivered from U.S. government stocks. (E)
See also Table 6-5.

McDonnell-Douglas, St. Louis, Missouri

Links to South Africa:
McDonnell-Douglas may still have a licensing/distribution agreement with its former subsidiary CMC Computer Machinery (Pty.) Ltd. (F1)

Links to Central America:

Arms Sales:

Douglas C-47 Skytrain/C-117	El Salvador (5)/(A); (7)/(B3)
	Guatemala (8)/(A); (10)/(B3)
	Honduras (6)/(A); (11)/(B3)
Douglas AC-47	El Salvador (2)/(B3)
Douglas C-54 Skymaster	El Salvador (2)/(A)
	Guatemala (1)/(A); (1)/(B3)
	Honduras (1)/(A); (2)/(B3)
Douglas C-118B Liftmaster	El Salvador (1)/(B3)
Douglas DC-6	El Salvador (2)/(B3)
Douglas DC-6B	Guatemala (1)/(B3)

Recent Transactions:
One converted DC-3 worth $1.5 million, delivered to El Salvador in December of 1984. (D1)
Eight Douglas C-47s with machine guns were being delivered in April 1985 to El Salvador. (D4)

The Nicaraguan contras were given a DC-4 cargo aircraft as a "gift," a transaction reported in August 1985. (D6)

See also Table 6-5; Table 6-6.

Links to the Nuclear Weapons Industry:

McDonnell-Douglas produced the nuclear-armed Genie missile, an air-launched missile designed to destroy aircraft. The company has also worked on the Tomahawk cruise missile program and the Ballistic Missile Defense program. (G)

Affiliations of Corporate Directors:

William H. Danforth is chancellor of Washington University, St. Louis.

Selected Institutional Owners:

Name	Shares Held	Filing Date
College Retirement Equities	343,700	[3]
WI Investment Board	272,200	[3]
NY State Common Retirement	271,900	[3]
First Wachovia Corporation	267,864	[3]
NY State Teachers Retirement	202,700	[3]
CA State Teachers Retirement	186,339	[3]
University of TX System	41,600	[3]
MD State Retirement	31,000	[1]
OH School Employee Retirement	30,800	[3]
Harvard College	30,200	[3]
Grinnell College	18,800	[5]
FL State Board/Administration	13,000	[2]
CO Public Employee Retirement	7,300	[3]
University of CO	4,200	[5]
Alma College	4,000	[5]
MI State Treasurer	2,300	[3]

SOURCE: *Notice of Annual Meeting of Stockholders,* April 28, 1988, and *Proxy Statement,* dated March 21, 1988, McDonnell-Douglas Corporation.

Mobil Oil Corporation, New York, New York

Links to South Africa:

Mobil Oil has direct investments in South Africa through these subsidiaries/affiliates: Mobil Oil Southern Africa (Pty.) Ltd.; Condor Oil (Pty.) Ltd.; Mobil Oil Refining Co. Southern Africa (Pty.) Ltd.; South African Oil Refining Co. (Pty.) Ltd. (33.3 percent interest); SONAREP (SA), (Pty.) Ltd.; Socony (Pty.), Ltd.; Vialit (Pty.) Ltd.; Westchester Insurance Co. (Pty.) Ltd.; and Superior Oil Co. (F1)

Links to Central America:

See Section 5.5; Table 5-9.

Affiliations of Corporate Directors:

Lewis M. Branscomb, is director, Science, Technology and Public Policy, John F. Kennedy School of Government, Harvard University.

Samuel Curtis Johnson is a trustee of Cornell University.

Allan E. Murray is a member of the advisory council, Columbia University Graduate School of Business. He is also a member of the Council on Foreign Relations.

Richard Frank Tucker is a trustee of Cornell University; chairman of the board of overseers Cornell University Medical School.

Selected Institutional Owners:

Name	Shares Held	Filing Date
NY State Common Retirement	4,984,000	[3]
College Retirement Equities	2,781,300	[3]
TX Teacher Retirement System	2,199,168	[3]
OH State Teachers Retirement	2,082,900	[3]
NY State Teachers Retirement	2,040,500	[3]
MI State Treasurer	1,856,100	[3]
CA State Teachers Retirement	1,708,719	[3]
CO Public Employee Retirement	702,700	[3]
First Wachovia Corporation	438,087	[3]
FL State Board/Administration	402,500	[2]
MD State Retirement	314,300	[1]
Ford Foundation	250,000	[3]
Howard Hughes Medical Institute	250,000	[3]
Rice, William Marsh University	217,652	[3]
OH School Employee Retirement	196,600	[3]
University of Chicago	188,845	[6]
University of TX System	147,700	[6]
Mineworkers Pension Scheme	134,060	[3]
Young Men's Christian Association	110,000	[3]
Aid Assoc For Lutherans	105,500	[3]
Columbia University	61,500	[5]
Lutheran Brotherhood	50,000	[3]
Wellesley College	47,000	[5]
University of MN-14	39,000	[5]
Knights of Columbus	37,000	[3]
Smith College-8	32,500	[5]
Bowdoin College	20,400	[5]
University of VA	20,000	[5]
Boston University	17,300	[5]
Case Western Reserve	15,400	[5]
Lehigh University	15,000	[5]
Mt. Holyoke College	14,300	[5]
Colby College	13,100	[5]
MA Institute of Technology	7,250	[2]
Williams College	3,900	[5]
Albright College	2,000	[5]

SOURCE: *Notice of Annual Meeting,* May 12, 1988 and *Proxy Statement,* March 14, 1988, Mobil Oil Corporation; *Who's Who in America, 45th Edition, 1988-89* (Wilmette, Illinois: MacMillan Directory Division, 1988).

Monark Boat Co. (subsidiary of Monark Industries, Inc., Monticello, Arkansas)

Links to Central America:

Arms Sales:

A contract for ten forty-one foot patrol boats manufactured by Monark Boat Company to be acquired by El Salvador was reported in January 1988. The contract was worth $3.6 million. (D14)

Monsanto, St. Louis, Missouri

Links to South Africa:
Monsanto has direct ownership in South Africa through Monsanto South Africa (Pty.) Ltd. and G.D. Searle SA (Pty.) Ltd. (F1)

Links to Central America:
See Table 3-2; Table 3-4.

Affiliations of Corporate Directors:
Marguerite R. Barnett is chancellor of the University of Missouri-St. Louis.
Richard J. Mahoney is a trustee of Washington University.
Buck Mickel is a life trustee of Clemson University and Converse College.
John B. Slaughter is chancellor of the University of Maryland at College Park.
Stansfield Turner is a former director of the CIA (1977-1981).

Selected Institutional Owners:

Name	Shares Held	Filing Date
College Retirement Equities	1,133,400	[3]
TX Teacher Retirement System	958,600	[3]
NY State Common Retirement	594,000	[3]
OH State Teachers Retirement	460,000	[3]
First Wachovia Corporation	391,394	[3]
NY State Teachers Retirement	349,400	[3]
CA State Teachers Retirement	324,523	[3]
WI Investment Board	118,900	[3]
University of TX System	105,500	[3]
MD State Retirement	56,000	[1]
Mineworkers Pension Scheme	50,500	[3]
Young Men's Christian Association	50,000	[3]
FL State Board/Administration	50,000	[2]
OH School Employee Retirement	41,400	[3]
Harvard College	30,800	[3]
CO Public Employee Retirement	14,000	[3]
Simmons College	14,000	[5]
Colby College-3	9,000	[5]
Mt. Holyoke College	8,400	[5]
University of Idaho	8,000	[5]
Duke Endowment	5,000	[3]
MI State Treasurer	4,500	[3]
University of CO	1,200	[5]
Colgate University-17	1,100	[5]

SOURCE: *Notice of Annual Meeting of Shareholders,* April 22, 1988 and *Proxy Statement,* dated March 11, 1988, Monsanto.

Motorola Inc., Schaumberg, Illinois

Links to South Africa:
Motorola products are distributed and manufactured under license by Altech in South Africa. (F1)

Links to Central America:

Arms Training:
NARMIC found that six technicians from El Salvador were trained in the use of Motorola Communications Systems in May of 1983. The training occurred at the Motorola International Training Facility in Ft. Lauderdale, Florida. (B2)

See also Table 6-6.

Affiliations of Corporate Directors:
George M.C. Fisher is a member of the board of directors of the University of Illinois Foundation and a trustee of Brown University.

Robert W. Galvin is chairman of the board of trustees of the Illinois Institute of Technology.

Lawrence Howe is a trustee of Loyola University.

Stephen L. Levy is a director of the Polytechnic Institute of New York.

Walter E. Massen is vice president for research and for Argonne National Laboratory, University of Chicago.

Arthur C. Nielsen, Jr. is a life trustee of the University of Chicago.

William J. Weisz is a member of MIT's development committee.

B. Kenneth West is chairman of the board of trustees of the University of Chicago.

Selected Institutional Owners:

Name	Shares Held	Filing Date
College Retirement Equities	1,547,500	[3]
NY State Common Retirement	1,291,400	[3]
TX Teacher Retirement System	884,500	[3]
MI State Treasurer	834,350	[3]
NY State Teachers Retirement	637,400	[3]
CO Public Employee Retirement	504,400	[3]
CA State Teachers Retirement	458,844	[3]
First Wachovia Corporation	362,434	[3]
OH State Teachers Retirement	137,600	[3]
University of TX System	118,900	[6]
FL State Board/Administration	115,000	[2]
University of Chicago	115,811	[6]
MD State Retirement	98,600	[1]
OH School Employee Retirement	59,100	[3]
Harvard College	56,600	[3]
Knights of Columbus	46,000	[3]
Duke Endowment	22,000	[3]
University of Rochester	17,700	[3]
Boston University	13,500	[5]

SOURCE: *Notice of Annual Meeting of Stockholders,* May 2, 1988, *Proxy Statement,* dated March 18, 1988, Motorola.

Northrop Corporation, Los Angeles, California

Links to Central America:

Arms Sales:
Northrop was involved in the transfer of twelve F-5E Tiger II fighter aircraft to Honduras in 1983. The sale was not identified as likely to have been delivered from U.S. government stocks. (E)

Recent Transactions:
   A shipment of eight to twelve Northrop F-5E fighters was planned for Honduras according to a March 1987 agreement worth $70 to $100 million.(D12) Two of twelve F-5 fighters ordered were delivered in December 1987. (D15)
   See also Section 6.7; Section 6.8.

Links to the Nuclear Weapons Industry:
   Northrop has described itself as "a major contributor to the nation's strategic buildup." As a subcontractor and supplier, the company has contributed to the production and development of many weapons systems used in the delivery of nuclear weapons, including: the MX, B-1B, B-52, and the ALCM. Northrop helped design the Stealth bomber. In FY 1981, Northrop's prime contracts on primary nuclear weapons systems totaled at least $147 million. (G)

Affiliations of Corporate Directors:
   Howard Pfeiffer Allen is a trustee of Pomona College.
   William F. Ballhaus is a trustee of Harvey Mudd College and a member of the advisory council, School of Engineering, Stanford University.
   Richard J. Flamson, III (see Coca-Cola above).
   Ivan A. Getting is a director of the Environmental Research Institute of Michigan (ERIM).
   Thomas V. Jones is a trustee of the Institute for Stategic Studies, London, and a member of the University of Southern California, Associates.
   Tom Killefer is a member of the council, Rockefeller University.
   Kent Kresa is on the visiting committee, Department of Aeronautics and Astronautics, MIT.
   Robert L. J. Long is on the board of visitors, National Defense Unviersity.
   George T. Scharffenberger is chairman of the board of trustees of the University of Southern California and a trustee of Georgetown University.

Selected Institutional Owners:

Name	Shares Held	Filing Date
MI State Treasurer	1,687,000	[3]
College Retirement Equities	781,300	[3]
CO Public Employee Retirement	458,900	[3]
NY State Teachers Retirement	448,100	[3]
NY State Common Retirement	324,000	[3]
CA State Teachers Retirement	257,126	[3]
MD State Retirement	46,400	[1]
University of TX System	23,500	[6]
Harvard College	19,100	[3]
OH School Employee Retirement	13,500	[3]
Case Western Reserve	10,000	[5]
Georgetown University-18	8,500	[5]

SOURCE: *Notice of Annual Meeting of Stockholders,* May 18, 1988, and *Proxy Statement,* dated March 31, 1988, Northrop Corporation; *Who's Who in America, 45th Edition, 1988-89* (Wilmette, Illinois: MacMillan Directory Division, 1988).

Olin Corporation, Stamford, Connecticut

Links to South Africa:
   The Olin Corporation has direct investment in South Africa through Olin (Pty.) Ltd. and Aquachlor (Pty.) Ltd. (F1)

Links to Central America:

Arms Sales:
NARMIC has identified Olin Corporation as a firm whose ammunition supplies are used by Guatemala. (B1)

See also Table 6-4.

Affiliations of Corporate Directors:

Richard R. Berry is a trustee of the Atlanta University Center.

Robert R. Frederick is chairman of the board of trustees of Depauw University and a trustee of New York University.

Richard M. Furlaud is a trustee of the Rockefeller University.

Robert Holland, Jr. is vice chairman of the board of trustees, Spelman College and a trustee of the Atlanta University Center.

John W. Johnstone, Jr. is a trustee of Hartwick College.

Jack D. Kuehler is a member of the engineering advisory board at Cornell's College of Engineering and MIT's visiting committee for sponsored research. He is also a trustee of Santa Clara University.

Robert H. Sorensen is a member of the University of Bridgeport board of trustees.

Selected Institutional Owners:

Name	Shares Held	Filing Date
NY State Common Retirement	200,000	[3]
College Retirement Equities	94,000	[3]
CA State Teachers Retirement	67,637	[3]
MD State Retirement	46,000	[1]
University of VA	12,500	[5]
First Wachovia Corporation	9,366	[3]
University of TN	7,500	[5]

SOURCE: *Notice of Annual Meeting of Shareholders,* April 28, 1988, and *Proxy Statement,* dated March 15, 1988, Olin Corporation.

Procter & Gamble Corporation, Cincinnati, Ohio

Links to South Africa:

Procter & Gamble acquired Richardson-Vicks, Inc. (U.S.) whose subsidiary Pantene Group has a licensing agreement in South Africa with Premark. (F1)

Links to Central America:

See Section 5.5; Table 5-6.

Affiliations Of Corporate Directors:

Joshua Lederberg is president of the Rockefeller University.

Selected Institutional Owners:

Name	Shares Held	Filing Date
University of California	2,467,707	[3]
NY State Common Retirement	1,402,600	[3]
College Retirement Equities	1,003,000	[3]
NY State Teachers Retirement	815,000	[3]
CA State Teachers Retirement	806,661	[3]
OH State Teachers Retirement	677,300	[3]
TX Teacher Retirement System	635,100	[3]

CO Public Employee Retirement	372,000	[3]
Kentucky Teachers Retirement	231,000	[3]
First Wachovia Corporation	204,884	[3]
FL State Board/Administration	170,000	[2]
University of TX System	154,800	[6]
MD State Retirement	129,400	[1]
Rice, William Marsh University	128,030	[3]
University of Chicago	111,347	[3]
Harvard College	73,432	[3]
Mineworkers Pension Scheme	54,510	[3]
OH School Employee Retirement	52,500	[3]
Lutheran Brotherhood	50,000	[3]
Aid Association for Lutherans	42,000	[3]
University of Delaware	38,000	[3]
Young Men's Christian Association	14,872	[3]
Lehigh University	14,000	[5]
University of Rochester	13,500	[3]
MI State Treasurer	10,000	[3]
University of VA	10,000	[5]
University of MI	9,600	[5]
Duke Endowment	6,000	[3]
Mt. Holyoke College	5,200	[5]
Williams College	4,400	[5]
University of Houston	3,000	[5]

SOURCE: *Proxy Statement, Annual Meeting of Shareholders to be Held October 11, 1988.*

Raytheon Company, Lexington, Massachusetts

Links to South Africa:

Although the company announced its intention to end all ownership in South Africa, as of 1988 it still had a 15 percent interest in its former subsidiary Badger (Pty.) Ltd. in South Africa. (F1)

Links to Central America:

Arms Sales:

Beech Model T-34C Mentor	El Salvador (3)/(A); (3)/(B3)
Beech Baron	Honduras (1)/(B3)
Beech C-45 Expeditor	Honduras (2)/(B3)
Beech Super King Air 200	Guatemala (1)/(B3)

Links to the Nuclear Weapons Industry:

Most of Raytheon's military work has been in electronic systems used on a number of conventional and nuclear-related weapons such as missile, fire control, air traffic control, sonar, communications and electronic countermeasure systems for the services. In FY 1981, Raytheon received at least $84 million in prime contract awards for primary nuclear warfare systems and component sales. Another $140 million was awarded for secondary nuclear weapons-related systems. Raytheon has been involved in the Trident missile, strategic radar, B-1B bomber and B-52 bomber programs. (G)

Affiliations of Corporate Directors:

Harvey Brooks is Benjamin Pierce Professor of Technology and Public Policy (Emeritus), Harvard University.

Theodore L. Elliot, Jr. is Alex Swanberg distinguished visiting scholar, the Hoover Institution, Stanford University, and a former U.S. Ambassador.

Colman M. Mockler, Jr. (see Bank of Boston above).

Thomas L. Phillips is a trustee at Gordon College and Northeastern University.

Selected Institutional Owners:

Name	Shares Held	Filing Date
OH State Teachers Retirement	1,075,400	[3]
TX Teacher Retirement System	1,040,100	[3]
College Retirement Equities	874,410	[3]
NY State Common Retirement	598,000	[3]
First Wachovia Corporation	500,861	[3]
NY State Teachers Retirement	332,600	[3]
CA State Teachers Retirement	277,280	[3]
Kentucky Teachers Retirement	135,000	[3]
Harvard College	123,500	[3]
University of TX System	87,700	[6]
University of DE	62,000	[6]
OH School Employee Retirement	54,900	[3]
MD State Retirement	54,800	[1]
Mineworkers Pension Scheme	46,350	[3]
Knights of Columbus	35,000	[3]
Tulane University	28,000	[5]
Bucknell University	25,000	[5]
CO Public Employee Retirement	12,800	[3]
University of VA	10,000	[5]
University of TN	8,100	[5]
Wheaton College	7,000	[5]
Duke Endowment	6,500	[3]
Boston University	6,000	[5]
MI State Treasurer	4,100	[3]
Albright College	2,000	[5]
University of CO	1,600	[5]

SOURCE: *Notice of the Annual Meeting of Shareholders,* May 25, 1988 and *Proxy Statement,* April 20, 1988, Raytheon; *Who's Who in America, 45th Edition, 1988-89* (Wilmette, Illinois: MacMillan Directory Division, 1988).

Rhone-Poulenc, Paris, France

Links to Central America:

In December 1986, Rhone-Poulenc acquired the major portion of the agrochemicals business of Union Carbide's former subsidiaries in the pesticide business in Central America. The agrochemicals segment of Rhone-Poulenc manufactures methomyl (methavin) which is used on cotton, corn, fruits and vegetables and malathion which is used on vines and arborculture.

See also Table 3-2.

SOURCE: Phone interview with Antoine Puech, Rhone-Poulenc, Research Triangle Park, North Carolina, May 12, 1989; Form 20-F, Rhone-Poulenc, Securities and Exchange Commission, Washington, D.C., dated June 30, 1988.

Rockwell International Corporation, El Segundo, California

Links to Central America:

Arms Sales:

Rockwell International Turbo Commander	Guatemala (1)/(A)
North American T-6 Texan	El Salvador (6-8)/(B3)
Rockwell T-28 Trojan	El Salvador (8)/(B3)
Rockwll T-28A	Honduras (12)/(B3)
North American F-96E Sabre	Honduras (4)/(B3)
Rockwell Aero Commander 680	Guatemala (1)/(B3)

Recent Transactions:

The Collins Government Avionics Division in Cedar Rapids, Iowa, in December 1985 supplied $13.4 million for line items of spare parts applicable to the *ARN-118* tactical airborne communications and navigation system to El Salvador and ten other countries. (C)

The Collins Government Avionics Division was involved in a $10.6 million arms deal in June 1985 for twenty-one line items of various quantities applicable to the *AN/ARC-186* VHF AM/FM radio system used on various aircraft to Honduras and thirteen other countries. (C)

The Collins Government Avionics Division was involved in a $10.8 million arms deal in June 1985 which sent fifteen line items of spare parts applicable to the *ARN-118* tactical airborne communications and navigation system to Honduras and fifteen other countries. (C)

Links to the Nuclear Weapons Industry:

Rockwell's recent nuclear warfare-related programs include the MX missile, the B-1B bomber, the Trident submarine and the Navstar and Afsatcom satellite systems. (G)

Affiliations of Corporate Directors:

Robert Anderson is a trustee of the California Institute of Technology.

Donald R. Beall is a charter trustee of the University of Pittsburgh and a member of the University of California-Irvine, board of overseers.

Richard M. Bressler is a trustee of Dartmouth College.

Robin Chandler Duke is vice chairman of the Institute of International Education.

Fred L. Hartley is a trustee of the California Institute of Technology.

James Clayburn La Force, Jr. is dean of the Graduate School of Management, the University of California, Los Angeles.

Joseph F. Toot, Jr. is a member of the Associates of the Harvard Business School.

Selected Institutional Owners:

Name	Shares Held	Filing Date
College Retirement Equities	2,485,900	[3]
TX Teacher Retirement System	2,226,600	[3]
NY State Common Retirement	1,882,100	[3]
NY State Teachers Retirement	1,315,900	[3]
CA State Teachers Retirement	1,201,114	[3]
WI Investment Board	530,600	[3]
FL State Board/Administration	300,000	[2]
MD State Retirement	211,700	[1]
OH School Employee Retirement	184,000	[3]
University of TX System	123,800	[6]
University of DE	112,000	[6]
Harvard College	103,000	[3]
CO Public Employee Retirement	52,000	[3]
University of MI	39,400	[5]
University of Rochester	26,000	[3]

Trinity College	17,000	[5]
MI State Treasurer	15,900	[3]
University of WI	9,700	[5]
MI State University	9,600	[5]
University of CO	5,000	[5]
Hanover College	2,500	[5]
Colgate University-17	1,350	[5]

SOURCE: *Notice of Annual Meeting of Stockholders,* February 10, 1988, *Proxy Statement,* dated January 5, 1988, Rockwell International.

Rohm & Haas Co., Philadelphia, Pennsylvania

Links to South Africa:
Rohm & Haas continues sales and licensing ties to former affiliates in South Africa. (F1)

Links to Central America:
See Table 3-2.

Affiliations of Corporate Directors:
George B. Beitzel is a trustee of Amherst College.

George Morris Dorrance, Jr. is a trustee of the University of Pennsylvania.

Earl G. Graves is a member of the visiting committee, Harvard University, School of Government and a trustee of the Tuskegee Institute.

John H. McCarthur (see Chase Manhattan Bank above).

Gilbert S. Omenn is dean of the School of Public Health and Community Medicine at the University of Washington, Seattle.

Selected Institutional Owners:

Name	Shares Held	Filing Date
TX Teacher Retirement System	1,110,000	[3]
NY State Common Retirement	790,000	[3]
College Retirement Equities	642,600	[3]
CA State Teachers Retirement	336,733	[3]
NY State Teachers Retirement	303,600	[3]
University of TX System	241,800	[6]
OH School Employee Retirement	45,000	[3]
Harvard College	37,000	[3]
MD State Retirement	32,200	[1]
CO Public Employee Retirement	12,600	[3]
First Wachovia Corporation	8,100	[3]
MI State Treasurer	4,000	[3]
Mt. Holyoke College	3,012	[5]

SOURCE: *Notice of Annual Meeting of Stockholders,* May 2, 1988 and *Proxy Statement,* dated March 30, 1988, Rohm & Haas; *Who's Who in America, 45th Edition, 1988-89* (Wilmette, Illinois: MacMillan Directory Division, 1988).

S.C. Johnson & Son Inc., Racine, Wisconsin
Links to South Africa:
S. C. Johnson has direct ownership in South Africa through S. C. Johnson & Son, South Africa (Pty.) Ltd. (F1)
Links to Central America:
See Table 3-2.
Affiliations of Corporate Directors:
Samuel Curtis Johnson (see Mobil Oil Corporation above).
J. Paul Sticht (see Bell Helicopter/Textron above).

SOURCE: *Who's Who in America, 45th Edition, 1988-89* (Wilmette, Illinois: MacMillan Directory Division, 1988).

Shell Oil Company, Houston, Texas (69 percent subsidiary of Royal Dutch/Shell Group, The Hague, The Netherlands)
Links to South Africa:
The Parent Royal Dutch/Shell is tied to South Africa through these subsidiaries/affiliates: Shell South Africa; Abecol (Pty.) Ltd.; Dundee Road Products (Pty.) Ltd.; Petrocol (Pty.) Ltd.; Cera Oil South Africa (Pty.) Ltd.; Easigas (Pty.) Ltd.; Shell & British Petroleum South African Refineries (Pty.) Ltd.; Shell Southern Marketing (Pty.) Ltd.; Shell Southern Trading (Pty.) Ltd.; Styrochem (Pty.) Ltd.; Richards Bay Coal Terminal Co. Ltd.; Immelwade Investment (Pty.) Ltd. and Valvoline Oil Co. South Africa (Pty.) Ltd. (F1)
See also Section 5.1.
Links to Central America:
See Table 3-2; Table 3-4; Section 5.5; Table 5-9.
Affiliation of Corporate Directors (Shell, U.S.A.):
John F. Bookout, Jr. is active in the chancellors council, University of Texas.
William A. Marquard is a trustee of the University of Pennsylvania and on the board of overseers, Wharton School of Business, University of Pennsylvania.

SOURCE: *Who's Who in America, 45th Edition, 1988-89* (Wilmette, Illinois: MacMillan Directory Division, 1988).

Smith and Wesson, Springfield, Massachusetts
Links to Central America:
See Table 6-4.

Texaco, Inc., White Plains, New York
Links to South Africa:
Texaco has a 50 percent interest in Caltex Petroleum Corporation whose South African subsidiaries include Caltex Oil (Pty.) Ltd. and a 34 percent interest in South African Oil Refining Co. (Pty.) Ltd. (F1)
Links to Central America:
See Section 5.5; Table 5-9.

Affiliations of Corporate Directors:

Robert A. Beck is a trustee of Syracuse University.

William C. Butcher is a member of the Brown University board of fellows and the Council on Foreign Relations.

Alfred DeCrane, Jr. is a member of the advisory council for the College of Arts and Letters of Notre Dame University.

Thomas S. Murphy is chairman of the New York University Medical Center Board.

Dr. Lorene L. Rogers is former president of the University of Texas at Austin (1974-1979).

Thomas A. Vanderslice is chairman of the board of trustees of Boston College.

L. Stanton Williams is a trustee of Carnegie Mellon University.

William Wrigley is a trustee of the University of Southern California.

Selected Institutional Owners:

Name	Shares Held	Filing Date
College Retirement Equities	2,901,000	[3]
NY State Common Retirement	2,855,000	[3]
WI Investment Board	1,130,700	[3]
NY State Teachers Retirement	960,800	[3]
CA State Teachers Retirement	848,172	[3]
FL State Board/Administration	323,000	[2]
MD State Retirement	185,800	[1]
First Wachovia Corporation	51,034	[3]
Lutheran Brotherhood	50,000	[3]
CO Public Employee Retirement	45,900	[3]
Boston University	32,500	[5]
University of TX System	30,000	[3]
University of TN	17,000	[5]
Case Western Reserve	15,000	[5]
MI State Treasurer	14,300	[3]
University of CO	9,100	[5]
Colby College-3	8,000	[5]
Alma College	4,800	[5]

SOURCE: *Notice of the Annual Meeting,* May 12, 1987, June 7, 1988 and *Proxy Statement,* dated April 17, 1987, April 21, 1988, Texaco.

Uniroyal Chemical Company Inc., Middlebury, Connecticut
(subsidiary of Avery, Inc., New York, New York)

Links to Central America:

See Table 3-2.

Uniroyal management was planning to purchase the company so that by August of 1989 it would no longer be a publicly traded concern.

Selected Institutional Owners (survey of Avery, Inc., affiliate of Triangle Industries):

Name	Shares Held	Filing Date
University of Minnesota	6,000	[5]

SOURCE: Phone interview with Bob Petrausch, Uniroyal Chemical Company, Middlebury, Connecticut, May 15, 1989.

United Brands Co., Cincinnati, Ohio (subsidiary of American Financial Corporation, Cincinnati, Ohio)

Links to Central America:
See Section 5.5; Table 5-2; Table 5-4.

Affiliations of Corporate Directors:
Carl Henry Linder is on the board of advisors of the Business Administration College, the University of Cincinnati.

Selected Institutional Owners (survey of United Brands):

Name	Shares Held	Filing Date
CA State Teachers Retirement	128,286	[3]
College Retirement Equities	56,700	[3]

SOURCE: *Who's Who in America, 45th Edition, 1988-89* (Wilmette, Illinois: MacMillan Directory Division, 1988).

Sikorsky Aircraft Division, Stratford, Connecticut
(subsidiary of United Technologies Corporation, Hartford, Connecticut)

Links to South Africa:
United Technologies Corporation has direct ownership in South Africa through its 51 percent interest in Otis Elevator Co. Ltd. (F1)

Links to Central America:

Arms Sales:

Sikorsky Model S-55/H-19D Chickasaw	Guatemala (3)/(A)
	Honduras (3)/(A)
Sikorsky UH-19 Helicopter	Guatemala (3)/(B3)
	Honduras (3)/(B3)

See also Table 6-6.

Recent Transactions:
The Hamilton Standard Division in Windsor Locks, Connecticut, was involved in a $8.6 million arms deal (September 1986) for spare parts applicable to *C-130* aircraft propellers to Honduras and eleven other countries. (C)

Links to the Nuclear Weapons Industry (United Technologies):
United Technologies has been a major producer of equipment for secondary nuclear weapons systems through its manufacture of Pratt & Whitney engines for nuclear-capable aircraft. The company has worked on the MX and Minuteman missile programs as well. (G)

Affiliations of Corporate Directors (United Technologies):
Antonia Handler Chayes is a fellow of the Harvard Center for International Affairs and the Council on Foreign Relations.

Robert H. Malott is a trustee of the University of Chicago.

Robert L. Sproull, former president of the University of Rochester, is presently professor of physics at the University.

Jacqueline G. Wexler, president of the National Conference of Christians and Jews, is a former president of Hunter College of the City University of New York.

Selected Institutional Owners (survey of United Technologies):

Name	Shares Held	Filing Date
WI Investment Board	2,600,600	[3]
College Retirement Equities	1,579,300	[3]
NY State Common Retirement	1,450,200	[3]
CO Public Employee Retirement	624,600	[3]
First Wachovia Corporation	607,308	[3]
NY State Teachers Retirement	562,200	[3]
CA State Teachers Retirement	529,774	[3]
FL State Board/Administration	340,000	[2]
Harvard College	312,400	[3]
University of TX System	263,900	[6]
Kentucky Teachers Retirement	187,000	[3]
MD State Retirement	100,600	[1]
Mineworkers Pension Scheme	71,200	[3]
OH School Employee Retirement	48,600	[3]
Williams College	28,120	[5]
University of MI	26,000	[5]
Colgate University	11,420	[5]
University of TN	11,000	[5]
University of MN-14	10,000	[5]
Wooster College	10,000	[5]
Boston University	10,000	[5]
MI State Treasurer	8,300	[3]
Alma College	6,000	[5]
Georgetown University-17	5,000	[5]

SOURCE: *Notice of Annual Meeting*, April 18, 1988 and *Proxy Statement*, March 9, 1988, United Technologies; *Who's Who in America, 45th Edition, 1988-89* (Wilmette, Illinois: MacMillan Directory Division, 1988).

Velsicol Chemical Corporation, Rosemount, Illinois
(subsidiary of Farley Industries, Chicago, Illinois)

Links to Central America:
See Table 3-2.
Affiliations of Corporate Directors:
William F. Farley is a trustee of Bowdoin College.

SOURCE: *Who's Who in America, 45th Edition, 1988-89* (Wilmette, Illinois: MacMillan Directory Division, 1989).

Westinghouse Electric Corporation, Pittsburgh, Pennsylvania

Links to South Africa:
Westinghouse has several licensees and distributors in South Africa including ESCOM for the Koeberg nuclear power plant. (F1)

Links to Central America:

Arms Sales:

NARMIC has linked the Westinghouse Defense and Electronics Systems Center in Baltimore, Maryland, to the supply of the AN/TPS-63 Tactical Surveillance Radar to Honduras in September of 1983. (B2)

Links to the Nuclear Weapons Industry:

Westinghouse has been a major contributor to the MX, Trident and cruise missile programs. The company has also worked on nuclear-related and "dual capable" sustems such as the Awacs program, the F-16 fighter and attack submarines. Westinghouse received $135 million in contract awards for primary nuclear systems in FY 1981. The company makes the launch tubes which house the Trident submarine's ballistic missiles. In October 1983, Westinghouse won a contract to operate the Idaho National Engineering Laboratory which "reprocesses spent fuel from the Navy's nuclear propulsion program and from government research reactors producing highly enriched uranium." Westinghouse also manages these nuclear weapon production plants: the Hanford Reservation (near Richland, Washington), Savannah River (near Aiken, South Carolina), the Feed Materials Production Center (Fernald, Ohio) and Rocky Flats (near Denver, Colorado). (G)

Affiliations of Corporate Directors:

John B. Carter is a director of the Marymount College, Morehouse College, the Harvard Business School Board of Directors Associates and the Council for Financial Aid to Education.

Barbara Hackman Franklin (see Dow Chemical Company above).

Dr. Donald F. Hornig, former president of Brown University, is the Alfred North Whitehead professor of chemistry and director, Interdisciplinary Programs in Health, Harvard University.

Paul E. Lego serves on the board of the Carnegie-Mellon University and the University of Pittsburgh.

David T. McLaughlin (see Chase Manhattan Bank above).

John C. Marous is chairman of the board of trustees of the University of Pittsburgh and a lifetime member of the Council on Foreign Relations.

Richard M. Morrow is a trustee of the University of Chicago.

Hays T. Watkins is a rector of the College of William and Mary and a trustee of Johns Hopkins University.

Selected Institutional Owners:

Name	Shares Held	Filing Date
College Retirement Equities	1,433,400	[3]
NY State Common Retirement	1,225,000	[3]
CA State Teachers Retirement	662,735	[3]
State Street Boston Corporation	653,101	[3]
NY State Teachers Retirement	614,800	[3]
First Wachovia Corporation	263,877	[3]
Ford Foundation	200,000	[3]
OH School Employee Retirement	137,700	[3]
WI Investment Board	99,000	[3]
MD State Retirement	98,400	[1]
Harvard College	70,300	[3]
Columbia University	58,800	[5]
Lutheran Brotherhood	50,000	[3]
Aid Association for Lutherans	34,000	[3]
University of TX System	27,400	[6]
CO Public Employee Retirement	27,100	[3]
Duke Endowment	18,000	[3]
University of MI	10,000	[5]
MI State Treasurer	8,200	[3]

University of CO	6,600	[5]
OH State Universify-1	6,000	[5]
Drew University	6,000	[5]
Colgate University	4,500	[5]
Boston University	3,500	[5]

SOURCE: *Notice of 1988 Annual Meeting and Proxy Statement*, April 27, 1988, dated March 14, 1988.

Winchester International, New Haven, Connecticut

Links to Central America:
See Table 6-4.

W.R. Grace Corporation, New York, New York

Links to South Africa:
W.R. Grace maintains a license and technical assistance agreement with its former South African subsidiary. (F1)

Links to Central America:
J. Peter Grace, the chairman and chief executive officer of Grace, has been a board member of PRODEMCA (Friends of the Democratic Center in Central America). This organization sponsored a full-page advertisment in *The New York Times* supporting aid for the *contras*. The group also gave $100,000 to the right-wing Nicaraguan daily, *La Prensa*. J. Peter Grace has been the advisory committee chair of AMERICARES, a group founded by its current president and a director of W.R. Grace, Robert C. Macauley. AMERICARES has distributed medical aid to Guatemala using that country's armed forces. The aid was used as part of the military's resettlement program of "model villages" which are designed to defeat guerrilla resistance. AMERICARES is a major funder of the Knights of Malta which distributes "humanitarian aid" through "civic action" programs in Honduras, Guatemala and El Salvador and also assists the *contras*. J. Peter Grace has been chair of the U.S. chapter of Knights of Malta and a member of the board of governors of the Council for National Policy (see Coors above).

Affiliations of Corporate Directors:
George C. Dacey is a director of the University of New Mexico Foundation.
Edward W. Duffy is a trustee of Syracuse University.
George P. Gardner is a life member of the MIT Corporation.
Paul Paganucci is a trustee of Colby College.
Grace Sloane Vance is a trustee of Colgate University a member of the Rockefeller University council and vice chairperson of the board of WNET-TV, Channel 13 (New York).

Selected Institutional Owners:

Name	Shares Held	Filing Date
WI Investment Board	1,871,000	[4]
NY State Common Retirement	1,579,000	[4]
College Retirement Equities	1,197,000	[4]
NY State Teachers Retirement	434,000	[4]
CA State Teachers Retirement	376,000	[3]
University of TX System	192,000	[4]
FL State Board/Administration	140,000	[4]
First Wachovia Corporation	75,000	[4]

MD State Retirement	65,000	[1]
OH School Employee Retirement	38,000	[4]
Colby College	22,000	[5]
Harvard College	21,000	[4]
VA University	15,000	[5]
CO Public Employee Retirement	15,000	[4]
Tulane University	12,000	[5]
MI State Treasurer	5,000	[4]
Pitzer College	3,000	[5]
Salem Academy and College	2,200	[5]

SOURCE: Tom Barry, Deb Preusch and Beth Sims, *The New Right Humanitarians* (Albuquerque, NM: Inter-Hemispheric Resource Center, 1986); *Notice of Annual Meeting of Shareholders, May 10, 1988, and Proxy Statement,* dated March 31, 1988, the W. R. Grace Corporation.

SOURCES/LEGEND FOR UNIVERSITY ENDOWMENT:

[1]-Shares filed on December 31, 1987, Disclosure data base series, Dow Jones, New York, New York.

[2]-Shares filed on March 31, 1988, Disclosure data base series, Dow Jones, New York, New York.

[3]-Shares filed on June 30, 1988, Disclosure data base series, Dow Jones, New York, New York.

[4]-Shares filed on September 30, 1988, Disclosure data base series, Dow Jones, New York, New York.

[5]-Shares filed March 1988 through September 1988, *Guide to College Endowment Portfolios,* Section 2, College Endowment (Huntington, NY: Vickers Stock Research Corporation, 1988).

[6]-Shares filed September 1988, *Guide to College Endowment Portfolios,* Section 2, College Endowment (Huntington, NY: Vickers Stock Research Corporation, 1988).

SOURCES FOR ARMS CONTRACTORS AND SOUTH AFRICA CONNECTIONS DATABASE:
Sources A and B describe national inventories of weapons. Sources C and D describe corporate links in terms of direct sales, for example, Commercial Sales. As noted in table, Source E identifies which sales are likely to be transmitted through the U.S. government.

A-Tom Gervassi, *The Arsenal of Democracy III: America's War Machine* (New York: Grove Press, 1984).

B1-National Action Research on the Military Industrial Complex, *The Central American War: A Guide to the U.S. Military Buildup* (Philadelphia: American Friends Service Committee, April 1983).

B2-National Action Research on the Military Industrial Complex, *Up in Arms: U.S. Military Shipments to Central America* (Philadelphia: American Friends Service Committee, November 1984).

B3-National Action Research on the Military Industrial Complex, *Invasion: A Guide to the U.S. Military Presence in Central America* (Philadelphia: American Friends Service Committee, 1985).

C-*El Salvador,* Profile by DMS Market Intelligence Report, 1987; *Guatemala,* Profile by DMS Market Intelligence Report, 1986; *Honduras,* Profile by DMS Market Intelligence Report, 1987.

D1-*Defense and Foreign Affairs,* February 1985.

D2-*Defense and Foreign Affairs,* March 1985.

D3-*Defense and Foreign Affairs,* May 1985.

D4-*Defense and Foreign Affairs,* July 1985.

D5-*Defense and Foreign Affairs,* October 1985.

D6-*Defense and Foreign Affairs,* November 1985.

D7-*Defense and Foreign Affairs,* March 1986.

D8-*Defense and Foreign Affairs,* July 1986.

D9-*Defense and Foreign Affairs,* October 1986.

D10-*Defense and Foreign Affairs,* March 1987.

D11-*Defense and Foreign Affairs,* May 1987.

D12-*Defense and Foreign Affairs,* June 1987.

D13-*Defense and Foreign Affairs,* February 1988.

D14-*Defense and Foreign Affairs,* March 1988.

D15-*Defense and Foreign Affairs,* May 1988.

D16-*Defense and Foreign Affairs,* October-November 1988.

E-Paul L. Ferrari, Jeffrey W. Knopf, and Raul L. Madrid, *U.S. Arms Exports: Policies and Contractors* (Washington, D.C.: Investor Responsibility Research Center, Inc., 1987); Paul L. Ferrari, Raul L. Madrid and Jeff Knopf, *U.S. Arms Exports: Policies and Contractors* (Cambridge, MA: Ballinger Publishing Company, 1988).

F1-"Selected List of U.S. Companies with Licensing, Franchising or Distribution Agreements in South Africa," The Africa Fund, New York, 1988; "Select List of U.S. Companies with Direct Investment in South Africa," The Africa Fund, New York, 1988; Robert Knight and Roger Walke, *Unified List of United States Companies Doing Business in South Africa and Namibia,* Second Edition (New York: The Africa Fund, 1988).

F2-*International Directory of Corporate Affiliation 1987/88: "Who Owns Whom?"* (Wilmette, Illinois: National Register Publishing Co., 1987).

G-Kenneth A. Bertsch and Linda S. Shaw, *The Nuclear Weapons Industry* (Washington, D.C.: Investor Responsibility Research Center, 1984); *Approximate Current Employment On Operations & Maintenance at Department of Energy Installations, March 31, 1985,* by the Metal Trade Council of the AFL-CIO, from their annual conference proceedings on October 21-22, 1986, Washington, D.C. as published in Greg Bischak, "Facing the Second Generation of the Nuclear Weapons Complex: Renewal of the Nuclear Production Base or Economic Conversion?," *Bulletin of Peace Proposals,* Vol. 19, No. 1, 1988; Matthew L. Wald, "Westinghouse Concedes Error in Its Atomic Role," *The New York Times,* November 13, 1988; phone interview with Greg Bischak, Employment Research Associates, Lansing, Michigan, March 10, 1989.

General Reference: "Who Owns Whom," *Directory of Corporate Affiliations: 1989* (Wilmette, Illinois: National Register Publishing Company, 1988); *Standard & Poor's Register of Corporations, Directors and Executives* (New York: Standard & Poor's Corporation, 1989).

Appendix 2

Military Advisors and their Academic Affiliations

Members	Military Group	Academic Affiliation
Dr. Duane A. Adams	Army Science Board	Carnegie Mellon University (A)
Dr. Martin Alexander	Army Science Board	Cornell University (A)
Dr. Peter M. Banks	Jason	Electrical Engineering, Stanford University (B)
Dr. Judson R. Baron	USAF Scientific Advisory Board	Professor, Dept. of Aeronautics & Astronautics, MIT (C)
Dr. Delbert S. Barth	Army Science Board	University of Nevada (A)
Ivan L. Benett, Jr.	Defense Science Board (Senior Consultant)	Professor of Medicine, New York University Medical Center (D)
Dr. Frederick S. Billig	USAF Scientific Advisory Board	Applied Physics Laboratory, Johns Hopkins University (C)
Davis B. Bobrow	Defense Science Board (Senior Consultant)	Professor of Government and Politics, University of Maryland (D)
Dr. William B. Bridges	USAF Scientific Advisory Board	Carl F. Braun Professor of Engineering, California Institute of Technology (C)
Dr. E. Downey Brill, Jr.	Army Science Board	University of Illinois at Urbana-Champaign (A)
Dr. Curtis G. Callan, Jr.	Jason	Physics, Princeton University (B)
Dr. Kenneth M. Case	Jason	Theoretical Physics, Rockefeller University (B)
Mr. Thomas E. Cheatham	USAF Scientific Advisory Board	Harvard University (C)
Dr. Julian D. Cole	USAF Scientific Advisory Board	Department of Mathematical Sciences, Rensselaer Polytechnic Institute (C)
Professor Lynn Conway	USAF Scientific Advisory Board	Associate Dean of Engineering, University of Michigan (C)
Dr. John M. Cornwall	Jason	Physics, University of California, Los Angeles (B)
Dr. Roger F. Dashen	Jason	Physics, Princeton University (B)

Legend on p. 299.

Dr. Russ E. Davis	Jason	Oceanography, University of California, San Diego (B)
Dr. Alvin M. Despain	Jason	Electrical Engineering, University of California, Berkeley (B)
John M. Deutch	Defense Science Board (Senior Consulant)	Provost, MIT (D)
Dr. Earl H. Dowell	USAF Scientific Advisory Board	School of Engineering, Duke University (C)
Dr. Sidney D. Drell	Jason	Stanford Linear Accelerator, Stanford, California (B)
Paul R. Drouilhet, Jr.	Army Science Board	Lincoln Laboratory, MIT (A)
Dr. James R. Durig	Army Science Board	University of South Carolina (A)
Professor Freeman J. Dyson	Jason	Institute for Advanced Studies, Princeton, New Jersey (B)
Dr. B. David Edens	Army Science Board	Stephens College (A)
Dr. Andrew G. Favret	Army Science Board	Catholic University of America (A)
Dr. Stanley M. Flatte	Jason	Physics, University of California, Santa Cruz (B)
Dr. Norval Fortson	Jason	Physics, University of Washington, Seattle (B)
Dr. Michael H. Freedman	Jason	Mathematics, University of California, San Diego (B)
Dr. Edward A. Frieman	Jason	Oceanography, University of California, San Diego (B)
Dr. Elsa M. Garmire	USAF Scientific Advisory Board	Center for Laser Studies, University of Southern California (C)
Dr. Murray Gell-Mann	Jason	Theoretical Physics, California Institute of Technology
Professor Alfred Gessow	Army Science Board	University of Maryland (A)
Dr. Marvin L. Goldberger	Jason	Director, Institute for Advanced Studies, Princeton, New Jersey (B)
Dr. Michael C. Gregg	Jason	Department of Oceanography, University of Washington, Seattle (B)
Dr. Allen F. Grum	Army Science Board	Mercer University (A)
Dr. David A. Hammer	Jason	Nuclear Science and Engineering, Cornell University (B)
Dr. William Happer, Jr.	Jason, USAF Scientific Advisory Board	Department of Physics, Princeton University (B),(C)
Dr. Thomas H. Henriksen	Army Science Board	Stanford University (A)
Dr. Dennis R. Horn	Army Science Board	University of Idado (A)
Dr. Paul Horowitz	Jason	Physics, Harvard University (B)
Dr. James Jacobs	Army Science Board	Sandia National Laboratories (A)

Dr. Jonathan I. Katz	Jason	Washington University (B)
Dr. Joshua Lederberg	Defense Science Board (Member at Large), Jason	President, Rockefeller University (B) (D)
Dr. William L. Lehman	USAF Scientific Advisory Board	University of New Mexico (C)
Harold W. Lewis	Defense Science Board (Senior Consultant)	Professor of Physics, University of California at Santa Barbara (D)
Professor James W. Mar	USAF Scientific Advisory Board	Hunsaker Professor of Aerospace Education, MIT (C)
Dr. Harlan D. Mills	USAF Scientific Advisory Board	Department of Computer and Information Sciences, University of Florida (C)
Mr. Walter E. Morrow, Jr.	USAF Scientific Advisory Board, Defense Science Board (Member at Large)	Director, Lincoln Laboratory, MIT (C) (D)
Dr. Richard A. Muller	Jason	Physics, University of California, Berkeley (B)
Dr. Walter H. Munk	Jason	Geophysics, University of California, San Diego (B)
Dr. William A. Neal	Naval Research Advisory Committee	Professor and Chairman, Department of Pediatrics, West Virginia University (E)
Dr. David R. Nelson	Jason	Physics, Harvard University (B)
Dr. William M. Nierenberg	Jason	California Space Institute, University of California, San Diego (B)
Dr. Jerre D. Noe	Army Science Board	University of Washington (A)
Dr. Robert Novick	Jason	Physics, Columbia University (B)
Dr. Felix S. Palubinskas	USAF Scientific Advisory Board	Department of Physics, Bridgewater State College (C)
Dr. Paul F. Parks	Army Science Board	Auburn University (A)
Dr. Francis W. Perkins, Jr.	Jason	Astrophysical Science, Princeton University (B)
Dr. Allen M. Peterson	Jason	Electrical Engineering, Stanford University (B)
Dr. Percy A. Pierre	Army Science Board	Prairie View A&M University (A)
Professor R. Byron Pipes	Army Science Board	University of Delaware (A)
Dr. William H. Press	Defense Science Board (Member at Large), Jason	Chairman Department of Astronomy, Harvard University (B),(D)
Dr. Burton Richter	Jason	Physics, Stanford University (B)
Mr. Raymond N. Rogers	USAF Scientific Advisory Board	Los Alamos National Laboratory (C)
Dr. Marshall N. Rosenbluth	Jason	Physics, University of Texas, Austin (B)

Dr. Oscar S. Rothaus,	Jason	Mathematics, Cornell University (B)
Henry S. Rowen	Defense Science Board (Senior Consultant)	Professor, Stanford University (D)
Dr. Malvin A. Ruderman	Jason	Physics, Columbia University (B)
Mr. William F. Scanlin, Jr.	Army Science Board	Lawrence Livermore National Laboratory (A)
Dr. Daniel Schrage	Army Science Board	Georgia Institute of Technology (A)
Professor Robert R. Shannon	USAF Scientific Advisory Board	Director, Optical Sciences Center, University of Arizona (C)
Dr. Harold W. Sorenson	USAF Scientific Advisory Board	University of California, San Diego (C)
Dr. Alfred Z. Spector	Army Science Board	Carnegie-Mellon University (A)
Professor George Sperling	USAF Scientific Advisory Board	Psychology Department, New York University (C)
Dr. Edward B. Stear	USAF Scientific Advisory Board	Executive Director, the Washington Techology Center, University of Washington (C)
Dr. Paul J. Steinhardt	Jason	Physics, University of Pennsylvania
Professor Allen R. Stubberud	USAF Scientific Advisory Board	Electrical Engineering, Univeristy of California, Irvine (C)
Dr. Jeremiah D. Sullivan	Jason	Physics, University of Illinois, Urbana (B)
Dr. Edward Teller	USAF Scientific Advisory Board	Associate Director Emeritus, Lawrence Livermore National Laboratory (C)
Dr. Charles H. Townes	Defense Science Board (Senior Consultant), Jason	University Professor of Physics, University of California at Berkeley (B) (D)
Dr. Sam B. Treiman	Jason	Physics, Princeton University (B)
Dr. Frank E. Vandiver	Army Science Board	Texas A&M University (A)
Dr. John F. Vesecky	Jason	Electrical Engineering, Stanford University (B)
Dr. Kenneth M. Watson	Jason	Oceanography, University of California, San Diego (B)
Dr. Max L. Williams, Jr.	USAF Scientific Advisory Board	Dean Emeritus, School of Engineering, University of Pittsburgh (C)
Dr. Robert C. Williges	Army Science Board	Virginia Polytechnic Institute and State University (A)
Dr. Patrick Winston	Naval Research Advisory Committee	Professor of Computer Science, Director, Artificial Intelligence Laboratory, MIT (E)

Professor William L. Wolfe	Army Science Board	University of Arizona (A)
Dr. Henry T. Y. Yang	USAF Scientific Advisory Board	Dean, School of Engineering, Purdue University (C)
Dr. Fredrik Zachariasen	Jason	Theoretical Physics, California Institute of Technology (B)

LEGEND AND SOURCES:

(A): "Army Science Board Membership List," Army Science Board, Office of the Assistant Secretary of the Army, Research, Development, and Acquisition, Washington, D.C., June 1988.

(B): "Open Letter Regarding Jason," with attached membership list published in *The Nonviolent Activist*, Volume 5, Number 8, December 1988; Letter to author and response to author's Freedom of Information Act Request from W. M. McDonald, Director, Freedom of Information and Security Review, Office of the Assistant Secretary of Defense, Washington, D.C., December 2, 1988.

(C): "Membership List," USAF Scientific Advisory Board, United States Air Force, Washington, D.C., January 17, 1989.

(D): "Defense Science Board: Background, Biographical Sketches and Activities," Office of the Under Secretary of Defense for Acquisition, Washington, D.C., 1987.

(E): "Composition of Membership, Naval Research Advisory Committee," Department of the Navy, Washington, D.C., September 30, 1988; Letter to author and attached listing from E. J. Barry, Department of the Navy, Office of the Chief of Naval Research, Arlington, Virginia, October 25, 1988.

Appendix 3

The Post-Vietnam War Rise in University Defense Dependency

The tables below illustrate that universities now rely more heavily on national military-serving agencies for funding their basic and applied research. The tables indicate a steady rise in the share of federal funds coming from military-serving agencies after 1975, the last year of direct American military commitment to the Vietnam War. The term "obligations" refers to the amounts specified in contracts arranged between universities and the respective agencies. In contrast, the term "outlays" refers to actual dollars spent.

Federal Obligations for Basic Research
by University and College Performers, by Selected Agency
(in Thousands of Dollars)

Year	DOD (A)	NASA (B)	AEC/ERDA/DOE (C)	Total (D)	% Military (A+B+C)/(D)	% DOD (A)/(D)
1967	148,548	59,740	82,329	857,149	34	17
1968	132,461	38,223	71,499	835,079	29	16
1969	151,254	45,165	78,360	864,339	32	17
1970	127,099	34,102	79,212	808,095	30	16
1971	129,876	49,957	73,055	879,356	29	15
1972	130,132	40,514	64,639	1,021,385	23	13
1973	114,677	56,266	59,919	1,048,189	22	11
1974	106,279	61,285	57,436	1,144,748	20	9
1975	105,530	64,548	57,511	1,260,609	18	8
1976	112,003	67,157	68,270	1,341,738	18	8
1977	141,754	71,988	71,103	1,555,067	18	9
1978	167,865	88,341	85,514	1,759,234	19	10
1979	178,902	96,785	97,215	2,079,925	18	9
1980	208,336	112,751	116,009	2,320,253	19	9
1981	244,405	124,418	133,656	2,503,223	20	10
1982	305,365	125,876	135,198	2,727,126	21	11
1983	360,432	140,081	162,264	3,112,307	21	12
1984	405,373	148,442	184,183	3,530,806	21	11
1985	408,777	176,886	211,281	4,038,709	20	10
1986	475,013	182,928	227,360	4,132,073	21	11
1987	476,160	220,060	248,224	4,665,814	20	10
1988E*	496,796	239,358	265,891	4,927,106	20	10
1989E*	537,867	245,244	269,954	5,308,274	20	10

Federal Obligations for Applied Research
by University and College Performers, by Selected Agency
(in Thousands of Dollars)

Year	DOD (A)	NASA (B)	AEC/ERDA/DOE (C)	TOTAL (D)	% MILITARY (A+B+C)/(D)	% DOD (A)/(D)
1967	97,959	24,215	NA	454,991	**27	22
1968	74,863	23,273	17,565	466,737	25	16
1969	71,015	16,078	19,340	457,434	23	16
1970	45,429	31,303	17,372	468,351	20	10
1971	54,094	20,352	16,594	550,815	17	10
1972	46,492	7,731	16,398	621,418	11	7
1973	45,875	24,159	18,790	642,866	14	7
1974	60,706	23,674	28,224	813,519	14	7
1975	59,461	26,169	54,610	818,157	17	7
1976	79,500	30,679	48,053	907,997	17	9
1977	79,159	33,071	62,827	1,028,440	17	8
1978	74,927	27,957	89,246	1,168,805	16	6
1979	92,284	28,511	106,539	1,253,450	18	7
1980	104,354	33,353	108,125	1,378,818	18	8
1981	118,561	32,734	114,413	1,416,921	19	8
1982	107,320	29,976	100,615	1,318,311	18	8
1983	111,771	29,600	111,111	1,355,637	19	8
1984	133,235	28,445	127,172	1,498,865	19	9
1985	178,375	36,535	124,601	1,687,558	20	11
1986	232,388	41,906	106,909	1,751,371	22	13
1987	204,878	42,964	123,467	1,974,519	19	10
1988E*	265,541	42,335	125,715	2,124,185	20	13
1989E*	261,407	47,113	114,379	2,118,335	20	12

LEGEND:

(A)-DOD Obligations

(B)-NASA Obligations

(C)-Atomic Energy Commission (AEC) Obligations (1967-1973); Energy Research and Development Administration (ERDA) Obligations (1974-1976); Department of Energy (DOE) Obligations (1977-1989).

NA-Not Available

E*-Estimates

**-Calculation excludes AEC.

SOURCE: Author's calculations based on Tables 30A and 40A, "Federal Funds for Research and Development: Detailed Historical Tables: Fiscal Years 1955-1989," Division of Science Resource Studies, National Science Foundation, Washington, D.C., 1988-1989.

Appendix 4

The DOD-University Forum

Co-Chairmen

Donald Kennedy, president, Stanford University
Donald Hicks, Under Secretary of Defense for Research and Engineering

University Members

Steven C. Beering, president, Purdue University
Edward J. Bloustein, president, Rutgers, The State University
Richard M. Cyert, president, Carnegie-Mellon University
Marvin L. Goldberger, president, California Institute of Technology
Henry Koffler, president, University of Arizona
C. Peter Magrath, president, University of Missouri
Joseph M. Pettit, president, Georgia Institute of Technology
Percy A. Pierre, president, Prairie View A&M University
Frank H. T. Rhodes, president, Cornell University
Michael I. Sovern, president, Columbia University

University Association Members

Robert H. Atwell, president, American Council on Education
Robert L. Clodius, president, National Association of State Universities and Land-Grant Colleges
Robert M. Rosenzweig, president, Association of American Universities

Department of Defense Members

Lieutenant General James A. Abrahamson, director, Strategic Defense Initiative Organization
Thomas E. Cooper, Assistant Secretary of the Air Force (Research, Development and Logistics)
Robert C. Duncan, director, Defense Advanced Research Projects Agency
Ronald L. Kerber, deputy Under Secretary of Defense (Research and Advanced Technology)
Melvyn R. Paisley, Assistant Secretary of the Navy (Research, Engineering and Systems)
Jay R. Sculley, Assistant Secretary of the Army (Research, Development and Acquisition)
Leo Young, director, Research and Laboratory Management

SOURCE: U.S. Department of Defense, Washington, D.C., revised list, November 1986.

Appendix 5

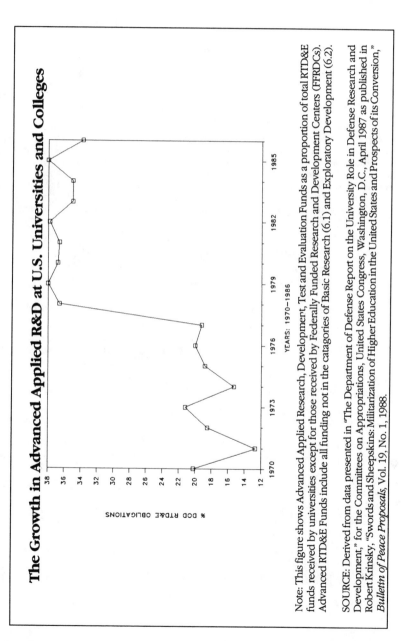

The Growth in Advanced Applied R&D at U.S. Universities and Colleges

Note: This figure shows Advanced Applied Research, Development, Test and Evaluation Funds as a proportion of total RTD&E funds received by universities except for those received by Federally Funded Research and Development Centers (FFRDCs). Advanced RTD&E Funds include all funding not in the catagories of Basic Research (6.1) and Exploratory Development (6.2).

SOURCE: Derived from data presented in "The Department of Defense Report on the University Role in Defense Research and Development," for the Committees on Appropriations, United States Congress, Washington, D.C., April 1987 as published in Robert Krinsky, "Swords and Sheepskins: Militarization of Higher Education in the United States and Prospects of its Conversion," *Bulletin of Peace Proposals*, Vol. 19, No. 1, 1988.

Appendix 6

Organizing Methodology and Resources

Overview of the University-Warfare Connection

The elaboration of university complicity in intervention and the warfare system provides the first step in explaining possible local handles for organizing efforts. Organizing which questions these links could help build the base for larger efforts aimed at institutional divestment from companies linked to intervention in Central America and at a national conversion program. A review of the connections elaborated in earlier chapters illustrates possible bases for such organizing. U.S. universities are connected to the process of interventionism in a number of ways. There are two varieties: direct and indirect intervention. Direct intervention consists of the support university personnel provide for the planning and research needs of companies and the government. Examples of such intervention include:

- Research on technologies that are used to weaken the economic power of Third World nations, e.g., biotechnology.

- Research for the Pentagon, DOE and NASA provides logistical support for the arms build-up and military power. Most publicized is Star Wars research although there are other connections through so-called "basic research."

- Faculty contracts for other national government agencies including the Agency for International Development which may promote co-optive land reform.

- Faculty research on counter-insurgency, research on terrorism, or published research which makes the ideological case for labeling Nicaragua a terrorist state or otherwise supports U.S. government foreign policy objectives in Central America.

- Faculty consulting and direct employment as state managers who direct foreign policy, e.g., national security advisors.

- Universities may also play a direct role in supporting the warfare State by allowing CIA, National Security Agency, military recruitment or ROTC programs on campus.

Indirect intervention refers to the support that universities give to corporations responsible for intervention in Central America. Such support can take the following forms:

- Investment in companies linked to intervention.

- Trustee ties to companies linked to intervention (a trustee is a corporate director of such a company).

- Business school and general university sanctioning of recruitment by such companies.

- Faculty research contracts or industry-university centers which carry out extended research for such companies.

- Corporate grants to the university.

- University use of banks and insurance companies linked to either intervention or companies themselves complicit in intervention.

What kinds of companies support intervention in Central America? Here are the significant criteria:

- Companies engaged in direct repression in Central America. For example, Bank of America has lent money to members of the Guatemalan oligarchy who are tied to death squads. Companies that resist trade union control and engage in capital flight/black mail also are part of this category, e.g., Coca-Cola in Guatemala.

- Agro-Chemical companies that promote the use of pesticides in Central America, which end up poisoning thousands of farm workers and their families. Many of these companies were tied to chemical warfare in Vietnam. Here the critical question becomes: What do these companies do to promote the responsible use of pesticides through advertising and product/label warnings? Do they actively resist the responsible pesticide management policy as they have done in Brazil?

- Transnational banks (including Citibank) and certain other transnationals (including banana, oil and rubber firms) play an important role in providing the social investment "glue" necessary to help reproduce repressive societies. These firms provide financial capital, large-scale investment, managerial resources and energy resources which assist the military states of El Salvador, Guatemala and Honduras.

- Companies whose weapons are sent directly to Central America or (as is more likely the case) whose weapons are sent to the Pentagon which then transfers them to the region. Here, the corporate responsibility still holds because: a) companies know to what use their weapons are put; b) such weapons may be particularly or exclusively useful for repression against civilians in the Third World; c) military corporations in the United States and Israel increasingly rely on arms exports; d) such exports are part of self-conscious "strategic planning."

- Finally, companies that sanction political distortions of progressive forces in Central America or legitimate intervention by the United States against the people of Central America, e.g., coverage by *The New York Times* of elections in El Salvador.

Information on University Corporate Ties

- *Recruitment data* can be found in business schools, administrative offices and university catalogues.

- *Endowment investment data* is compiled by two sources: the Vickers College Endowment Guide and the Dow Jones Disclosure data base.

- *University corporate research contract data* is collected by university industrial liason offices and should be available in the central administrative offices of the university.

- *Trustee ties to corporate boards* can be found in the proxy statement of specific corporations available in most business school libraries, *Who's Who in Finance & Industry, Who's Who in America,* and in university catalogues. One method for identifying corporate affiliations is to assemble a list of trustees from the catalogue and then compare this with the listing in *Who's Who in Finance & Industry,* 26th Edition, 1989-1990, MacMillan Directory Division, Wilmette, Illinois, projected publication date is September 13, 1989.

Information on University-Military Ties

Recruitment data such as whether your university has an ROTC program and the percentage of undergraduates enrolled should be available from the Financial Aid, ROTC, Admissions, and Registrar's Offices.

Academic ties to military agencies are documented by these Pentagon agencies:

USAF Advisory Board
Headquarters, United States Air Force
Washington, D.C. 20330-5430

Army Science Board
Department of the Army
Office, Assistant Secretary
Washington, D.C. 20310-0103

Naval Research Advisory Committee
ATTN: Code OONR
800 North Quincy Street
Arlington, VA 22217-5000

The Defense Science Board
Office of the Secretary of Defense for Acquisition
Washington, D.C. 20301

Defense research contracts are listed in *500 Contractors Receiving the Largest Dollar Volume of Prime Contract Awards for Research, Development, Test, and Evaluation,* Department of Defense, Washington Headquarters Services, Directorate for Information, Operations and Reports, Washington, D.C. Large universities have central administrative offices which track and compile faculty contracts. Using a freedom of information request you can receive "work-unit summaries" which describe faculty defense projects (see Cowan, below). Contact the Freedom of Information Act Focal Point, Defense Technical Information Center, Building 5, Cameron Station, Alexandria, VA, 22304.

Research Resources

Agro-Chemical Company Regulation and Policy

Pesticide Education & Action Project
P.O. Box 610
San Francisco, CA 954101
(415) 541-9140

National Coalition Against the Misuse of Pesticides
530 7th Street, S.E.
Washington, D.C. 20003
(202) 543-5450

National Toxics Campaign
37 Temple Place,
4th Floor
Boston, MA 02111
(617) 482-1477

Rural Advancement Fund International
P.O. Box 1029
Pittsboro, NC 27312
(919) 542-5292

National Conversion and Disarmament Economics

National Commission for Economic Conversion & Disarmament
P.O. Box 15025
Washington, D.C. 20003
(202) 544-5059

Employment Research Associates
115 West Allegan Street, Suite 810
Lansing, MI 48933
(517) 485-7655

University Militarization and Policy

Leonard Minsky
National Coalition for Universities in the Public Interest
c/o Newman and Newell
21 Dupont Circle, 4th Floor
Washington, D.C. 20036
(202) 547-8707

University-Military Action Guide Project
Rich Cowan
117 Rindge Avenue
Cambridge, MA, 02140
(617) 497-0870

Matt Nicodemus
968 F Street
Arcata, CA 95221
(707) 826-7033

Campus Watch
[Quarterly Newsletter on CIA in Academia]
PO Box 9623
Warwick, RI 02889

Guides to Military Research and the University

Rich Cowan, "Uncovering the Pentagon Connection: Does Your School Work for the Military?," *Science for the People,* Vol. 20, No. 5, November-December 1988.

"Special Issue: Science and the Military: Who's Pulling the Strings?," *Science for the People,* Vol. 20, No. 1, January-February 1988.

Roger Kerson, "Investigating the Investigators," *Radical Teacher,* No. 26, June 1984.

Notes

Chapter One: The Tripartite Alliance

1. *Enfoprensa,* Year 5—Number 6, February 13, 1987.

2. "U.S. Helicopters Used to Fly Guatemalan Troops to Battle," *The New York Times,* May 6, 1987.

3. Bob Stix, "U.S. Helicopters Airlift Guatemalan Combat Troops," *Report on Guatemala,* Vol. 8, Issue 2, May-June 1987.

4. "U.S. Helicopter Parts Sale to Guatemala Sure to Kill Indians and Worsen Refugee Flow to the United States," Council On Hemispheric Affairs, press release, Washington, D.C., February 13, 1984.

5. *Ibid.;* "Guatemala," *DMS Market Intelligence Report,* 1986; *Proxy Statement,* Textron Corporation, March 15, 1988. Swearer was to retire by the end of 1988, see "Brown University President to Quit Post Next Year," *The New York Times,* October 17, 1987.

6. See Chapter Six and Appendix One.

7. Kim McDonald, "Pentagon Plan Aims at Luring Students into Military-Related Doctoral Programs," *The Chronicle of Higher Education,* September 2, 1981.

8. John Gerassi, *North Vietnam: A Documentary* (New York: Bobbs-Merrill, 1968).

9. On Haiti, see Michael S. Hooper and Anne Manuel, "The U.S. Role in Haiti's Debacle," *The New York Times,* November 16, 1987.

10. See Chapter Seven.

11. See Section 6.1.

12. See Michael McClintock, *The American Connection,* Vol. 1 & Vol. 2 (London: Zed Books, 1985); Noam Chomsky, *Turning the Tide* (Boston: South End Press, 1985).

13. Jonathan Feldman and Robert Krinsky, "New Directions for the Peace Movement," ms., Columbia University, New York, New York, August 9, 1987; Tables No. 189, No. 234 and No. 235, in U.S. Bureau of the Census (108th edition), *Statistical Abstract of the United States: 1988* (Washington, D.C.: U.S. Government Printing Office, 1987), pp. 118, 140-141. Figures are for 1985.

Chapter Two: State and Corporate Repression in Central America

1. Ricardo Alejandro Fiallos, "Testimony of Captain Ricardo Alejandro Fiallos," Before the Foreign Operations Subcommittee of the House Appropriations Committee, April 29, 1981, in *El Salvador: A Gross and Consistent Pattern of Human Rights Abuses,* El Salvador Packet, Amnesty International, New York, 1983, hereafter, El Salvador Packet.

2. Noam Chomsky, *Turning the Tide* (Boston: South End Press, 1985), pp. 109-111.

3. Chris Norton, "El Salvador Government Reels From Rightist Blow," *Christian Science Monitor,* March 22, 1988; James LeMoyne, "Picture of Death Squads Seen In Key Salvadoran Notebook," *The New York Times,* December 2, 1987.

4. See Fiallos, "Testimony…," *op. cit.,* for a full description of the "parallel government."

5. Quoted in Chomsky, *op. cit.,* pp. 16-17.

6. "El Salvador Promotes Officers Tied to Killings," *The New York Times,* January 16, 1986.

7. "El Salvador: Abductions and Killings By 'Death Squads,' " press release, March 3, 1983, Amnesty International, in El Salvador Packet, *op. cit.*

8. Stephen Kinzer, "Ex-Aide in Salvador Accuses Colleagues on Death Squads," *The New York Times,* March 3, 1984.

9. Robert Perry, "Former Army Officer in Salvador tells of death squad killings," *Boston Globe,* February 13, 1986. See also Allan Nairn, "Confessions of a Death Squad Officer," *The Progressive,* March 1986.

10. Fiallos, "Testimony," in El Salvador Packet, *op. cit.*

11. *A Massacre in El Salvador's Morazan Province December 7-17, 1981, On President Reagan's Certification for Aid to El Salvador,* Two Statements By the Political-Diplomatic Commission of the F.M.L.N./F.D.R. of El Salvador (San Francisco: Solidarity Publications, March 1982), p. 44. For a confirmation of the military's participation in the massacre, see Nairn, *op. cit.,* p. 30.

12. Chomsky, *op. cit.,* pp. 21-22.

13. Dan Williams, "Salvadoran Civilians Become Pawns in a Changing War," *Los Angeles Times,* as cited in Christina Courtright, "Prelude to Operation Phoenix," ms. Medical Aid For El Salvador, Los Angeles, 1986; Janet Shenk, "El Salvador: Central America's Forgotten War," *Mother Jones,* July-August 1986, p. 70.

14. James LeMoyne, "Salvadoran Air Raid Reported in Town," *The New York Times,* February 1, 1987; *Notes on the Air War in El Salvador* (Los Angeles: Medical Aid for El Salvador, 1985), Updated July 10; p. 8; Lindsey Gruson, "Peace is Still a Long Shot in El Salvador," *The New York Times,* September 27, 1987. Maria Julia Hernandez, director of the archbishop's human rights office, estimates that 1,400 civilians were killed in military bombings and sweeps in the countryside in 1985. See Shenk, *op. cit.,* p. 70.

15. Flyer from the Northern California Caravan for Peace and Justice in Central America, San Francisco, 1986; Chris Norton, "Salvador's Army moves civilians in effort to oust rebels," *Christian Science Monitor,* February 6, 1986.

16. *Notes on the Air War, op. cit.;* Phone interview with Christina Courtright, Los Angeles, California, March 3, 1986.

17. This phrase appears as the title to an article by Alan Nairn and Jean-Marie Simon, "Guatemala's Bureaucracy of Death," *The New Republic,* June 30, 1986.

18. George Black, Milton Jamail and Norma Stolz Chinchilla, *Garrison Guatemala* (London: Zed Books, 1984), p. 2; Allan Nairn, "The Guatemala Connection," *The Progressive*, May 1986, p. 22; "Guatemalan Human Rights Commission: Monitoring Abuses and Denouncing Them Worldwide," *Guatemala!*, Vol. 7, No. 6, November-December 1986, p. 5.

19. Black, *et al., op. cit.,* p. 2.

20. This discussion is based on Shelton H. Davis, "State Violence and Agrarian Crisis in Guatemala," in Martin Diskin, ed., *Trouble in Our Backyard* (New York: Pantheon Books, 1983), pp. 155-171.

21. *Guatemala Update: Amnesty International's Human Rights Concerns in Guatemala since the August 1983 Coup which brought General Oscar Humberto Mejia Victores to Power* (London: Amnesty International, December 22, 1983), p. 2; Interview with Garcia Granados, quoted in *Special Update,* "Guatemala: The Roots of Rebellion" (Washington, D.C.: Washington Office on Latin America, October 1982) as cited in Susanne Jonas, "Contradictions of Revolution and Intervention in Central America in the Transnational Era: The Case of Guatemala," in *Revolution and Intervention in Central America,* Marlene Dixon and Sussane Jonas, eds. (San Francisco: Synthesis Publications, 1983), p. 289, hereafter, "Contradictions..."

22. Philip Bennett, "Violence still grips Guatemala," *The Boston Globe,* February 4, 1987; "The Cerezo Presidency A Year Later: He Reigns, But Does He Rule?," Council On Hemispheric Affairs, Washington, D.C., news release No. 87.6, February 6, 1987.

23. Stephen Kinzer, "Army's Hold in Guatemala Stirs Fear for Democracy," *The New York Times,* September 4, 1988. Kinzer also reported here that "officers who in the past were tied to urban death squads and military units that carried out massacres of peasants still hold second-level posts in the army, the National Police and the Treasury Police."

24. See references in Note 22 and "Guatemalan Human Rights Commission...," *op. cit.,* p. 6.

25. *Honduras: On the Brink* (New York and Washington, D.C.: Americas Watch, February 1984), p. 1.

26. Tom Barry and Deb Preusch, *The Central America Fact Book* (New York: Grove Press, 1986), p. 259, hereafter, Barry and Preusch.

27. *Oakland Times,* April 22, 1983; Stephen Kinzer, "Human Rights Is Also an Issue in Honduras," *The New York Times,* January 22, 1984; Steven Volk, "Honduras: On the Border of War," *NACLA Report on the Americas,* Vol. 15, No. 6, November-December 1981.

28. *Honduras: State for Sale* (London: Latin America Bureau, 1985), p. 78.

29. *Honduras: On the Brink, op. cit.*

30. James Le Moyne, "Honduras Reported to Raid Refugees," *The New York Times,* September 5, 1985.

31. Committee for the Defense of Human Rights, "The Human Rights Situation in Honduras, 1986," *Honduras Update,* Special Issue No. 1, May 1987, pp. 10ff.

32. *Honduras: On the Brink, op. cit.,* p. 2; Also see for example the case of Doris Benevidez, described in "Chronology: April 14-30, 1987," *Honduras Update,* Vol. 5, No. 8, May 1987, p. 7; and "The Build-Up's Other Side: Repression and Resistance," *El Salvador Alert!* New York: Committee in Solidarity with the People of El Salvador (CISPES), May 1984.

33. James LeMoyne, "Honduras Army Linked to Death Of 200 Civilians," *The New York Times,* May 2, 1987.

34. James LeMoyne, "In Human Rights Court, Honduras Is First to Face Death Squad Trial," *The New York Times,* January 19, 1988. For an update on repression in Honduras, see Julia Preston, "Honduras Accused of Death-Squad Operations," *The Washington Post,* November 1, 1988.

35. Tom Barry, Beth Wood and Deb Preusch, *Dollars and Dictators: A Guide to Central America* (New York: Grove Press, 1983), p. 165, *hereafter,* Barry *et al.*

36. Barry and Preusch, *op. cit.,* pp. 251, 264.

37. Robert Armstrong, "El Salvador: Why Revolution?," *NACLA Report on the Americas,* Vol. 14, No. 2, March-April 1980.

38. ANDES leader quoted in James Petras, "The Junta's War Against the People," *The Nation,* December 1980 in *El Salvador: The Roots of Intervention, A Special Reprint of Articles from the Nation,* New York, New York, 1980, 1981.

39. Petras, *ibid.*

40. Paul Desruisseaux, "Its Campus Patrolled by Guardsmen, Salvadoran University Survives in 'Exile,' " *The Chronicle of Higher Education,* September 14, 1983.

41. Paul Desruisseaux, "Occupied Salvadoran University May Reopen," *The Chronicle of Higher Education,* April 27, 1984.

42. Phone interview with Sandy Smith, U.S. Campaign for the University of El Salvador, Washington, D.C., February 22, 1986.

43. Interview with spokesperson for the University of El Salvador, New York, New York, August 1984.

44. "The President's Education," *Economist,* July 27, 1985, as quoted in Chomsky, *op. cit.,* p. 113.

45. Sally Macdonald, "Life of a Salvador student leader: on the run from death squads," *The Seattle Times,* November 6, 1985.

46. *Ibid.;* Smith interview, *op. cit.*

47. Chris Norton, "A comeback for the death squads," *In These Times,* July 22-August 4, 1987. See also Sandy Smith and Howard Frumkin, "Destroyed University Struggles to Rebuild," *Links,* May-June 1985.

48. "Ignacio Martin Baro, Leader of a College Under Fire," interview by David P. Hamilton, *The Tech,* Massachusetts Institute of Technology, Cambridge, Massachusetts, April 26, 1985.

49. Gene I. Maeroff, "New Scholarships Aim to Improve U.S. Standing in Central America," *The New York Times,* January 12, 1986.

50. "Without Education There Can Be No Democracy...," brochure, U.S. Campaign for the University of El Salvador, 1985-86.

51. "Books not Bombs for the University of El Salvador...," flyer of the New England Central American Network; Phone interview with Doug Calvin, Washington, D.C., January 30, 1989.

52. Gordon L. Bowen, "Guatemala: A New Form of Totalitarianism?," *Commonweal,* February 10, 1984, p. 77.

53. *Guatemala!,* Vol. 2, No. 3, Feburary 1, 1981.

54. *Guatemala Update, op. cit.,* p. 5.

55. Letter to the author from America Ugarte, director of *Enfoprensa,* September 18, 1985.

56. *Enfoprensa,* Year 3—Number 4, September 13, 1985; Year 3—Number 35, September 20, 1985. A report this year stated that "at least seven University of San Carlos student activists have been kidnapped and murdered during the past school year." See Jon Reed, "Despite terror, Guatemalan students protest openly," *In These Times,* January 25-31, 1989.

57. *State for Sale, op. cit.,* p. 5.

58. Jefferson C. Boyer, "Growing Repression in 'Democratic' Honduras," *Honduras Update,* November-December 1983.

59. *Ibid.*

60. See Noam Chomsky, *American Power and the New Mandarins* (New York: Pantheon, 1969).

61. See Philip Bennett, "Food crisis seen shaking support for Sandinistas," *The Boston Globe,* August 17, 1986.

62. Edgar Chamorro, "Inside the Nicaraguan 'Contras': A Former Leader Speaks," *On Guard,* Vol. 1, No. 1, 1986.

63. "The Central American Peace Plan—One Year Later," *Update,* Vol. 7, No. 26, August 16, 1988. For one of the first political obituary's of the contras, see Stephen Kinzer, "In U.S. and in Latin America, Contras Seem to Be History," *The New York Tmes,* December 13, 1988.

64. See Peter Kornbluh, *The Price of Intervention* (Washington, D.C.: Institute for Policy Studies, 1987); Caleb Rossiter, "The Financial Hit List," *International Policy Report,* February 1984; Jim Morrell, "Redlining Nicaragua: How the U.S. Politicized the Inter-American Bank," *International Policy Report,* December 1985.

65. Mark Green with Michael Waldman, *Who Runs Congress?* (New York: Dell, 1984), pp. 170-171.

66. See Kornbluh, *op. cit.,* for more on the Reagan Administration's use of the media.

67. Kornbluh, *op. cit.,* p. 13.

68. *Ibid.*

69. Chamorro quoted in "Interview with Ex-Contra Leader Edgar Chamorro Upon His Return to Nicaragua," *Update,* Vol. 6, No. 37, November 13, 1987.

70. See Holly Sklar, *Washington's War on Nicaragua* (Boston: South End Press, 1988).

71. William I. Robinson and Kent Norsworthy, "Nicaragua: The Strategy of Counterrevolution," *Monthly Review,* Vol. 37, No. 7, December 1985.

72. "Are the Contras Defeated?," *Central American Bulletin,* Vol. 5, No. 8, June 1986.

73. For an extended analysis of the relationship between the U.S. Government and El Salvador as well as an analysis of the U.S. as "super-government," see Central American University research team, "Duarte: Prisoner of War," in *NACLA: Report on the Americas,* Vol. 20, No. 1, January-March 1986.

74. *Ibid.,* p. 15.

75. *Ibid.*

76. "Interview: Salvador Deserter Discloses Green Beret Torture Role," *Covert Action Information Bulletin,* No. 16, March 1982. Another account of a U.S. adviser who gave advise on torture to interrogation officers from the National Guard, National Police, and Treasury Police intelligence departments is given in Nairn, "Confessions of a Death Squad Officer," *op. cit.,* pp. 27-28.

77. Philip Taubman, "Top Salvador Police Official Said to be a C.I.A. Informant," *The New York Times,* March 22, 1984. See also Stephen Kinzer, "Ex-Aide in Salvador Accuses Colleagues on Death Squads," *op. cit.*

78. Allan Nairn, "Behind the Death Squads," *The Progressive,* May 1984, front cover page.

79. *Ibid.,* p. 20.

80. Michael McClintock, *The American Connection: Volume I: State Terror and Popular Resistance in El Salvador* (London: Zed Press, 1985), p. 207.

81. *Ibid.,* p. 341.

82. Nairn, "Behind the Death Squads," *op. cit.,* p. 20. ANSESAL was abolished by the reformist junta in 1979 but was succeeded by "Department 5," the civic affairs department of the army general staff, as an assassination operation. See Nairn, "Confessions of a Death Squad Officer," *op. cit.,* p. 28.

83. Stephen Kinzer and Stephen Schlesinger, *Bitter Fruit: The Untold Story of the American Coup in Guatemala* (New York: Doubleday, 1982); Paul L. Goepfert, "Democratic Opening," *The Progressive,* November 1985; Black, *et al., op. cit.;* Michael McClintock, *The American Connection, Volume II: State Terror and Popular Resistance in Guatemala* (London: Zed Books, 1985); Chomsky, *Turning the Tide, op. cit.*

84. George Black, "Under the Gun," *NACLA: Report on the Americas,* Vol. 19, No. 6, November-December 1985, p. 21; Chomsky, *Turning the Tide, op. cit.,* p. 155.

85. "Honduras: Opposition to the U.S. Rises," *Central America Bulletin,* Vol. 6, No. 6, June 1987; Interview with Eric Shultz, Honduran Information Center, Somerville, Massachusetts, September 18, 1987.

86. *The Central American War: A Guide to the U.S. Military Buildup* (Philadelphia: NARMIC, Revised April 1983); Bingaman quote appears in Hendrick Smith, "U.S. Latin Force in Place If Needed, Officials Report," *The New York Times,* March 23, 1984; Bob Stix, "U.S. Helicopters Airlift Guatemalan Combat Troops," *Report on Guatemala,* Vol. 8, Issue 2, May-June 1987; Peter Kornbluh, *op. cit.,* p. 77; Cynthia Arnson and Flora Montealegre, "Background Information on U.S. Military Personnel and U.S. Assistance on Central America," Institute for Policy Studies Update #7, November 1982; Michael T. Klare, "Maneuvers in Search of an Invasion," *The Nation,* June 9, 1984; Joseph B. Treaster, "Honduras Vows to Counterattack If Sandinistas Refuse to Pull Back," and Richard Halloran, "U.S. Positions Battalion 42 Miles From Nicaragua," *The New York Times,* March 20, 1988.

87. Armstrong, *op. cit.*

88. "Experience Supports Confidence in El Salvador as Site for MNCs," *Business Latin America,* April 15, 1981. Strikes have been outlawed in the San Bartolo free trade zone where companies have been able to operate tax-free.

89. Barry and Preusch, *op. cit.,* p. 221.

90. Barry, *et al., op. cit.,* p. 189.

91. Theodore H. Moran, "The Cost of Alternative U.S. Policies Toward El Salvador, 1984-1989," in *Central America: Anatomy of Conflict* (New York: Permagon Press, 1984); Barry *et al., op. cit.,* p. 189. The ties between U.S. corporate investment and Salvadoran capital are numerous. The wave of U.S. dominated investment which took place in the 1960s took the form of joint ventures with the Salvadoran bourgeoisie. A 1974 study showed that foreign capital was involved in at least half of all Salvadoran businesses, usually joint ventures with local capitalists. See Barry, *et al.*

92. "Eight Chiefs of State to Address Miami Conference," *In Action, A bi-monthly newsletter of Caribbean/Central American Action,* September-October 1981; "David Rockefeller Elected to C/CAA Chairmanship," *In Action,* May-June 1983; James LeMoyne, "Duarte Winning Support Abroad, Using Democratic Credentials," *The New York Times,* July 25, 1984; Council of the Americas, *Annual Report,* New York, 1982. See Chapters Three, Five, Six and Appendix One on the links of these firms to repression and intervention.

93. *The New Right Humanitarians* (Albuquerque, NM: The Resource Center), First Edition.

94. Chuck Bell, "Evergreen's El Salvador Contacts: The Death Squad Connection," *The Alliance,* Vol. 5, No. 10, October 1985.

95. Henry Weinstein, "California Union to Aid Textile Workers' Strike in El Salvador," *Los Angeles Times,* September 22, 1986.

96. Barry, *et al., op. cit.,* p. 126.

97. *Ibid.*, p. 127.

98. Figure 9 in John E. Lind, *The Debt Crisis and Credit Risk in Countries with Human Rights Abuses* (San Francisco: Northern California-Interfaith Center on Corporate Responsibility, 1983), p. 11.

99. Allan Nairn, "Bank of America Subsidizing Terror in Guatemala," *Washington Report on the Hemisphere,* Council On Hemispheric Affairs, Washington, D.C., Vol. 2, No. 2, February 23, 1982.

100. "Bank of America Leaves the American Chamber of Commerce," *Prophets and Profits,* NC-ICCR Newsletter, March 1984.

101. Nairn, "Bank of America Subsidizing Terror...," *op. cit.*

102. *Ibid.*

103. *Ibid.* The loan was received while Lucas served as Minister of Defense from 1974-1978. Lucas became President in 1978.

104. Nairn, "Bank of America Subsidizing Terror...," *op. cit.*

105. Roger Burbach and Patricia Flynn, "Agribusiness Targets Latin America," *NACLA Report on the Americas,* Vol. 12, No. 1, January-February 1978; Barry, *et al., op. cit.*

106. Jonas, "Contradictions...," *op. cit.,* p. 303; Robert Morris, "Coca-Cola and Human Rights in Guatemala," *ICCR Brief,* New York, New York, November 1980.

107. Jonathan Fried, "Guatemala Labor: Coke Boycott Wins (For Now)," *NACLA Report on the Americas,* Vol. 14, No. 5, September-October 1980.

108. *We will neither go nor be driven out,* A Special Report by the IUF Trade Union Delegation on the Occupation of the Coca-Cola Bottling Plant in Guatemala, North American Regional Organization of the IUF, Washington, D.C., p. 1.

109. *Ibid.,* p. 16.

110. *Ibid.,* p. 1.

111. Allan Nairn, "Coca-Cola backs down in Guatemala dispute," *Multinational Monitor,* July 1980.

112. "Coca-Cola Information," news release no. 2, International Union of Food and Allied Workers Associations, Geneva, March 20, 1984; Lecture by Steve Abrecht, Consultant, Locker/Abrecht Associates Inc., April 1984, New York, New York; *We will neither go nor be driven out, op. cit.,* p. 7.

113. *We will neither go nor be driven out, op. cit.,* p. 16.

114. Stephen Kinzer, "Guatemala Unions Watch Plant Feud," *The New York Times,* July 10, 1984; phone interview with Jonathan Fried, New York, New York, August 1984; "Coca-Cola Violates Agreement," *Enfoprensa: Information on Guatemala,* July 6, 1984. As part of the May Agreement, Coke was to search for a new owner and workers were no longer to occupy the plant. Workers were to remain in the plant to maintain the grounds and operations and in exchange would receive some compensation.

115. Jonathan Fried, "U.S. Unionists Support Coke Plant Occupation," *Guardian,* April 11, 1984; Jonathan Fried, "Guatemala: Coca-Cola Wins International Support," *Guardian,* April 25, 1984.

116. Jonathan Fried, "Labor: Solidarity with Guatemala's Coca-Cola Workers," *Guardian,* May 23, 1984. In Norway, food and beverage workers carried out a one-day work stoppage in support of the Guatemala Coke workers on May 7, 1984. They threatened to repeat the action until the Coke problem was resolved for its workers.

117. "Coke Workers Sign Agreement," in *Guatemala!*, n.d.; *Press,* news publication of the IUF, March 11, 1985; Anna Eisner, "Guatemalan Unions: Testing the Water," *NACLA: Report on the Americas,* Vol. 20, No. 4, July-August 1986.

118. Eisner, *ibid.*

119. Eisner, *ibid.;* Barry and Preusch, *op. cit.,* pp. 247-248.

120. Juan C. Arancibia, *Honduras: Un Estado Nacional?* (Tegucigalpa: Editorial Guaymuras, 1984), as cited by Tom Barry, *Roots of Rebellion: Land and Hunger in Central America* (Boston: South End Press, 1987), pp. 56-59.

121. *State for Sale, op. cit.,* p. 45.

122. *Ibid.,* p. 44.

123. Barry and Preusch, *op. cit.,* p. 266; *La Presna,* April 21, 1987 report cited in "Chronology: April 14-30, 1987," *Honduras Update,* Vol. 5, No. 8, May 1987.

124. *State for Sale, op. cit.,* pp. 21-28; Barry and Preusch, *op. cit.,* p. 253.

125. *State for Sale, op. cit.,* p. 22.

126. *Ibid.,* p. 53.

127. *Ibid.,* p. 81.

128. Barry, *et al., op. cit.,* pp. 17, 21.

129. *Ibid.,* pp. 19, 170.

130. *Ibid.,* p. 264.

131. *Ibid.,* p. 17. For more detailed information about Castle & Cooke's economic influence in Central America, See Chapter Five.

132. *Ibid.,* p. 21.

133. *Ibid.*

134. Larry Rich, "Castle & Cooke, Inc.: An Agribusiness Case Study," *ICCR Brief,* New York, July 1980.

135. Roger Burbach, "Union Busting: Castle & Cooke in Honduras," *NACLA Report on the Americas,* Vol. 11, No. 8, November-December 1977.

136. Steve Volk, "Honduras: On the Border of War," *NACLA Report on the Americas,* Vol. 15, No. 6, November-December 1981.

137. Barry, *et al., op. cit.,* pp. 231-232.

138. Burbach, *op. cit.*

139. Barry and Preusch, *op. cit.,* p. 266.

Chapter Three: Agro-chemical Companies: From Napalm in Vietnam to Pesticide Poisoning in Central America

1. General studies of pesticide poisoning include: *An Environmental and Economic Study of the Consequences of Pesticide Use in Central American Cotton Production* (Final Report), Guatemala, Instituto Centro Americano De Investigacion Y Technologica Industrial (ICAITI), January 1977; David Weir, "Global Pesticide Issues," in *The Pesticide Handbook: Profiles for Action,* Second Edition (Penang, Malaysia: International Organization of Consumers Unions, 1986). Reference to Central America poisonings from: Tom Barry, *Roots of Rebellion* (Boston:

South End Press, 1987), p. 92. Also, see data presented in the text and referenced under Note 33. Pre-revolution Nicaragua had an estimated 3,000 poisonings a year from 1962 to 1972. See L.A. Falcon and R. Smith, *Guidelines for Integrated Control of Cotton Pests* (Rome: Food and Agriculture Organization of the United Nations, 1973) as cited in Douglas L. Murray, "Social Problem-Solving in a Revolutionary Setting: Nicaragua's Pesticide Policy Reforms," *Policy Studies Review*, Vol. 4, No. 2, November 1984, p. 220. Bull estimate appears in David Bull, *A Growing Problem: Pesticides and the Third World Poor* (Oxford: Oxfam, 1982), p. 38.

2. J.B. Neilands, "Napalm Survey," in *The Wasted Nations: Report of the International Commission of Enquiry into United States Crimes in Indochina, June 20-25, 1971,* Frank Browning and Dorothy Forman, eds. (New York: Harper and Row, 1971), p. 34. According to Neilands, from "January 1969 through June 1971 an estimated 125,000 tons of napalm was employed by U.S. forces in Indochina."

3. *Ibid.*, p. 32. In 1965, Dow Chemical began napalm production in its Torrence, California plant. Dow continued to supply napalm until late 1969. See *ibid.*, pp. 31-33.

4. Seymour M. Hersh, *Chemical and Biological Warfare* (New York: Bobbs-Merrill, 1968), pp. 62-63, 254.

5. Merle Ratner, "What About All These Victims of Agent Orange?," *Guardian*, May 30, 1984.

6. F. J. Delmore quoted in John Lewallen, *Ecology of Devastation: Indochina* (Baltimore: Penguin Books, 1971), p. 63.

7. *Ibid.*, p. 65.

8. *Ibid.*, p. 114.

9. Robert Morris, "Agent Orange/2,4,5-T and Dow Chemical," ICCR Brief, *The Corporate Examiner,* Newsletter of the Interfaith Center on Corporate Responsibility, June 1982.

10. Margot Hornblower, "Emergency Ban is Ordered for 2 Weed Killers," *The Washington Post,* March 2, 1979 as cited in *ibid.*

11. Lewallen, *op. cit.;* Ratner, *op. cit.*

12. Morris, *op. cit.*

13. Todd Ensign, "Action—At Last—on Agent Orange," *Guardian*, February 22, 1984. In May of 1984, the seven chemical companies which produced Agent Orange agreed to pay $180 million into a fund which would go to settle the claims of all Vietnam War veterans injured by exposure to the herbicide. See Todd Ensign, "Fair Deal for Agent Orange Vets?," *Guardian,* May 16, 1984.

14. "U.S. Verterans Agency Revises Its Agent Orange Pamphlet," *The New York Times,* May 26, 1982, as cited in Morris, *op. cit.*

15. Lewallen, *op. cit.*, p. 116; Morris, *op. cit.* See also Harrison Wellford, *Sowing the Wind* (New York: Grossman Publishers, 1972), pp. 195-202.

16. "In Secret 1965 Meeting: Dioxin Makers Admitted 'Problem,' " *Citizen Soldier,* May 1983.

17. Philip Shabecoff, "Chemical Industry's Influence Is Studied," *The New York Times,* April 22, 1983.

18. David Stone, Graduate Student, Department of History, "Dow and the University," in *Dow Chemical: Three Views,* ms., New York University, New York, New York, 1968.

19. See Chapters Six and Seven for an elaboration of the universities' role in the "military division of labor."

20. Quoted in Hersh, *op. cit.*, p. 261.

21. Liberation News Service, "Students Battle Cops," *New Left Notes,* October 23, 1967.

22. Quoted in Hersh, *op. cit.*, p. 261.

23. "Napalm: The Image Maker," *Forbes*, March 15, 1969.

24. Bill Keller, "The Bidding to Make Poison Gas," *The New York Times*, September 1, 1985.

25. Phone interview with Todd Ensign, *Citizen Soldier*, New York, New York, August 4, 1987; Keller, *op. cit*. A recent report noted that Dow Chemical's increased exposure in consumer markets has made the company more sensitive to consumer and political concerns about its investments and actions. See Claudia H. Deutsch, "Dow Chemical Wants to Be Your Friend," *The New York Times*, November 22, 1987.

26. "Fact Sheet: Pesticides and the Third World," Sierra Club International Earthcare Center, New York, New York, May 1983.

27. Quoted in David Weir and Mark Schapiro, *Circle of Poison: Pesticides and People in a Hungry World* (San Francisco: Institute for Food and Development Policy, 1981), p. 7.

28. Magda Renner quoted in Alicia Culver, "New Global Campaign to Exterminate Dirty Dozen Pesticides," *Multinational Monitor*, Vol. 16, No. 13, September 1985.

29. Barry, *op. cit.*, p. 92.

30. Letter from David Schieber, dated August 29, 1983, in Sierra Club International pesticide files, New York, New York.

31. Jon Steinberg, "Pesticides in Central America: For Export Only," *Links*, published by the National Central America Health Rights Network (NCAHRN), Vol. 4, No. 1, Spring 1987.

32. Weir and Schapiro, *op. cit.*, p. 14.

33. *An Environmental and Economic Study...*, *op. cit.*, pp. 88, 91. Data on parathion from Weir and Schapiro, *op. cit.*, pp.32-33.

34. Tom Barry and Deb Preusch, *The Central America Fact Book* (New York: Grove Press, 1986), p. 158.

35. *An Environmental and Economic Study...*, *op. cit.*, pp. 88-91. Such conditions also lead to poisonings because when field workers wash their equipment, they frequently use the only source of water available, irrigation ditches: "From there the water may flow into the streams where the workers and their families as well as their neighbors bathe and drink. Since the majority have no toilets, they use the fields, and often use the poisoned vegetation to wipe themselves." See Steinberg, *op. cit*. An International Labor Organization study also concluded that, "Well nourished, comfortably housed workers, enjoying adequate rest and hygiene are less vulnerable to toxic chemicals than persons who are burdened with malnutrition, disease and fatigue." "Guide to Health and Hygiene in Agricultural Work," (Geneva: International Labor Organization, 1979), p. 94 as quoted in Barry, *op. cit.*, p. 93.

36. "Fact Sheet: Pesticides and the Third World," *op. cit.*; GAO, "Better Regulation of Pesticide Exports and Pesticide Residues in Imported Food Is Essential," Washington, D.C., 1979, cited in Barry and Preusch, *op. cit.*, pp. 158-159.

37. Martin Abraham and Lawrie Mott, "Your Daily Dose of Pesticide Residues," Fact Sheet of the "Dirty Dozen Campaign," PAN International, San Francisco, California. A report issued in May of 1987 by the National Academy of Sciences found that the nation's food supply was inadequately protected from cancer-causing pesticides. See Philip Shabecoff, "Code on Pesticides Urged for Nation," *The New York Times*, May 21, 1987.

38. Bull *op. cit.*, p. 6; press release, United Nations Environment Programme, New York Liason Office, March 21, 1984; *Transnationals Information and Exchange-Europe*, No. 15, 1983. For an overview of the pesticide problem in the Third World, see Weir and Schapiro, *op. cit.*; Bull, *op. cit.* and *The Careless Technology: Ecology and International Development*, M. Taghi Farvar and John P. Milton, eds. (Garden City, NY: The Natural History Press, 1972).

39. David Weir, "The Global Pesticide Threat," *Multinational Monitor*, September 1985, p. 9; data on Central American imports from Murray, *op. cit.*, p. 220. Regarding Table 3-1, the figures

on the increase in the value of Nicaragua's insecticide and herbicide imports are not good proxies for the increase in the amount of pesticides imported. For example, in 1982, the volume of imported pesticides dropped to 45 percent of the preceeding year. However, "although insecticide imports decreased, insecticide costs increased dramatically, a result of the shift away from the relatively inexpensive organochlorines to the very expensive synthetic pyrethroids, as well as a more general increase in petrochemical prices." See Sean L. Swezey, Douglas L. Murray and Rainer G. Daxl, "Nicaragua's Revolution in Pesticide Policy," *Environment*, Vol. 28, No. 1, January-February 1986, p. 35. Tom Barry estimates that for Central America as a whole, "during the last decade the cost of pesticide imports increased sevenfold, while the amount imported only increased by half... The price of imported fertilizers jumped five-fold during the 1970s, but import volume increased by only 25 percent." See Barry, *op. cit.*, p. 40.

40. Bull, *op. cit.*, p. 3, p. 5. Quote on UN study from Swezey, *et al.*, p. 30. Quote on effect of pesticide reductions from Murray, *op. cit.*, p. 222.

41. Bull, *op. cit.*, p. 10. Swezey, *et al.* report on the Nicaraguan case: "...insects considered innocuous in the mid-1950s, now freed from their natural controls, became new secondary pests." See Swezey, *et al.*, *op. cit.*, pp. 9, 29. In 1938, scientists knew of only seven insect and mite species that had developed a resistance to pesticides. By 1984, that number had reached 447, and included most of the world's pests. See Sandra Postel, "Defusing the Toxics Threat: Controlling Pesticides and Industrial Waste," *Worldwatch Paper: 79* (Washington, D.C.: Worldwatch Institute, September 1987), p. 19.

42. Bull, *op. cit.*

43. Bull, *ibid.*, p. 12.

44. *Ibid.* A 1984 interview by Tom Barry of Gilberto Galindo, manager of a cotton plantation in Guatemala, confirmed that this pattern continued into the 1980s. According to Galindo, "The insects here have grown stronger, and it is due to the heavy use of chemicals. Not only are the insects stronger than the chemicals, but we now have problems with new kinds of insects that are attacking our crops." See Barry, *op. cit.*, p. 93.

45. Bull, *op. cit.*, p. 81. One study found that in 1979 almost 50,000 tons of chemicals were sprayed annually onto cotton, coffee, bananas, flowers and non-traditional vegetables, i.e., export cash crops. See SIECA, *Compendio Estadistico,* 1981, as cited in Barry, *op. cit.*, p. 104.

46. William R. Furtick and Ray F. Smith, "World Problems of Pesticides" in *The Agromedical Approach to Pesticide Management,* UC/AID, 1976, p. 10, quoted in Bull, *op. cit.*, p. 81.

47. Bull, *op. cit.*, pp. 83-84, 87. Data on Nicaragua from Swezey, *et al.*, *op. cit.*, p. 29.

48. Bull, *op. cit.*, p. 87.

49. *Ibid.*, p. 92.

50. *Ibid.*, p. 92, 93, 121, 122.

51. The 75 percent figure is from Shelley A. Hearne, *Harvest of Unknowns: Pesticide Contamination in Imported Foods* (New York: Natural Resources Defense Council, 1984), p. 21 as cited in Barry, *op. cit.*, p. 95. Information on Standard Fruit suit in Barry, *ibid.*, p. 99.

52. Ray F. Smith and J. Lawrence Apple, "Principle of Integrated Pest Control," in *Short Course on Integrated Pest Control for Irrigated Rice in South and South East Asia,* Philippines, 1978, quoted in Bull, *op. cit.*, p. 126. See also Edward C. Wolf, "Beyond the Green Revolution: New Approaches for Third World Agriculture," *Worldwatch Paper: 73* (Washington, D.C.: Worldwatch Institute, October 1986).

53. Michael Hansen, *Escape from the Pesticide Treadmill,* Preliminary Report, Institute for Consumer Policy Research, Consumers Union, May 1986, p. 24.

54. Quote on 40 percent reduction from Joseph Collins and Donna Kelly, "Nicaragua: Getting Off the Pesticide Treadmill," *Multinational Monitor,* September 1985; Hansen, *op. cit.*, pp.

25-26; interview with Juan Jose Rodriguez, Centro Nacional de Proteccion de Vegetal, Managua, Nicaragua, September 3, 1987.

55. Hansen, *op. cit.,* p. 4, p. 5.

56. Lex Gillespie, "Brazil's Silent Spring: An Interview with Magda Renner," *Multinational Monitor,* September 1985; Catherine Caufield, "Companies Defy Brazilian Pesticide Law," *New Scientist,* August 11, 1983, p. 393.

57. Letter to author from Giselda Castro, Vice-President Acao Democratica Femina Gaucha (ADFG), Porto Alegre, May 14, 1984.

58. "Pesticides and Pills: For Export Only," Film script by Robert Richter, Part One: Pesticides, Transcript of Television Broadcast on Public Broadcasting Service, October 5, 1981, Appendix 1, in Ruth Norris, ed. *Pills, Pesticides & Profits* (Croton-on-Hudson, NY: North River Press, 1982).

59. "News Briefs," *Latinamerica Press,* February 16, 1984.

60. Pat Roy Mooney, "The Law of the Seed," *Development Dialogue,* Nos. 1 & 2, September 1983, p. 97. Another source estimates that over the next twenty years, estimated global sales *per annum* of biotechnology-based agricultural inputs could range as high as $50 to $100 billion. See J. Murrary and L. Teichner, *An Assessment of the Global Potential of Genetic Engineering in the Agribusiness Sector* (Chicago: Policy Research Corporation and Chicago Group, Inc., 1981), as cited in Martin Kenney and Frederick H. Buttel, "Biotechnology: Prospects and Dilemmas for Third World Development," *Development and Change,* Vol. 16, 1985, p. 66, *hereafter,* Kenney, *et al.*

61. For a further explanation of this point of view, see below and the comments of Susan George as published in "Biotechnology," *Meeting the Corporate Challenge,* TIE Report 18/19, John Cavanagh, *et al.,* eds. (Amsterdam: Transnational Information Exchange, February 1985).

62. Frederick H. Buttel, Martin Kenney and Jack Kloppenburg, Jr., "From Green Revolution to Biorevolution: Some Observations on the Changing Technological Bases of Economic Transformation in the Third World," *Cornell Rural Sociology Bulletin Series,* August 1983, Bulletin No. 132, p. 7.

63. Weir and Schapiro, *op. cit.,* p. 43.

64. Constance Matthiessen and Howard Kohn, "In Search of the Perfect Tomato," *The Nation,* July 7-14, 1984.

65. "Green Revolution #2: Biotechnology's New Plants Can't Grow Agricultural Solutions," *Dollars and Sense,* December 1985, p. 12. The agro-chemical companies and other transnationals have become "the new seed monopolies" and are completely dominating research, production and marketing. A report in 1982 stated that more than twenty international companies belonging to monopoly groups with a yearly turnover of more than $500 million had started businesses in seed growing. These included: ITT, Occidental Petroleum, Cargill, Union Carbide, Continental Grain Co., Monsanto, FMC, Celanese, Diamond Shamrock, Pfizer, Olin, Upjohn, Central Soya, Anderson Clayton, International Multifoods, Purex, Dekalb Agresearch Inc., Pioneer Hi-Bred International Inc. (U.S.); Tate & Lyle (Great Britain); Royal Dutch Shell (Great Britain/Netherlands); Sandoz, Ciba-Geigy Ltd. (Switzerland) and EMC-group (France). See Horst Schilling, "The New Seed Monopolies," *Raw Materials Report,* Vol. 1, No. 3, 1982. See also Mooney, *op. cit.,* especially Table 23, p. 96 and Table 24, p. 99, for additional information on TNCs' links to the seed industry.

66. Erol Black, "Seeds of Destruction?," *Monthly Review,* Vol. 31, No. 11, April 1980.

67. Kenney, *et al., op. cit.,* p. 68.

68. George, as quoted in Cavanagh, *op. cit.,* p. 23.

69. Wolf, *op. cit.,* p. 35.

70. Weir and Schapiro, *op. cit.,* p. 44.

71. "Newsnotes: Seed Embargo," *Science for the People,* January-February 1986, p. 4. For an earlier assessment, see Table 6, Mooney, *op. cit.,* p. 26. He found that 55 percent of the world's collected germplasm was banked in the North (i.e., industrialized market-economy and centrally-planned states) and 31 percent was banked in the South (i.e., Group of 77 nations and the People's Republic of China). See also "A Report on Germplasm Embargoes," RAFI Communique, October 1988 published by the Rural Advancement Fund International, Pittsboro, North Carolina.

72. Keith Schneider, "U.S. Opposes Plan to Store Agricultural Genes," *The New York Times,* November 28, 1985, p. 1, p. A19.

73. Wolf, *op. cit.,* p. 33.

74. Matthiessen and Kohn, *op. cit.* For university ties to biotechnology, see Martin Kenney, *Biotechnology* (New Haven: Yale University Press, 1986).

75. Dennis Gaffney, "Getting the Business: Academic-Corporate Biotechnology Ties Make Some Uneasy," *The Boston Tab,* Vol. 6, No. 42, July 1, 1986; Academic Industry Program, Government-University-Industry Research Roundtable, *New Alliances and Partnerships in American Science and Engineering* (Washington, D.C.: National Academy Press, 1986), p. 16.

76. David F. Noble and Nancy E. Pfund, "Business Goes Back to College," *The Nation,* September 20, 1980.

77. George, as quoted in Cavanagh, *op. cit.,* p. 23.

78. Kenneth A. Smith, "Industry-University Research Programs," *Physics Today,* February 1984.

79. Katherine Bouton, "Academic Research and Big Business: A Delicate Balance," *The New York Times Magazine,* September 11, 1983, p. 63.

80. *New Alliances and Partnerships in American Science and Engineering, op. cit.,* p. 4.

81. Smith, *op. cit.*

82. Noble and Pfund, *op. cit.*

83. Donald Kennedy, "Government Policies and the Cost of Doing Research," *Science,* 227, February 1, 1985, pp. 480-484, cited in *New Alliances and Partnerships in American Science and Engineering, op. cit.* p. 7. See also the collected articles in "Research and the Academy," *Thought & Action,* Vol. 1, No. 1, Fall 1984. For more on university-corporate ties, see also: Frederick H. Buttel, J. Tadlock Cowan, Martin Kenney, Jack Kloppenburg, Jr., "Biotechnology in Agriculture: The Political Economy of Agribusiness Reorganization and Industry-University Relations," in H. K. Schwarzeller (ed.), *Research in Rural Sociology and Development* (Greenwich, CT: JAI Press, 1981), draft copy; J. Tadlock Cowen and Frederick H. Buttel, "U.S. State Governments and the Promotion of Biotechnology R&D: A Case Study of the Emergence of Subnational Corporatism," paper prepared for presentation at the annual meeting of the British Sociological Association, Cardiff, Wales, March 1983; "The DNA Business and Campus Questions," *The Boston Globe,* November 3, 1980.

84. Smith, *op. cit.*

85. *New Alliances and Partnerships in American Science and Engineering, op. cit.,* p. 1.

86. Philip M. Boffey, "Industry Takes Dominant Science Role," *The New York Times,* July 17, 1984; See also "Research and the Academy," *Thought and Action, op. cit.*

87. Robert H. Malott, "Corporate Support of Education: Some Strings Attached," *Harvard Business Review,* July 1978, pp. 133, 137, as quoted in Philip L. Bereano, "Making Knowledge a Commodity: Increased Corporate Influence on Universities," *IEE Technology and Society Magazine,* December 1986, p. 11.

88. Albert Meyerhoff, "Agribusiness on Campus," *The Nation,* February 16, 1980 as cited in Bereano, *op. cit.*

89. Dorothy Nelkin and Richard Nelson with Casey Kiernan, "University-Industry Alliances," Government-University-Industry Roundtable, Columbia University, New York, New York, ms. See also *New Alliances and Partnerships in American Science and Engineering, op. cit.*

90. See *Thought and Action, op. cit.* and Bereano, *op. cit.* Leonard Minsky and the National Coalition for Universities in the Public Interest, in Washington, D.C., have monitored several faculty cases of harassment and firings related to changing patterns in the university.

91. "International Code of Conduct on the Distribution and Use of Pesticides," Adopted on November 22, 1985 at the 23rd Session of the Conference of the Food and Agriculture Organizations of the United Nations (FAO), reprinted in *The Pesticide Handbook: Profiles for Action, op. cit.,* pp. 199- 214. Quote on importance of labeling from Swezey, *et al., op. cit.,* p. 35.

92. Rodriguez interview, *op. cit.;* "Acuerdos De La Reunion De San Jose—Costa Rica Para Unificar Criterios Sobre Etiquetados Y Registros De Plaguicidas," Centro Nacional de Protec-cion de Vegetal.

93. "International Code of Conduct...," *op. cit.,* p. 212.

94. In Nicaragua, color-coded labels provide assistance to illiterate workers and a law now requires all instructions for pesticide use to be in Spanish. All advertising by pesticide firms are regulated by laws administered by the Nicaraguan government and designed to promote social responsibility. Companies have to submit their advertising to the office of pesticide registration. However, some advertisers still carry on the past practice of making misleading claims about their products. Rodriguez interview, *op. cit.;* see also Barry, Chapter Five: "Chemical Craze," *op. cit.*

95. Sweezy, *et al., op. cit.,* p. 33; Murray *op. cit.,* p. 227.

96. Barry, *op. cit.,* p. 101.

97. Murray, *op. cit.,* p. 226.

98. Care's workplace health and safety project has encouraged the installation of "closed" pesticide systems which limit workers' exposure to pesticides by using interlocking tubes, containers and pumping devices. Personal protective equipment is provided to farm workers in high-risk jobs at airfields on the farms where concentrated chemicals are mixed and loaded into spray planes. Farmworkers are trained and educated in health and safety methods, the use of closed systems and such equipment. The program also trains workers and inspectors in health education techniques, pesticide identification, workplace monitoring and illness investigation. [Interview with Dominique Hoppe, Care International, Managua, Nicaragua, August 1987.] See also "The Pesticide Health and Saftey Program," mimeo, Care International, Managua, Nicaragua, May 1987. Multinationals now in Nicaragua have carried out some conscientious actions with regard to pesticide problems. For example, they have set up classes which train field representatives once a year in the safe use of pesticides. Companies involved in such training include FMC (U.S.), Ciba-Geigy (Switzerland), Bayer and Schering (West Germany). Such companies also publish brochures on pesticide health and safety [Rodriguez interview, *op. cit.*]. Other firms linked to the pesticide trade in Nicaragua include: Hercules (U.S.), Monsanto (U.S.), Agroquimicas de Guatemala (Owned by Witco Chemical Corporation, U.S.) and Quimica Estrella (Argentina). [Information on Hercules from: Barry and Preusch, *op. cit.* Information on Monsanto from: "Roundup: Herbicida de Monsanto," pesticide label. Other companies from: "Chlordimeform: Nombre Comercial No. Registro Fecha Procedencia," document photocopy, dated February 16, 1986, Ministerio de Desarrollo Agropecuario, Nicaragua.]

99. Matthew Rothschild, "New Coalition Forms to Combat Pesticide Abuse," *Multinational Monitor,* July 1982.

100. Alicia Culver, "New Global Campaign to Exterminate Dirty Dozen Pesticides," *Multinational Monitor,* September 1985; Monica Moore, "PAN: The International Grassroots Organization for Pesticide Reform," *The Journal of Pesticide Reform,* Spring 1986.

101. Phone interview with Dan Carter, United Farm Workers, Washington, D.C., October 31, 1988.

102. Phone interview with Rev. Sharon Streater, Farm Labor Organizing Committee, Toledo, Ohio, October 25, 1988; "Chemical Fact Sheet For: Chlorothalonil (tetrachloroisophthalonitrile)," Environmental Protection Agency, Washington, D.C., draft circulated, circa 1984.

103. Phone interview with Elise Wilson, Yardley, Pennsylvania, November 1, 1988; Bob Condor, "Special Report: Killer Courses," *Golf Magazine,* December 1986; Sharon Begley with Mary Hager, "Keep Off the Grass," *Newsweek,* May 16, 1988. According to Wilson, the death of her brother, George Prior, through chlorothalonil poisoning was confirmed by military officials.

104. "U.S. Produces 833 Pounds of Toxic Waste Per Person Yearly," *Bangor Daily News,* October 7, 1986.

105. *Corporate Profile: Dow Chemical Company,* unpublished study by the Chemical Industry Responsibility Project, Cambridge, Massachusetts, November 1985.

106. *Corporate Profile: Monsanto Company,* unpublished study by the Chemical Industry Responsibility Project, Cambridge, Massachusetts, November 1985; *Corporate Profile: Union Carbide Corporation,* unpublished study by the Chemical Industry Responsibility Project, Cambridge, Massachusetts, November 1985.

107. Dick Russell with Russell King, "Politics of ozone: delay in the face of disaster," *In These Times,* August 17-30, 1988; Sarah Clark, *Protecting the Ozone Layer: What You Can Do,* Environmental Defense Fund, New York, New York.

108. Robert A. Rice and Joshua N. Karliner, "Militarization: The Environmental Impact," EPOCA/Green Paper No. 3, September 1986; *Central America Report,* November-December 1984.

109. Mary Jo McConahay and Robin Kirk, "Over There," *Mother Jones,* February-March 1989.

110. One report noted that if tolerant seeds for roundup were developed, annual sales could increase by $150 million. See "Herbicide Tolerance," *RAFI Communique,* November 1987.

111. Mooney, *op. cit.,* p. 5.

Chapter Four: Foreign Capital: Dependency or Development?

1. For a critique of divestment relevant to this sort of thinking, see Lars Waldorf, "After the Pullout," *The New Republic,* December 29, 1986.

2. See Andre Gunder Frank, *Crisis In The Third World* (New York: Holmes & Meier Publishers, 1981), p. 104; Mario Ponce, "Honduras: Agricultural Policy and Perspectives," in *Honduras Confronts its Future,* Mark B. Rosenberg and Philip L. Shepherd, eds. (Boulder, CO: Lynne Rienner Publishers, Inc., 1986), p. 146.

3. James F. Petras and and Morris H. Morley, "Economic Expansion, Political Crisis and U.S. Policy in Central America," in *Revolution and Intervention in Central America,* Marlene Dixon and Susanne Jonas, eds. (San Francisco: Synthesis Publications, 1983), p. 195.

4. Solon Barraclough and Peter Marchetti, "Agrarian Transformation and Food Security in the Caribbean Basin," Chapter Ten in *Towards an Alternative for Central America and the Caribbean,* George Irvin and Xabier Gorostiaga, eds. (London: George Allen & Unwin, 1985),

hereafter, Irvin and Gorostiaga. Data on Costa Rica from *Country Development Strategy Statements: Data Abstract* (Washington, D.C.: Agency for International Development, 1982) as cited by Tom Barry, *Roots of Rebellion* (Boston: South End Press, 1987), p. 16.

5. Joseph Collins and Frances Moore Lappe, "Food Self-Reliance," Chapter Eight in *Self-Reliance: Strategy for Development,* George Galtung, Peter O'Brien and Roy Preiswerk, eds. (London: Bogle-L'Ouverture Publications, Ltd., 1980), p. 140.

6. Oxfam America, "Facts for Action," No. 12 (Boston: Oxfam, n.d.).

7. Barraclough and Marchetti, *op. cit.,* p. 157.

8. *Ibid.*

9. *Ibid.,* p. 160.

10. *Ibid.;* Edelberto Torres-Rivas, "Central America Today: A Study in Regional Dependency," pp. 1-33 in *Central America: Trouble in Our Backyard,* Martin Diskin, ed. (New York: Pantheon, 1983).

11. Oxfam, *op. cit.*

12. Author's calculations based on U.S. General Imports CIF and General Exports FOB in 1986 as published in the *1986 International Trade Statistics Yearbook,* Vol. 1 (New York: United Nations, 1988), pp. 1010, 1013.

13. Robert G. Williams, *Export Agriculture and the Crisis in Central America* (Chapel Hill, NC: The University of North Carolina Press, 1986), pp. 23, 19; *Fibres & Textiles: Dimensions of Corporate Marketing Structure* (Geneva: United Nations: 1981), p. 38. In 1950, the eight *municipios* that would grow more than 90 percent of Guatemala's cotton a decade later achieved average yields that were 50 to 100 percent more than the national average. Total cropland in these *municipios* expanded by 52,000 acres by the census period from 1963 to 1964. However, despite this dramatic increase in land under cultivation, land dedicated to corn cultivation declined by 25,000 acres. Cotton cultivation expanded to 192,000 acres, consuming 70 percent of the *muncipios'* cropland. This pattern of cotton displacing corn was repeated in El Salvador: "the two largest corn producing *municipios* in the early 1950s (San Miguel and Jiquilisco) were transformed into the two largest cotton producers by the early 1970s." Edelberto Torres-Rivas described the impact of cotton by writing that "the introduction of cotton in El Salvador is most tragic from the viewpoint of the country's displaced population." For the campesinos, the expansion of cotton production came at the cost of "a large margin of hunger and hopelessness." See Williams, *op. cit.,* p. 55; Edelberto Torres-Rivas, "El Desarrollo de la Agricultura en Centroamerica," in Conferacion Universitaria Centroamericana (CSUCA), "Documentos de Estudios" (San Jose), July 22-23, 1982 and CIERA and INIES, "El Subsistema del Algodon, Causas y Consecuencias" (San Salvador), 1980, p. 32, quoted in Tom Barry and Deb Preusch, *The Central America Fact Book* (New York: Grove Press, 1986), p. 153, *hereafter,* Barry and Preusch.

14. Susanne Jonas, "Guatemala: Land of Eternal Struggle," Chapter One in *Latin America: The Struggle with Dependency and Beyond,* Ronald H. Chilcote and Joel C. Edelstein, eds. (Cambridge, MA: Schenkman Publishing Co., 1974), p. 187.

15. Shelton H. Davis, "State Violence and Agrarian Crisis in Guatemala," pp. 155-171 in Diskin, *op. cit.,* p. 160.

16. Phillip L. Russell, *El Salvador in Crisis* (Austin, TX: Colorado River Press, 1984), p. 61.

17. Oxfam, *op. cit.*

18. Ponce, *op. cit.,* p. 133.

19. *Ibid.,* pp. 133, 136.

20. *Ibid.,* p. 141.

21. Davis, *op. cit.*, p. 160.

22. Oxfam, *op. cit.* Data on El Salvador from: University of Central America, San Salvador, "La Fase III de la Reforma Agraria y Las Condiciones de Vida de Sus Beneficiarios—Seminario Permanente Sobre la Economic Nacional del Departamento de Economia" (San Salvador); *Proceso* (El Salvador) September 12, 1983, p. 9, as cited in Barry *op. cit.*, p. 17. In data collected by Barry covering the 1980s, the following percentages reflected the proportion of the rural population in absolute poverty ("the inability to afford food providing minimum nutritional requirements") : Costa Rica (40 percent), El Salvador (70 percent), Guatemala (60 percent), Honduras (77 percent), and Nicaragua (57 percent). See Barry, *op. cit.*, Table 7, p. 16.

23. George Black, in collaboration with Milton Jamail and Norma Stoltz Chinchalla, *Garrison Guatemala* (London: Zed Books, 1984); Petras and Morley, *op. cit.;* Quote is from *Fibres and Textiles, op. cit.*, p. 38.

24. Table 4-6 and pp. 160-161, p. 178 in Ray A. Goldberg, *Agribusiness Management for Developing Countries-Latin America* (Cambridge, MA: Ballinger, 1974) as summarized in Susan George, *Feeding the Few: Corporate Control of Food* (Washington, D.C.: Institute for Policy Studies, 1979), p. 51; Russell, *op. cit.*, p. 62.

25. Roger Burbach and Patricia Flynn, *Agribusiness and the Americas* (New York: Monthly Review Press, 1980).

26. U.S. multinational interests have also organized and helped reproduce the agro-export system by encouraging nontraditional exports such as vegetables, flowers, shrimp and beef. U.S. investors buy produce grown by local farmers and export it to the United States. The Latin American Agribusiness Development Corporation (LAAD) has promoted the production of nontraditional exports by distributing Agency for International Development funds and investing in over 160 businesses in Central America. LAAD was formed by Bank of America in 1970 and is composed chiefly of U.S. banks and agribusiness interests. Past projects include the financing for U.S. subsidiaries which process and freeze broccoli, cauliflower and Okra grown by Indian farmers in Guatemala and investments in livestock in Guatemala, Costa Rica, Honduras and Nicaragua. Aside from BOA, other LAAD companies include Castle & Cooke, Monsanto and Chase Manhattan. See Barry and Preusch, *op. cit.*, pp. 155-157. Norma Stoltz Chinchilla and Nora Hamilton, "Prelude to Revolution: U.S. Investment in Central America," Chapter Seven in *The Politics of Intervention in Central America*, Roger Burbach and Patricia Flynn, eds. (New York: Monthly Review Press, 1984), pp. 227-228. A review of the cotton industry illustrates how TNCs and the oligarchy have used their control of land, technological inputs, marketing and distribution systems to the detriment of the average farm worker. In Central America, TNC-linked fertilizer and insecticide companies captured a significant share of the wealth generated by the cotton economy. A merchant profit was earned on sales, an industrial profit was earned by hiring workers to both mix and package the compounds, and an excess profit was earned by agribusiness supply houses: "profits of growers were transferred to the agribusiness supply houses because of the artificially high prices permitted by protective tariffs." During the 1960s most of the export trade in Guatemala was handled by local cotton merchants, a large portion of whom represented U.S. firms. The bulk of cotton grown in Guatemala was produced on large estates. In 1964, farms larger than 1,100 acres cultivated 62 percent of the cotton. In El Salvador, during the period from 1972 to 1973, one fourth of the cotton crop was controlled by eighteen families through land ownership and rental. A review of a list of Salvadoran families that had harvested a thousand or more bales in 1972-1973 reveals that: "The majority of the top cotton-growing families in El Salvador fall within the top thirty land-owning families, and all of those on the list, with the exception of [two], fall within the top fifty coffee-exporting families." Such owners of large haciendas along the coastal plain received the greatest concentration of the wealth produced by cotton cultivation in Central America. But while the economic elites benefited from cotton cultivation, the peasants were not given a minimal share of the agro-export income. Peasants who once grew food on small farms for family consumption or sharecropped on larger plots of land were

displaced when the land became profitable for cotton production. Cotton growers, or others with privileged access to land titling institutions in the capital, evicted the peasants, leaving them uprooted and homeless. See Williams, *op. cit.*, pp. 32-73.

27. Torres-Rivas, "Central America Today…," *op. cit.*, p. 12; Table 28 in C.V. Vaitsos, *The Role of Transnational Enterprises in Latin American Economic Integration Efforts: Who Integrates, and with Whom, How and for whose Benefit?*, UNCTAD, January 6, 1983, p. 59.

28. See *Selected Data on U.S. Direct Investment Abroad, 1950-1976*, Bureau of Economic Analysis, U.S. Department of Commerce, Washington, D.C., February 1982, p. 17; *U.S. Direct Investment Abroad: Balance of Payments and Direct Investment Position Estimates, 1977-1981*, Bureau of Economic Analysis, U.S. Department of Commerce, Washington, D.C., November 1986, p. 1; *U.S. Direct Investment Abroad: 1982 Benchmark Survey Data*, Bureau of Economic Analysis, U.S. Department of Commerce, Washington, D.C., December 1985, p. 51.

29. Vaitsos, *op. cit.*, pp. 10-11. See also Salvador Umana, *et al., El Salvador: Recent Economic Developments* (Washington, D.C.: International Monetary Fund, December 12, 1985); World Bank, *El Salvador: Country Economic Memorandum* (Washington, D.C.: World Bank, 1986).

30. Albert O. Hirschman, *A Bias for Hope* (New Haven: Yale University Press, 1971).

31. *Ibid.;* Edelberto Torres-Rivas, "The Central American Model…," in *Revolution in Central America* (Boulder, CO: Westview Press, 1983); Barry and Preusch, *op. cit.;* Chinchilla and Hamilton, *op. cit.*

32. Jonas, *op. cit.*, pp. 177-178.

33. *Ibid.*, p. 178, 183.

34. *Ibid.;* Chinchilla and Hamilton, *op. cit.*, p. 240.

35. Marc W. Herold, From "Riches to 'Rags': Finanzkapital in El Salvador, 1900-1980," ms., Whittemore School of Business and Economics, University of New Hampshire, Durham, New Hampshire, February 29, 1980. Note, however, that when Texas Instruments announced plans in October 1985 to lay off workers because of a recession in the semiconductor industry, one of the plants slated to go was in El Salvador. See Peter Coy, "Massive Layoffs Announced," *The Oakland Tribune*, October 26, 1985.

36. Russell, *op. cit.*, p. 57.

37. For a critical assessment of dependency theory and the limits of the "surplus-extraction thesis," see John Weeks, "The Limits to Accumulation in Backward Countries: A Critique," Chapter One in *Limits to Capitalist Development: The Industrialization of Peru, 1950-1980* (Boulder: Westview Press, 1985).

38. Russell, *op. cit.*, p. 52.

39. This section is based on Chinchilla and Hamilton, *op. cit.;* Quote appears on p. 219.

40. Russell, *op. cit.*, p. 52.

41. Joseph Moscarella, "Economic Integration in Central America," Chapter Seventeen in *Latin American Economic Integration*, Miguel S. Wionczek, ed. (New York: Frederic A. Praeger, 1966) p. 264; Chinchilla and Hamilton, *op. cit.*, p. 220. However, in judging the value of protectionism, John Weeks notes that: "While import-substitution industries would not have been viable without tariff protection, studies show that the differential between intra-CACM prices and world prices were relatively modest…As a result, the relative profitability of production for extra-regional export and intraregional trade did not change dramatically." See John Weeks, "An Interpretation of the Central Ameican Crisis," *Latin American Research Review*, Vol. 21, No. 3, 1986, p. 43.

42. Russell, *op. cit.*, p. 53.

43. Chinchilla and Hamilton, *op. cit.;* Russell explains that when the market began functioning, "its planning body received more money from the US than it did from all the Central American nations combined. In 1965 and 1966 the US contributed 54% of the total budget of the nine Central American Common Market Agencies, while the Central American nations themselves only contributed 13%," quoted in Russell, *op. cit.,* p. 53.

44. Jonas, *op. cit.,* pp. 183-184.

45. Russell, *op. cit.,* p. 53.

46. Chinchilla and Hamilton, *op. cit.,* p. 220.

47. Herold, *op. cit.*

48. Russell, *op. cit.,* p. 53.

49. Torres-Rivas, "The Central American Model...," *op. cit.;* Torres-Rivas, "Central America Today," *op. cit.* See also Ronald Muller, "(More) on Multinationals: Poverty is the Product," *Foreign Policy,* Vol. 13, 1973-1974, p. 4, quoted in Thomas J. Biersteker, *Distortion or Development?: Contending Perspectives on the Multinational Corporation* (Cambridge, MA: MIT Press, 1978), pp. 85-88.

50. Russell, *op. cit.,* p. 53.

51. Barry and Preusch, *op. cit.,* p. 167. Chinchilla and Hamilton, *op. cit.,* p. 222; J. Vaupel and J. Curhan, *The Making of the Multinational Enterprise* (Boston: Harvard University, 1969); D. Tobis, "La falacia de las inversiones norteamericanas en Centroamerica," in *La inversion extranjera en Centroamerica,* Editorial Universitaria Centroamericana (EDUCA), 1974, pp. 206-210, as cited in C. V. Vaitsos, *op. cit.* p. 58.

52. Jonas, *op. cit.,* p. 182.

53. SIECA, *La Situacion Actual del Sector Industrial de Centroamerica y Algunas Propuestas de Medidas para su Reactivacion* (Guatemala: SIECA, 1983), p. 5, as cited in Barry and Preusch, *op. cit.,* p. 167.

54. Tom Barry, Beth Wood and Deb Preusch, *Dollars and Dictators* (New York: Grove Press, 1983), p. 9.

55. Biersteker, *op. cit.,* p. 8.

56. Barraclough and Marchetti, *op. cit.,* p. 158. This situation changed during the depression when the price of coffee fell dramatically and the coffee elite sought supplementary income by industrializing the country. Further incentives for industrialization came in the 1960s, after the fall of coffee prices in the late 1950s.

57. Vaitsos, *op. cit.,* p. 52 and p. 9 (as cited in Barry and Preusch, *op. cit.,* p. 165).

58. Table 27 in *ibid.,* calculated from data in R. Lopez Porra, "Empresas de accion o capital multinacional en Centroamerica," *Revista de la Integracion,* No. 12, January 1972.

59. Table 26 in *ibid.,* p. 53.

60. Victor Bulmer-Thomas, "Central American Integration, Trade Diversification and the World Market," in Irvin and Gorostiaga, *op. cit.,* p. 200.

61. Quoted in Herold, *op. cit.;* Rusell, *op. cit.*

62. UNCTAD, *Trade and Development Report* (New York: United Nations, 1986), p. 34.

63. Bulmer-Thomas, *op. cit.,* pp. 201 ff.

64. Collins and Lappe, *op. cit.,* p. 140.

65. Burbach and Flynn, "Agribusiness and the Americas," *op. cit.,* p. 134.

66. Vaitsos, *op. cit.,* p. 54. Technological imports are a particular problem because "buying a radio implies something about future purchases of parts and servicing; this will be true, *a*

fortiori, when buying electric generators and blueprints for building petrochemical plants." See Collins and Lappe, *op. cit.,* p. 139.

67. Russell, *op. cit.,* pp. 55, 57.

68. Frank, *op. cit.,* pp. 103-104.

69. Torres-Rivas, "Central America Today...," *op. cit.,* p. 13.

70. UNCTAD, *Trade and Development Report* (New York: United Nations, 1985), p. 62.

71. Table 3 in Torres-Rivas, "The Central American Model...," *op. cit.,* p. 146; Torres-Rivas, "Central America Today...," *op. cit.,* p. 15; data on Honduras appears in Committee for the Defense of Human Rights in Honduras, Section 2.2, Economic Situation, "The Human Rights Situation in Honduras, 1986," *Honduras Update,* Special Issue No. 1, May 1987, p. 7.

72. Collins and Lappe, *op. cit.,* p. 143; Frank, *op. cit.,* pp. 148ff.; Salvador Umana, *et al., op. cit.;* phone interview with IMF official, Washington, D.C., April 6, 1989. For an update and references to the debt situation in Central America, see Romulo Caballeros, "External Debt in Central America," *Cepal Review,* [Santiago, Chile] No. 32, August 1987; Peter Passell, "Costa Rica's Debt Message," *The New York Times,* February 1, 1989 and *World Debt Tables: External Debt of Developing Countries, 1987-1988 Edition,* Volume II Country Tables (Washington, D.C.: The World Bank, 1988). Barry, *op. cit.,* pp. 80-81, reports on the IMF and the trade-debt cycle with respect to the overproduction of coffee.

73. Carlos F. Diaz-Alejandro, "Delinking North and South: Unshackled or Unhinged?," in *Rich and Poor Nations in the World Economy,* Albert Fishlow, ed., *et al.* (New York: McGraw-Hill Book Co., 1978), p. 43.

74. The data released by the Department of Commerce only report the book value or historical costs of U.S. investment, not the value of a business upon resale; use a minimum investment level of $500,000; exclude the value of less tangible assets such as management and licensing; and do not include the assets of foreign affiliates. See Barry and Preusch, *op. cit.,* p. 13.

75. Xabier Gorostiaga, "Towards Alternative Policies for the Region," in Irvin and Gorostiaga, *op. cit.,* p. 14.

76. Barry and Preusch, *op. cit.,* pp. 24-25.

77. Interview with FDR Representatives, New York, New York, Fall 1986.

78. Barry and Preusch, *op. cit.,* p. 213.

79. "Conflict and Conflict Resolution in Central America," *Bulletin of Peace Proposals,* Vol. 17, No. 3-4, 1986, p. 430.

80. *Ibid.;* Data on El Salvador from Jozef Goldblat and Victor Millan, "The Central American crisis and the Contradora search for regional security," *SIPRI Yearbook: 1986* (New York: Oxford University Press, 1986), p. 527.

81. "Conflict and Conflict Resolution in Central America," *op. cit.*

82. Raul Moncarz, "The Poverty of Progress in Honduras," in Rosenberg and Shepherd, *op. cit.,* p. 116.

83. Umana, *et al., op. cit.,* p. 1.

84. *Ibid.*

85. Secretaria General del Consejo Nacional de Planificacion Economica de Guatemala, *Plan de Desarrollo 1971-1975,* Guatemala 1971; C.V. Vaitsos, *op. cit.,* p. 55.

86. Frank F. Clairmonte and John Cavanagh, "Corporate Power in selected food commodities," *Raw Materials Report,* Vol. 1, No. 3, 1982, p. 35. A report on banana pricing and value added shares specific to Central America found that, "of the retail price in consuming nations, only 14 percent is returned to Central America—mostly in the form of wages and taxes. The

remaining 86 percent goes to the foreign corporations that grow, ship, ripen, distribute, and retail the bananas." See "Bargaining Position and Distribution of Gains in the Banana Exporting Countries, Especially Honduras and Panama" (Santiago de Chile: CEPAL, 1982), p. 135 as cited in Barry, *op. cit.,* pp. 76-77.

87. See Jorge Sol comments in "El Salvador: Can the Duarte Experiment Work?," *NACLA: Report on the Americas,* Vol. 19, No. 1, January-February 1985; *Changing Course: Blueprint for Peace in Central America and the Caribbean* (Washington, D.C.: Institute for Policy Studies, 1984).

88. *Changing Course, ibid.,* p. 73.

89. See "A Program for Development," in *ibid.,* pp. 72-78.

90. For a more detailed explanation on the links between economic development and repression, see Chapter Five.

Chapter Five: Towards Selective Divestment: Using Corporate Pressure Against the State

1. Carole Collins, "Divestment Campaigns," in *Meeting the Corporate Challenge, TIE Report* 18/19, John Cavanagh, *et al.,* eds., February 1985, p. 41.

2. Barry Mitzman, "The Divestiture Demonstrations," *The Nation,* May 13, 1978; "210 stage Nassau Hall sit-in," *The Daily Princetonian,* April 14, 1978; Anne Mackay-Smith, "Protests shake east coast colleges," *The Daily Princetonian,* April 17, 1978; Crystal Nix, "Many in U.S. Protest on South Africa," *The New York Times,* October 12, 1985.

3. Jon Wiener, "Students, Stocks and Shanties," *The Nation,* October 11, 1986.

4. Joseph Schwartz, "Making the Economy Scream," *Democratic Left,* New York, New York, Vol. 13, No. 3, May-June 1985.

5. Michael Isikoff and Peter Behr, "U.S. Business Debates S. Africa Ties," *Washington Post,* August 25, 1985.

6. Schwartz, *op. cit.*

7. Collins, *op. cit.,* p. 42; Lars Waldorf, "After the Pullout," *The New Republic,* December 29, 1986.

8. Steven V. Roberts, "Senate, 78 to 21, overrides Reagan's Veto and Imposes Sanctions on South Africa," *The New York Times,* October 3, 1986.

9. Nicholas D. Kristof, "U.S. Sanctions May Not Hurt South Africa Economy Much," *The New York Times,* October 4, 1986; Barnaby J. Feder, "IBM To Pull Out From South Africa as Problems Grow," *The New York Times,* October 22, 1986.

10. Clair Brown and Michael Reich, "South-Africa Free Investment: Divestiture can improve portfolio performance," *Dollars & Sense,* December 1985.

11. Collins, *op. cit.,* p. 45.

12. Michael West, " 'Waiting for Derek': The Anti-Apartheid Struggle at Harvard," forthcoming in *How Harvard Rules,* Jack Trumpbour, ed. (Boston: South End Press, 1989).

13. Dennis Kneale, "Firms With Ties to South Africa Strike Back at Colleges That Divest," *The Wall Street Journal,* December 10, 1986.

14. *Ibid.*

15. Tamar Levin, "Gauging the Real Impact of Leaving South Africa," *The New York Times,* October 24, 1986; See also Tamar Levin, "Divestment: Did U.S. Companies Meet Test," *The New York Times,* October 26, 1986.

16. Collins, *op. cit.*, p. 42.

17. "U.S. Solidarity for South Africa," *South Africa Labor Bulletin*, Vol. 2, No. 5, April-May 1986; Matthew Walker, "The Cost of Doing Business in South Africa: Anti-Apartheid Coalition Boycotts Shell," *Multinational Monitor*, Vol. 7, No. 7, April 15, 1986.

18. Midnight Notes Collective, "Substruction in the Class/Room Struggle," *Midnight Notes*, Jamaica Plain, Massachusetts, No. 8, August 1985; Collins, *op. cit.*, p. 43.

19. David Beresford and Hamish McRae, "Barclay pulls out of South Africa," *The Guardian*, London, November 24, 1986; "Initial Assessment of Barclay's Disinvestment from South Africa," mimeo, Anti-Apartheid Movement, London, Great Britain, n.d.; "Press Release," Anti-Apartheid Movement, London, Great Britain, n.d. Despite the announced divestment, other banking connections to South Africa through management services and technical cooperation continued.

20. "The Anatomy of A Bank Campaign," *SCAR NEWS*, Vol. 4, No. 1, February 1987; Patrick Bond, "On Building Solidarity to Confront the Debt Crisis: How First and Third World Community Activists Can Work Together to Gain Concessions from Major Banks," mimeo, The Philadelphia Reinvestment Research Group, Philadelphia, Pennsylvania; *The Community Reinvestment Act: A Citizen's Action Guide* (Washington, D.C.: Center for Community Change, March 1981); Patrick Bond, "From Divestment to Reinvestment," *Dollars and Sense*, June 1987.

21. Edelberto Torres-Rivas, "Central American Model...," in *Revolution in Central America*, Stanford Central America Action Network, ed. (Boulder, CO: Westview Press, 1983), p. 148.

22. Joseph Collins and and Francis Moore Lappe, "Food Self-Reliance," Chapter Eight in *Self-Reliance: Strategy for Development*, George Galtung, Peter O'Brien and Roy Preiswerk, eds. (London: Bogle-L'Ouverture Publications, Ltd., 1980), p. 141.

23. Marc C. Herold, "From Riches to 'Rags': Finanzkapital in El Salvador, 1900-1980", ms., Whittemore School of Business and Economics, Durham, New Hampshire, February 29, 1980.

24. Annette Fuentes and Barbara Ehrenreich, *Women in the Global Factory* (Boston: South End Press, 1983), p. 11.

25. For example, in 1982, the largest company by sales rank in Nicaragua was "Pennwalt-Hercasa Chemicals," a chemicals company owned by Hercules in the U.S. In 1982, the company's sales or turnover was $82 million. The seventh ranked "Milca" Company, a soft-drink bottler owned by Coca-Cola, had sales of $21.6 million in 1982. See *Statistical Abstract of Latin America*, James W. Wilkie and Adam Perkal, eds., Vol. 24 (Los Angeles: UCLA Latin American Center Publications, University of California, 1985). Other U.S. corporations doing business in post-revolutionary Nicaragua have included: Citibank, NA; Coca-Cola; Exxon; IBM World Trade Corp.; Monsanto; and Union Carbide among others. See Jason Adkins, "U.S. Business in Nicaragua," *Multinational Monitor*, Vol. 6, No. 4, April 1985.

26. See, for example, Carlos F. Diaz-Alejandro, "Open economy, closed polity?" in *Latin America in the World Economy*, Diana Tussie, ed. (Hampshire, England: Gower Publishing Co., Ltd., 1983).

27. Carlos F. Diaz-Alejandro, "Delinking North and South: Unshackled or Unhinged?," in *Rich and Poor Nations in the World Economy* Albert Fishlow, *et al., eds.* (New York: McGraw-Hill Book Co., 1978), p. 112.

28. See Diaz-Alejandro, "Delinking North and South...," *op. cit.*

29. Theodore H. Moran, "Multinational corporations and dependency: a dialogue for dependentistas and non-dependentistas," *International Organization*, Vol. 32, No. 1 (Madison, WI: The University of Wisconsin Press, Winter 1978).

30. Manuel Castells, "High Technology, World Development, and Structural Transformation: The Trends and the Debate," Vol. 11, No. 3, *Alternatives*, July 1986, p. 313.

31. Torres-Rivas, "The Central American Model...," *op. cit.*, p. 143; Ward Morehouse, "Technological Autonomy and Delinking in the Third World: Confronting the Unholy Alliance of Power, Privilege and Technology in Rich and Power Countries," in *The New International Division of Labor, Technology and Underdevelopment Consequences for the Third World,* Dieter Ernst, ed. (Frankfurt: Campus Verlag, 1980), pp. 531ff. Morehouse builds on the notion of selective delinking found in Diaz-Alejandro, "Delinking North and South," *op. cit.*

32. Nicholas D. Kristof, "Curbs Give Way to Welcome For Multinational Companies," *The New York Times,* May 11, 1985.

33. Diaz-Alejandro, "Delinking North and South...," *op. cit.*, p. 106.

34. For data on capital flight in Central America, see James F. Petras and Morris H. Morley, "Economic Expansion, Political Crisis and U.S. Policy in Central America," in *Revolution and Intervention in Central America,* Marlene Dixon and Susanne Jonas, eds. (San Francisco: Synthesis Publications, 1983), pp. 190ff., pp. 201-202; Jason Adkins, "Nicargua—Prologue," *Multinational Monitor,* Vol. 6, No. 4, April 1985.

35. James LeMoyne, "Salvador Rebels Widen Their War," *The New York Times,* January 10, 1986.

36. Philip L. Russell, *El Salvador in Crisis* (Austin, TX: Colorado River Press, 1984), p. 59.

37. Editors of *Estudios Centroamericanos* special report, "Duarte: Prisoner of War," *NACLA: Report on the Americas,* Vol. 20, No. 1, January/March 1986, p. 35.

38. Russell, *op. cit.*

39. Monty Neil of Harvard's School of Education has written about the limits of "de-linking" along these lines. The editors of *Estudios Centroamericanos* write that, "The FMLN has devoted little thought to the costs of economic recovery, and has not worked out where the money will come from to resurrect the country from the ashes of a prolonged war," "Duarte...," *op. cit.*, p. 38. However, this criticism does not mention the concern about foreign investment in the Salvadoran left.

40. Russell, *op. cit.*, p. 57.

41. For a critical discussion on this point see James E. Austin and John C. Ickis, "Managing after the revolutionaries have won," *Harvard Business Review,* May-June 1986; James E. Austin and John C. Ickis, "Management, Managers, and Revolution," *World Development,* Vol. 14, No. 7, 1986, pp. 775-790.

42. Two discussions of how to change the terms under which transnationals operate in the Third World through "selective divestment" can be found in Albert O. Hirschman, *A Bias For Hope* (New Haven: Yale University Press, 1971) and John Sheahan, "Market-Oriented Economic Policies and Political Repression in Latin America," *Economic Development and Cultural Change,* Vol. 28, No. 2, January 1980. In an essay on divestment, Hirschman wrote, "a policy of selective liquidation and withdrawal of foreign private investment is in the best mutual interests of Latin America and the United States. Such a policy can be selective with respect to the countries and to economic sectors and it ought to be combined with a policy of encouraging new capital outflows, also on a selective basis and with some safeguards." See Hirschman, *op. cit.*, p. 233. Sheahan proposed that Third World nations adopt "an active screening process to get some of the real gains of foreign investment and on a very selective basis." See Sheahan, *op. cit.*, p. 290.

43. Michael Urquhart, "U.S. Unionists Join in Salvadoran Peace Meeting," *Labor Notes,* No. 95, January 1987; Presentation by FENASTRAS spokeswoman, transcribed by Leonard Sklar, San Salvador, El Salvador, July 31, 1987.

44. "The Universal Declaration of Human Rights," Adopted and Proclaimed by General Assembly Resolution 217 A (III) of December 10, 1948, as published in *Human Rights: A Compilation of International Instruments* (New York: United Nations, 1983).

45. "Central American Peace Accord," transcribed by the Press Office of the Ministry of Foreign Affairs, Managua, August 7, 1987, as published in *Envio* [English edition], Instituto Historico Centroamericano, Managua, Nicaragua, Vol. 6., No. 74, August 1987, pp. 46-52.

46. *Ibid.,* p. 50. For disparate reports on Central American nations' support for the contras, see Eric Shultz, "Honduras, First to Non-Comply," *Honduras Update,* Vol. 5., No. 12, September 1987; Neil A. Lewis, "Duarte Seems to Back Contra Aid Halt," *The New York Times,* October 16, 1987; Neil A. Lewis, "Honduran Urging Halt in Contra Aid," *The New York Times,* October 22, 1987; "Ilopango: Supply Base for the Contras," *Venceremos,* No. 1, December 1987-January 1988; and James LeMoyne, "Costa Rica in Ultimatum to Contras," *The New York Times,* January 14, 1988. One report describes Costa Rica's support for the contras as follows: "Contra forces still operate from Costa Rica and leaders of the contra political directorate work and live in Costa Rica without censure from the government, although this violates the Esquipulas [Arias] Accords." See "The Central American Peace Plan—One Year Later," *Update,* Vol. 7, No. 26, August 16, 1988.

47. Marlene Dixon, "Dual Power: The Rise of the Transnational Corporation and the Nation-State: Conceptual Explanations to Meet Popular Demand," *Contemporary Marxism,* No. 5, Summer 1982, p. 138.

48. "Accepting Repression in Guatemala," Vol. 7, No. 14, *Multinational Monitor,* October 1986.

49. Susanne Jonas, "Guatemala: Land of Eternal Struggle," Chapter One in *Latin America: The Struggle with Dependency and Beyond,* edited by Ronald H. Chilcote and Joel C. Edelstein (Cambridge, MA: Shenkman Publishing Co., 1974), pp. 191-192.

50. Peter B. Evans, "National Autonomy and Economic Development: Critical Perspectives on Multinational Corporations in Poor Countries," in *Transnational Relations and World Politics,* Robert O. Keohane and Joseph S. Nye, eds. (Cambridge, MA: Harvard University Press, 1971).

51. The analysis presented here generally follows points raised by Allan Nairn at a lecture given at Hunter College, New York, New York, February 20, 1988.

52. Mehdi Shafaeddin, "Import Capacity as a Bargaining Tool of Developing Countries," *Trade and Development,* No. 5, 1984, pp. 59-60.

53. Hirschman argued that Third World nations could use divestment to promote the redistribution of economic and political power. He proposed that assets divested by a TNC be held by an intermediary such as a newly created "Inter-American Divestment Corporation." This Corporation could then sell "a substantial portion, perhaps a majority of the equity of the erstwhile foreign firms to white-and blue-collar workers." Foreign investment could also be "vacated, without any compensation." See Hirschman, *op. cit.,* p. 245.

A report issued in 1986 by the "Presidential Task Force on Project Economic Justice," explains ways in which employee ownership can be promoted in Central America. The report recommends that some businesses owned by the governments of the region be sold to their employees. U.S. bank debt to these nations would be exchanged for equity in the *parastatals,* and the equity would be sold to an employee ownership plan. At, La Perla, a large planatation in Guatemala, landowners have set up a mechanism resembling a U.S. Employee Stock Ownership Plan (ESOP) to transfer 40 percent ownership to the workers. See "International Interest in Employee Ownership Growing," *The Employee Ownership Report,* November-December 1986.

Depending on technological and managerial inputs, firms transferred to workers may do better under worker ownership. Studies have shown that worker owned firms have superior performance in productivity and profit measures in certain ranges of industry. The economic limits of transfers of TNC ownership to nationals in the Third World has been noted by Arghiri Emmanuel: "Two-thirds of all the capital in Canada belongs to foreigners, 80 percent of whom are Americans. On the other hand, India is the example *par excellence* where industrialization was carried out by the local bourgeoisie. It is not very clear what the Canadian people—who are among the richest in the world—would stand to win if the 'centres of decision' moved from the skyscrapers of Manhattan to the office blocks of Montreal, or what the people of India—among the most poverty-stricken of the world—would stand to lose further if her capitalists handed over their factories to others holding a Japanese or German passport." See "The Multinational Corporations and Inequality of Development," in *Multi-National Corporations and Third World Development*, Pradip K. Ghosh, ed. (Westport, CT: Greenwood Press, 1984), pp. 101-102. Of interest also on nationalization is Jorge I. Dominguez, "Latin American national business and behavior toward multinational enterprises," in *Economic Issues and Political Conflict: US-Latin American Relations*, Jorge I. Dominguez, ed. (London: Butterworth Scientific, 1982), pp. 17, 58.

54. Some activists have favored church shareholder actions, others church divestment, as a way to pressure corporations. Divestment may be appropriate when part of a larger movement by governments, universities and other investors. However, in isolation, church divestment actions have often been ignored or welcomed by corporations who feel more threatened by shareholder protests. For more on church social responsibility actions, see Rev. Christian T. Iosso, "Disarming Church Portfolios: Divestment as a Strategy for Witness in an Increasingly Militarized Economy," *ICCR Brief*, December 1982, published by the Interfaith Center on Corporate Responsibility, New York, New York.

55. On the failure of the Arias Plan to address the roots of the crisis in Central America, see David Finkel, "Central America's Peace Plan & the U.S. Solidarity Movement," *Against the Current*, Vol. 2, No. 5, November-December 1987 and Noam Chomsky, "Is Peace At Hand?," *Zeta Magazine*, Vol. 1, No. 1, 1988. Other signs that the agreement was breaking down or would fail with regard to El Salvador could be seen in the following press stories: James LeMoyne, "Central American Pact Aids Those in Power," *The New York Times*, November 29, 1987; Douglas Farah, "Duarte's Party Divided as Key Election Nears," *The Washington Post*, December 28, 1987 and Douglas Farah, "Salvadoran Insurgents Vow To Launch Major Offensive," *The Washington Post*, January 5, 1988.

56. Barry and Preusch, *The Central America Fact Book* (New York: Grove Press, 1986), pp. 148ff.; *The World Banana Economy, 1970-1984*, FAO Economic and Social Development Paper 57 (Rome: Food and Agricultural Organization of the United Nations, 1986), pp. 8, 40.

57. *The World Banana Economy, op. cit.*, p. 40; *International Trade Statistical Yearbook*, Vol. II (New York: United Nations, 1986).

58. Table 59, "Summary: Organization of Banana Imports and Distribution, Selected Markets 1984," in *The World Banana Economy, op. cit.*, p. 81.

59. Castle & Cooke Form 10-K, For Fiscal Year Ended December 28, 1985, Prepared for the Securities and Exchange Commission, Castle & Cooke, Inc., Honolulu, Hawaii.

60. Tom Barry, *Roots of Rebellion* (Boston: South End Press, 1987), p. 75. Here, it is worth noting the activities of the U.S. Overseas Private Investment Corporation (OPIC) which has insured a portion of U.S. private investments in Central America against political risks. OPIC insurance coverage programs provide coverage for the loss of investment due to expropriation, nationalization or confiscation by action from a foreign government. OPIC also protects against loss due to war, revolution or insurrection. Historically, the organization has encouraged foreign capital to remain in Central America although recently, its coverage has decreased. Between 1948 and September 30, 1980, OPIC and its predecessor agencies provided expropriation insurance for over $430 million and war risk insurance of about $345 million to U.S. investors in Central America. See Marcelo Alonso, *et al., Central America in Crisis* (Washington, D.C.: The Washington Institute for Values in Public Policy, 1984), pp. 111, 149.

61. Castle & Cooke Form 10-K, *op. cit.*; Barry and Preusch, *op. cit.*; "Table 2922: Honduras Corporate Business Activity," *Statistical Abstract of Latin America, op. cit.*, p. 687.

62. *The World Banana Economy, op. cit.*, p. 11.

63. *Ibid.*, p. 70. For more on UPEB and company threats to leave Central America, see Barry, *op. cit.*, pp. 74-75.

64. Castle & Cooke Form 10-K, *op. cit.*

65. Renny Golden and Michael McConnell, "The 'Price' of Coffee," *World Hunger Actionletter,* World Hunger/Global Development Program of the American Friends Service Committee, New York, New York, March-April 1985.

66. *Ibid.*

67. Address by Guillermo Diaz Salazar, Minister of Foreign Trade in El Salvador, Boca Raton, Florida, February 10, 1981, as quoted in "From Beans to Bullets...Salvadoran Coffee," brochure, Albuquerque, New Mexico, Global Justice, n.d; Quoted in Golden and McConnell, *op. cit.*

68. "Controversial Solution to Coffee Crisis," *Central America Report,* November 5, 1982, pp. 340-342, as quoted in "From Beans to Bullets...," *op. cit.*

69. Golden and McConnell, *op. cit.*

70. *Latin America Weekly,* November 6, 1981, as quoted in *ibid.* In 1985-1986, the value of coffee exports (FOB) was $322 million for Costa Rica, $620 million for El Salvador, $482 million for Guatemala and $286 million for Honduras. See Table VI-4 in *Quarterly Statistical Bulletin,* No. 38, April-June 1986 (Preliminary), Section VI: Values, published by the International Coffee Organization, December 15, 1986.

71. Barry and Preusch, *op. cit.*, p. 147.

72. *Ibid.*, pp. 146-147.

73. Table 2 in Victor Bulmer Thomas, "Central American Trade Diversification and the World Market," Chapter Eleven in *Towards and Alternative for Central America and the Caribbean,* George Irwin and Xabier Gorostiaga, eds. (London: George Allen Unwin, 1985), p. 195.

74. Phone interview with Jeff Epstein, *World Coffee & Tea Journal,* West Haven, Connecticut, January 7, 1987.

75. Barry and Preusch, *op. cit.*, p. 221.

76. Comparable data on oil imports from another source reveals the increasing reliance of El Salvador on imported oil:

Crude Petroleum as a Percent of Total Imports

Country	Percent
El Salvador	11.2 (a)
Guatemala	6.8 (b)
Honduras	13.6 (a)
Costa Rica	11.2 (c)

a-1979; b-1978; c-1980.

SOURCE: *Boletín Estadístico de la OEA* and *International Financical Statistics,* as published in Table 3.16, Marcelo Alonso, et al, *Central America in Crisis* (Washington: Washington Institute for Values in Public Policy, 1984), p. 145.

77. Interview with Nomonde Ngubo, United Mine Workers of America, "Working Against Apartheid: Trade Unions in South Africa," *Multinational Monitor*, Vol. 7, No. 7, April 15, 1986; "Table 2920: Guatemala Corporate Business Activity," *Statistical Abstract of Latin America, op. cit.*, p. 686; Barry and Preusch, *op. cit.*, p. 342; Russell, *op. cit.*, p. 66; Robert Henriques Girling and Luin Goldring, "U.S. Strategic Interests in Central America: The Economics and Geopolitics of Empire," in *Revolution in Central America, op. cit.* p. 195.

78. "Table 2920: Guatemala Corporate Business Activity," *Statistical Abstract of Latin America, op. cit.*

79. Barry and Preusch, *op. cit.*, p. 248.

80. "Table 2920: Guatemala Corporate Business Activity," *Statistical Abstract of Latin America, op. cit.*; Barry and Preusch, *op. cit.*, p. 247.

81. John E. Lind, *The Debt Crisis and Credit Risk in Countries with Human Rights Abuses* (San Francisco: Northern California Interfaith Committee on Corporate Responsibility, 1983).

82. See Table "How Student Borrowing Has Grown in 15 Years" and Jean Evanglauf, "Students' Borrowing Quintuples in Decade, Raising the Specter of a 'Debtor Generation,'" *The Chronicle of Higher Education*, Vol. 33, No. 17, January 7, 1987. On radical alternatives for debtor nations, see John Gerassi, "A Modest Proposal on how the Sardines can become Piranas," Paper delivered at the 24th annual convention of the International Studies Association, Mexico City, April 6, 1983.

83. "Guatemala and Britain Resume Relations," *Enfoprensa*, Year 5—Number 1, January 9, 1987.

84. *Statistical Abstract of Latin America, op. cit.*; "Castle & Cooke Form 10-K," *op. cit.*

85. See Lindsey Gruson, "Latin Presidents Announce Accord on Contra Bases," *The New York Times*, February 15, 1989.

86. PSI survey of September 1983 as published in "Business Opportunities in Costa Rica," a publication of the Costa Rican Coalition of Development Initiatives, San Jose Costa Rica, n.d., Foreign Commercial Service, report prepared for the American Embassy, San Jose, "Marketing in Costa Rica," *Overseas Business Reports*, OBR 86-01, International Trade Administration, U.S. Department of Commerce, Washington, D.C., January 1986.

87. Department of State Airgram, Subject: Investment Climate Statement, Reference: USDOC 7267, From American Embassy, Tegucigalpa, To: U.S. Department of Commerce, August 20, 1980; "1985 Investment Climate Statement for Honduras," Economic Section, U.S. Embassy, Tegucigalpa, Honduras, February 1985.

88. Sheet, "Honduras as a site for offshore apparel manufacturing, typical average expected monthly costs (1988)," distributed by FIDE (Foundation for Investment and Development of Exports), Tegucigalpa, Honduras.

89. "Investment in Guatemala," Non-traditional Products Exporters Association, Guatemala, August 1988.

90. The daily minimum wage for residents of San Salvador and the metropolitan area is $3.60; for the rest of the country, it is $3.40. See "Why El Salvador?" Salvadoran Foundation for Economic and Social Development (FUSADES), San Salvador, El Salvador and Miami, Florida, August 1988.

91. For information on trade unions in Central America, see James Dunkerley and Chris Whitehouse, *Unity is Strength: Trade Unions in Latin America, A Case for Solidarity* (London: Latin America Bureau, 1980); David Moberg, "Labor inches out of the long repression," *In These Times*, January 25-31, 1989 and various issues of *NACLA: Report on the Americas*, published by the North American Congress on Latin America, New York, New York.

92. See Xabier Gorostiaga, "Towards Alternative Policies for the Region," in *Towards an Alternative for Central America and the Carribbean, op. cit.,* p. 16. See Chapter Six below for a fuller exposition of the limits of anti-corporate efforts.

93. For a critique of the Caribbean Basin Initiative, see Barry, *op. cit.* and *Revolution and Intervention in Central America,* Roger Burbach and Patricia Flynn, eds. (New York: Monthly Review Press, 1984).

Chapter Six: The Warfare State and the University

1. A blatant example of U.S power in this regard was seen in January when the President's national security adviser warned the leaders of four Central American countries "that they could face serious economic and political consequences if Congress [let] the contras collapse." See Neil A. Lewis, "4 Latin Presidents Cautioned by U.S. on Contras' Fate," *The New York Times,* January 13, 1988. See also Mark A. Uhlig, "Honduras Shifting to U.S. Stand, Won't Evict Contras From Bases," *The New York Times,* March 23, 1989.

2. Caspar W. Weinberger, *Annual Report to the Congress: Fiscal Year 1988* (Washington, D.C.: U.S. Government Printing Office, 1987); Howard Morland, "A Few Billion for Defense: Plus 250 Billion More for Overseas Military Intervention," *New Policy Papers* 1, Coalition for a New Foreign and Military Policy, Washington, D.C.,; William Hartung, "Weapons For The World: It's Time To Change The Rules," *CEP Newsletter,* Council on Economic Priorities, New York, New York, N87-8, August 1987.

3. Richard J. Barnet, *Roots of War* (New York: Penguin Books, 1972), p. 184.

4. Roger Burbach and Marc Herold, "The U.S. Economic Stake in Central America and the Caribbean," *The Politics of Intervention,* Roger Burbach and Patricia Flynn, eds. (New York: Monthly Review Press, 1984), pp. 191-192.

5. Harry Magdoff, *The Age of Imperialism* (New York: Monthly Review Press, 1966), p. 14 as quoted in Robert Henriques Girling and Luin Goldring, "U.S. Strategic Interests in Central America: The Economics and Geopolitics of Empire," in *Revolution in Central America* (Boulder, CO: Westview Press, 1983), p. 188.

6. Shultz quoted in Peter Kornbluh, *Nicaragua: The Price of Intervention* (Washington, D.C.: Institute for Policy Studies, 1987), p. 3. For a fuller explanation of the "demonstration effect," see Noam Chomsky, *Turning the Tide* (Boston: South End Press, 1985).

7. Alexander Haig quoted in Xabier Gorostiaga, "Towards Alternative Policies for the Region," in *Towards an Alternative for Central America and the Caribbean* (London: George Allen & Unwin, 1985), p. 20.

8. Barnet, *op. cit.,* describing the views of Michael Hudson, p. 191.

9. *Ibid.,* p. 191.

10. *Ibid.,* p. 192; Josh Cohen and Joel Rogers estimate that total U.S. military operations in Central America—including airstrips, manuevers, equipment and personnel—now cost American taxpayers $9.5 billion per year, see Joshua Cohen and Joel Rogers, "Central America Policy: The True Cost of Intervention," *The Nation,* April 12, 1986, p. 513; Joshua Cohen and Joel Rogers, *Inequity and Intervention,* (Boston, MA: South End Press, 1986); and "Central America: The Right to Eat," *Food First,* pamphlet, updated edition.

11. Gorostiaga, *op. cit.,* pp. 14, 15. Some authors believe that both geopolitical and economic interests are important, arguing that U.S. defense interests and fear of left-wing regimes are shaped by service to corporate profitability in Latin America as a whole, or that interventions serve as a warning to all Third World states. However, the central point here is that U.S. military intervention and state manipulation of multi-lateral lending institutions exist regardless of whether the Central American region itself is profitable. Thus, disengaging TNCs from Central

America does not necessarily prevent intervention of the U.S. military apparatus. However, the interactions between domestic disruption in the U.S. (caused by divestment protests, etc.), economic sabotage/capital flight overseas and international solidarity actions may make such military intervention more difficult as has been argued throughout the text.

12. Richard J. Barnett writes that: "Classic theories of economic imperialism, which view the state as an agent of the most powerful domestic economic interests, underestimate the independent role of the national-security bureaucracy which in the United States has taken on a life and movement of its own. It has the money and power at its disposal to develop within very broad limits its own conception of the national interest." See *Intervention and Revolution* (New York: The New American Library, 1972), p. 29 and Martin Shaw, "War, Imperialism and the State System: a Critique of Orthodox Marxism for the 1980s," in *War, State and Society,* Martin Shaw, ed. (London: McMillan, 1984), p. 49, pp. 51, 54. Other radical theorists like Ernest Mandel, Robin Murray, Bob Rowthorne and Harry Magdoff have developed a more advanced view regarding the division of labor between state managers and corporate managers. Some on the left argue that we cannot successfully restructure the war-making institutions without restructuring capitalism itself. But the Left has often reduced intervention and the political seizure of power over Central America by the U.S. military to imperialism and economic interests, leaving us with a diffuse critique of the system. This in turn provides no handles for organizing or focal points for leverage in that system (see Chapter Eight).

13. *Report of the Congressional Committees Investigating the Iran-contra Affair (hereafter, Iran-Contra Affair),* 100th Congress, 1st Session (Washington, D.C.: Government Printing Office, 1987), p. 8.

14. Arthur Liman memo quoted in Alfonso Chardy, "Reagan aides and the 'secret' government," *The Miami Herald,* July 5, 1987. According to testimony given by Col. North, the CIA Chief envisioned an "overseas entity" that would be "independent of appropriated monies." Fox Butterfield reports that this implied "that it would be free from normal Congressional oversight and control, and able to conduct operations like the secret arms sales to Iran and diversion of profits to support the Nicaraguan rebels." See Fox Butterfield, "A Correction: Times Was in Error On North's Secret Fund Testimony," *The New York Times,* July 13, 1987.

15. Chardy, *op. cit.*

16. Noam Chomsky, "The November 1986 Elections," ms., Cambridge, MA, November 10, 1986 [English translation of article submitted to *Il Manifesto*]. A July 16, 1987 news report noted the flip side of the equation, that such indirect terror can sometimes backfire. It described how the Iran-contra affair would damage Reagan's Presidency for the rest of his term and weaken the Republican Party. See Bernard Weinraub, "Major Setback to Reagan and Party Seen," *The New York Times,* July 17, 1987. However, the essential point is that the warfare state remained undamaged. Thus, Senator Warren B. Rudman, Republican Vice-Chairman of the Senate panel, said by the end of the hearings that the committees probably would not recommend any new laws to tighten control over covert operations. He added, "I haven't seen anything wrong with the system, but there was something wrong with the people." Later reports that Congress was thinking of subjecting the President's national security appointments to Senate confirmation or that a joint Congressional committee comprising a few House and Senate leaders would be created to be "kept apprised of all Administration activities" still would leave the national security apparatus intact, even if these modest proposals were made law. See Fox Butterfield, "Inquiry Shortens List of Witnesses Still to Testify," *The New York Times,* July 19, 1987 and Peter Grier and Peter Osterlund, "New phase for 'the hearings,' " *Christian Science Monitor,* July 21, 1987.

17. Alexander Hamilton, "Grounds for Limitations on Control Over Armies," Paper No. 26, in *The Enduring Federalist,* Edited and Analyzed by Charles A. Beard (Garden City, NY: Doubleday & Co., Inc., 1948), p. 106.

18. Neil A. Lewis, "A Windfall for Reagan: Threats and Use of Nicaraguan Defector Force a Compromise Over Aid to Contras," *The New York Times,* December 22, 1987. The Congress

has also used its authority over the budget to gain concessions from the executive branch. Gary M. Stern of the Center for National Security Studies argues that the Boland Amendment was passed only because it was attatched to a massive continuing resolution. However, the concentrated economic authority of the Pentagon has often given the executive branch the upper hand in foreign policy disputes. See also Note 21.

19. *Iran-Contra Affair, op. cit.,* p. 17.

20. Robert Borosage, "Para-Legal Authority and Its Perils," *Law and Contemporary Problems,* Vol. 40, No. 3, Summer 1976, p. 175. The CIA's authority in this regard has been based on section 102 (d) (5) of the National Security Act's "other functions" clause: "it shall be the duty of the Agency to perform such other functions and duties related to intelligence affecting the national security as the National Security Council may from time to time direct."

21. See Chapter Three in Marcus Raskin, *Notes on the Old System* (New York: David McKay Company, Inc., 1974). See also Harold Hongju Koh, "Why the President (Almost) Always Wins in Foreign Affairs: Lessons of the Iran-Contra Affair," *The Yale Law Journal,* Vol. 97, No. 7, June 1988.

22. *Foreign and Military Intelligence, Book 1, Final Report of the Select Committee to Study Governmental Operations with Respect to Intelligence Activities,* U.S. Senate, 94th Congress, 2d Session, Report No. 94-755, April 26, 1976, p. 159 as quoted in *Covert Operations and the Democratic Process* (Washington, D.C.: Center for National Security Studies, July 1987), p. 4.

23. Quoted in Borosage, *op. cit.,* p. 179.

24. Jay Peterzell, "Timely Does Not Mean Never: Notice to Congress of the Iran Arms Deal," *First Principles,* Vol. 12, No. 2, April 1987.

25. Ronald Reagan, quoted in Kornbluh, *op. cit.,* p. 1.

26. Richard F. Grimmett, "Covert Actions: Congressional Oversight," *Issue Brief,* Congressional Research Service, Washington, D.C., Updated October 7, 1987.

27. Paul Joseph, *Cracks in the Empire* (Boston: South End Press, 1981), pp. 153, 163.

28. Fred Halliday, *Beyond Irangate: The Reagan Doctrine and the Third World* (Amsterdam: Transnational Institute, 1987), pp. 20-21.

29. On the role of defense contractors as submanagements to the Pentagon, see Seymour Melman, *Pentagon Capitalism* (New York: McGraw-Hill, 1970). Interests tied to universities play a pivotal role in legitimating warfare state objectives. For example, "on the two occasions when American and Soviet negotiators appeared closest to an agreement on a [nuclear test] ban," objections raised by the nation's two principal nuclear weapons laboratories at Livermore, California and Los Alamos, New Mexico, led to the defeat of Senate approval required for ratification. The principal contractor at Los Alamos is the University of California. See Josephine Anne Stein and Frank von Hippel, "Laboratories vs. a Nuclear Ban," *The New York Times,* March 28, 1986.

30. Michael T. Klare, *The University-Military Complex: A directory and related documents* (New York: North American Congress on Latin America, 1969). Among the technologies supported by Defense research are the laser (Townes and Shawlow, Columbia University, 1953), the Viterbi algorithm (UCLA, 1967), shock-free wing design (Seebass, University of Arizona, 1978). The Defense Department supported much of the early laser research, including the chemical laser (Pimentel, University of California at Berkeley, 1965), the unstable resonator (Siegman, Stanford University, 1967), the free-electron laser (Madey, Stanford University, 1977), and the collective-mode electron laser (Schlesinger, Columbia University, 1979). See Leo Young, "The University Link," *Defense/83,* Washington, D.C., February 1983.

31. David Noble, *Forces of Production* (New York: Oxford University Press, 1984), p. 11.

32. Daniel Kelves quoted in *ibid.*

33. Kelves quoted in *ibid.,* p. 12.

34. Robert Borosage, "The Making of the National Security State," in *The Pentagon Watchers,* Leonard S. Rodberg and Derek Shearer, eds. (Garden City, NY: Doubleday and Company, 1970), pp. 3-63.

35. "WPB Aide Urges U.S. To Keep War Set-Up," *The New York Times,* January 20, 1944.

36. Chomsky, *Turning the Tide, op. cit.,* p. 209ff.; Robert Reich, "High Technology, Defense and International Trade," in *The Militarization of High Technology,* John Tirman, ed. (Cambridge, Massachusetts: Ballinger Publishing Co., 1984).

37. Melman, *Profits Without Production* (New York: Alfred A. Knopf, 1983), p. 85.

38. Eisenhower quoted in Appendix A in *Pentagon Capitalism, op. cit.,* p. 234.

39. Borosage, "The Making of the National Security State," *op. cit.,* pp. 29-30.

40. David Noble, "Academia Incorporated," *Science for the People,* January-February 1983.

41. James Ridgeway, *The Closed Corporation: American Universities in Crisis* (New York: Random House, 1968), p. 139.

42. Table 3 in "The Department of Defense Report on the University Role in Defense Research and Development," for the Committees on Appropriations, United States Congress, Washington, D.C., April 1987, p. 14. See Chapter Seven for an explanation of 6.1 research and the links between NASA, DOE and the warfare state.

43. Howard Ehrlich, "Taking Stock: The U.S. Military Buildup," *Defense Monitor,* Vol. 13, No. 4, 1984, p. 7; "The University-Military Research Connection," *Thought & Action,* Vol. 1, No. 1, Fall 1984, p. 118; *Defense Monitor,* p. 6; Melman, *Pentagon Capitalism, op. cit.,* p. 100.

44. Stanton A. Glantz and Norm V. Albers, "Department of Defense R&D in the University," *Science,* November 1974, as quoted in *Going for Broke: The University and the Military-Industrial Complex* (Ann Arbor, MI: Committee for Non-Violent Research, 1982), p. 6.

45. *Going for Broke, ibid.,* pp. 6, 9.

46. Seymour Melman, *Profits Without Production, op. cit.,* p. 178, as cited in Mario Pianta, "New Technologies Across the Atlantic: US Leadership or European Autonomy?" Report prepared for the United Nations University Peace and Global Transformations Subprogram (draft), April 1986; see also Note 52.

47. "Basic Research Program," Prepared by the Office of the Deputy Under Secretary of Defense for Research and Engineering, Department of Defense, distributed by U.S. Government Printing Office, n.d., pp. 9, 17, 19, 33.

48. Melman, *Pentagon Capitalism, op. cit.,* p. 90.

49. "Basic Research Program," *op. cit.,* p. 35.

50. *Strategic Computing: New-Generation Computing Technology: A Strategic Plan for its Development and Application to Critical Problems in Defense* (Washington, D.C., Defense Advanced Research Projects Agency, October 28, 1983); *Strategic Computing: Second Annual Report: New Generation Computing Technology: A National Strategy for Meeting the National Security Challenge of Advanced Computer Technology* (Washington, D.C.: Defense Advanced Research Projects Agency, February 1986).

51. Susan Wright, "The Military and the New Biology, *Genewatch* (Boston: Committee for Responsible Genetics), Vol. 2, No. 2, May-August 1985; Steve Farber and Tom Hsu, "MIT Researches Biological Warfare," *The Thistle,* Vol. 1, No. 2, September 17, 1987.

52. For an account of the impact of superpower possession of nuclear weapons on the Third World and Europe, See Alva Myrdal, *The Game of Disarmament* (New York: Pantheon Books, 1982). A recent study on the impact of SDI on Europe is: Mario Pianta, *New Technologies Across the Atlantic: US Leadership or European Autonomy?* (Sussex: Wheatsheaf Books, 1988).

Comprehensive treatments of the impact of nuclear weapons on the Third World include: *The Deadly Connection: Nuclear War & U.S. Intervention,* Joseph Gerson, ed. (Philadelphia: New Society Publishers, 1986) and Noam Chomsky, "Which Way for the Disarmament Movement: Interventionism and Nuclear War," in *Beyond Survival: New Directions for the Disarmament Movement,* Michael Albert and David Dellinger, eds. (Boston: South End Press, 1983).

53. Noam Chomsky, *Turning the Tide* (Boston: South End Press, 1985), p. 207ff.; Daniel Ellsberg, "Introduction, Call to Mutiny," in *Protest and Survive,* E.P. Thompson and Dan Smith, eds. (New York: Monthly Review Press, 1981), p. vi; Chomsky, "Which Way for the Disarmament Movement," *op. cit.,* p. 251.

54. Frank Barnaby, "Microelectronics and War," in Tirman, *op. cit.,* pp. 45, 46. The importance of universities can be seen in trends in military research and development: "A very large part of the huge sums currently spent on armaments now pays for modernizing them rather than increasing their numbers. These qualitative increases depend upon military R&D and trends in them are important determinants of the amount and types of armament in the future." See "Military Research and Development," Chapter Two in *Bulletin of Peace Proposals,* Vol. 17, No. 3-4, 1986, p. 235.

55. Ridgeway, *op. cit.,* p. 126; Table 1, "DOE Research Laboratories: Primary Nuclear Weapons Labs," March 31, 1985, in Greg Bischak, "Facing the Second Generation of the Nuclear Weapons Complex: Renewal of the Nuclear Production Base or Economic Conversion?" *Bulletin of Peace Proposals,* Vol. 19, No. 1, 1988.

56. Bischak, *ibid.*

57. Robert Krinsky, "Swords and Sheepskins: Militarization of Higher Education in the United States and Prospects of its Conversion," in *Bulletin of Peace Proposals, op. cit.;* Thomas C. Schelling, "What Went Wrong With Arms Control?" *Foreign Affairs,* Winter 1985-86, p. 226 as quoted in Krinsky.

58. Seymour Melman, *The Peace Race* (London: Victor Gollancz Ltd., 1961), pp. 20, 21. For more on the problems with arms control and nuclear deterrence theory, see "Nuclear Deterrence, Nuclear War-Fighting and Nuclear Disarmament," Chapter Twenty-two in *Bulletin of Peace Proposals,* Vol. 17, No. 3-4, *op. cit.*

59. Inga Thorsson, *In Persuit of Disarmament: Conversion from Military to Civilian Production in Sweden,* Vol. 1A (Stockholm: Allmänna Förlaget, 1984), p. 38; Robert C. Johansen, "Toward A Dependable Peace: A Proposal for an Appropriate Security System," *World Policy Paper,* No. 8, World Policy Institute, New York, pp. 6-7.

60. Robert Schaeffer, "The 5% Solution," *Nuclear Times,* Vol. 6, No. 1, September-October 1987, pp. 22, 24 and 26.

61. Matthew L. Wald, "College Heads Endorse a World Peace Curriculum," *The New York Times,* December 17, 1986, p. A 14.

62. United States Arms Control and Disarmament Agency, *Toward A World Without War: A Summary of United States Disarmament Efforts—Past and Present* (Washington, D.C.: U.S. Government Printing Office, October 1962), p. 9.

63. *Defense Science Boards: A Question of Integrity,* Twenty-Seventh Report by the Committee on Government Operations together with additional views, U.S. House of Representatives, 98th Congress, 1st Session, November 28, 1983 (Washington, D.C.: U.S. Government Printing Office, 1983), pp. 1-11.

64. Ehrlich, *op. cit.,* pp. 119-120; Tony Kaye, "JASON Studies Top Defense issues" and "JASON's Military Record," *Columbia Daily Spectator,* April 12, 1982; Oliver Mathey, "Counterpoint: What JASON *Really* means," *Columbia Daily Spectator,* March 16, 1987.

65. Ehrlich, *ibid.,* p. 120; Unpublished study by Randall Dodd, Jonathan Feldman, Kate Hill and Adele Oltman, ms., Columbia University, New York, New York, 1987.

66. The Trilateral Commission (North America), Annual Report, and list of "North American Members" as of March 15, 1985, New York, New York.

67. Quoted in Ehrlich, *op. cit.*, p. 120.

68. For more on the "National Security State," see Marcus G. Raskin, *The Politics of National Security* (New Brunswick, New Jersey: Transaction Inc., 1979).

69. Frank Donner, *The Age of Surveillance* (New York: Alfred A. Knopf, 1980), p. 160.

70. *The Abuses of Intelligence Agencies,* Jerry J. Berman and Morton H. Halperin, eds. (Washington, D.C.: Center for National Security Studies, 1975), p. 135.

71. Donner, *op. cit.,* p. 269

72. "Princeton-CIA-Middle East," *Counterspy,* Vol. 4, No. 1; "10 African-Studies Centers Reject Ties with Spy Agency," *The Chronicle of Higher Education,* November 18, 1981.

73. Stephen Engelberg, "C.I.A. Says It Has Restored Link to Campuses to Get More Advice," *The New York Times,* January 20, 1986.

74. Jon Weiner, "The C.I.A. Goes Back to College," *The Nation,* December 12, 1987, p. 719.

75. Fox Butterfield, "Scholar to Quit Post at Harvard Over C.I.A Tie," *The New York Times,* January 2, 1986, p. A12; "Spence Issues Report on CIA Contracts with Nadav Safran," *Harvard University Gazette,* January 10, 1986.

76. John Roosa, "Tufts University: Students Counter Spies," *The National Reporter,* Vol. 9, No. 1, Winter 1985.

77. The ATAP link to the death squad members was discoved by Dan Siegel, former associate of the Institute for Policy Studies. This material is covered in Hope Edelman, "Blowing the Whistle," *Campus Voice,* Knoxville, Tennessee, Winter 1986.

78. Gillam Kerley, "Do You Feel a Draft," *The Progressive,* March 1985.

79. "Justices Uphold Linking of Aid to Draft Signup," *The New York Times,* July 6, 1984.

80. "Youth System Urged," *The New York Times,* November 16, 1984. The latest "youth service" proposals before Congress have been criticized as a program which increasingly ties work or military service to financial aid. Previous programs which did not have such strings attached are being cut back. Thus, students are forced to rely on the new programs (out of economic necessity) even though they are "voluntary." For background, see Rick Maze, "National service plans attacked from left and right," *Army Times,* April 24, 1989.

81. Daniel A. Buford, "High School Militarism: A Case for Counter Recruitment," *CALC Report,* January-February 1984; Cassandra Tiresias, "Draft Juggernaut Ready to Roll," *Fellowship,* June 1984; Richard J. Crohn, "The Draft Waiting in the Wings," *Fellowship,* April-May 1984; Osha Davidson, article on ROTC in *In These Times,* October 1-7, 1986. A September 1985 report by the Defense Department describes this agency's programs aimed at high schools: "To encourage students to seek careers in science and technology, promising high school students are offered summer research experiences/apprenticeships in DOD laboratories or with university researchers under contract to DOD. Over the past five years, more than 2,000 students have participated. In the summer of 1984, DOD tested a new program, modeled after the DOD high school apprenticeship program, to enable high school science and math teachers to have summer research experiences in DOD laboratories to enhance their teaching of science and math." See Office of the Secretary of Defense, *Basic Research Program* (Washington, D.C.: U.S. Government Printing Office, September 1985), p. 4.

82. Buford, *op. cit.*

83. *Time,* February 16, 1987.

84. *Report of the DOD-University Forum, op. cit.,* p. 33, pp. 36-37.

85. Students Against Intervention in Central America, "ROTC: The Issue is Central America," *The Daily Californian*, September 26, 1985.

86. "What's In It For You: Navy," U.S. Navy Brochure, n.d. (circa 1984).

87. "Counter-Recruitment Work Can Link CALC Issues," memo., Clergy and Laity Concerned, New York, NY, n.d.; Buford, *op. cit.*

88. "Racism and the Draft," fact sheet, Committee Against Registration and the Draft, Washington, D.C., n.d.

89. *Equal Opportunity Assessment: 1984,* Office of the Deputy Chief of Staff for Personnel, Department of the Army, Washington, D.C., n.d.; "Today's Army Fails as Mecca for Jobless Youth Seeking Skills," fact sheet, Militarism Resource Project, Philadelphia, PA, n.d.

90. *Equal Opportunity Assessment: 1984, op. cit.;* "Thinking About Enlisting?" brochure produced by Draft and Pre-enlistment Counseling Project, Eugene, OR, n.d. For a more comprehensive look at the relationship between militarism and racism, see Jack O'Dell, "Racism: Fuel for the War Machine," Albert and Dellinger, *op. cit.*

91. *Equal Opportunity Assessment: 1984, op. cit.;* "Thinking About Enlisting," *op. cit.;* "Women...Uncle Sam Wants You?" brochure produced by Committee Against Registration and the Draft, Washington, D.C., n.d.; Kerely, *op. cit.* More information on the links between the gender system and the military can be found in Leslie Cagan, "Feminism and Militarism," in Albert and Dellinger, *op. cit.,* and Betty A. Reardon, *Sexism and the War System* (New York: Teachers College Press, 1985).

92. *Basic Research Program, op. cit.;* Kim McDonald, "Pentagon Fellowships," *The Chronicle of Higher Education,* September 2, 1981.

93. *University Research Initiative, op. cit.;* "Los Alamos National Laboratory Seeks Candidates for Two Postdoctoral Programs," flyer circa 1986.

94. "All about engineering and computers and you and electronics at Hughes," promotional brochure, Hughes Aircraft Corporation, circa 1985. One estimate for Hughes Aircraft's dependency on the military was 76 percent, see Table 7, "Contractor Dependency on the Department of Defense, 1975-9," as published in *Defended to Death,* Gwyn Prins, ed. (London: Penguin Books, 1983), p. 150.

95. "All about engineering...," *op. cit.*

96. "Opportunity," promotional brochure, General Electric, Professional Recruiting and University Relations Office, Schenectady, New York, August 1984.

97. Warren F. Davis, "On the Number of Engineers and Scientists Serving the Defense Sector," a contribution to *The War Against the Economy: The Military-Industrial Complex,* A Colloquim Sponsored by the Columbia University Seminar on the Political Economy of War and Peace, Columbia University, New York, New York, January 26, 1985.

98. Michael T. Klare, *The American Arms Supermarket* (Austin: University of Texas Press, 1984), pp. 56-57.

99. *Ibid.,* p. 56.

100. *Ibid.,* p. 93.

101. *Ibid.,* p. 94.

102. *Ibid.,* p. 56.

103. Quote, "In order...," from p. 64, *ibid.* Quotes thereafter from: pp. 64-67.

104. The distinctions between weapons which can be used for internal repression and external defense or aggression clearly break down at some point, especially given the links between death squad activities and armed forces. In combatting defense contractors' arguments that their weapons are developed to provide for the defense of borders, it is useful to document

how certain weapons systems are *dedicated* in function for internal repression i.e. it is built into the design of these weapons. Another useful distinction has been drawn by Johan Galtung between "offensive" and "defensive" weapons: "Defensive weapons systems are defined as those that have a limited range and destruction area and for that reason can (essentially) only be used on one's own territory; offensive weapons are all the others." See Johan Galtung, "Transarmament: from Offensive to Defensive Defense," *Journal of Peace Research,* Vol. 21, No. 2, 1984. Galtung's work helps explain how less fixed weapons systems such as planes and tanks can be viewed as dedicated to offensive war, although here, too, arise logical inconsistencies.

105. The Military Assistance Program (MAP) accelerated precisely as elite planners attempted to control the internal social order in Latin America:

> The programme became intensified after the visit of [Nelson] Rockefeller to Latin America [in 1969], where he encountered considerable turbulence. His evaluation of the unrest was that there was a need for stronger government. He claimed that pluralistic forms of government would often be incapable of maintaining the proper balance between development and stability in nations undergoing the process of modernization. The question, he argued, was less one of democracy or lack of it, than of an orderly way of doing things. He argued that the United States should learn to live with military strongmen in Latin America, and to understand that a new type of military man was coming to the fore and becoming a major force for constructive change in the American republics.

See Asborn Eide, "Proliferation and Trade: The Transfer of Arms to Third World Countries and Their Internal Uses," *International Social Science Journal,* Vol. 26, No. 1, 1974 as published in *Making the Connection: Disarmament, Development and Economic Conversion: A Reader* (New York: United Nations, January 1985), pp. 72-73.

106. "Police Aid to Central America: Yesterday's Lessons, Today's Choices," Arms Control and Foreign Policy Caucus, U.S. Congress, Washington, D.C., mimeo, August 13, 1986, pp. 6, 7-8.

107. *Ibid.*

108. Under the Arms Export Control Act of 1976, the U.S. president is authorized to control the export and import of defense supplies and services and provide guidelines governing parties involved in the export or import of such military supplies and services. The "U.S. Munitions List," established by the president, details the military articles and services under his control. See Klare, *op. cit.,* pp. 55-56.

109. *Foreign Military Sales, Foreign Military Construction Sales and Military Assistance Facts as of September 30, 1985* (Washington, D.C.: Data Management Division, Comptroller, DSAA, n.d.); Michael T. Klare and Cynthia Arnson, *Supplying Repression* (Washington, D.C.: Institute for Policy Studies, 1981).

110. Klare, *op. cit.,* p. 186.

111. *Foreign Military Sales..., op. cit.*

112. Tom Gervasi, *The Arsenal of Democracy III (New York: Grove Press, 1984),* pp. 120-121; *Invasion: A Guide to the U.S. Military Presence in Central America* (Philadelphia: NAR-MIC/American Friends Service Committee, 1985).

113. Klare, *op. cit.,* p. 189.

114. Gervasi, *op. cit.,* pp. 218-219.

115. *Invasion..., op. cit.*

116. Gervasi, *op. cit.,* pp. 280-281; *Invasion..., op. cit.*

117. Klare, *op. cit.*, pp. 82-84.

118. J. L. Fried, *et al, Guatemala in Rebellion* (New York: Grove Press, 1983) as cited by Benjamin Beit-Hallahmit, *The Israeli Connection: Who Israel Arms and Why* (New York: Pantheon Books, 1987), p. 82.

119. See *Defense and Foreign Affairs Weekly* for a listing of these arms shipments. Brazil, like Israel, has ties to the U.S. arms industry: "Weapons from Brazil, the South's biggest exporter, will soon go into production under license in the US, where companies are keen to build a Brazilian-designed armoured car, and aim to start joint development of a new tank for the 1990s." See Francis Khoo, "Gunning for the big time," *South*, No. 79, May 1987. In 1984, Honduras ordered eight EMB-312 Tucano trainer aircraft from Brazil (delivered in 1985) [Appendix 17B., "Register of the trade in major conventional weapons with industrialized and Third World Countries, 1985," *SIPRI Yearbook: 1986* (Oxford: Oxford University Press, 1986), p. 379]. An analysis of the EMB-312 Tucano aircraft described the following links between subsystems and foreign producers:

Foreign Producers of Tucano Aircraft Subsystems

Subsystem	Producer	Country
Avionics (including communications)	Collins	USA
Ejection Seats	Martin Baker	UK
Engine	Pratt & Whitney or Garrett	Canada USA
Landing Gear	Piper	USA
Propeller	Harztell	USA
Wheels and Wheelbrakes	Parker-Hannifin	USA

SOURCE: Stockholm International Peace and Research Institute data, as published in Michael Brzoska and Thomas Ohlson, "The trade in major conventional weapons," *SIPRI Yearbook: 1986* (London: Oxford University Press, 1986), Table 17.5, p. 339.

120. Milton Jamail and Margo Gutierrez, "Getting Down to Business," *NACLA Report on the Americas,* Vol. 21, No. 2, March-April 1987, p. 25.

121. M. Peled, "Israel and the Arms Market," *Ha'aretz,* August 5, 1985 [Hebrew], p. 9, as cited in Beit-Hallahmi, *op. cit.*, p. 78.

122. *Ibid.*, p. 85.

123. J. Hunter interview with Francisco Guerra y Guerra, *Israeli Foreign Affairs,* January 1985 as cited in *ibid.*, p. 86.

124. *SIPRI Yearbook 1980,* p. 97 as cited in Jamail and Gutierrez, *op. cit.*, p. 29.

125. *SIPRI Yearbook 1981* (London: Taylor and Francis, 1981) and C. Lusane, "Israeli Arms in Central America," *Covert Action,* Winter 1984, pp. 34-37 as cited in Beit-Hallahmi, *op. cit.,* p. 85.

126. *Ibid.,* p. 80; *SIPRI Yearbook 1980,* p. 97 as cited in Milton Jamail and Margo Gutierrez, "Guatemala: The Paragon," in *NACLA, op. cit.,* p. 33.

127. G. Kessary, "Pesakh Ben-Or: Business in the Dark," *Maariv,* December 13, 1985 [Hebrew] as cited in Beit-Hallahmi, *op. cit.,* p. 80.

128. *Ibid.,* p. 81.

129. E. Cody, "Salvador, Israel Set Closer Ties," *Washington Post,* August 7, 1983, p. 7, as quoted in *ibid.,* p. 81.

130. Cynthia Arnson, "Israel and Central America," *New Outlook,* March-April 1984, p. 20 and *Diario de Centro America* (Guatemala City), November 5, 1981 as quoted and cited by Jamail and Gutierrez, "Guatemala," *op. cit.,* p. 33.

131. Beit-Hallahmit, *op. cit.,* p. 88.

132. H. Anderson, "The CIA Blows an Asset," *Newsweek,* September 3, 1984, as cited in *ibid.,* p. 93. See also Jane Hunter, "Israel: The Contras' Secret Benefactor," *NACLA, op. cit.*

133. "Backdoor Help for Contras, Replaces Congress-Voted Aid," *This Week: Central America and Panama* (Guatemala City), September 17, 1984 and *The New York Times,* September 4, 1984 as cited in Hunter, *op. cit.,* p. 22.

134. "An Israeli Connection?" *Time,* May 7, 1984. See also *Christian Science Monitor,* January 13, 1987 as cited by Hunter, *op. cit.,* p. 24 which quotes a report in *Ha'aretz* that Israeli advisers trained contras at U.S. Army bases in Honduras.

135. Milton Jamail and Margo Gutierrez, "A Special Relationship," *NACLA, op. cit.,* p. 16.

136. Beit-Hallahmi, *op. cit.,* p. 95.

137. Thomas L. Friedman, "How Israel's Economy Got Hooked On Selling Arms Abroad," *The New York Times,* December 7, 1986.

138. *Ibid.*

139. Alex Mintz, Department of Political Science, the Hebrew University of Jerusalem and Department of Political Science, University of Illinois, and Daniel Maman, Department of Sociology, the Hebrew University of Jerusalem, "Center vs. Periphery in Israel's Military-Industrial Sector: Implications for Civil-Military Relations," paper presented at the "Section on Military Studies/ISA" meetings, Urbana, Illinois, November 7-9, 1985; Table 17.3 in Michael Brzoska and Thomas Ohlson, "The trade in major conventional weapons," *SIPRI Yearbook 1986* (New York: Oxford University Press, 1986), p. 336.

140. See various articles by Jamail and Gutierrez in *NACLA, op. cit.* and Beit-Hallahmi, *op. cit.*

141. Jamail and Gutierrez, "A Special Relationship," *op. cit.,* p. 17. Israel also depends on the U.S. government for a subsidy for its arms industry. It is accorded the unusual privilege of using U.S. FMS credits to purchase armaments from its own military industries. The United States permits Israel to co-produce weapons systems under this program. [Phone interview with Sheila Ryan, New York, New York, July 24, 1987; Sheila Ryan, "U.S. Military Contractors in Israel," *Middle East Report,* January-February 1987, p. 17.]

142. Ryan, *ibid.*

143. *Ibid.*

144. *Excelsior,* October 11, 1983; *Enfoprensa,* January 6, 1984; *The New York Times,* July 7, 1984; Latin American Newsletters, *Special Report,* March 1983, as cited in Ryan, *op. cit.,* p. 20. A report in 1986 noted that "Tadiran has clearly targeted the U.S. market. Its 1984 sales there—including civilian electronics, such as switchboards—were $30-million, in 1985, $60

million, and it has a target of $130 million for 1986, of which some $80 million would be military and $50 million civilian." The report notes that Elbit purchased an infrared and thermal imaging firm called Iframetrics as a subsidiary in Bedford, Massachusetts. See "Israel Tightens the Belt," *Defense and Foreign Affairs,* February 1986.

145. In addition to the well publicized cases of beatings and killings of civilians in the occupied territories, an article alluding to torture by Shin Beth internal security service agents noted a report which claimed that they had been acting according to established norms. See "Israel Cabinet Defers Issues of Security Agency," *The New York Times,* November 2, 1987.

146. Phone interview with Toni Verstandig, House Foreign Affairs Committee, and Barry Sklar, Senate Foreign Relations Committee, U.S. Congress, Washington, D.C., July 17, 1987.

147. Ehrlich, *op. cit.,* p. 120. See Appendix One for investments of College Retirement Equities Fund.

148. *Good Money: The Newsletter of Social Investing and Inventing,* May-June 1985.

149. "Questions and Answers About Pax World Fund," promotional brochure; "Semi-Annual Report, June 30, 1985," Prospectus, April 25, 1985, Pax World Fund, Portsmouth, New Hampshire.

Chapter Seven: Growing Pentagon Hegemony Over Universities

1. Peter David, "Pentagon to Renew University Links," *Times Higher Education Supplement,* March 19, 1982. See also *The Defense Monitor,* Vol. 13, No. 4, 1984; Kim McDonald, "Pentagon to Allot $319.5-million for Basic Research at Universities," *The Chronicle of Higher Education,* Vol. 23, No. 2, September 9, 1981. See *Report of the Defense Science Board Task Force on University Responsiveness to National Security Requirements,* Office of the Under Secretary of Defense for Research and Engineering, Washington, D.C., January 1982.

2. David, *ibid.*

3. Michael T. Klare, "The Reagan Doctrine: Reagan's $1.5 trillion military buildup goes hand in glove with a new, aggressive war-making strategy," *Inquiry,* March-April 1984; *The FY 1986 Defense Budget: The Weapons Buildup Continues* (Washington, D.C.: Defense Budget Project, Center on Budget and Policy Priorities, April 1985).

4. Table 5 in John P. Holdren and F. Bailey Green, "Military Spending, The SDI, and Government Support of Research and Development: Effects on the Economy and the Health of American Science," *F.A.S. Public Interest Report,* Vol. 39., No. 7, September 1986, pp. 7-9. The most recent estimates are that *75 percent* of federal funding for R&D is military. Another important survey article is: Joel S. Yudken and Barbara Simons, "Computer Science Research Funding: Issues and Trends," *Abacus,* Vol. 5, No. 3, Spring 1988, pp. 60-66.

5. P.B. Stares, *The Militarization of Space,* as cited in Carl Barus, "Military Influence on the Electrical Engineering Curriculum Since World War II," *IEEE Technology and Science Magazine,* Vol. 6, No. 2, June 1987, p. 5. See Lloyd J. Dumas, "University Research, Industrial Innovation, and the Pentagon," in *The Militarization of High Technology,* John Tirman, ed. (Cambridge, MA: Ballinger Publishing Co., 1984) and Holdren and Green, *op. cit.,* for estimates on NASA's impact on university research and the proportion of NASA which is military in nature. An accurate estimation of the military proportion of NASA's university contracts is an open question of course. One could argue for example that "100 percent" of the faculty contracts from NASA are from a military-serving agency.

6. Bhupendra Jasani, "The Expansion of the Arms Race into Outer Space," *Bulletin of Peace Proposals,* Vol. 17, No. 3-4, 1986, p. 331.

7. Mario Pianta, "Star Wars Economics," Paper for the Conference: 'The State of Star Wars,' Transnational Institute, Amsterdam, January 23-25, 1987. See also W. Hartung, *et al.*, *The Strategic Defense Initiative: Costs, Contractors and Consequences* (New York: Council On Economic Priorities, 1984).

8. Mark Zieman, "Growing Militarization of the Space Program Worries U.S. Scientists," *Wall Street Journal*, January 15, 1986. This article cites a General Accounting Office report which states that "in the past three years, up to 20% of NASA's budget has been spent directly on military application."

9. Bob Alvarez, Memorandum, "Perpetuating the Romance with Atom: An Assessment of Spending for the U.S. Department of Energy During the Reagan Era (FY 1981-FY 1989)," Environmental Policy Institute, Washington, D.C., June 6, 1988.

10. Interview with John Rudolph, Department of Energy, Fall 1987; Letter from Richard E. Stephens, Director, Division of University and Industry Programs, Office of Field Operations Management, Office of Energy Research, Department of Energy, March 4, 1987 and attached photocopy: "Department of Energy: University R&D Funding (By Program Office)." See also *Guide to Energy R&D Programs for Universities and Other Research Groups* (Washington, D.C.: Department of Energy, Office of Energy Research, June 1984).

11. An example of this critical link between nuclear power and nuclear weapons was reported in a September 16, 1980 article in *The New York Times*, "Lack of Plutonium for Warheads Stirs Debate on Increasing Output," by Richard Burt. The story explains that President Carter had approved several new nuclear weapons for deployment in the 1980s, such as the MX mobile missle, the Trident submarine-launched rocket and air- and sea-launched cruise missiles. However, Pentagon officials and military specialists on Capitol Hill said it was "highly unlikely that the warheads for those systems could be made without starting up old reactors at Barnwell, S.C., and a reprocessing plant in Hanford, Wash." In the first term of the Reagan Administration, the Secretary of Energy "had proposed to transfer virtually all the plutonium being used in the Department's Civilian Breeder Reactor Program into nuclear weapons." See Richard Ottinger, "The Links Between Nuclear Power and Weapons Proliferation," in proceedings of *The Second Biennial Conference: On the Fate of the Earth*, Washington, D.C., September 19-23 (San Francisco, CA: Earth Island Institute, 1985), p. 77.

12. Alvarez, *op. cit.*

13. "Markey Releases Analysis of Reagan Energy Budget: The Militarization of Energy Department Marches On," press release, Office of Ed Markey, U.S. House of Representatives, Washington, D.C., January 12, 1987; Michael R. Gordon, "Most Energy Funds for Military Uses," *The New York Times*, January 13, 1987. Alvarez, *op. cit.*, found that 56.8 percent of DOE's budget was defense-related in 1987.

14. Dumas, *op. cit.*, p. 124 ff., i.e. in 1980, $2.5 billion of an estimated $8.2 billion of R&D funded by all sources and performed at universities and related FFRDCs was military in nature.

15. Seth Shulman, "Poisons from the Pentagon," *The Progressive*, November 1987, p. 18; Richard Jannaccio, "The University of Wisconsin Hatches Toxins," *The Progressive, ibid.*, p. 20. More recently still, an article on the Star Wars budget stated, "Some researchers maintain...that defense officials might find it beneficial to reduce money for basic research. The Universities receiving Star Wars money are fairly well distributed geographically...The Pentagon might let them feel the pinch...as a way to generate more political support for a higher budget next year." See Collen Cordes, "Many Scientists Welcome the Reluctance of Congress to Back Large Increases for 'Star Wars' Research," *The Chronicle of Higher Education*, December 16, 1987, pp. A17-A18.

16. Richard De Veaux, Assistant Professor, program in Statistics and Operations Research, Princeton University, as quoted in "Professors and the Pentagon," *Currents*, program aired on WNET-TV, Public Broadcasting Service, New York, April 16, 1987.

17. Hicks quoted in *Science,* April 25, 1986 as cited in Holdren and Green, *op. cit.,* p. 15.

18. Steve Slaby, Professor of Civil Engineering, Princeton University; Terry Matilsky, Professor of Astrophysics, Rutgers University, as quoted in "Professors and the Pentagon," *op. cit.*

19. Barus, *op. cit.,* p. 5, p. 7. See also N. Balabanian, "The essential focus of engineering education—the individual student," *IEEE Trans. on Education,* Vol. E-12, March 1969, pp. 1-3.

20. Holdren and Green, *op. cit.,* p. 14.

21. Holdren and Green, *ibid.,* suggest that the Mansfield Amendment has made military-sponsorsed university research even less applicable to basic science needs. See the related arguments dealing with spinoffs below.

22. Seymour Melman, *Profits Without Production* (New York: Alfred A. Knopf, 1983), p. 83.

23. Kim McDonald, "House-Senate Committee Backs Big Increase in Funds for Military Research at Universities," *The Chronicle of Higher Education,* August 7, 1985, p. 17.

24. Leo Young, "The University Link," *Defense/83,* Washington, D.C., February 1983, p. 5.

25. "Remarks Prepared for Delivery by The Honorable Caspar W. Weinberger, Secretary of Defense at the ADA Expo 1986 Conference, Charleston, West Virginia, Wedenesday, November 19, 1986," press release, Office of Assistant Secretary of Defense (Public Affairs), Washington, D.C., November 19, 1986.

26. From 1956 to 1963 government spending for total research increased by 20 percent, or more, almost every year. "After 1963, the rate of growth began to diminish. By 1965, with increased pressure on the budget from the Vietnam War, the growth of federal research outlays was sharply curtailed…" See Seymour Melman, *Pentagon Capitalism* (New York: McGraw Hill Book Co., 1970), p. 90.

27. Cynthia Arnson, "Cold War in the Caribbean," *Inquiry,* December 10, 1979. For more information on post-Vietnam interventionism, see also James Petras, "The Revival of Interventionism," *Monthly Review,* Vol. 31, No. 9, February 1980; "US Foreign Policy in the 1980s," *Monthly Review,* Vol. 31, No. 11, April 1980; Michael T. Klare, *Beyond the "Vietnam Syndrome": US Interventionism in the 1980s* (Washington, DC: Institute for Policy Studies, 1981); Noam Chomsky and Edward Herman, *The Political Economy of Human Rights* (Boston: South End Press, 1979); Noam Chomsky, *Towards a New Cold War* (New York: Pantheon Books, 1982).

28. Arnson, *op. cit.*

29. Clive Cookson, "Universities ask for new defense pact," *Times Higher Education Supplement,* April 17, 1981.

30. See John H. Cushman, "Bigger Role Urged for Defense Dept. in Economic Policy," *The New York Times,* October 19, 1988.

31. Michael T. Klare, "The Reagan Doctrine," *op. cit.*

32. *Who Rules Columbia?* (New York: North American Congress on Latin America, 1968), p. 20.

33. Mary Kaldor, *The Baroque Arsenal* (New York: Hill and Wang, 1981), p. 55ff.; Irving Brinton Holley, Jr., *U.S. Army in World War II, Special Studies,* Vol. 7 (Washington, D.C.: Office of the Chief of Military History, Department of the Army, 1964), p. 22 as quoted in Kaldor, pp. 56-57.

34. See Ann Markusen, *Defense Spending and the Geography of High Tech Industries: Working Paper 423* (Berkeley: University of California, Institute of Urban and Regional Development, 1984); Ann Markusen, "The Militarized Economy," *World Policy Journal,* Vol. 3, No. 3, Summer 1986; Ann Markusen and Robin Bloch, "Defensive Cities: Military Spending, High Technology and Human Settlements," in *High Technology, Space and Society,* Manuel Castells, ed. (Beverly Hills: Sage Publications, 1985), p. 108.

35. Markusen and Bloch, *ibid.*

36. Klaus Engelhardt, "Conversion of military research and development: Realism or wishful thinking?" *International Labour Review,* Vol. 124, No. 2, March-April 1985, p. 184.

37. "A Frightening New Number Game," *US News & World Report,* September 28, 1987 as cited in Marek Thee, "Recovering Research and Science," in *Perestroika: Global Challenge* (Nottingham, England: Spokesman Books, 1988), p. 84.

38. Warren F. Davis, "On the Number of Engineers and Scientists Serving the Defense Sector," a contribution to *The War Against the Economy: The Military-Industrial Complex,* A Colloquim Sponsored by the Columbia University Seminar on the Political Economy of War and Peace, Columbia University, New York, New York, January 26, 1985. One study gives evidence that civilian jobs in some categories may still be higher paying than those in defense firms. The College Placement Council, which collects information on starting salaries from placement offices, calculated offers to bachelors degree recipients by industry. According to the Council, in 1986 salary offers for engineering students in the military-related computer and aerospace industries trailed those of other sectors, especially the petroleum and chemical industries. The MIT Career Services Office also has collected data appearing to corroborate such claims. See Seth Shulman, "Knocking the Military Habit: Exploding the Myths of an Armed Society," *Science for the People,* November-December 1986, pp. 14-15. However, the increased defense dependency of high-tech sectors suggests that, regardless of the level of pay, engineering students will be increasingly channeled into military work.

39. Ronald Reagan as quoted in "Star Wars: Is It a Mission Possible?" *Changes,* September-October 1985.

40. Pianta, *op. cit.*

41. Noam Chomsky, *Turning the Tide* (Boston: South End Press, 1985), p. 209ff., Robert Reich, "High Technology, Defense and International Trade," Tirman, *op. cit.;* Robert Reich, "High Tech, A Subsidy of Pentagon, Inc.," as quoted in Chomsky, *op. cit.*

42. John Pike, *The Strategic Defense Initiative: Areas of Concern* (Washington, D.C.: Federation of American Scientists, 1985), p. 4, as quoted in Mario Pianta, "New Technologies Across the Atlantic: US Leadership or European Autonomy?" Report prepared for the United Nations University Peace and Global Transformations Subprogram (draft), April 1986.

43. Pianta, *op. cit.; Star Wars: The Economic Fallout,* Rosy Nimrody, ed. (Cambridge, Massachusetts: Ballinger Publishing Company, 1988), pp. 28, 36.

44. *Ibid.,* pp. 82, 86.

45. George C. Wilson, "SDI Was 'Oversold' Cheney Says," *Washington Post,* March 29, 1989; Michael R. Gordon, "Bush Plans to Cut Reagan Requests for Key Weapons," *The New York Times,* April 24, 1989.

46. *Ibid.;* William Hartung and Rosy Nimroody, "Pentagon Invades Academia," *CEP Newsletter* Council on Economic Priorities, New York, New York, January 1986. A report noted, "the IST office has already committed $62 million in long-term contracts to support six research consortia involving twenty-nine universities in sixteen states." See Nimroody, *op. cit.,* p. 84.

47. Quoted in *ibid.*

48. Quoted in "Senators and scientists object to SDI costs and uncertainties," *Physics Today,* July 1985.

49. Keith B. Richburg, "'Star Wars' Sparks New Campus Debate," *Washington Post,* July 29, 1985.

50. Judith Axler Turner, "Illinois 'Star Wars' Rift Embroils Army Lab, Supercomputer, Chancellor," *The Chronicle of Higher Education,* August 7, 1985.

51. Philip M. Boffey, "Censorship Action Angers Scientists," *The New York Times,* September 5, 1982.

52. Ann Markusen, "The Militarized Economy," *op. cit.*

53. Melman, *Pentagon Capitalism, op. cit.,* p. 101; Markusen and Bloch, *op. cit.,* p. 110.

54. *Industry and University: New Forms of Co-Operation and Communication* (Paris: Organisation for Economic Co-Operation and Development, 1984).

55. Robert Leavitt, *"By the Sword We Seek Peace": Military Spending and State Government in Massachusetts,* ms. (Boston: Massachusetts, 1986), p. 48.

56. *Going For Broke* (Ann Arbor, MI: Committee for Nonviolent Research, 1982).

57. *Planning a Government Procurement Outreach Center* (Washington, D.C.: The Academy for State and Local Government, September 1985); Office of Economic Adjustment, "Department of Defense Support for the President's Private Sector Initiatives Program," Dec. 3, 1984 as quoted in Robert Krinsky, "Community programs aid Pentagon," *Bulletin of the Atomic Scientists,* Vol. 42, No. 8, October 1986, p. 38. The author has benefited from discussion with Robert Krinsky in outlining the ideas in this section.

58. *FY-1987 Defense Small Business Innovation Research Program (SBIR),* Program Solicitation No. 87.1 (Washington, D.C.: SBIR Program Office, U.S. Department of Defense, October 1, 1986); "A Major Source of Money for Columbia Researchers with Small Business Ties," Vol. 8, No. 3, *OPG Newsletter* Office of Projects and Grants, Columbia University, New York, New York, November 18, 1985.

59. Hartung and Nimroody, *op. cit.*

60. *Ibid.* However, even NSF has military links: "In Washington, the National Science Foundation, Department of Energy, NASA, and DOD regularly consult, coordinate, and even trade and share project funding." See Paul Selvin and Charles Schwartz, "Publish & Perish," *Science for the People,* Vol. 20, No. 1, January-February 1988.

61. James Botkin, Dan Dimancescu, Ray Stata, with John McClellan, *Global Stakes* (New York: Penguin Books, 1984), pp. 52, 49-72, 61-62.

62. Monty Neil, ms. on universities and defense R&D, Harvard University, Cambridge, MA, n.d.; "Research Universities and the National Interest," A Report from Fifteen University Presidents, Ford Foundation, New York, 1977, as cited in Neil; National Science Foundation (NSF), *The Five-Year Outlook on Science and Technology, 1981* (Washington, D.C.: US Government Printing Office, 1982), p. 1 as cited in Neil; Botkin, *et al., op. cit.,* p. 63. See also "Campus Buildings are Decaying, Survey Says," *The New York Times,* October 18, 1988.

63. Jack Ruina, "Memo to Faculty" and "Report of the Ad Hoc Committee on the Military Presence at MIT," Enclosure G, MIT, Cambridge, Massachusetts, May 15, 1986; J.R. Baron, *et al.,* "Lincoln Laboratory Review Committee Interim Report," Enclosure H, MIT, Cambridge, Massachusetts, February 24, 1986.

64. In a review on the "Cost and Evaluation of Operations in American Universities," in the early 1970s, Seymour Melman found that the administrative expenses of colleges and universities had increased dramatically from the early 1950s to the early 1960s. In the academic year 1951-52, the ratio of general administrative expenses to instruction and department research was 22 percent for state universities and colleges. For private universities and colleges the corresponding ratio was 36 percent. By the academic year 1963-64, these figures had jumped to 27 percent and 46 percent respectively. See Seymour Melman, "Cost and Evaluation of Operations in American Universities," in *Higher Education in the United States,* Otto Feinstein, ed. (Lexington, MA: D.C. Heath and Company, 1971).

65. "Indirect Costs" are university costs which defense-serving agencies, such as the Defense Department, NASA and DOE reimburse; these are "costs associated with maintaining the capability to perform research; for example, maintenance of facilities, utilities, or administrative salaries." A GAO report released in Feburary 1986 details how the defense agencies underwrite

such costs for research contracts. See *University Funding: Federal Funding Mechanisms in Support of University Research* (Washington, D.C.: General Accounting Office, February 1986).

66. For example, the universities have turned to the Defense Department to underwrite a major program sponsoring the acquisition of equipment to underwrite the deterioration of the nation's science capability after years of neglect (see Section 7.5).

67. Ruina, *op. cit.;* Baron, *et al., op. cit.*

68. *The Department of Defense FY 1986 University Research Initiative Program Overview,* Department of Defense, Washington, D.C. *(hereafter, University Research Initiative)*, p. 1.

69. *Going For Broke, op. cit.,* p. 17. Such university defense entrepreneuring is not confined to the University of Michigan. For example, in the Spring of 1987, the University of Wisconsin hired Philip Sobocinski, a retired Army colonel and former deputy commander of the Army Medical Research Institute of Infectious Diseases, to "help professors tailor their research to serve the Pentagon—and bring funding to the school." See Jannaccio, *op. cit.,* p. 20.

70. *Going for Broke, op. cit.,* pp. 15, 11.

71. *Ibid.,* p. 11, p. 22.

72. *Ibid.,* p. 6, p. 9.

73. *Ibid.,* p. 10.

74. Botkin, *et al.,* p. 50.

75. *Report of the DOD-University Forum,* Calendar Year 1984 (Washington, D.C.: Office of the Under Secretary of Defense for Research and Engineering, December 1984), p. 34.

76. For background on the secondary labor market and associated race and class issues, see Richard Edwards, *Contested Terrain* (New York: Basic Books, 1979). For a discussion of the division of labor in the military and the "production model of war," see James William Gibson, *The Perfect War: Technowar in Vietnam* (Boston: The Atlantic Monthly Press, 1986).

77. Jean Evangelauf, "Students' Costs Will Rise 7 Pct., Nearly Twice the Inflation Rate," *The Chronicle of Higher Education,* Vol. 30, No. 24, August 14, 1985.

78. Table 7 in *Trends in Student Aid: 1980 to 1986* (New York: The College Board, 1986), p. 11.

79. Table 17 in *The Polarization of America: The Loss of Good Jobs, Falling Incomes & Rising Inequality* (Washington, D.C.: Industrial Union Department, AFL-CIO, 1986), p. 60.

80. These figures reflect changes in constant 1982 dollars. See Table 6 in *Trends in Student Aid, op. cit.*

81. Table 4 in *ibid.*

82. "Federal Student Aid Funding FY 1970-87," a study by the American Council on Education, Washington, D.C., March 17, 1987.

83. Susan T. Hill, "Participation of Black Students in Higher Education: A Statistical Profile from 1970-71 to 1980-81," *Integrated Education,* Vol. 22, Nos. 1-3, January-June 1984, p. 53.

84. Gaynelle Evans, "Social, Financial Barriers Blamed for Curbing Blacks' Access to College," *The Chronicle of Higher Education,* August 7, 1985.

85. See Robin Wilson, "Low-Income Students at Black Colleges Facing Aid Gap," *The Chronicle of Higher Education,* April 15, 1987; Table 5 in *Access to College: The Impact of Federal Financial Aid Policies at Private Historically Black Colleges* (Washington, D.C.: The National Institute of Independent Colleges and Universities, 1987), p. 19.

86. Kim McDonald, "Pentagon Boosts Financial Support for ROTC," *The Chronicle of Higher Education,* September 16, 1981; Richard Halloran, "R.O.T.C., Shunned No More, Grows Increasingly Selective," *The New York Times,* July 20, 1987, p. 1.

87. One turning point was the end of the draft in 1973, see Halloran, *ibid.*

88. *Handbook of Labor Statistics,* U.S. Department of Labor, Bureau of Labor Statistics, Bulletin 2217, Washington, D.C., June 1985; U.S. Bureau of the Census, *Statistical Abstract of the United States* (106th & 107th edition), Washington, D.C., 1985, 1986.

89. Gibson, *op. cit.,* has an interesting compilation on this topic, including these studies: Ralph Guzman, "Mexican Casualties in Vietnam," *La Raza,* 1 (1971); Lawrence M. Baskir and William A. Strauss, *Chance and Circumstance: The Draft, the War and the Vietnam Generation* (New York: Alfred A. Knopf, 1978). From 1965 to 1969, blacks on average represented a little more than 9 percent of the total armed forces. But, the percent of total Vietnam battle deaths registered by blacks from 1961 to 1969 was *12.9 percent.* Blacks suffered 24 percent of army deaths in Vietnam in 1965. See *Statistical Abstract of the United States: 1970* (91st edition) (Washington, D.C.: U.S. Bureau of the Census, 1970), p. 258; Baskir and Strauss, *op. cit.,* p. 8.

90. Senator John C. Stennis, in "Hearings on Authorization for Military Procurement, Research and Development, Fiscal Year 1970," Ninety-first Congress, first session, p. 1553, as quoted in Richard F. Kaufman, *The War Profiteers* (Garden City, NY: Anchor Books, 1972), p. 235.

91. *Report of the DOD-University Forum,* Calendar Year 1984 (Washington, D.C.: Office of the Under Secretary of Defense for Research and Engineering, December 1984), p. 32.

92. *The Department of Defense FY 1986 University Research Initiative Program Overview,* Department of Defense, Washington, D.C. *(hereafter, University Research Initiative); Science,* July 1986.

93. Recent reports have noted that the URI was in danger of being phased out. Congress decreased funding from $100 million in 1986 to $35 million in 1987, see "The Department of Defense University Research Interdisciplinary Initiative is in Trouble," Vol. 9, No. 8, *OPG Newsletter,* Office of Projects and Grants, Columbia University, New York, New York, November 18, 1985. However, there are always new projects waiting in the wings. A Pentagon committee recommended that the government establish eight university centers for research and training in semiconductor technology which would cost $50-million a year. See Judith Axler Turner, "Pentagon Panel Suggests Establishment of Centers for Semiconductor Research," *The Chronicle of Higher Education,* February 25, 1987.

94. A 1974 report by a committee of the National Academy of Engineering stated that: "With a few exceptions the vast technology developed by Federally funded programs since World War II has not resulted in widespread 'spinoffs' of secondary or additional applications of practical products, processes and services that have made an impact on the nation's growth, industrial productivity, employment gains and foreign trade." See National Academy of Engineering Committee on Technology Transfer and Utilization, "Technology Transfer and Utilization, Recommendations for Reducing the Emphasis and Correcting the Imbalance" (Washington, D.C.: National Academy of Engineering, 1974), p. i, as cited in Dumas, *op. cit.,* p. 143. More recent data debunking the spinoff myth is found in an Office of Technology Assessment report described in Bob Davis, "U.S. Agency Sees Japanese Firms Ready to Win Superconductor Products Race," *The Wall Street Journal,* June 20, 1988. Marek Thee notes that "many technological achievements now associated with military R&D have in fact originated in civilian R&D." These include the transitor, which was developed in 1948 by Bell Labs and then sold to the military. See Thee, *op. cit.,* pp. 98-101.

95. Melman, *Profits Without Production, op. cit.;* for arguments that "large, rapid increases in the SDI Research, Development, Test, and Evaluation (RDT&E) budget...will drive up the price of scarce resources needed for civilian R&D," see Frank R. Lichtenburg, "The Impact of the Strategic Defense Initiative on U.S. Civilian R&D Investment and Industrial Competitiveness," Graduate School of Business, Columbia University, January 1988.

96. Neil, *op. cit.;* John Tirman, "The Militarization of Route 128," *The Boston Globe Magazine,* August 15, 1982.

97. Office of the Secretary of Defense, *Basic Research Program* (Washington, D.C: U.S. Government Printing Office, September 1985), p. 4.

98. "1986 R&D Budget: Prosperity for defense, pain for national labs," *Physics Today,* April 1985, pp. 59-65, as cited by Jay Stowsky, "Competing with the Pentagon," *World Policy Journal,* Vol. 3, No. 4., Fall 1986, p. 698.

99. Robert Krinsky, "Swords and Sheepskins: Militarization of Higher Education in the United States and Prospects of its Conversion," *Bulletin of Peace Proposals,* Vol. 19, No. 1, 1988. See also *The Department of Defense Report on the University Role in Defense Research and Development,* For the Committees on Appropriations, United States Congress, Washington, D.C., April 1987.

100. Stowsky, *op. cit.,* p. 698.

101. *Ibid.* The diversion of technical and scientific resources to the military has led to a relative decline in U.S. inventive capabilities as evidenced by decreasing U.S. patent activity vis-à-vis foreign nations. See Dumas, *op. cit.,* pp. 143-144, for a presentation of the statistics and arguments.

102. See Stowsky, *op. cit.,* p. 701 and Warren F. Davis, "The Pentagon and the Scientist," in Tirman, *op. cit.,* pp. 157-159.

103. Noble, *Forces of Production, op. cit.;* on cost-minimizing versus cost-maximizing, see Melman, *Profits Without Production, op. cit.,* pp. 133-135.

104. David Noble, "The Social and Economic Consequences of the Military Influence on the Development of Industrial Technologies," in *The Political Economy of Arms Reduction,* Lloyd J. Dumas, ed. (Boulder, CO: Westview Press, 1982), p. 103.

105. Earl Yang, lecture delivered to Corliss Lamont Seminar on Economic Conversion, Department of Industrial Engineering and Operations Research, Columbia University, New York, New York, November 11, 1986. On the detrimental impact of military R&D on productivity, see also "The Relationship Between Federal Contract R&D and Company R&D," *Papers and Proceedings,* American Economic Association, 1984, pp. 73-78; Nathan Rosenberg, "Civilian 'Spillovers' from Military R&D," in Sanford Lakoff and Randy Willoughby, eds., *Strategic Defense and the Western Alliance* (Lexington, Massachusetts, Lexington Books, 1987).

106. Lloyd J. Dumas, "Military Spending and Economic Decay," in *The Political Economy of Arms Reduction, op. cit.,* p. 17; See also Seymour Melman, *Profits Without Production, op. cit.*

107. Dumas, "Military Spending and Economic Decay," *op. cit.*

108. *Ibid.*

109. Paul Lewis, "Military Spending Questioned," *The New York Times,* November 11, 1986.

110. The protests against the military in the 1980s are described in Chapter Eight. The important point seems to be that the collapse of the more confrontational and larger movement against the Vietnam War has encouraged various agencies of the National Security State to expand links on campus, or at least act more visibly about their university connections.

111. The authors of *Going for Broke, op. cit.,* write that in Ann Arbor, Michigan, there is four to five times more military research performed off-campus, at local high-technology firms, than there is within the University of Michigan. The implications of such findings are discussed in Chapter Eight.

112. *Ibid.,* p. 7.

113. Peter David, *op. cit.*

114. Kim McDonald, "Pentagon Boosts Financial Support for ROTC," *op. cit.*

115. Matthew Rothschild, "Central Employment Agency," *The Progressive,* Feburary 1984.

Chapter Eight: A Disarmament Strategy for the University

1. This section is based on interviews with former student leaders at Cornell, Tufts and the University of Iowa. See also "Students Protesting CIA Recruiting," AP Wire Story, *The New York Times*, March 14, 1984; James McGrath Morris, "CU protestors blow whistles on the CIA," *The Ithaca Journal*, March 14, 1984; Bernie McEvoy, "Protestors Stop CIA Speech," *The Tufts Observer*, Tufts University, Vol. 19., No. 6, October 5, 1984; "Tufts wimps out with its CIA ban," Editorial, *The Boston Herald*, October 24, 1984; "Brown Students Vote on Atom War 'Suicide Pills,'" *The New York Times*, October 11, 1984; Cory Dean, "Student Activism Alive at Brown U.," *The New York Times*, February 14, 1985; Mike O'Keefe, "Boulder: Three Hundred Protest CIA recruitment; Police Riot," *Guardian*, December 3, 1986, p. 3; "Anti-CIA Protestors at Amherst College Acquitted by Jury," *The Chronicle of Higher Education*, April 22, 1987.

2. Oscar Hernandez, "Tufts, Harvard, MIT Physicists Oppose Star Wars," ms. Department of Physics, Harvard University, Cambridge, MA, n.d.; Keith B. Richburg, "'Star Wars' Sparks New Campus Debate," *The Washington Post,* July 29, 1985; Fred Kaplan, "3,700 scientists refuse SDI funds," *The Boston Globe*, May 14, 1986.

3. Colleen Cordes, "6,500 Scientists Vow to Boycott Studies Aided by 'Star Wars,'" *The Chronicle of Higher Education*, May 21, 1986.

4. Seth Shulman, "Stopping Star Wars," *Science for the People*, Vol. 18, No. 1, January-February, 1986, p. 14.

5. Oscar Hernandez, ms. on Star Wars and the university. See also Oscar Hernandez, article on Star Wars in *How Harvard Rules,* Jack Trumpbour, ed. (Boston: South End Press, 1989).

6. Kaplan, *op. cit.*

7. "FAS Statement on Improper University Research Practices," *F.A.S. Newsletter,* Vol. 21, No. 1, January 1968, p. 1.

8. See Chapter Seven.

9. *Hearings on Military Posture and HR 5968 (HR 6030), Department of Defense Authorization for Fiscal Year 1983,* Before the Armed Services Committee (Washington, D.C.: U.S. Government Printing Office, 1982). On October 26th, 1986, the front page of *The New York Times* business section ran a short item titled, "Disinvestment II?" which suggested that because many large U.S. firms had decided that week to pull out of South Africa, many activist groups in the United States would look to new targets. The piece quoted Benjamin Weiner, a political-intelligence consultant who suggested that, "the targets will be pro-American, capitalist countries with imperfect democracies, like South Korea or Chile." See "Prospects: Disinvestment II?" *The New York Times*, October 26, 1986.

10. See Kirkpatrick Sale, *SDS* (New York: Random House, 1973).

11. "Universities Plot Repression of Student Movement," *Unity*, Student Supplement, October 11, 1985, p. S3; Howard Levine and David Pickell, "Conference Explores Campus 'Disruption', *The Daily Californian*, September 18, 1985, p. 1.

12. Melissa Crabbe, "Protest Closes Career Center for One Hour," *Daily Californian,* February 27, 1986, p. 3; p. 10.

13. Lisa Peatie, "The Peace Movement," ms., Department of Urban Studies and Planning, MIT, Cambridge, MA, 1986.

14. Seymour Melman, "A Road Map, Not a STOP Sign: Politics of Peace" (mimeo), Department of Industrial Engineering and Operations Research, Columbia University, New York, New York, September 25, 1986, and as published in *The Demilitarized Society* (Montreal: Harvest House Publishers, 1988). For related arguments, see Joshua Cohen and Joel Rogers, *Rules of*

the Game (Boston: South End Press, 1986) and Bob Overy, *How Effective Are Peace Movements* (Montreal: Harvest House, 1982).

15. *Why Mass Action?: A Strategy for Stopping the U.S. War Against Nicaragua and Ending U.S. Intervention in Central America and the Caribbean,* pamphlet, Issued by the Emergency National Council Against U.S. Intervention in Central America/The Caribbean (ENC), Cleveland, Ohio, November 1986.

16. Norman Fruchter, "Protest, Power and the People," *Liberation,* No. 15 February-April 1971, p. 69.

17. Sale, *op. cit.* An important case where general anti-war protest affected a corporate lab is described in George C. Wilson, "Bell Leaving Missiles After 25 Years; War Protest Influenced Decision," *The Washington Post,* May 20, 1970.

18. Melman, *op. cit.*

19. Noam Chomsky, "The November 1986 Elections," ms., Cambridge, MA, November 10, 1986 [English translation of article submitted to *Il Manifesto*]; See also Noam Chomsky, *Turning the Tide* (Boston: South End Press, 1985).

20. See Seymour Melman, "Problems of Conversion from Military to Civilian Economy: An Agenda of Topics, Questions and Hypotheses," *Bulletin of Peace Proposals,* Vol. 16, No. 1, 1985 and Jonathan Feldman, *An Introduction to Economic Conversion* (Washington, D.C.: National Commission for Economic Conversion and Disarmament, May 1988).

21. Sara Evans, *Personal Politics* (New York: Vintage Books, 1980), p. 219.

22. *Ibid.,* p. 218.

23. While the anti-intervention movement certainly is built upon groups that form in universities, churches and unions, the full power of linking the anti-intervention project to the political terrain of the university has yet to be fully explored, see Chomsky, *op. cit.* for a related discussion.

24. Frances Fox Piven and Richard A. Cloward, *Poor People's Movements* (New York: Vintage Books, 1979), p. 22.

25. Gordon Adams, "Undoing the Iron Triangle: Conversion and the 'Black Box' of Politics," in *Economic Conversion: Revitalizing America's Economy,* Suzanne Gordon and Dave McFadden, eds. (Cambridge, MA: Ballinger Publishing Co., 1984), p. 149 and Feldman, *op. cit.*

26. On the relationship between productivity, industrial competence and labor retention, see Seymour Melman, *Dynamic Factors in Industrial Productivity* (New York: John Wiley, 1956) and *Profits Without Production* (New York: Alfred A. Knopf, 1983). On the possibilities of the "recentralization" of capital in advanced capitalist nations, see Michael J. Piore and Charles F. Sabel, *The Second Industrial Divide* (New York: Basic Books, 1984). On the relationship between declining import penetration and domestic reflation, see CEPG Group, "Academic criticisms of the CEPG analysis," *Cambridge Economic Policy Review,* Vol. 6, No. 1, Chapter Four, pp. 35-42, 1980; Francis Cripps and Wynne Godley, "Control of imports as a means to full employment and the expansion of world trade: the UK's case," *Cambridge Journal of Economics,* Vol. 2, 1978, pp. 327-334; John M. Culbertson, *Free Trade and the Future of the West* (Madison, WI: 21st Century Press, 1985). Transnationals may still have *political* reasons for choosing overseas production. Nevertheless, conversion is a necessary condition for expanding the sphere of domestic production and reinvigorating the industrial base. See John Ullmann, *Economic Conversion: Indispensable for America's Economic Recovery* (Washington, D.C.: National Commission for Economic Conversion and Disarmament, April 1989).

27. See Jonathan Feldman, "Converting the Military Economy through the Local State: Local Conversion Prospects in Massachusetts," *Bulletin of Peace Proposals,* Vol. 19, No. 1, 1988; Ann Markusen, "The Militarized Economy," *World Policy Journal,* Summer 1986.

28. A news report during the presidential campaign reported that "Michael Dukakis says he will reverse the Reagan course, slashing research funds for Star Wars and a $3 billion Air Force air-breathing jet and putting the money into civilian research." See Bob Davis, "Dukakis, Bush Duel on Science-Policy Promises as Scientists Fret Over Funding, Focus of Research," *The Wall Street Journal*, August 9, 1988.

29. Wendy Batson, David McFadden, Diane Thomas-Glass and Jim Watson, *Shaping Alternatives at Lawrence Livermore Laboratory: A Preliminary Analysis* (San Francisco: U.C. Nuclear Weapons Labs Conversion Project, Second Edition, October 1979).

30. The development of such a conversion planning scenario for nuclear power and weapons has been developed by Greg Bischak, "Facing the Second Generation of the Nuclear Weapons Complex," *Bulletin of Peace Proposals*, Vol. 19, *op. cit.*

31. Greg Bischak, an economist with Employment Research Associates in Lansing, Michigan, has proposed the development of a "portfolio" of alternative research and development work with an emphasis on basic research. The ideas presented here build on this suggestion.

32. *California and the 21st Century: Foundations for a Competitive Society*, Vol. 1, A Report of the Senate Select Committee on Long Range Policy Planning, Senator John Garamendi, Chair (Sacramento, CA: Joint Publications, January, 1986), pp. 51, 60-61.

33. Mario Pianta, "High Technology Programmes: For the Military or for the Economy?" *Bulletin of Peace Proposals*, Vol. 19, *op. cit.* See also Philip W. Anderson, " 'Super' Science Squeezes 'Small' Science," *The New York Times*, February 8, 1988. Other models for alternative technology projects can be found in Ken Darrow and Rick Pam, *Appropriate Technology Sourcebook: Vol. I*, Revised Edition (Stanford, CA: Volunteers in Asia, Februrary 1981) and *Appropriate Technology Sourcebook: Vol. II* (Stanford, CA: Volunteers in Asia, January 1981). See also the various books authored by Barry Commoner and Amory Lovins, *Soft Energy Paths* (London: Penguin, 1977).

34. On defense cuts, see Feldman, *An Introduction...*, *op. cit.;* Richard Halloran, "Carlucci Orders $33 Billion in Cuts for Armed Forces," *The New York Times*, December 5, 1987 and Cordes, *op. cit.;* Collen Cordes, "Many Scientists Welcome the Reluctance of Congress to Back Large Increases for 'Star Wars' Research," *The Chronicle of Higher Education*, December 16, 1987, pp. A17-A18; John H. Cushman, "Pentagon Official Proposes Cost Cut for Space Weapon," *The New York Times*, September 8, 1988; and Greg Bischak, "Pentagon Legerdemain," letter to *The New York Times*, December 22, 1987; Bischak reports that the $33 billion "is largely the difference between former Defense Secretary Caspar W. Weinberger's bloated request and the more modest proposal of Frank C. Carlucci." However, the budget deficit is likely to bring substantial defense decreases and failing that economic ruin.

35. "Research Emergency," *The New York Times*, April 30, 1970. Department of Defense RDT&E Obligations to Academic Institutions fell from $1.063 billion in FY 1964 to $.634 billion in FY 1970 and $.421 billion in FY 1975 (in constant 1987 dollars). See *The Department of Defense Report on the University Role in Defense Research and Development*, For the Committees on Appropriations, United States Congress, Washington, D.C., April 1987.

36. On DOD-University Forum "lobbying" activities, see Robert Krinsky, "Swords and Sheepskins: Militarization of Higher Education in the United States and Prospects of its Conversion," *op. cit.;* On the "academic pork barrel," see Colin Norman, "Congress Approves Deals for Ten Universities," *Science*, Vol. 231, January 17, 1986, p. 211; Robert C. Cohen, "Trimming fat from the academic pork barrel," *Christian Science Monitor,* September 21, 1986. An April 1987 article noted: "Little federal money is available through competitive programs to build or renovate academic research buildings. Instead, universities that want to upgrade their research facilities have increasingly lobbied Congress for individual attention," see Colleen Cordes, "Higher-Education Groups Seek to Calm Furor over Surge in 'Pork-Barrel' Science," *The Chronicle of Higher Education*, April 22, 1987. While universities may claim that have no economic choice but to continue their economic ties to the military, an interesting case of alternative social

investment is described in: "Yale Plans to Invest $50 million in New Haven," *The New York Times*, May 21, 1987, pp. A1, B2. On Los Alamos, see "Los Alamos National Laboratory: Research in Support of Technological Competitiveness," Energy and Research Applications, Summary of Briefing, January 28, 1988. Regarding Sovern's comments, see "Sovern Asks Watch on Bush Pledge," *Columbia University Record*, Vol. 14, No. 16, January 27, 1989.

37. Lars Gordon Bjork, *Organizational Environment and the Development of a Research University*, Ph.D. Thesis, The University of New Mexico, May 1983. The members of the proposed consortium included: Arizona State University, the University of Arizona, Idaho University, Montana College of Mining, Technology and Science, South Dakota School of Mines and Technology, South Dakota State University, the University of Montana, the University of Nebraska, the University of Nevada, the University of New Mexico and the University of South Dakota.

38. *Ibid.,* p. 114.

39. *Ibid.,* and phone interview with Lars Gordon Bjork, Columbia, South Carolina, Spring 1987.

40. These ideas build on a discussion with Joel Yudken, former program director at the Center for Economic Conversion and presently a technology consultant in Stanford, California.

41. Seymour Melman, *Profits Without Production* (New York: Alfred A. Knopf, 1983).

42. Pianta, *op. cit.* Even science designed for peaceful uses can be exploited by the military. The conversion of the local and national economy will create barriers to such technology transfer. For more on these questions, see Joseph Weizenbaum, "Not Without Us," and Natasha Aristove, Chester Regen and Elliott Smith "Ethical Dilemmas: Between A Rock and A Hard Place," *Science for the People*, November-December 1986.

43. Yudken, *op. cit.,* Increased funding for civilian research bureaucracies is an essential part of a conversion strategy. One positive development is the reorganization and expansion of the National Bureau of Standards into the "National Institute of Standards and Technology." This could serve as the prototype of an alternative to DARPA. See the "Technological Competitiveness" section of the 1988 Trade Bill, Public Law 100-418, August 23, 1988.

44. The Weiss Bill also requires a one year prenotification of plans to cut back or terminate a defense contract or military base. Planning assistance is provided together with income support and retraining programs for communities and workers while a conversion is underway. See Lloyd J. Dumas, "Making Peace Possible: The Legislative Approach to Economic Conversion," in Gordon and McFadden, *op. cit.,* pp. 67-88; *Defense Economic Adjustment Act: HR 813,* 100th Congress, 1st Session, January 28, 1987 and Jonathan Feldman, Robert Krinsky and Seymour Melman, *Criteria for Economic Conversion Legislation*, First Edition (Washington, D.C.: National Commission for Economic Conversion and Disaramament, December 1988). Stephanie Saul, "Washington Briefing: Easing the Pain of Defense Cuts," *Newsday,* February 20, 1989.

45. Interview with Mel King, Cambridge, MA, May 12, 1987; House Bill No. 909, The Commonwealth of Massachusetts, January 1988; phone interview with Mark Judge, Boston, Massachusetts, July 1987; "The East Bay Conservation Corps Program: Briefing Information," Oakland, CA, East Bay Conservation Corps, September 1986. The Future Corps bill states that "interns who complete one year of service...shall earn a tuition voucher in an amount equivalent to the cost of two years of tuition, room, board, and fees at any of the public institutions of higher education under the governing authority of the board of regents. Future corps interns who complete two years of service shall earn a tuition voucher in an amount equivalent to the cost of four years of tuition, room, board, and fees."

46. On this notorious misinterpretation of Vietnam, see Noam Chomsky, *American Power and the New Mandarins* (New York: Random House, 1967) and his "The Remaking of History," in *Towards a New Cold War* (New York: Pantheon Books, 1982), pp. 134-153.

47. Seymour Melman, "The Peaceful World of Economics I," *Journal of Economic Issues,* Vol. 6, No. 1, March 1972, p. 36.

358 / UNIVERSITIES IN THE BUSINESS OF REPRESSION

48. See Marcus Raskin, *Draft Treaty for a Comprehensive Program for Common Security and General Disarmament*, revised and edited by Matthew Hooberman (Washington, D.C.: Institute for Policy Studies, July 1986) and Robert Krinsky, *An Introduction to Disarmament* (Washington, D.C.: National Commission for Economic Conversion and Disarmament, May 1988).

49. See Noam Chomsky, "Objectivity and Liberal Scholarship," in *American Power and the New Mandarins, op. cit.;* "Institutional neutrality: is the university value-free?" Chapter One in *The University Crisis Reader*, Vol. One: The Liberal University Under Attack (New York: Random House, 1971), pp. 59-77. A clearer idea of how cultural institutions service the warfare state and how they can be transformed politically can be seen in examining the media's links to intervention. The Seattle Central America Media Project developed in response to the need to improve the accuracy and adequacy of local news coverage of Central America. In contrast to conservatives' claims that national and local newspapers are guilty of a left-wing bias when covering the region, the Media Project found that news coverage by local papers and the national media is biased in the opposite direction. The Media Project has used its documentation about media bias to change the direction of news coverage through letters to the editor, phone calls, meetings with editorial boards and other lobbying activities. Another progressive organization, Fairness & Accuracy in Reporting (FAIR), based in New York City, also monitors news bias in the national media and engages in similar activities. Some groups have engaged in direct action against the media's complicity in right-wing activities. The most dramatic example occured in the 1960s in Berlin when students burned newspapers, overturned delivery trucks and blocked the distribution of papers in the streets.

50. For a comprehensive outline of these arguments, see Jane E. Kirtley, "Openness in Government and Freedom of Information," in *Winning America,* Marcus Raskin and Chester Hartman, eds. (Boston: South End Press, 1988), pp. 65-74.

51. *Report of the Congressional Committees Investigating the Iran Contra Affair*, 100th Congress, 1st Session (Washington, D.C.: Government Printing Office, 1987).

52. *Official Accountability Act of 1987: HR 3665*, 100th Congress, 1st Session, November 20, 1987; John Conyers, "HR 3665: To Reassert the Rule of Law," ms., Office of Congressman John Conyers, Washington, D.C., 1988.

53. Gary M. Stern, "Covert Paramilitary Operations," *First Principles*, Vol. 13, No. 1, February-March 1988, p. 14.

54. Memorandum, "RE: Campaign to Abolish Covert Operations: Substantive Strategy," *Center for National Studies,* Washington, D.C., March 15, 1989. The Center for National Security Studies is a project of the national, Washington, D.C. office of the American Civil Liberties Union. This office has been criticized for failing to oppose Pentagon "gag orders" (or security clearance provisions) designed to silence Pentagon employees critical of Defense Department policies. The national ACLU office has also been criticized for other policies regarding covert operations. See Chapter Fifteen, "Carpet Bombing the Constitution," in A. Ernest Fitzgerald, *The Pentagonists* (Boston: Houghton Mifflin Company, 1989), pp. 258-278; "Editorial," *Covert Action Information Bulletin*, No. 14-15, October 1981, p. 5; "Editorial," *Covert Action Information Bulletin*, No. 22, Fall 1984, p. 3. These observations suggest that a successful movement to disarm covert operations institutions would require grassroots pressure on liberal policy groups. A successful effort to organize nationally against covert operations has been waged by the group connected to the Association of National Security Alumni in Washington, D.C.

55. See Simcha Bahiri, "Displacing milk and honey," *Jerusalem Post*, August 12, 1986 for arguments on the detrimental impact of defense expenditure to Israel. See, also Paul Quigley, "Arms Exports: The 'Stop Gap' Alternative to Pentagon Contracts?" *Bulletin of Peace Proposals*, Vol. 19, *op. cit.*

Index

About the Author

Jonathan Feldman is Program Director at the National Commission for Economic Conversion and Disarmament in Washington, D.C. He attended Bard College and the Massachusetts Institute of Technology and was a Corliss Lamont Fellow in Economic Conversion at Columbia University. He has worked as an organizer and researcher in Boston, Detroit, New York, Omaha, and Washington, D.C.

About South End Press

South End Press is a nonprofit, collectively run book publisher with over 150 titles in print. Since our founding in 1977, we have tried to meet the needs of readers who are exploring or are already committed to the politics of radical social change. Our goal is to publish books that encourage critical thinking and constructive action on the key political, cultural, social, economic, and ecological issues shaping life in the United States and in the world. In this way, we hope to give expression to a wide diversity of democratic social movements and to provide an alternative to the products of corporate publishing.

If you would like to receive a free catalog of South End Press books or get information on our membership program—which offers two free books and a 40% discount on all titles—please write us at South End Press, 116 St. Botolph Street, Boston, MA 02115.

Other titles of interest

Necessary Illusions: Thought Control in Democratic Societies

Noam Chomsky

Roots of Rebellion: Land and Hunger in Central America

Tom Barry

New Voices: Student Political Activism in the '80s and '90s

Tony Vellela

How Harvard Rules: Reason in the Service of Empire

edited by John Trumpbour

Liberating Theory

co-authored by Michael Albert, Leslie Cagan, Noam Chomsky, Robin Hahnel, Mel King, Lydia Sargent, and Holly Sklar